KT-510-267

SUCCESSFUL GARDENING

CARING FOR YOUR PLANTS

Published by The Reader's Digest Association Limited.

Reprinted 1994

Consultant editor: Lizzie Boyd

Typeset by SX Composing Limited in Century Schoolbook

PRINTED IN SPAIN

ISBN 0 276 42088 8

Opposite: Good garden management shows in weed-free flower beds, proper pruning and well-trimmed lawns.

Overleaf: Greenhouse gardening protects a wealth of exotic plants, half-hardy annuals and tender food crops.

PUBLISHED BY THE READER'S DIGEST ASSOCIATION LIMITED
LONDON NEW YORK MONTREAL SYDNEY CAPE TOWN

Originally published in partwork form
by Eaglemoss Publications Limited

SUCCESSFUL GARDENING
CARING FOR YOUR PLANTS

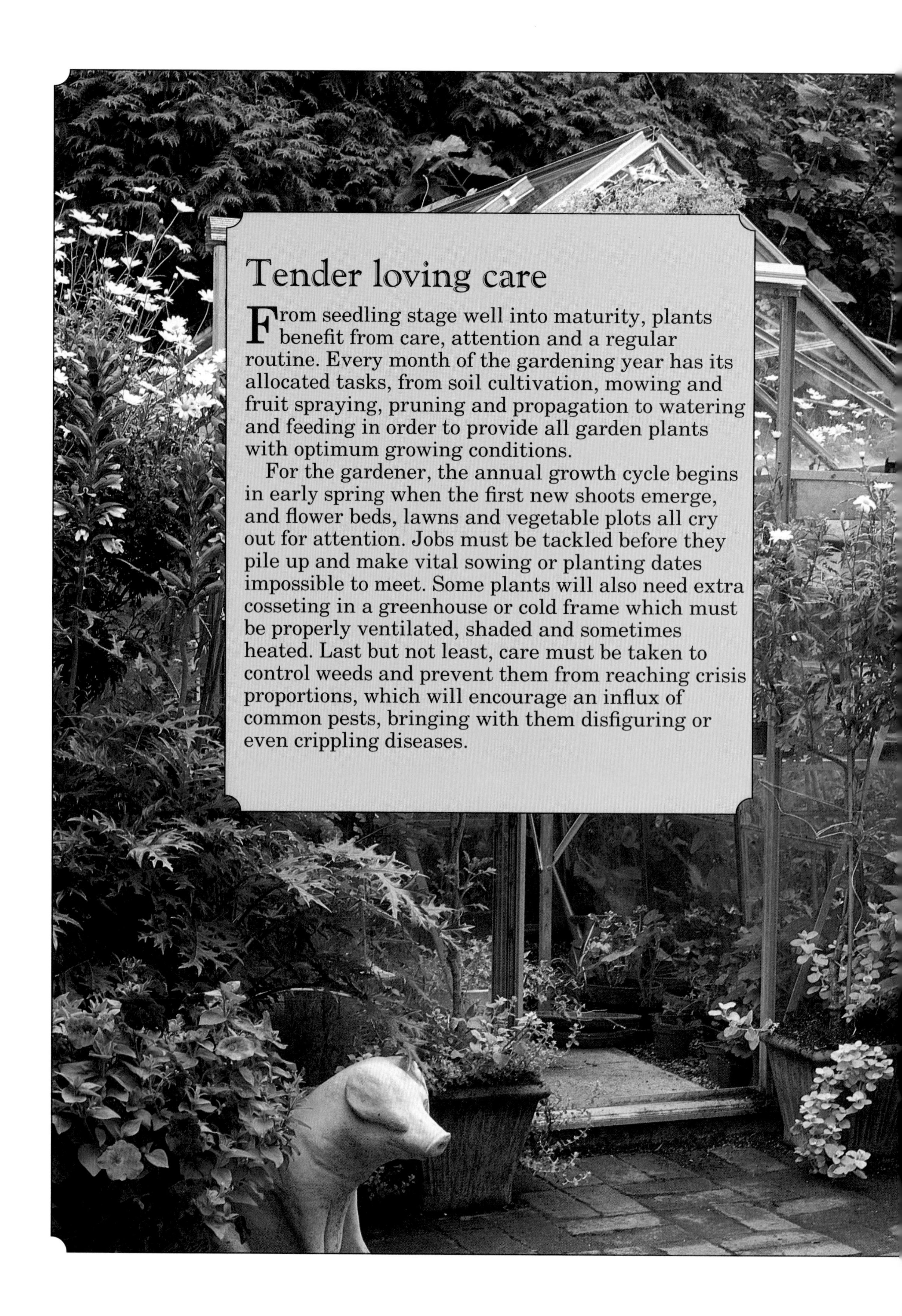

Tender loving care

From seedling stage well into maturity, plants benefit from care, attention and a regular routine. Every month of the gardening year has its allocated tasks, from soil cultivation, mowing and fruit spraying, pruning and propagation to watering and feeding in order to provide all garden plants with optimum growing conditions.

For the gardener, the annual growth cycle begins in early spring when the first new shoots emerge, and flower beds, lawns and vegetable plots all cry out for attention. Jobs must be tackled before they pile up and make vital sowing or planting dates impossible to meet. Some plants will also need extra cosseting in a greenhouse or cold frame which must be properly ventilated, shaded and sometimes heated. Last but not least, care must be taken to control weeds and prevent them from reaching crisis proportions, which will encourage an influx of common pests, bringing with them disfiguring or even crippling diseases.

CONTENTS

Garden management

Growing under glass

Weeds and weed control

Troubles in the flower garden

Troubles in the kitchen garden

Autumn colours The crimson and scarlet leaves of *Euonymus alatus* herald the close of the gardening year.

Garden management

Time is the gardener's most valuable asset – time to perform the many jobs that ensure perfect flowering plants, velvet lawns and succulent vegetable crops. The following pages constitute a work plan that summarizes month by month the jobs that need to be done in the gardening year.

Spring is by far the busiest time. Transforming winter dreariness into the lushness of summer can seem a daunting prospect without a flexible routine that takes into account the vagaries of the British climate. There are seeds to be sown, fruit trees to be sprayed and roses to be pruned. Soon there is fresh growth everywhere and seedlings develop into young plants that need to be fed and watered. Then, as spring merges into the long summer days, the results of early work show in bright flowers and heady scents, fresh young vegetables and ripening fruits. At last there is a little more time to propagate favourite plants, dead-head roses or just contemplate additions to flower beds and borders.

The mellow days of autumn bring new tasks: harvesting fruit and vegetables, digging over the soil and planting out perennials, bulbs, shrubs and trees. Autumn is also the time for laying new lawns, preparing rose beds and planting hedges. The good gardener doesn't wait for the first frost before bringing bedding plants like begonias, fuchsias and pelargoniums under cover or lifting tender dahlia and gladioli tubers. As the garden dies down there are leaves to be stacked for rich leaf-mould and long evenings to be spent in planning next year's garden adventures.

Early spring Clumps of brilliant crocus goblets open wide at the first touch of spring sunshine.

EARLY SPRING

As the days lengthen and warmer sun dries out the soil, planting can begin and the gardener's year gets under way.

Early spring weather invariably has the most pronounced variations from day to day, and the widest variations from year to year. The contrast between weather in the north and south of Britain is at its greatest.

Cold, strong winds in the wake of depressions from the Atlantic bring hail, sleet and snow, especially to high ground. But the sun's rays are beginning to grow stronger and sunshine hours are increasing, so that in a sheltered spot, in bright sun, it is warm. Though showers may be widespread, the overall rainfall in early spring can be quite low.

Temperatures at midday can be quite moderate, but at night they may fall dramatically, and there may be freezing fog. Air frost is possible on most nights, especially when there is a clear sky.

Take every advantage of dry spells in early spring to complete soil cultivation. But don't be misled by short periods of warm weather into thinking that spring has finally arrived. It is often safer

▼ **Early spring companions** The yellow-green flower clusters of *Helleborus lividus corsicus* set off to perfection the clear pink blooms of double-flowered camellias.

LAWN MAINTENANCE

Re-seed worn areas in the lawn, first levelling any depressions and raking to a fine tilth.

Aerate the lawn thoroughly, raking it vigorously a number of times in directions at right angles to each other. This will scatter worm casts, remove dead grass, debris and moss, and allow air and water to enter the surface of the turf.

Towards the end of early spring, if the weather is warm and not too dry, apply a proprietary spring fertilizer as evenly as possible.

Make the first spring mowing when the grass is about 6-7.5cm (2½-3in) high, setting the mower blades high. The weather should be dry. First scatter any worm casts with a rake or besom. Always mow with the grass box on at this time of year – clippings left on the turf surface will encourage disease.

Attend to lawn edges, cutting with a half-moon edging tool and using a plank laid on the grass as a straight-edge guide. Stand on the plank and cut away from you slightly to prevent crumbling of the lawn edge.

Where a lawn edge has crumbled or become worn, cut out the damaged area as a square or rectangle and turn it round so that there is sound turf at the edge. Sow grass seed on the bare patch and cover lightly with sifted soil.

Fusarium patch disease can occur in early spring. It is recognized by collapsed areas of fawn-coloured, waterlogged, dead grass, eventually with pinkish white fungal threads developing over the patch. Treat with a proprietary mercury-based fungicide. A number of applications may be necessary. To harden the grass and make it more resistant to disease, apply a lawn sand preparation, following the manufacturer's recommended doses.

To control most lawn weeds, apply a proprietary selective lawn weedkiller – containing mecoprop or dicamba with 2,4-D or a mixture of these chemicals – one or two weeks after the spring fertilizer application. To get the best effect, apply selective weedkillers during periods of active growth in damp, fairly warm and still conditions.

If moss is a problem, apply a proprietary lawn moss killer – which is often combined with a fertilizer.

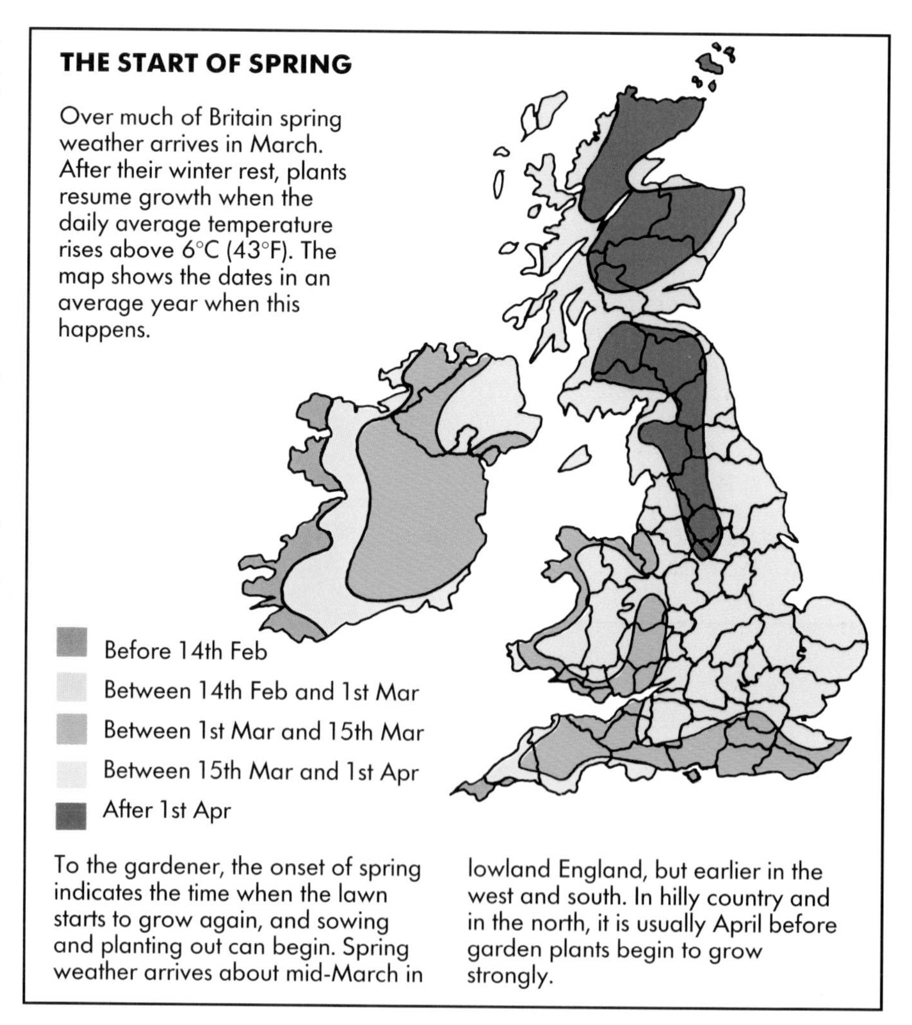

THE START OF SPRING

Over much of Britain spring weather arrives in March. After their winter rest, plants resume growth when the daily average temperature rises above 6°C (43°F). The map shows the dates in an average year when this happens.

To the gardener, the onset of spring indicates the time when the lawn starts to grow again, and sowing and planting out can begin. Spring weather arrives about mid-March in lowland England, but earlier in the west and south. In hilly country and in the north, it is usually April before garden plants begin to grow strongly.

to delay sowing and planting than to be caught by a subsequent cold spell that can mean disaster for young plants and seedlings.

Try to establish a routine that follows the progress of the seasons so that all gardening tasks receive equal attention.

Garden borders

A well-planned herbaceous or mixed border can be the focal point of a garden, giving a succession of blooms from early spring to the first frost of late autumn.

Tough, relatively trouble-free and long-lived, hardy herbaceous perennials need a modicum of work for a maximum of results. Many will produce some sort of show even when they are neglected, but for the best results early to mid spring is the time to start their routine care.

Clear away any debris which has accumulated around shrubs and the crowns of dormant perennials. However, avoid treading on naturally heavy, wet soil or on soil that is sticky from thawing frost or from rain – your weight will compress the soil, which will become waterlogged if there is more rain, or will dry hard if there is a period of dry weather, because the essential air spaces within the soil have been lost.

Prune trees and large shrubs which overhang herbaceous borders if not done in winter.

Watch out for slugs during mild weather – the smaller grey slugs can destroy herbaceous plants. They usually retreat to cover during the day, but slime trails reveal their presence. Destroy these pests by drowning them in beer or salt water or by scattering slug pellets.

In about the second week of early spring, it should be safe to remove the covering of leaves or straw packed around tender plants for frost protection. Leave it in place if the plants are still dormant and the weather is poor.

Overgrown clumps of perennials should be lifted and divided in spring, but this operation can be left for another month unless the soil is workable, weather conditions reasonably fine and the plants show signs of early growth.

In fact, most perennials benefit from being routinely divided every few years. The plants most likely to show early signs of regrowth are those which flower in early summer, including delphiniums and lupins.

Where perennial weeds – such as ground elder and couch grass – are found among the crowns of perennials, it is advisable to lift and divide the plants as soon as possible in spring before the weeds have time to get an even firmer hold. Using a border fork, dig up the entire clump. Shake the plants free of soil and, if the crowns are large and tough, carefully divide them using two forks back to back as levers. Break off and discard any woody parts and replant the divisions only when you have removed every trace of the weeds.

New stock can also be planted now – container-grown perennials and shrubs are readily available from nurseries and garden centres, and packaged plants can be bought by mail-order. Or, plant out your own stock raised from seed.

Using a hand trowel, dig a hole large enough to contain the plant's roots without cramping them. On light, dry soil, fill the hole with water, but watering is rarely needed in early spring on medium or heavy soil, which is still damp from winter. When the water has drained away, set the plant in position and firm down soil around the roots with your fingers. Draw drier soil around the base of the plant, firming it level.

Annuals Sow the hardiest types of annuals outdoors in the flowering site if weather and soil conditions are favourable. Suitable plants include candytuft (*Iberis*), clarkia, gypsophila, cornflower (*Centaurea*), godetia, poppy (*Papaver*) and pot marigold (*Calendula*).

To help both seeds and seedlings combat pests and diseases in the early stages, dress the seeds before sowing with a proprietary powder, shaking the powder and seeds together in the packet. To make subsequent weeding and thinning easier, sow the seeds in rows.

Bulbs, corms and tubers Remove flower heads from narcissi and daffodils as they fade. Cut just below the dead head, leaving the stalk intact – all remaining green tissues help build up the bulb's strength for the next year.

The last of the bulbs grown in pots or bowls indoors have finished flowering now. Plant them outdoors, removing intact the bulbs and the fibre or compost in which they were grown to encourage growth that will replenish the bulbs for future flowering.

As these bulbs are unsuitable for forcing again, plant them in clumps between shrubs, perennials or rock plants, depending on their flowering height. Narcissi, daffodils, hyacinths, crocuses and some of the smaller irises can all be planted out in this way to flower again one to two years later and in subsequent springs. Tulips are less likely to succeed, but may flower again for a year or two.

Weather and soil conditions permitting, plant gladiolus corms between the second and fourth weeks of early spring. Also complete the planting of lily bulbs.

Lift, divide and replant overgrown clumps of snowdrops. They are easier to establish at this time of year, while still in leaf, than in autumn.

Roses

Complete the planting of roses as early in spring as possible, preferably in beds prepared during the autumn or winter. If the beds have not been prepared, dig them to spade depth, mixing in plenty of well-rotted compost or manure and adding a dressing of bone-meal.

EARLY SPRING SHRUB PRUNING

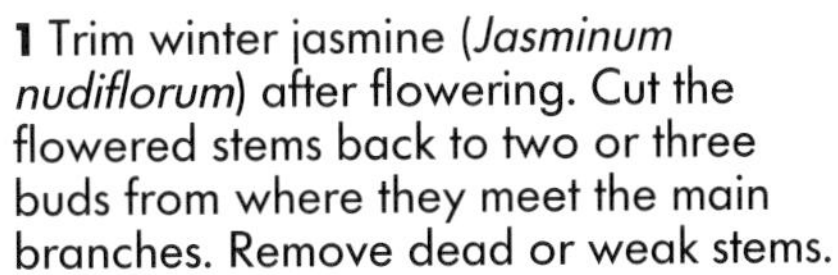

1 Trim winter jasmine (*Jasminum nudiflorum*) after flowering. Cut the flowered stems back to two or three buds from where they meet the main branches. Remove dead or weak stems.

2 Reduce *Buddleia davidii* to a low framework of branches, from which new shoots will grow and flower in summer. Cut back the previous year's stems to two or three buds from base.

Prune bush and standard roses before planting to make them easier to handle. Also cut back damaged roots and roots more than 30cm (1ft) long.

In mild districts, start pruning established roses at the beginning of early spring during frost-free weather. In gardens prone to late, hard frosts, delay pruning until the end of early spring. Pruning is essential for healthy, well-shaped growth with a good show of flowers.

Shrubs and trees

Plant deciduous shrubs and trees at any time during early spring, provided that the soil is not frozen or waterlogged and that the weather is reasonably fine. Container-grown shrubs and trees, which are planted with an unbroken soil ball, can be put in now, or at any other time of year.

Dig a hole large enough to hold the roots comfortably, making sure that the top-most roots will be covered by 10cm (4in) of soil. Then position the shrub carefully with its stem vertical. With trees and tall shrubs, insert a stout stake next to the root ball (not through it). Gently replace the soil, firming it down as you go and finally treading round it. Mulch with well-rotted compost, manure or bark.

Where staking is necessary, secure the main stem or trunk with proprietary tree or shrub strap-and-buckle ties – rose ties are also suitable – or use improvised ties made from old nylon stockings or strips of plastic furnishing fabric. The stake must be left in place until the new plant is well established, otherwise windrock will prevent the roots from getting a firm hold in the ground.

◄ **Spring pruning roses** Hybrid Tea (large-flowered) and floribunda (cluster-flowered) bush roses should be pruned as soon as frosts are over. Cut out dead, diseased, spindly and crossing stems and prune the remainder back by half or one-third their length, making a sloping cut to an outward facing bud.

TAKING DAHLIA CUTTINGS

1 Early spring is the ideal time to propagate overwintered dahlias. Spray the tubers daily with tepid water to encourage new shoots. When these are 7.5-10cm (3-4in) long, cut them off close to the base.

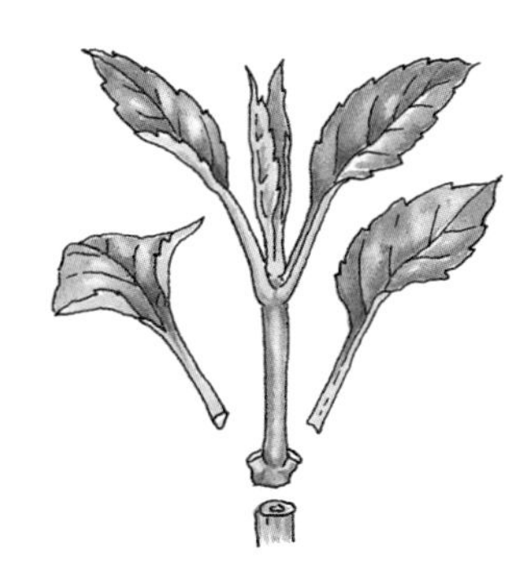

2 Remove the lower pair of leaves, and make a clean cut across the stem just below the joint from which they were growing. Dip the cutting in fresh hormone rooting powder – buy new powder each year since it deteriorates.

3 Insert each dahlia cutting about 2.5cm (1in) deep in a small pot filled with John Innes potting compost No. 1 or a proprietary potting compost. Or insert several cuttings in a box of compost. Water in thoroughly.

4 To conserve moisture and warmth, place polythene bags over the pots or boxes, or place the containers in large boxes covered with glass. Keep the cuttings shaded until they have begun to root – indicated by renewed growth.

Propagating shrubs Layering is a simple method of propagation at this time of year for lax-stemmed shrubs, such as *Amelanchier canadensis*, celastrus, lilac (*Syringa*), wintersweet (*Chimonanthus*), and all species of rhus except *Rhus typhina*.

Peg down the selected branches into sandy loam, either in pots sunk in the soil or in the open ground at the base of the parent plant. The rooting process usually takes a year or more, after which the layers can be separated from the parent and replanted.

Some shrubs, including *Amelanchier canadensis*, produce offsets, and these can be severed in early spring. Pot the offsets in a proprietary compost until the autumn, and then transplant them to their flowering positions.

Divide the roots of rose of Sharon (*Hypericum calycinum*) and perennial sweet peas (*Lathyrus*), replanting the separated pieces in their flowering positions. Rooted suckers of kerria can be separated and replanted in a similar way.

Some other shrubs are raised easily from seeds, which can be sown in early spring in a cold frame or in a cool greenhouse. Sow seeds of clematis, cotoneaster, genista, laburnum and wisteria in boxes or pots of seed compost, lightly covering the seeds with sifted compost. Place them in a closed cold frame.

Seeds of eccremocarpus and shrub mallow (*Lavatera olbia* 'Rosea'), sown in the same manner and placed in a greenhouse propagating frame with a temperature of 13-18°C (55-64°F), will germinate quicker than those sown in a cold frame.

When the seedlings are large enough to handle, prick them out into individual pots and grow them on in an open cold frame.

Camellias can be increased by taking 2.5cm (1in) long leaf cuttings in early spring. Insert them in potting compost in a propagating frame, maintaining a temperature of 13-16°C (55-61°F) until well rooted. Transfer rooted cuttings to individual pots and keep them in a cold, shaded frame until the following spring.

Take 5-7.5cm (2-3in) long root cuttings of *Campsis radicans*, *Rhus typhina* and Californian tree poppy (*Romneya coulteri*). Insert the cuttings singly in pots of compost and put in a propagating frame at a temperature of about 13°C (55°F). When the cuttings have rooted, repot the new plants and leave them in an open cold frame to grow on.

Pruning shrubs If the winter has been severe – with hard frosts and heavy snowfalls – some of the more tender deciduous shrubs, such as cistus, hebe, *Hydrangea macrophylla*, laburnum and potentilla, will need light pruning to remove dead, damaged or weak stems.

Other shrubs, such as berberis, ivy (*Hedera*) and *Hypericum patulum*, will produce more vigorous growth after a light thinning out of old wood to maintain shape.

Caryopteris clandonensis, deciduous *Ceanothus* species and *Hypericum calycinum* should have the previous year's shoots removed almost to the ground. Cut hardy fuchsias, *Buddleia davidii* and shrub mallow (*Lavatera*) hard back to live wood at the base from which new shoots will appear.

As soon as winter jasmine (*Jasminum nudiflorum*) and the early flowering shrub honeysuckle (*Lonicera fragrantissima*) have finished flowering, cut back the flowered stems – unless this was done already in late winter. With willows (*Salix*) and dogwoods (*Cornus alba*) grown for winter bark, cut stems hard back to promote fresh growth of brightly coloured stems.

Hedges With the exception of broad-leaved evergreens, early spring is the last opportunity in the gardening year to plant hedges grown from bare-rooted plants. If planted later, the young growth already on the plants may wilt and die while the roots try to become established.

Weeds begin to grow in early spring. Remove them from the bottoms of all hedges by pulling them up or by hoeing. Use a Dutch hoe for preference, as it is easier to push one of these tools round the congested bases of hedging plants than to use a draw hoe, which requires a chopping action. Pull up all large, deep-rooted perennial weeds by hand.

If chemical weed control is preferred, use a paraquat and diquat mixture weedkiller, taking care to keep the liquid off the leaves and stems of the hedging plants.

It is particularly important to keep newly planted hedges free from weeds, which compete with the plants by taking moisture and nourishment from the soil. Weeds may also shade the lower branches of hedging plants and either kill them or reduce their growth.

Complete the hard pruning of any large, old hedges not finished in late winter.

The fruit garden

In most years, this is the last opportunity for planting fruit trees and bushes. Also finish pruning established and autumn-planted plants as soon as possible, and always before bud-burst stage.

Feed established trees and bushes growing in cultivated soil. All soft fruits, except strawberries, benefit from a dressing of farmyard manure. Do not feed trees growing in grass until late spring, and feed then only if the fruit set is good. Newly planted trees and shrubs should not need any feeding in their first season after planting if the ground has been properly prepared.

With apple trees at bud-burst stage, control apple scab by spraying with benomyl or carbendazim. Control newly hatched pests – apple blossom weevil, capsid bug, greenfly and winter moth caterpillar – by spraying with HCH. But use only anti-scab spray if the trees have been winter-washed with tar-oil.

With pears at green cluster and white bud stage, control pear scab by spraying with benomyl, carbendazim or mancozeb.

Control cherry tree pests by

FRUIT BUD STAGES

1 The stages of fruit tree bud development provide a key to the timing of spray applications for controlling pests and diseases. At bud-burst stage, the tips of the small bud scales begin to separate.

2 At green cluster stage there are small green flower buds in the centre of the opening foliage. The growth rate varies from year to year – this is why it is impracticable to determine spraying dates by the calendar.

3 At pink or white bud stage, the flowers are not yet open but the petals are showing pink or white. Don't spray when the flowers are fully open because you will kill pollinating insects such as bees.

4 Petal fall stage is when nearly all the blossom has fallen. After this stage fruitlets begin to swell – known as fruitlet stage. Learn to recognize each of these stages, since spraying at the wrong time can be ineffective.

◀ **Early potato planting** In the south, and provided the soil is not too wet, plant from mid-March onwards. Plant in trenches 30cm (1ft) wide and 23cm (9in) deep, spacing the tubers 30-35cm (12-14in) apart. Cover them with soil to form a ridge over each row.

Dutch crocuses (*Crocus vernus* hybrids) are ideal for naturalizing in grass, perhaps in an informal swathe at the edge of a lawn, or in rougher grass in a semi-wild garden or on a bank. Flower colour ranges from intense purple, through shades of mauve and lilac, to vivid yellow or pure white. Named varieties are available, or buy packs of mixed colour corms.

To ensure that the corms build up strength for the following year's flowers, do not mow the lawn for the first time until the crocus leaves have died down. If left undisturbed, naturalized crocuses will eventually form dense clumps.

Other early spring flowers A wide selection of bulbs is available for early spring colour. These include Dutch hyacinths (*Hyacinthus orientalis* hybrids), grape hyacinths (*Muscari* species), narcissi and daffodils, early tulips and many of the dwarf irises, such as *Iris danfordiae*.

These bulbs provide vivid colour in all shades, so there is plenty of scope for planting colour themes or multicoloured plantings. Biennial polyanthus primulas (*Primula polyantha*) make ideal bedding partners for many bulbs, as do common English daisies (*Bellis perennis* Monstrosa varieties).

For taller early spring colour, there are several attractive shrubs to choose from – such as pink, red or white camellias, sweet-scented daphnes, flowering currant (*Ribes sanguineum*), Japanese quince (*Chaenomeles*) and yellow forsythia. The white-flowered *Magnolia stellata* will flower while quite young as a small shrub; with age it will develop into a small, multi-trunked tree.

spraying with dimethoate or heptenophos at bud-burst stage.

Feed apple, pear, plum and cherry trees in open ground with sulphate of ammonia, or nitro-chalk if the soil is acid. Do the same for bush and cane fruits. Black currants benefit from an additional dressing of sulphate of potash every year.

The vegetable garden

Early spring is a good time to start growing vegetables. If you haven't got space for a wide variety of crops, grow salads and some of the less common vegetables.

In relatively mild areas, select a sheltered, moisture-retentive site to sow salad onions, lettuce (such as 'All The Year Round' or 'Webb's Wonderful') and radishes.

Plant asparagus plants, unless the ground is saturated. If you receive asparagus plants by mail-order and planting is impossible, make a shallow trench and bury the roots under 10-15cm (4-6in) of soil, marking them with pegs.

Jerusalem artichokes can be planted towards the end of early spring or at the beginning of mid spring. They are perennial, invasive and need plenty of space. Kohl rabi can be sown now, as well as summer spinach to give early pickings from late spring.

Of the more common vegetables, onion sets can be planted now or at the beginning of mid spring. Also complete the planting of shallots as soon as possible; and there is still time to sow early round-seeded peas.

To grow an early crop of Brussels sprouts in fairly mild areas, purchase hardened-off plants from a nursery and plant them in fertile soil. In colder areas, only set out young plants of Brussels sprouts which have been over-wintered outdoors.

Sow parsnip seeds at the start of early spring in mild areas, or at the end of early spring in colder districts. Sow seeds of leeks, late summer cabbages and maincrop Brussels sprouts in a nursery bed for planting out later.

In milder areas, plant early potatoes from the middle of early spring onwards, provided the soil is not saturated.

Also in milder areas, sow short-rooted carrots if cloches and a fertile, sheltered site are available.

MID SPRING

As spring weather reaches across the country, the garden bursts into life and cries out for attention.

The general weather pattern is much the same as for early spring, and differences between the south and north of Britain are still quite marked. Showers – sometimes of sleet or snow – are common, but snowfalls rarely settle for long.

Cold, grey weather is again possible, and the nights may be very frosty. But the sun is strong enough to outweigh the effects of the cold nights and plant growth begins in earnest.

Mid spring is a busy time in the garden, but wet spells can cause considerable hold-ups – especially if gardening is mostly restricted to the weekends. A dry period can be helpful, but take extra care to see that young plants don't run short of soil moisture.

Garden borders

Plant late-flowering herbaceous perennials and those which are slow to make new growth – Michaelmas daisies (*Aster novi-belgii*) and red-hot pokers (*Kniphofia*).

LAWN MAINTENANCE

To improve old and badly worn lawns, mow, aerate, apply spring fertilizer, scarify with a springy wire rake and, where necessary, over-seed at the rate of 15g (½oz) per sq m/yd. Apply a light top dressing of loamy soil 3-6mm (⅛-¼in) deep. Roll the lawn if it is dry, but leave it if wet.

Apply spring fertilizer to all established lawns if this has not been done already.

Continue to mow little and often, especially if the weather is warm and showery. Lower the cutting blades 6mm (¼in) at a time at each successive mowing, but do not cut the grass shorter than 10-12mm (⅜-½in) high – the lower height for very fine turf.

Use a light roller to firm the surface of the turf if the mower roller is inadequate, but remember that over-use of the roller tends to compact the surface and keep out water and air. Never roll heavy soils.

Some 7-10 days after applying a fertilizer, and at least three days before or after mowing, apply a selective weedkiller. Dig out persistent perennial weeds and coarse grasses by hand – a daisy grubber will be useful for this. Apply a proprietary mosskiller, or a fungicide for the control of fusarium disease, if necessary.

To level a hump or fill a hollow in the lawn, make an H-shaped cut in the grass, with the cross-piece of the H over the hump or hollow. Roll back the turf and remove or add soil as necessary. Roll the turf back into position, tamp down well and sift a little soil into the cracks.

Complete the routine division and replanting of border perennials if you didn't do this in early spring. Michaelmas daisies deteriorate fairly quickly, and finer flowers and healthier growth come from young plants. So lift and divide these plants every few years, keeping only the healthiest shoots from the outside of each clump. The taller rudbeckias, helianthus, monardas and heleniums need similar treatment.

◄ **Flowering cherry** The naked branches of Cheal's weeping cherry (*Prunus* 'Kikushidare Sakura') are clothed with glorious clusters of deep pink flowers in mid spring. Beneath are other true spring harbingers – bright blue grape hyacinths, red tulips and multi-coloured primulas.

Towards the end of mid spring, stake delphiniums before their heavy flower spikes reach half their expected ultimate height. Insert a sturdy bamboo cane or a 2.5cm (1in) diameter wooden stake into the ground behind each plant.

Tie garden string round the stake once with a single knot, and then make a knotted loop round the spike, allowing ample room for the stems to swell as they grow. As the spikes lengthen, tie them at intervals of about 45cm (1½ft). The shorter, more branching Belladonna delphiniums can be supported with pea sticks.

Insert pea sticks in and around other shorter-growing but equally weak-stemmed plants, such as pyrethrums. Proprietary wire hoop plant supports are also ideal. Once kinks develop in weak stems, they can never be straightened, and the effect of support later in the season is unsightly.

Stake pinks (*Dianthus*), if necessary, by pushing small branched twigs into the ground so that the flower stems can grow up through them.

By the end of mid spring most herbaceous plants have emerged from winter dormancy, so winter losses can be assessed. But remember that some tuberous-rooted plants don't emerge for another few weeks. Fill any definite gaps with new plants – annuals and other bedding plants can be used to great effect.

The last week of mid spring is also a good time to plant out healthy overwintered dahlia tubers in warm and sheltered areas. Discard any tubers which are completely shrivelled or have rotted at the crown.

Continue to dead-head early bulbs, leaving the flower stalks and all leaves intact.

As the ground warms up, apply mulching material to beds and borders. If any tender plants become frosted, try to get at them before the sun reaches them. Cover them with newspaper or sacking, or spray cold water on them – surprisingly, this allows them to thaw out more gradually.

Renew slug pellets around susceptible plants, and look out for early attacks of aphids and other pests. Spray with a systemic insecticide where necessary.

Annuals Complete seed purchases as soon as possible. Many near hardy annuals can be sown outdoors in mid spring if weather and soil conditions are favourable. These include cosmos, gaillardia, lavatera, stocks (*Matthiola*), sunflower (*Helianthus*), scabious and annual phlox.

Dust the seeds with a proprietary fungicidal dressing before sowing, and fork into the soil a dressing of general flower fertilizer if this was not done earlier.

Complete the indoor sowing of half-hardy annuals. Move to a cold frame any well grown, early-sown half-hardy annuals. Keep the frame closed at first, opening it progressively as the weather improves and the plants become hardened.

Take special care with the more tender plants. In the case of French and African marigolds, bedding dahlias and ageratums, cover the cold frame with sacking if a hard frost is forecast. There is more frost protection near the centre of the frame than round the edges.

Yellowing of leaves may occur among some boxes of plants in frames. This often indicates slight starvation and is best overcome by watering weekly with a liquid flower fertilizer.

Plant early spring-sown sweet peas as soon as they are growing strongly. Start restricting growth on cordon-grown sweet peas when they are 23-30cm (9-12in) high. Select the strongest leading shoot on each plant, and carefully cut off the remainder with a sharp knife.

JOBS IN THE FLOWER GARDEN

1 Support pinks (*Dianthus*) by inserting twiggy sticks close to the clump so that the stems can grow up through and around the supports. Staking in this way is most likely to be needed with tall-growing varieties, especially on rich soil and in gardens subject to heavy rainfall or strong winds.

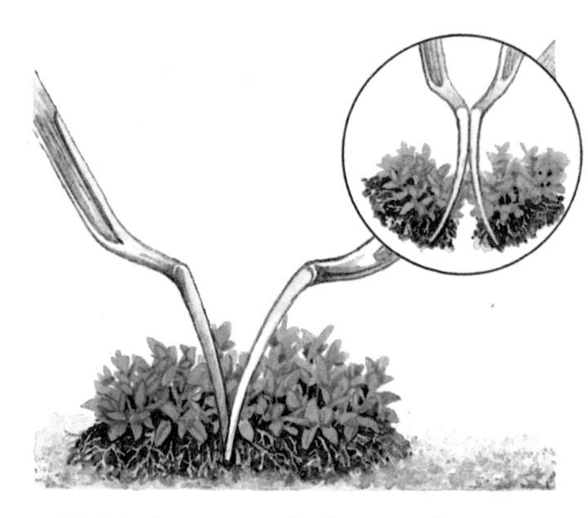

2 Divide large, tough clumps of herbaceous perennials, which have been lifted from the ground, by thrusting in two garden forks, back to back, and levering them apart. Use a strong, sharp knife to divide plants which have thick fleshy root growths. Pull small clumps apart by hand.

3 Hoe the ground around perennials and shrubs to keep them free from weeds. These soon appear once the ground begins to warm up. If necessary, use a contact weedkiller. Ensure that the soil is reasonably moist and then apply a mulch of garden compost, spent mushroom compost or forest bark.

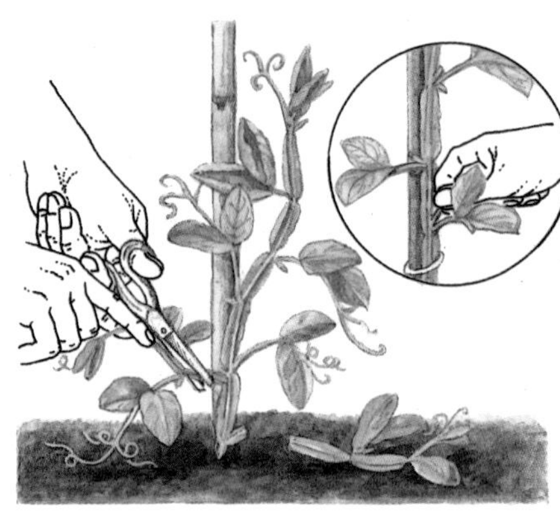

4 Begin restricting the growth of cordon sweet peas. When they are 23-30cm (9-12in) tall, select the strongest shoot on each plant and cut off the remainder of the growths. Tie the leader shoot to the cane. Remove all tendrils and side-shoots as soon as they are big enough to handle.

Tie the leader loosely to the cane, leaving ample room for the stem to thicken. From this stage onwards, carefully remove all the tendrils while they are still small. Also remove all side-shoots which form in the leaf axis.

Naturally grown sweet peas need no restriction. Remove the cloches from rows of sweet peas sown outdoors in mid autumn.

Roses
Complete all outstanding pruning of roses as soon as possible. Feed established roses with a proprietary rose fertilizer, scattering a handful per sq m/yd over the surface of the beds, except for a 15cm (6in) radius circle round the main stem of each plant. Hoe in the fertilizer.

Mulch established rose beds by covering the soil with at least a 2.5cm (1in) thick layer of well-rotted compost or manure. Alternatively, apply a 12mm (½in) layer of grass clippings, but don't use mowings from a lawn which has been treated with weedkiller. Use forest bark or composted coir for newly planted roses – they don't need the strong fertilizer content of compost or manure at this stage.

Pull up weeds by hand, but don't hoe them off since roses have shallow roots that may easily be damaged. Alternatively, control weeds by applying dichlobenil or alloxydium sodium, ensuring that the chemical doesn't come in contact with the rose stems.

During prolonged dry weather, water newly planted roses – 5 litres (1 gallon) per plant – to prevent them shrivelling. Although the normal planting season is past, container-grown roses may be bought from garden centres for transplanting into the open ground.

Shrubs and trees
Plant evergreen shrubs during showery spells when the soil is well-moistened. Continue to plant deciduous wall shrubs, such as clematis, honeysuckle, jasmine, ornamental vines and wisteria.

Water newly planted trees and shrubs during dry spells. Mulch around these plants with black polythene or grass clippings to reduce water loss from the soil.

Propagate *Hydrangea paniculata* and magnolias by pinning down layers. These can be severed and replanted when rooted, after one to two years.

Trees and shrubs which have finished flowering may require some light pruning. Shorten branches and cut off dead flower spikes and old weak shoots of *Chaenomeles japonica* and spring-flowering clematis.

Cut back forsythia after flowering to within one or two buds of the old wood. The arching stems of *Forsythia suspensa* often root of their own accord where they come in contact with the ground. Sever the rooted pieces from the parent and plant them elsewhere.

Hedges Plant broad-leaved evergreen hedging plants, such as holly (*Ilex*), laurel (*Prunus laurocerasus*) and escallonia. On free-draining soils, water the plants well during dry spells.

The fruit garden
Apple, pear, plum and cherry trees generally flower in mid spring. Look out for pests on the flowers or young fruitlets, but do not spray with insecticides while the flowers are open, because you will kill pollinating insects. Wait until the petals fall.

The greatest hazard at this time of year is frost damage to the flowers. Protect wall-trained trees and soft fruit bushes against slight frost by covering with muslin or fine netting.

Frost damage may also be reduced slightly if the soil is kept bare, firm and damp, since this type of soil absorbs the sun's heat

JOBS IN THE KITCHEN GARDEN

1 Transplant late summer cabbages to their final cropping rows. Make the holes with a dibber and dust each hole with calomel to protect against club root disease. Set the plants with their bottom leaves at soil level, firming them in well and watering them plentifully immediately afterwards.

2 Harvest forced rhubarb sticks. Lift off the bell forcing jar, upturned bucket or barrel. Pull the pink-red stems from the plant, grasping them close to the base and pulling away from the crown with a slight twisting motion. Do not cut rhubarb sticks with a knife – the remaining base will rot.

3 Peach flowers often open before pollinating insects are really active. To ensure a good crop, hand-pollinate peach flowers with a camel-hair paintbrush at about midday every day during flowering. Gently dab yellow pollen from one flower to another on the same tree.

4 Protect the flowers of peaches, nectarines and other early-flowering wall shrubs from frost damage by draping the plants with small-mesh netting or muslin sheets. Insert tall canes at an angle in front of the plants to form a support for the screen. Roll up the screen during the day.

better than dry soil and will release any absorbed heat at night. Water dry soil, especially for low-growing crops like strawberries.

With apples, if bad weather has delayed growth so that bud-burst takes place in mid spring, apply a spring spray as recommended for early spring. At pink bud stage, spray against apple scab with benomyl or carbendazim – especially if the weather is wet with alternating periods of rain and relatively high temperatures.

At early white bud stage, spray pear trees with benomyl, carbendazim or mancozeb against pear scab, and also spray with dimethoate or permethrin if greenfly or caterpillars are a problem.

On fan-trained cherries, plums, damsons, peaches and nectarines cut out shoots growing directly towards or away from the wall as new growth starts. Spray with dimethoate to control aphids.

Help the setting of peach and nectarine flowers by applying a fine spray of water. If red spider mites are seen on peaches or nectarines, spray with dimethoate once all the petals have fallen.

Make sure that pollinating insects can reach strawberry flowers on plants under cloches. Remove flowers from runners that are not well enough established to fruit this year, and from autumn-fruiting varieties. Watch for aphids and spray with pirimicarb if necessary. Top-dress strawberries with sulphate of ammonia, or nitro-chalk on acid soil, if the plants are slow to start into growth, but keep the rate low or the foliage will be too heavy.

The vegetable garden

Plant onion sets and sow salad crops, parsley and other herbs when the soil is sufficiently dry to work to a fine tilth. In colder areas, plant early potatoes (this should have been done in early spring in milder areas).

Sow seeds of late summer cauliflowers, winter cabbages and broccoli in a nursery bed for planting out in late spring or early summer.

Sow seeds of wrinkle-seeded varieties of peas in their cropping positions – they should be ready for harvesting in 12 weeks.

Set out plants of late summer cabbages sown in early spring. Plant with a dibber and dust the planting holes with calomel as a precaution against club root disease.

Early in mid spring, remove the soil from globe artichokes earthed up last autumn, replacing it with a layer of manure or compost. If garden compost is used, first sprinkle a light dressing of sulphate of ammonia over the ground. Plant new globe artichokes in soil that has been manured recently.

Cut asparagus from beds that are at least two years old when the growths are 10-15cm (4-6in) above the soil. Using a sharp knife, cut about 5-7.5cm (2-3in) below ground and go over the bed two or three times each week.

After about the second week of mid spring, sow maincrop carrots on ground manured for a previous crop. Rake in a general fertilizer before sowing.

Towards the end of mid spring, sow globe-rooted beetroot in soil that has received a medium dressing of manure or compost, first soaking the seeds in tepid water overnight.

Protect emerging potato leaves from frost damage by earthing up with a draw hoe. When the ridges can be made no higher, have straw at hand to cover the shoots if frost threatens. Remove the straw cover the next morning when the frost has thawed.

In mild areas, sow seeds of French beans from the third week of mid spring onwards and cover them with cloches.

Pasque flower (*Pulsatilla vulgaris*) produces a tufted clump of soft ferny leaves from which slightly nodding goblet-shaped flowers appear in mid-spring, standing 20-30cm (8-12in) high. The typical petal colour is rich mauve-purple, but varieties are available with pale mauve, pink, red or white flowers. They always have a prominent boss of golden yellow stamens in the centre. When the flowers fade, pretty silken seedheads develop, which resemble those of clematis.

Other mid spring flowers

Bulbs continue to dominate the scene when it comes to mid spring colour – choose from the hundreds of varieties of narcissi, tulips, hyacinths, fritillaries and grape hyacinths (*Muscari*). For a powerful sweet scent, lily-of-the-valley (*Convallaria*) cannot be beaten.

Blue gentians, gold doronicums, pink, red or white mossy saxifrages and white arabis bring colour to the rock garden. And in the shrubbery, there are red or white Japanese quinces (*Chaenomeles*), yellow forsythia, creamy fothergilla, pure white *Magnolia stellata* and orange *Berberis darwinii*.

LATE SPRING

Dry and sunny days mark an end to really bad weather and plants soon make up for checks caused by a cold start to the year.

On average, late spring has some of the driest spells of the year in Britain, and in the south the second week of late spring is one of the sunniest. However, thunderstorms are often more frequent than earlier in spring, and these may be accompanied by squally winds. In the north of Britain, snow showers still occur, but snow cover rarely persists for long.

Anticyclone conditions may give hot, tranquil weather in late spring, with daytime temperatures occasionally reaching as high as 27°C (80°F) in southern Britain. But clear nights often bring late frosts, especially if mid spring has been drier than usual. Eastern regions may experience morning fog and low cloud, giving a grey chilly start to the days.

Late spring is often a stabilizing period during which slow-to-start plants respond quickly to milder conditions and soon make up for any lost time caused by previous poor weather.

Garden borders

Continue hoeing between perennials and shrubs to kill weeds while they are still small. Also continue to stake and support tall plants, such as delphiniums, which are liable to be damaged by winds or rain near flowering time.

Pinching out To check the growth of perennials that are inclined to grow too tall, and to make the plants branch out, pinch out the tips. Plants which respond well to this treatment are those that form a leafy clump opening into heads of flowers – such as phlox, golden rod (*Solidago*), helenium, Michaelmas daisies (*Aster*) and rudbeckias.

When a plant has reached about a quarter of its expected height, and at least a month before flowering time, pinch out the leading shoots. This may reduce the ultimate height by a quarter, but will not reduce the flowering period – although it may retard flowering by a week or two.

LAWN MAINTENANCE

Apply a liquid high-nitrogen lawn feed to green up the grass. This dressing is especially valuable if the spring fertilizer has been given early.

Water the lawn thoroughly in dry weather. Continue regular mowing, but first check the mower blades for sharpness and correct the setting if necessary. Set the height of cut not lower than 12mm (½in) and keep edges neatly trimmed.

In good growing weather, continue to deal with weeds regularly and apply fungicides for disease control.

However, if plants are more than three years old and are producing a large number of shoots, that tend to bear inferior blooms, or if you are in a cold district where retarded flowering would be undesirable, it is better to thin out some of these shoots. The

▼ **Late spring symphony** Golden laburnum is draped with long chains of pea-like flowers in late spring and early summer – to be followed by poisonous seed pods. Mature trees provide splendid support for the vigorously rambling, pale pink *Clematis montana*.

JOBS IN THE FLOWER GARDEN

1 Plant out half-hardy annuals as soon as danger of frost has passed. Lay the plants in position to satisfy yourself that the placings are balanced, then dig holes deep enough for the roots, firm in the plants and water them well.

2 Use a sharp knife to remove surplus shoots from the centre of clumps of older perennials, cutting the growths as close to the ground as possible and selecting the weakest ones only. Remove up to half the total number.

3 Water young but established plants during dry spells by using the puddling method. First scrape soil away to form a low bank round the plant. Add water until a puddle forms, then level the soil once the water has drained away.

4 To encourage bushier, branching growth from herbaceous perennials that tend to grow tall, pinch out the leading shoot tips. Do this at least one month before flowering. Ultimate height may be reduced by a quarter.

shoots which are left on the plant will become more vigorous.

Thin out the shoots at the same time as pinching out shoot tips, or preferably a little earlier. Remove the weakest shoots, concentrating on those at the centre of the crown. Where the shoots are dense, take out up to half the total, severing them close to the ground.

Watering Young plants may require watering during dry spells. Where only a few new kinds have been planted among established plants, use the puddling method.

Scrape away 2.5cm (1in) of the dry topsoil to make a low bank all round the plant or group. Fill the trough once with water – or twice if the soil is very dry. When the water has soaked away, push back the soil with a rake or hoe.

If a whole newly planted bed is too dry, use a sprinkler or a rose on a watering can or hosepipe. Make sure that the water comes out as a fine spray and not in large drops which tend to pan the soil surface. It is the roots of plants that need water, so be prepared to water the ground a second or even third time.

As soon as the surface begins to dry a little, scratch over with a rake to restore the tilth necessary for aeration.

Chrysanthemums Plant out garden varieties when all danger of frost is past, using pot-grown plants raised from cuttings, or bought in stock. Insert a cane at each planting hole and tie the stem loosely in place; water well.

Bulbs and tubers Dead-head daffodils, tulips, hyacinths and irises as they finish flowering. If it is necessary to make way for summer bedding, lift daffodils and tulips now, but otherwise wait until early summer.

Heel in lifted bulbs in a temporary bed in a spare corner of the garden so that they can die back gradually. First take out a trench about 30cm (1ft) deep. Lay a length of fine wire or plastic netting in the bottom and then lay the bulbs on the netting. Fill the trench with soil so that it covers the lower half of the stems.

By the beginning of mid summer the stems and leaves will have shrivelled and the bulbs can be lifted for storage. Use the netting as a lever – a sharp pull should lift all the bulbs at once.

Plant crinum bulbs 15-20cm (6-8in) deep in a south-facing border. Or plant them in tubs which can be moved under cover during the autumn in cold regions.

Plant out young dahlia plants – either your own rooted cuttings or bought plants – when danger of frost is over. Dormant dahlia tubers should have been planted out in mid spring, but in colder areas plant them in the first week of late spring.

Tall dahlias need staking as their stems are generally too weak to support the heavy flower heads satisfactorily. For each dahlia, drive a stout stake into the ground at the back of the planting hole before inserting the tuber.

As the stems grow, tie them loosely to the stakes with garden string or raffia. Label each plant. If night frost is forecast, protect the young plants with sheets of newspaper, removing these the next morning.

Annuals Tie cordon-grown sweet peas to their canes as they grow. Continue to pinch out side-shoots and tendrils as they appear. Pinch out the first few flowers while they are tiny, but leave the little stems, bearing more buds, which will soon appear.

There is still time to make outdoor sowings of hardy and half-hardy annuals, such as alyssum, calendula, candytuft, cosmos, gaillardia, nasturtium, phlox and tagetes. Hardy biennials can also be sown now in nursery beds.

In mild areas, planting out of

half-hardy annuals can begin as soon as the risk of frost has passed. Don't be persuaded into planting earlier than this by the flood of bedding plants appearing in garden centres – they often bring out stock before outdoor planting conditions are really suitable. If in doubt, it is safer to wait until the first week of early summer.

Water borders and beds cleared of spring bedding before setting out half-hardy annuals.

Give the hardened-off plants a good watering. Remove them from their containers with as much root as possible. Most garden centres sell annuals in strips or boxes made from thin plastic or polystyrene, each plug containing a single plantlet. Remove plants from polystyrene strips by pushing up from the base, those from plastic plugs by pulling the plastic down and away from the fragile root ball.

▲ **Bedding schemes** Mark out a plan for bedding annuals with trails of sand to define the divisions between one variety and the next. Make a rough estimate of the number of each variety available and ensure that, with the correct spacing, the layout can be filled to give a well-balanced effect.

Taller growing varieties should go towards the back or centre of the bed, with shorter ones at the front and edges. Plant the taller growing types first, treading on the soil as little as possible – use a plank if necessary.

TENDING ROCK GARDEN PLANTS

1 Destroy weed seedlings between rock garden and alpine plants by hoeing carefully during dry weather. An onion hoe is the ideal size and shape for this purpose. Pull up larger perennial weeds by hand.

2 After flowering, trim aubrieta, mossy saxifrages and other vigorous rock plants to encourage fresh, compact growth. This may also promote a second flush of flowers later in the season and will prevent self-seeding.

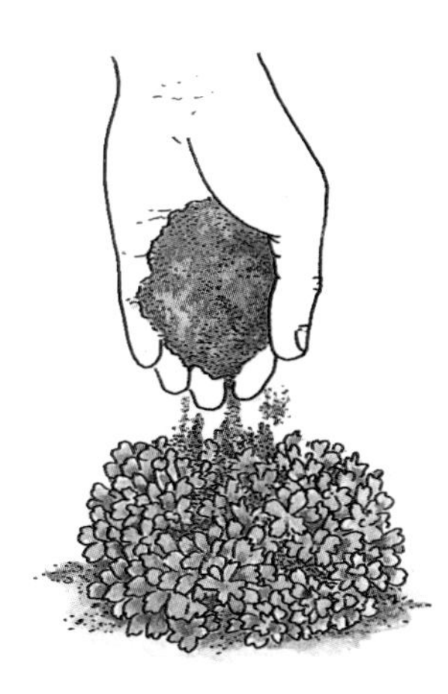

3 Sedums, saxifrages and other clump-forming or hummocky rock plants benefit from a sprinkling of fine soil mixed with sand and granular fertilizer. Work this in among the rosettes with your fingers, firming it lightly.

◀ **Lime-hating rhododendrons** In gardens with acid soil, late spring is synonymous with rhododendrons and azaleas. They burst into glorious colours, from palest pastels to fiery hues of reds and blues, and thrive in the shelter of woodland. After flowering, carefully twist off the faded heads by hand, without damaging the new growth buds at the base.

If you have raised your own seedlings, ease the whole soil and root mass out of the seed tray and cut the plants apart with a knife.

After planting each batch, water with a sprinkler or fine-rose watering can, giving them a good soaking – light watering of young annuals merely results in attracting their roots to the surface.

Rock garden plants

Late spring is the peak period for colour in the rock garden, but weeds are also growing strongly. Use an onion hoe to eliminate small annual weeds. Pull up by hand and destroy any larger perennial weeds. Also remove any unwanted self-sown seedlings of aubrieta, mossy saxifrages and other rock garden plants.

After flowering, trim off the stalks and surplus growth from fast-growing species. This will promote new compact growth and may encourage more flowers – especially with aubrieta.

Sprinkle a mixture of fine soil, sand and granular fertilizer among the green rosettes of sedums and saxifrages if they appear ragged. Allow the mixture to trickle on to the plants through your fingers, then work it in below the leaves and stems. Push further material underneath trailing stems.

Alternatively, if the weather is damp, lift the plants, dig and fertilize the soil, and replant them deeper than previously in close-set bunches.

Roses

Be prepared to spray regularly to combat rose pests. Spray both sides of the leaves and the stems, using a sprayer that delivers a fine mist. Use proprietary rose insecticides and fungicides – or any type which specifies on the label that it is suitable for roses – following the manufacturer's instructions.

Aphids (mainly greenfly), caterpillars, black spot and mildew are the major rose pests and diseases to watch out for. Routine protective spraying gives better results than spraying to eradicate an established outbreak.

Shrubs and trees

During showery weather, complete the planting of evergreens. Keep them moist at the roots after planting, and spray the foliage with water in the evenings during dry or windy weather.

With shrubs that have finished flowering – such as kerria, pieris, flowering currant and spring-blooming spiraeas – dead-head,

PROPAGATING HERBS

Propagate thyme by taking 7.5-10cm (3-4in) long cuttings from the previous year's growth, cutting cleanly just below a node. Remove the lower leaves (*above*) and then insert the cuttings, several to a pot, in a proprietary compost. Stand the pot in a cool spot outdoors; cover with a cloche when it is cold or windy. Marjoram, rosemary and sage can be propagated in the same way.

Herbs which make runners, such as mint (*above*), are best propagated by cutting the runners into sections, each with a shoot and roots. Replant them separately.

shorten long stems, and thin out or completely remove weak shoots. Also dead-head rhododendrons and azaleas by snapping off the stalks with your fingers, taking care that the new growth buds at the base of the old flower cluster are not damaged in the process.

Hedges Clip hedges of *Lonicera nitida* monthly from now until the end of early autumn to keep them neatly shaped and prevent them from breaking open as they grow. Some other hedges, such as common privet, also need regular clipping to look their best.

Clip hedges of forsythia and flowering currant after the flowers have died. Do not clip them again until the following year, otherwise the flower buds will be removed and the spring display lost.

The fruit garden

There is still a risk of frost damage, but trees are now making more growth which will help to protect the flowers. Soil temperatures are also rising so that low-growing fruits are less likely to be frosted than earlier on.

Most fruits contain a high proportion of water and benefit from watering in dry spells. To avoid producing too much growth, water mainly after flowering during the fruit-swelling stage.

If fruit set appears good on tree fruits such as apple, pear, plum and cherry, apply 15-30g (½-1oz) per sq m/yd of sulphate of ammonia or nitro-chalk. This will help to swell the fruit and form fruit buds for next year. Do not feed if the trees are not fruiting – they will make too much leaf growth and extension shoots.

Continue to spray against apple and pear scab disease every 10-14 days, especially in a wet spring. Also spray apple trees against apple blossom weevil, caterpillars and aphids, especially if a winter-wash or bud-burst spray have been missed. At petal-fall stage, control apple sawfly with fenitrothion, HCH or pirimiphos-methyl, red spider mite and woolly aphids with malathion or dimethoate.

New raspberry canes should now be growing up strongly. Pull out unwanted shoots which are causing overcrowding in the row or growing in the space between rows. If fruit set appears good, apply a mulch to conserve moisture. Apply 30g (1oz) per sq m/yd of sulphate of ammonia, or nitro-chalk on acid soil.

Blackberries, loganberries and hybrid berries should be producing new shoots from the ground, which will bear next year's crop. To check the spread of disease from old canes to the new, keep them apart as much as possible by training them along separate wires or in opposite directions. Feed these plants in the same way as raspberries, but increase the amount of nitrogenous fertilizer to 60g (2oz) per sq m/yd.

With black currants, if fruit set appears good, apply 30g (1oz) per sq m/yd of sulphate of ammonia or nitro-chalk. Apply carbendazim three weeks after the first spray against big bud mite.

Feed cordon gooseberries and bush red and white currants with up to 15g (½oz) per sq m/yd of dried blood. Feed bush gooseberries with up to 30g (1oz) per sq m/yd of sulphate of ammonia or nitro-chalk. Apply derris or pyrethrum to gooseberries just before the flowers open to control sawfly.

TRAINING RUNNER BEANS

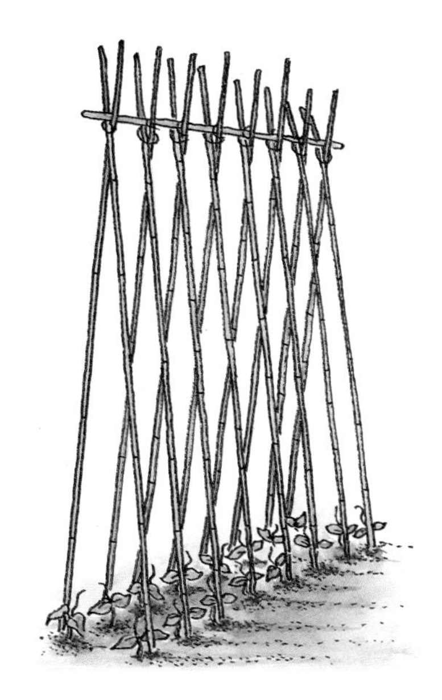

1 Provide bean poles or tall canes alongside the plants, setting them at an angle. Tie opposing poles together near their tops. For added strength and rigidity, lay a horizontal strut across the top and secure it to the uprights.

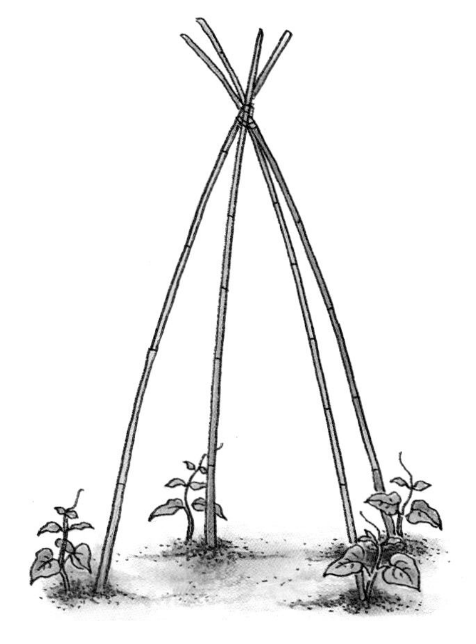

2 A wigwam of poles or canes provides an alternative means of supporting runner beans where space cannot be spared for a bean row. This system is also more attractive in a small garden, but the yield may be reduced slightly.

THINNING PEACHES

1 Left unthinned, peaches may bear numerous small fruits of poor quality. Start thinning fruit in late spring, removing any small or misshapen fruits. Those remaining will grow larger and more succulent.

2 Once thinned out, the small peach fruits on wall-trained trees should be spaced 7.5-10cm (3-4in) apart on the branches. Further fruit thinning, to a spacing of about 23cm (9in), will be needed in early summer.

Control weeds among cane and bush fruits by hoeing carefully.

Apply benomyl to open strawberry flowers to protect the fruit against grey mould. Protect developing strawberry fruits by putting down chopped straw, black polythene matting or by using bituminized paper collars.

The vegetable garden
Sow maincrop carrots, if this was not done in mid spring. Continue to cut asparagus spears.

If you want to grow outdoor crops of marrows or courgettes, prepare the site at the beginning of late spring by digging holes 30cm (1ft) square and 90cm (3ft) apart. Place a forkful of well-rotted manure in each hole before replacing the soil until it forms a mound. At the end of late spring sow three seeds on each soil mound, later removing the two weakest seedlings.

About the second week of late spring, sow French beans outdoors. During the last two weeks of late spring sow runner beans, preferably on a site prepared earlier. Insert bean poles or support canes before sowing.

Set out plants of late summer cauliflowers which were sown in mid spring, planting them 60cm (2ft) apart. Plant with a dibber and dust each hole with calomel as a precaution against club root disease. Set the plants with their bottom leaves at soil level, firming them in with the heel and watering immediately afterwards.

In cool northern areas, plant out Brussels sprouts. Make further sowings of summer spinach and salad crops for a steady supply.

Cloches and frames Remove cloches from spring cabbages, carrots, lettuces and broad beans, in several stages over three weeks, so that the plants harden off gradually. First move the cloches 5cm (2in) apart, doubling the gap at intervals of four or five days.

To grow cucumbers under cloches or in frames, prepare the site as for outdoor marrows. Sow the seeds a week or two afterwards. When the seeds germinate, remove surplus seedlings and ventilate the cloches or frames during the day.

In cool northern areas, sow runner beans under glass in the middle of late spring for planting out in the open during the second week of early summer.

Common lilac (*Syringa vulgaris*) is unparalleled by any other garden shrub for its beauty, elegance and rich colour in late spring. Named varieties and hybrids, sometimes listed under *Syringa × hyacinthiflora*, come in a range of colours in addition to the typical lilac-mauve, mauve-purple, pinkish mauve, wine red, creamy white and pure white.

Growing up to 3.5m (12ft) in height, with a spread of up to 3m (10ft), lilac is best suited to a large shrubbery or it can be grown as a specimen plant. The distinctively and strongly scented flowers are borne in pyramid-shaped clusters up to 23cm (9in) long.

Other late spring plants
Azaleas and rhododendrons are among the most popular of late spring shrubs, but they are generally successful only on acid, peaty soils. There are hundreds of species and varieties to choose from, coming in a vast range of colours and sizes – make sure you check the ultimate size of any plant carefully before buying to avoid problems later on.

For a strong orange-blossom scent and starry white flowers, choose the evergreen Mexican orange (*Choisya ternata*). This compact shrub does well in a large container or against a sunny wall.

Weigela florida and its hybrids burst into pink, red or white blossom in late spring, making an informal backdrop for lower-growing flowers such as mauve or pink crane's-bills (*Geranium*), aquilegia, blue forget-me-not (*Myosotis*), red-mauve honesty (*Lunaria annua*) and late tulips.

Rock gardens abound with flowering plants in late spring. The most stunning displays are given by *Alyssum saxatile, Aubrieta deltoidea, Iberis semperflorens* and *Phlox subulata.*

EARLY SUMMER

The sun is at its strongest now and plant growth is rapid, so try to maintain soil moisture and keep down weeds.

During early summer winds tend to be light and there are alternating periods of bright, clear sunshine and rainy but warm, muggy weather. Nevertheless, this is usually the driest period of the year. During strong sunshine, afternoon temperatures may soar to 27°C (80°F), but night temperatures can fall to 10°C (50°F).

This combination of weather offers ideal conditions for plant growth – weeds as well as ornamentals and crops. The soil dries out quickly and moisture must be replenished by frequent watering during prolonged sun. Pests and diseases also thrive at this time and must be dealt with quickly.

Roses

Early summer sees the beginning of the rose-flowering season, generally starting with the older shrub types and true species, then followed by the modern bush rose and climber varieties.

Many Hybrid Tea (large-flowered) roses have flowering shoots on which two or three side buds are produced in addition to the main bud at the top. If you want high quality blooms with long stems suitable for cutting, remove the small side buds as soon as it is possible to pick them off with finger and thumb. This procedure is known as disbudding.

Pull away briar shoots on the main stems of standard roses at the point where growth emerges. Remove sucker shoots appearing through the ground in rose beds.

Hoe the soil around roses to improve aeration and remove weeds, but don't slice deeper than 12mm (½in) or so, since rose roots grow close to the surface and are easily damaged by harsh hoeing.

Mulch roses with garden compost, well-rotted manure, forest bark or lawn clippings. But don't use lawn clippings if the grass has been treated with weedkiller

LAWN MAINTENANCE

Apply a supplementary lawn fertilizer if this was not given in late spring. Mow the lawn regularly, adjusting the height of the mower blades according to the weather. During periods of drought, raise the blades and cut without the grass box in place - the clippings will act as a mulch and help to retain moisture.

Summer drought can cause significant damage to a lawn which receives constant wear, so spike it well to enable any rain or hose water to penetrate deeply to the roots. Use a garden fork or special lawn aerator, and carry out the work when the ground is soft after rain or watering.

Continue treatment with lawn weedkillers as necessary, except during prolonged dry spells.

▼ **Herbaceous borders** Early summer is the highlight of herbaceous borders, with fresh green foliage to offset vibrant flower colours. The hardy crane's-bills (*Geranium* sp.) are covered in a profusion of blooms that range in colour from white and pale pink through crimson and purple to shades of blue. Their dense growth habit also helps to suppress any weed growth in the border.

ROSE CARE

1 Pinch out the side buds from the flowering shoots of Hybrid Tea roses if you want the best quality, largest blooms from the terminal buds. This is essential if you want long-stemmed blooms for picking or exhibition. Watch out for aphids on the buds and spray with a rose insecticide when necessary.

2 Suckers arising from the rootstock of grafted roses will drain the plant's strength. These are distinguished by their very thorny stems and lusher green but smaller leaves. Cut suckers flush from where they sprout from the rootstock. If necessary, scrape away the soil to expose the point of origin.

During dry weather, water miniature and patio roses growing in containers. All other roses tolerate normal spells of dry weather without harm.

Spray roses with systemic rose insecticide if aphids appear, and with rose fungicide at regular intervals as a precaution against mildew, rust and black spot diseases. With all rose ailments, prevention is easier than cure.

Garden borders

Herbaceous borders should remain colourful from early summer to early autumn if the plants have been carefully chosen.

Where early flowering herbaceous perennials are fading, cut them down to within 7.5cm (3in) of the ground and clear away any unsightly support sticks. This encourages a fresh crop of foliage, which will provide attractive ground cover for the rest of the summer. In some cases, a second flush of flowers may develop later in the season.

Lay a 2.5cm (1in) thick mulch of leaf-mould or forest bark between moisture-loving and shade-loving plants to hold the soil moisture and to keep down weeds.

Chrysanthemums Stop garden varieties by removing the growing tips of plants as soon as break buds show in the leaf axils on the main stem. This will induce side-shoots which will flower earlier than if they were allowed to break naturally. Stop all plants no later than the third week of early summer or the flowers will be too late to avoid autumn frosts.

Do not allow chrysanthemums to become dry at the roots. Early in the month, hoe in a dressing of sulphate of ammonia at 15g (½oz) per sq m/yd to promote growth.

Bulbs Towards the end of early summer in warm districts start lifting spring bulbs on which the leaves have turned yellow.

Tulips need to be lifted regularly to maintain their health, but most other bulbs – including daffodils – require dividing and replanting in fresh soil only if show-quality flowers are wanted or if the plants have become so crowded that they produce only masses of leaves.

In mild regions, plant anemone corms (*Anemone coronaria* 'De Caen') for autumn or winter show.

When dahlia tubers have begun to grow – two or three weeks after planting – pinch out the tip of each leading shoot. This will encourage the production of side shoots and make bushy plants that will give a long succession of flowers. When the shoots have reached a height of about 45cm (1½ft) tie them to the stakes with garden string or raffia. Lay a thick mulch around dahlias and water the plants well.

Annuals Complete the planting of half-hardy bedding annuals, waiting until all risk of late frosts has passed in cold or low-lying regions. Water the cleared borders or beds and the hardened-off plants before setting these out in the flowering positions.

During prolonged dry weather, water thoroughly all recently planted half-hardy annuals, and hardy annuals sown earlier, to help them make sufficient growth before flowering starts.

Give support to the taller-growing annuals when they reach a height of 15-23cm (6-9in). This is especially important in exposed situations. Use twiggy pea sticks slightly shorter than the eventual height of the plants, pushing them in among the individual clumps so that the plants conceal them while at the same time gaining support from them.

Spray bedding plants monthly with a systemic insecticide to control aphids and other sap-sucking insects. Hoe regularly to control weeds.

Biennials Sow hardy biennials, such as wallflowers, if this was not done in late spring. They can be raised outdoors or under glass.

As soon as they reach manageable size, set out in a nursery bed biennial seedlings which are at present in seed boxes or outdoor seed beds. Plant them 15-23cm (6-9in) apart so that they have enough space to make sturdy, bushy plants for setting out in their final positions in early autumn.

Alternatively, sow wallflowers and sweet Williams directly in their flowering site at the end of early summer. Sow thinly and prick out surplus seedlings as soon as possible to leave remaining plants 15-23cm (6-9in) apart.

Rock garden plants

Continue to weed and hoe the rock garden, placing weeds straight into a bucket or box to prevent seeds from being scattered.

Trim dead flowers from aubrietas and saxifrages to prevent unwanted self-seeding. Dead-heading of other rock plants is unnecessary, but clipping with shears keeps the garden tidy. At

► **Planting leeks** By mid summer transplant leek seedlings. First trim off the top quarter of the leaf tuft and the bottom half of the roots. Then drop each plant into a hole made with a dibber. Do not firm the plants in, but puddle them in with a generous amount of water from a watering can, so that the soil is washed into and over the roots from the sides of the holes.

the same time, trim back excessive growth on trailing plants. In the case of species which root as they spread, thrust an old knife vertically into the soil, then pull out the severed portions.

Shrubs and trees

Prune deciduous shrubs, such as deutzia, cutting out shoots that have just flowered. This will encourage strong new growth to develop and ripen for next year.

As soon as brooms (*Cytisus*) have finished flowering, cut back the shoots to prevent seedpod production. But do not cut into the old wood – it may refuse to send out new shoots and the plants will remain dormant or even die.

Dead-head lilacs (*Syringa*) and thin out weak shoots. If you grow senecios for their silvery foliage effect, remove the flower heads as soon as they appear.

Propagate *Chaenomeles japonica* and clematis by layering lax shoots into pots of a proprietary compost sunk into the ground.

Many hedges need the first trim of the year in early summer. Escallonia hedges, if trimmed now, will produce a fine show of pink or white flowers on new growth during late summer and early autumn. Continue to weed or hoe at the base of hedges.

The fruit garden

Control weeds around the base of

LIFTING AND STORING BULBS

1 Lift spring bulbs such as daffodils and tulips by using a garden fork. To avoid damaging them, insert the fork well clear of the clump and deep enough to get right under the roots.

2 After lifting, spread the bulbs out to dry in shallow boxes, leaving the old leaves and roots in place for now. Stand them in a well ventilated shed until all moisture has evaporated.

3 Once they are bone-dry, gently peel away the dead skins and cut or pull off the roots and shrivelled leaves. Do not remove the inner skins to expose white flesh. Store the bulbs in a cool shed.

4 Some bulbs, such as narcissi and daffodils, multiply by offset bulblets. Gently break these away from the parent bulbs and store them separately for planting later in a nursery bed.

fruit trees and keep grass short by mowing. Slacken the ties on newly planted fruit trees if they are getting tight – otherwise they will strangle the trunk. Where birds are a constant pest, cover fruit trees with netting.

Watch out for aphids on apple, pear, plum, damson and peach trees; these insects can be controlled by spraying with a systemic insecticide. Red spider mite can be controlled with dimethoate. Bronzing and early falling leaves are sure signs of fruit tree red spider mite.

Continue spraying regularly with benomyl or carbendazim against apple and pear scab. Apply pirimiphos-methyl or fenitrothion against codling moth caterpillar and tortrix caterpillar on apples. Where fruit set is heavy, thin out the fruit for the first time, but remember that there can be a heavy natural drop quite soon, so do not over-thin at this stage.

Check plums, damsons and cherries for signs of silver leaf – the shoots have a metallic appearance. Cut out all affected branches right back to healthy growth where no brown staining is evident in the cut wood.

On fan-trained plums and cherries, pinch out the tips of laterals not required for extension or as replacements, when they have made about seven leaves.

Having de-shooted wall-trained peaches and nectarines in late spring, tie in the remaining shoots to the framework as they develop.

Train new shoots of blackberry, loganberry and hybrid berries so that they are separate from the old fruiting stems.

Control weeds around all cane fruits by shallow cultivation, taking care not to damage the crop's roots. Alternatively, pull out weeds by hand. Cover bush and cane fruits with netting to deter birds.

Apply derris or malathion to cane fruits ten days after flowering to prevent raspberry beetle attack. Water cane fruits well in dry weather while the fruit is swelling.

If gooseberry bushes are carrying a heavy crop, thin the fruit to improve the size of the remaining fruit, and use the thinnings for cooking. At the end of early summer, pinch out the tips of the longest new lateral shoots to about five leaves. Treat gooseberry bushes with derris or pyrethrum to protect against defoliating gooseberry sawfly.

Destroy strawberry fruits attacked by grey mould, which is common in damp spells. Deter slugs and snails with a deep straw mulch. Protect the fruit from birds. Propagate strawberries by anchoring runners.

The vegetable garden

Plant Brussels sprouts for harvesting in late winter, and also winter cabbages and broccoli. Plant self-blanching celery as soon as possible in early summer in well-manured soil.

Plant leeks, choosing the thickest seedlings if you have a surplus, and cut the tops back by a quarter of their length and the fibrous roots by about half.

In cool regions, sow swedes for eating during the following winter, dusting the seed drills with calomel as a precaution against club root disease. Thin swede seedlings early and dust them with HCH to protect against flea beetle attack.

Towards the end of early summer, sow spinach beet for eating in autumn to spring.

Plant marrows if seeds were not sown directly in the prepared bed earlier. Also plant outdoor tomatoes in their cropping beds or grow bags. Insert canes or other means of support alongside tomato plants, although bush varieties need no support. Water the young plants immediately and give further thorough waterings every few days if the weather remains dry. Give a liquid feed weekly.

Continue to sow salad crops to maintain supplies during late summer. There is still time to sow batches of peas and French beans.

Peonies are among the most beautifully formed of all garden flowers, their satiny petals providing rich shades of red and pink, or soft creams and white, often with a prominent boss of golden stamens in the centre. Once the flowers have faded, these plants remain attractive right through until the autumn because their leaves are also very decorative. *Paeonia officinalis* 'J. C. Weguellin' has vivid magenta-crimson, single flowers; or choose from the wide range of single, semi-double and double hybrids of *P. lactiflora*.

Other early summer flowers are wide-ranging – herbaceous perennials and old-fashioned roses being most prominent. Aquilegias, campanulas, delphiniums and geraniums provide a wealth of blue and mauve flowers and heights from just a few inches to 1.5m (5ft) or more. Dicentra, erigeron and lupins add pink and white flowers to the early summer scene, while hypericum and eschscholzia are valued for their hotter oranges and yellows.

MID SUMMER

With perennials and annuals in full bloom and the sun at its hottest, watering is often the most important job.

The warmest mid summer days reach temperatures of at least 24°C (75°F), especially in inland areas of southern Britain. But this can also be the wettest part of summer – hilly areas of the north and west often receive heavy rain and thunderstorms for several hours at a time. Humid, hazy spells are common, and night temperatures rarely fall below 10°C (50°F) in inland gardens.

High humidity and frequent rain produce ideal conditions for the spread of disease. To ensure good control of such diseases, dust or spray susceptible plants, such as Michaelmas daisy and solidago, with fungicides as routine – once a disease has taken a firm hold, it is usually too late to expect control measures to succeed.

Garden beds and borders

In very dry weather, water liberally to extend the flowering season, but do not give so much water that leaf growth is encouraged at the expense of flowers. It is better to give a lot of water once or twice a week than a small volume every day, since the latter method encourages the roots to grow towards the surface, where they dry out more quickly and find little nutrient.

LAWN MAINTENANCE

During prolonged dry weather, water the lawn thoroughly once or twice a week, in the morning or evening – a lot of water applied infrequently is more beneficial than a little water every day. Apply water at the rate of 10-20 litres (2-4 gallons) per sq m/yd so that it penetrates to at least 15cm (6in) deep. Brown patches may develop where weeds begin to infest weakened areas.

If the lawn is compacted, spike the surface with a garden fork or lawn aerator before watering. If necessary, apply a selective lawn weedkiller during warm, moist weather, but never in full sun.

▼ **Mid summer glory** An annual rainbow of vivid colour comprises red poppies, magenta-pink silene, golden rudbeckias, yellow chrysanthemums, blue echiums and cornflowers, and indigo larkspurs.

LAYERING CORDON SWEET PEAS

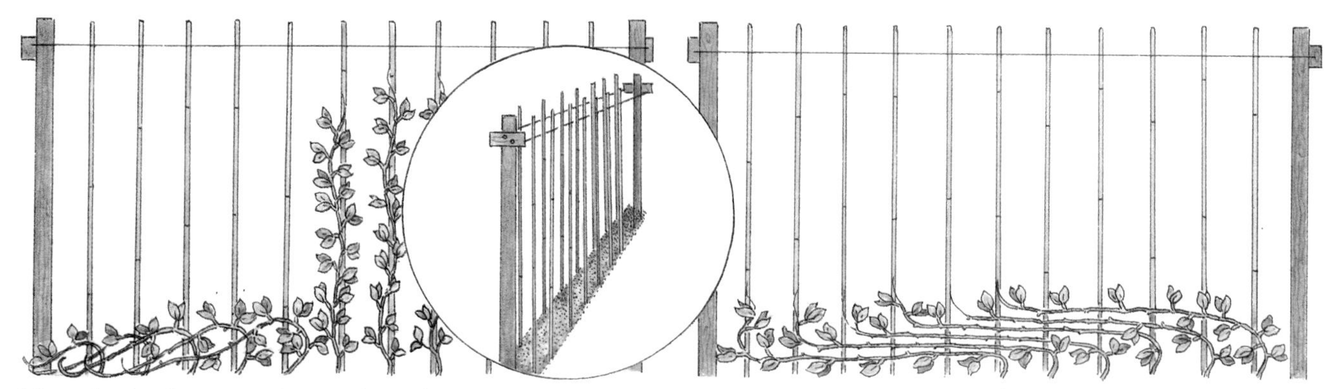

1 Layering is often carried out with cordon sweet peas to improve flower quality. When the plants are 1.5m (5ft) high, starting at one end of a row, unfasten the ties on the first four to six plants and gently lay the stems on the ground.

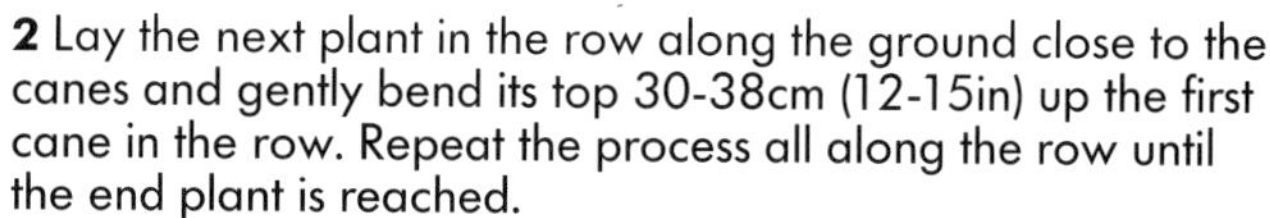

2 Lay the next plant in the row along the ground close to the canes and gently bend its top 30-38cm (12-15in) up the first cane in the row. Repeat the process all along the row until the end plant is reached.

3 Secure the stem of each plant with two or three wire ring, raffia or string ties. At this stage, the end plants, which were the first to be unfastened from their canes, are still left lying on the ground.

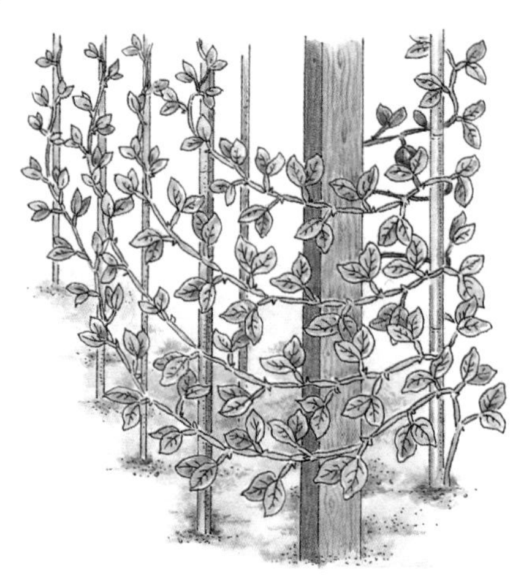

4 Bring the first plants from the second row round the end post and tie them to the vacant canes. Finally, secure the untied first row plants to the vacant second-row canes. Continue to pinch out all tendrils and side-shoots.

Give support to taller-growing plants well before they show signs of flopping over – though this should have been done in late spring or early summer. Continue to tie upright plants to their stakes or supports as they grow. Also check that the lower ties are not strangling the stems, which will have thickened by now.

Continue to spray border plants and annuals every four weeks to control aphids and other sap-sucking insect pests. Hoe regularly to control weeds.

Biennials Early in mid summer, direct-sow wallflowers and sweet Williams where they are to flower the following year. (Mid summer is too late to sow these biennials in nursery beds.)

As soon as they reach manageable size, set out in a nursery bed seedlings of hardy wallflowers, sweet Williams (and hardy perennials) which are at present in seed boxes or outdoor seedbeds.

Annuals and perennials The lives of many flowering plants – especially annuals – are shortened if they are allowed to form seed-heads or pods. So dead-head all plants as soon as the flowers fade, unless you specifically want seed-heads for their decorative value later in the year, or you want to collect the seeds for sowing next year. Removing the old flower heads also keeps the garden colourful and attractive.

Continue cutting back early flowering border perennials. Some kinds, such as *Achillea taygetea* and *Salvia* × *superba*, will produce a second flush of flowers by late summer if they are cut back quite severely just before the main flowering is over. In warm, sheltered gardens, delphiniums and lupins may also flower again if cut down right to ground level.

However, do not cut back herbaceous peonies that have flowered; just remove the dead flower heads – the foliage is ornamental, and peonies need to die back naturally.

Chrysanthemums Keep the plants well watered and give a monthly liquid feed of a general fertilizer. On all but spray and pompon varieties, if large blooms are required, reduce each plant to five flowering shoots by breaking off the weaker shoots.

Bulbs and corms Lift and store spring bulbs, such as tulips, daffodils and hyacinths, if this was not done in early summer.

Plant autumn-flowering bulbs now – they provide a touch of unusual form among shrubs and trees at a time when flowers are fairly scarce. Excellent types include *Amaryllis belladonna, Nerine bowdenii, Sternbergia lutea* and *Colchicum*, as well as autumn-flowering *Crocus* species.

Stake gladioli plants individually if you want straight stems for cutting. Use wire rings, string or raffia for securing the main stems to the stakes.

Order spring-flowering bulbs as soon as possible – daffodils in particular benefit from early autumn planting.

If dahlias are slow in growth – they should be about 60cm (2ft) tall by the middle of summer – feed them every two weeks with liquid fertilizer. Always apply the feed to the soil when it is damp. In dry weather, water the soil first.

To obtain long stems and good flowers for cutting, disbud a proportion of each dahlia plant's stems. At the top of each main shoot is a crown bud, with two smaller buds just below. Remove the lower two buds. Alternatively, to obtain a large number of smaller flowers, remove the crown bud, leaving the two lower ones to grow on.

At the beginning of mid summer dig up and divide dwarf and intermediate bearded irises if they have been undisturbed for three years. Tall bearded irises need the same treatment from the end of mid summer onwards, when they have finished flowering.

When replanting bearded irises, cut the best single rhizomes from the old clumps and plant them in a sunny site in soil which has had well-rotted manure or compost as well as some general fertilizer dug into the top 23cm (9in). Leave the tops of the rhizomes above ground level and press the soil firmly on to the roots below. This will ensure that the rhizome gets baked and well ripened in the sun.

After planting the iris rhizomes, cut off the top half of the leaves to lessen moisture loss and possible loosening in the soil by the wind rocking the plants to and fro.

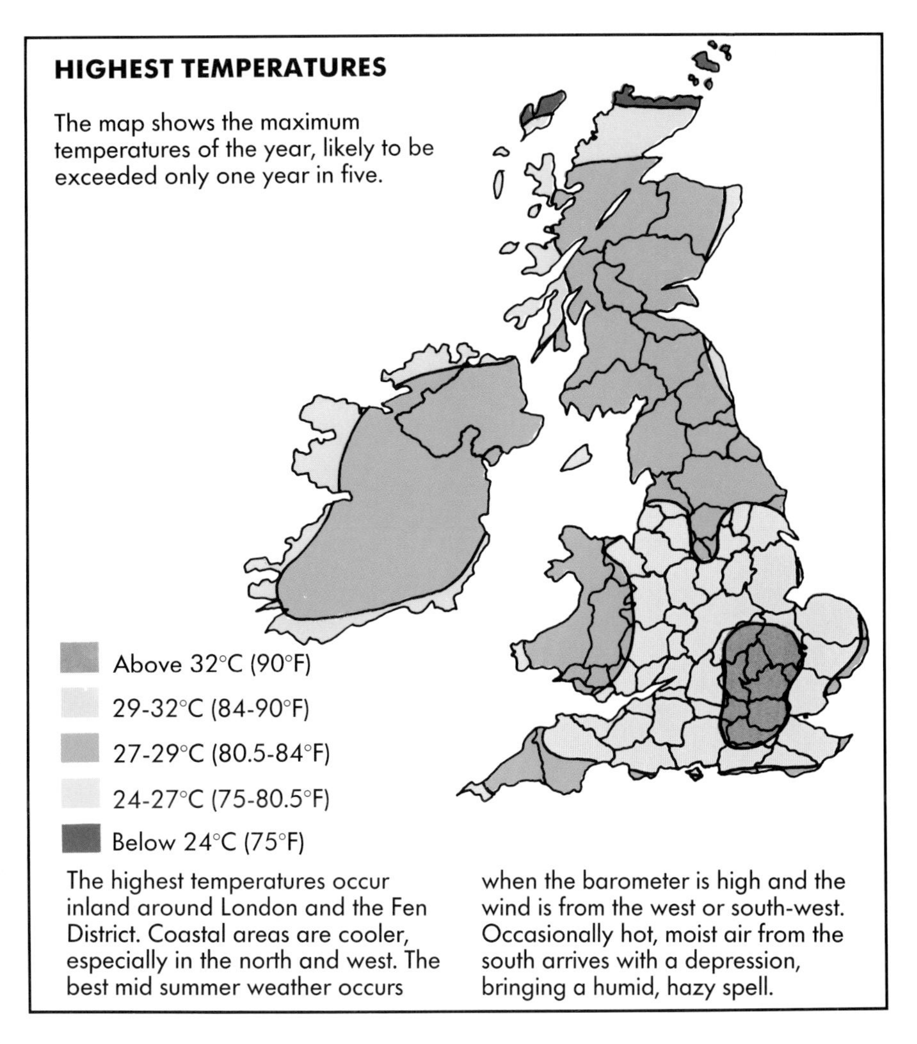

HIGHEST TEMPERATURES

The map shows the maximum temperatures of the year, likely to be exceeded only one year in five.

The highest temperatures occur inland around London and the Fen District. Coastal areas are cooler, especially in the north and west. The best mid summer weather occurs when the barometer is high and the wind is from the west or south-west. Occasionally hot, moist air from the south arrives with a depression, bringing a humid, hazy spell.

Roses

Summer pruning consists of cutting blooms for home decoration, and dead-heading – both procedures encourage new, strong shoots to grow in the directions required to maintain shapely plants. They also assist the next flush of blooms to develop on repeat-flowering plants.

When cutting blooms from newly planted roses, do not cut stems longer than required. Ideally, remove only one-third of the flowering stem produced this season. Roses need all their leaves to produce enough food for the next flowers. Dead-head back to a compound leaf with flower buds in the axil.

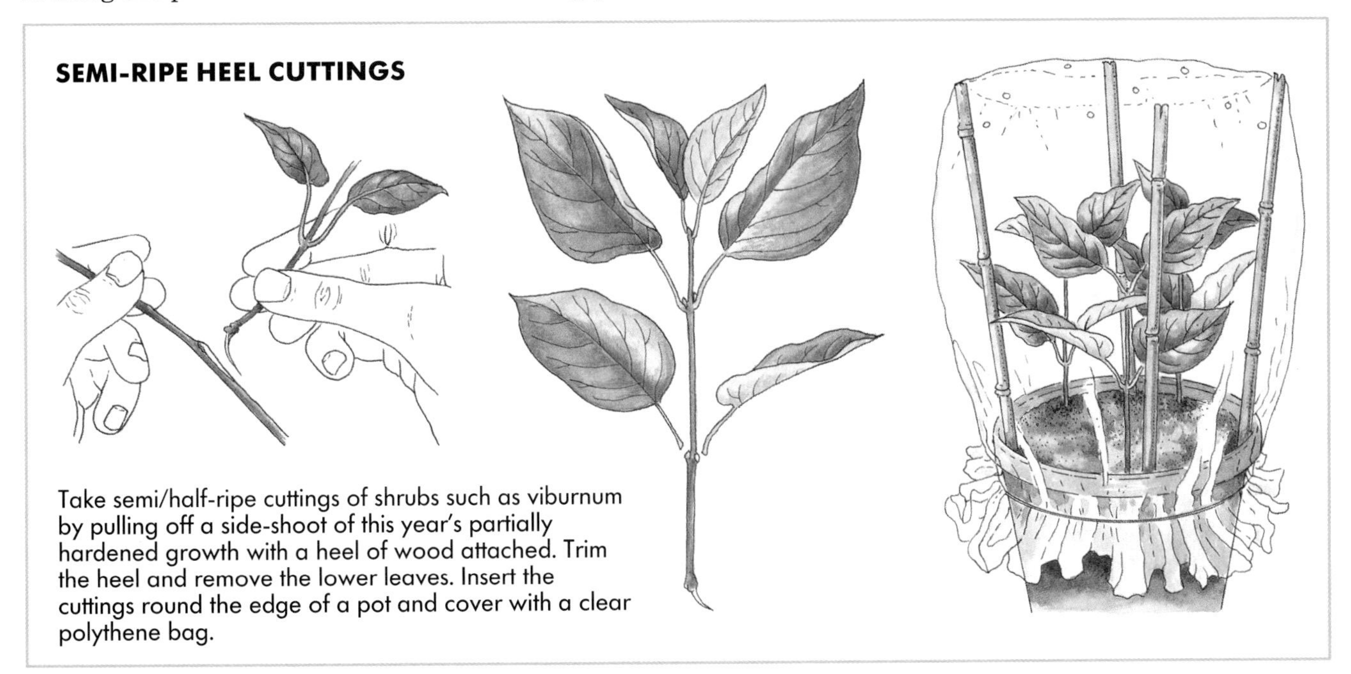

SEMI-RIPE HEEL CUTTINGS

Take semi/half-ripe cuttings of shrubs such as viburnum by pulling off a side-shoot of this year's partially hardened growth with a heel of wood attached. Trim the heel and remove the lower leaves. Insert the cuttings round the edge of a pot and cover with a clear polythene bag.

As soon as the first batch of rose blooms is over, feed the plants with a proprietary rose fertilizer, hoeing it into the surface soil. Spray regularly with rose insecticide and fungicide.

Shrubs and trees

After flowering, prune deciduous shrubs – such as *Philadelphus* – by removing faded flowers and cutting out thin and weak shoots.

Watch for sucker growth on grafted rhododendron and azalea hybrids. In bad cases, the wild rhododendron rootstock will take over. Using secateurs, cut off all sucker growth as soon as it is noticed.

Take cuttings of *Buddleia alternifolia*, callicarpa, campsis, cistus, clematis, cotoneaster, deutzia, euonymus, *Hydrangea paniculata, Hydrangea petiolaris*, mahonia, spiraea and viburnum. Root these in a cold frame.

Root cuttings of camellia, elaeagnus, honeysuckle (*Lonicera*), hypericum, pyracantha and rhus in pots under glass. Layer shoots of passion flower (*Passiflora*) and wisteria in pots sunk in the ground.

Sweet peas (*Lathyrus odoratus* varieties) come in a wide range of colours, including pastel and vivid shades, except yellows and oranges. The most familiar types climb to 1.5-3m (5-10ft). But for a small garden, the dwarf bushy types are ideal and need no support. 'Bijou' is an early flowering mixture, reaching just 45cm (1½ft) in height.

Other mid summer flowers suitable for growing in association with dwarf sweet peas include cornflower (*Centaurea*), godetia, larkspur (*Delphinium consolida*), lavatera, petunia and verbena.

The fruit garden

Most of the soft fruits are bearing produce now and will need attention after picking. Other fruit crops are nearing maturity.

Continue to watch for codling moth attack on apples, and for red spider mite on apples and pears, spraying as necessary. Treat small outbreaks of woolly aphid by brushing with malathion, pirimiphos-methyl or dimethoate. If the fruit has been well protected until now against apple and pear scab, later attacks will not mark it seriously, so further spraying for this disease is unnecessary.

Complete the thinning of apple and pear fruit as soon as natural drop is over, reducing the number of fruits to one from each cluster and with a final spacing of 10-15cm (4-6in). Support branches of trained apples, pears and other top fruit which are heavily laden, either by a stake for each branch or by ties from a centre post.

Summer prune cordon, espalier and dwarf pyramid apples and pears, dealing with the pear trees first because they are ready before the apples. Spread the job of pruning over the next eight weeks. While working on trained trees, check that the ties are not cutting into stems and branches.

As soon as picking of plums and damsons has been completed, prune the trees. Continue to tie in new growths which are being kept as replacements on wall-trained peaches and nectarines.

Pick raspberries as they ripen. Once all the fruit has been harvested, cut off the old canes close to the ground to leave room for the new growths which will carry next year's crop. Tie new growths to the support wires.

With blackberries and loganberries, train in new shoots, keeping them separate from the fruiting shoots. Apply derris or malathion against raspberry beetle ten days after flowering.

Pick black currants as they mature. Prune the bushes after picking if necessary, leaving the robust new shoots intact. Watch out for reversion disease.

Pick gooseberries as they ripen, but look out for sawfly larvae, which defoliate the bushes.

Tidy strawberry beds after picking. Strip off and burn the old leaves. Remove runners – unless they are wanted to produce more plants – and apply fertilizer.

The vegetable garden

Complete the planting of leeks as soon as possible, if not already done. Also complete the planting of late Brussels sprouts, winter cabbages and broccoli by the end of the second week of mid summer.

Sow large winter radishes and, in mild areas, sow swedes during the first two weeks of mid summer. Late sowings of round-seeded peas and globe beetroot will mature in mid autumn. And there is still time to sow spinach beet.

Pinch out the side-shoots which grow from the leaf axils of cordon tomato plants. Do not pinch out side-shoots from bush tomatoes, but cover the ground beneath them with straw or black plastic to keep the fruits off the ground.

At the end of mid summer lift and store onions.

LATE SUMMER

Watering, lawnmowing and dead-heading continue to be important jobs, and there are plenty of crops to harvest.

The weather in late summer usually follows the same trends as mid summer. Spells of anticyclone weather may raise the daytime temperature to 27°C (80°F) or above, and they often end in severe thunderstorms. Westerly winds arriving with a depression often bring long periods of dull weather and lots of rain, especially in the hilly areas of north and west Britain.

The nights are lengthening considerably by late summer, and night temperatures are getting lower. Dewfall can be heavy and this aggravates plant disease problems. However, dry, cool, clear nights may also occur – in the north of Britain night temperatures can approach freezing point in sheltered valleys.

The last weeks of summer often bring high winds, so check plant stakes regularly. Also repair all gaps in hedges and fences so that the garden is better protected against wind damage.

In the south-east of England, the total rainfall during late summer rarely exceeds the amount of water taken up by plants, so regular watering is necessary – especially with shallow-rooted plants, such as bedding annuals and vegetables, which can't reach moisture in the subsoil. Unshaded gardens with a south-facing aspect are most vulnerable to the effects of low rainfall.

Garden borders

Continue dead-heading annuals to keep them tidy and encourage more flowers. However, perennials flowering after mid summer are unlikely to flower a second time if cut back. Remember that the dead flowers may develop into attractive seed heads, and that tufts of bare, cut-down stalks can look very unsightly, so consider whether it is worth leaving the plants alone.

After tall plants have finished flowering, dead-head them, cut off any tall weak stems, and then remove the supports if they are too obtrusive. The remaining stems should be strong enough to support themselves.

Continue to spray perennials and annuals every four weeks with insecticide and fungicide, especially if they are susceptible to aphid infestation or mildew disease. Aster, calendula, dahlia, petunia, solidago and sweet pea,

LAWN MAINTENANCE

Continue to mow the lawn regularly, trim edges, and water well once or twice a week during prolonged periods of drought. Also apply a proprietary lawn fungicide for disease control if necessary, and a selective lawn weedkiller during good weather.

▼ **Late summer borders** The huge straw-coloured flower sprays of feather grass (*Stipa gigantea*) are the focal point in this herbaceous border backed by dark green tree and shrub foliage. They sway gently above orange turk's-cap lilies and trusty perennials like border phlox, monarda and liatris whose range of pinks and contrasting flower forms are highlighted by pure white Shasta daisies (*Chrysanthemum maximum*).

for instance, are particularly vulnerable to attack.

Mulch and, if necessary, feed and water sweet peas to extend flowering over a long period. If you do not apply a new mulch, hoe between plants to eliminate competing weeds. Cut sweet pea blooms regularly – they last well in water indoors. Never allow blooms to fade and droop on the plants, or to form seed pods, otherwise the flowering period will be reduced drastically.

Dig over neglected beds and borders before the end of summer, hoeing off or turning over all annual weeds while the sun is still warm so that they will die rapidly. Pull up by hand or fork out any perennial weeds, trying to leave as few of their roots in the ground as possible – this is easier when the soil is moist. Cut back plants which have outgrown their space, even if this means sacrificing the remaining flowers.

Plant out well grown perennial seedlings raised under glass. They should be moved to a nursery bed where they will get good light and plenty of space – not to their final positions, which may be rather cramped at this time of year. The young plants will be ready for moving again, to their final positions, during autumn or next spring.

Chrysanthemums Before the third week of late summer, complete the disbudding of outdoor chrysanthemums, which are grown for single-stemmed, extra-large blooms. Give a liquid feed, but stop fertilizing once the buds show colour. Keep the plants well supported to allow for the increasing weight of the flowering stems.

Bulbs, corms and tubers Replant lifted daffodil and narcissus bulbs by the end of late summer, unless they are to be used for spring displays in beds which cannot be cleared of summer bedding until autumn. These bulbs recommence their root growth in late summer and benefit from early planting. Plant all but the smallest bulbs 15cm (6in) deep.

Also plant madonna lily (*Lilium candidum*) as soon as possible, with not more than 5cm (2in) of soil above each bulb.

Feed dahlias with liquid fertilizer, and keep the plants carefully tied to avoid wind damage. Continue to spray dahlias against blackfly and other pests.

PROPAGATING LILIES FROM BULBILS

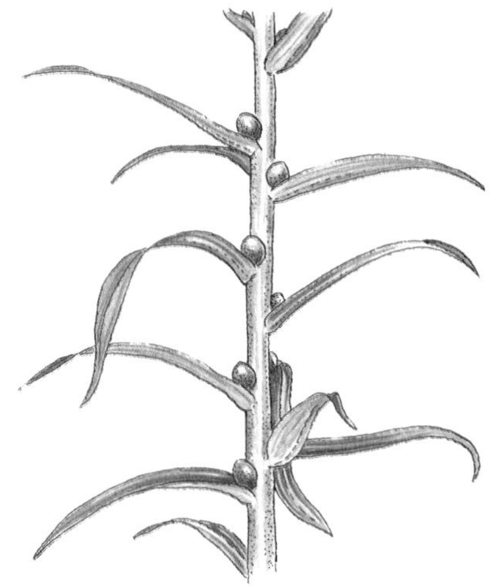

1 Tiger lilies (*Lilium tigrinum*), *Lilium sargentiae* and some hybrid lilies produce bulbils (small bulbs) on their stems, nestling in the axils of the leaves. Gather the dark coloured bulbils when they fall at a touch.

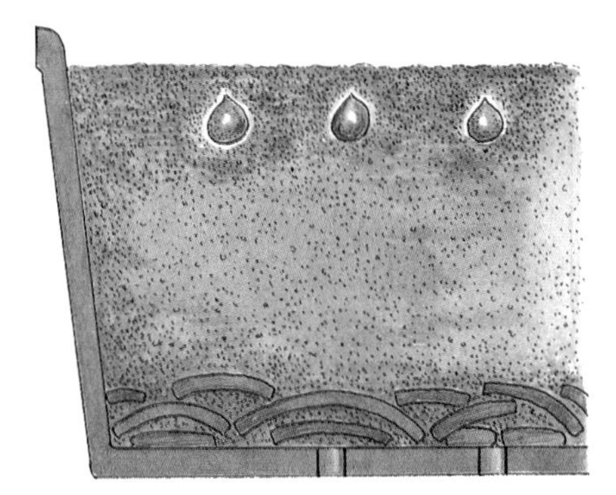

2 Plant the bulbils about 5cm (2in) apart in a deep seed box filled with a proprietary potting compost. Either cover the bulbils with 12mm (½in) of compost or just press them into the surface with your fingertips.

Cut gladioli for indoor decoration when the first flower on the spike is just opening. Leave at least four leaves when cutting, otherwise the new corm developing from the old one for next year's flowers will be deprived of its source of nourishment.

Rock garden plants

Take cuttings of rock garden plants which are becoming straggly with age, or which are producing too few flowers – such as helianthemums, rock pinks (*Dianthus*), achilleas, mossy saxifrages and most of the shrubby types. All these have finished flowering by the start of late summer.

A shaded cold frame or cloche will provide enough protection. (Don't put rock plant cuttings in a greenhouse unless you have a mist propagation unit.) Dig the soil well, reducing it to a fine tilth, and lighten heavy soil by mixing in sand. Spread a surface layer of sharp sand for good drainage.

There are four main types of alpine cuttings:

☐ Tip cuttings are made from the top section of non-flowering shoots, cut off cleanly just below a leaf node. Lengths vary from 4cm (1½in) to 7.5cm (3in), depending on the habit of the plant. Trim leaves from the lower half.

☐ Heel cuttings are obtained by pulling off short growths from a larger branch. Torn gently downwards, they will come away with a little tailpiece or heel. Pare away any ragged wood and trim the leaves from the lower half of the shoot before putting in the soil.

☐ Basal cuttings are made by severing shoots at, or just below, ground level. These need little trimming and may already show traces of new roots.

☐ Root cuttings are pieces of fleshy root, taken while the plant is dormant. Prepare them by cutting the roots into sections about 5cm (2in) long.

Roses

Continue to remove blooms as they fade. Do not apply rose fertilizers after the end of mid summer since they would encourage late, soft growth that would not harden before the first frost.

If greenfly appear on shoots or flower buds, spray with a systemic rose insecticide. Also continue to spray regularly with rose fungicide against black spot and rust.

Shrubs and trees

Prune shrubs that have just finished flowering by shortening the flowering shoots and thinning out old and weak wood. Shrubs needing this treatment include evergreen ceanothus, escallonia, lavender (*Lavandula*), senecio and deciduous species of honeysuckle (*Lonicera*).

Well established, vigorous wisteria may need cutting back. Take out the tips of young shoots after they have made three or four leaves, to contain growth.

TAKING ROCK PLANT CUTTINGS

1 The four types of material used for propagating rock garden plants and alpines are tip cuttings, heel cuttings, basal cuttings and root cuttings. All of these can be rooted in a cold frame or under cloches.

2 Insert the lower halves of tip, heel and basal cuttings in small holes made with a dibber, pointed stick or pencil. Firm them in gently with your fingers. Level the surface of the bed and water thoroughly.

3 Unless the cuttings are grown in a cold frame, protect them with a cloche. Close the ends and shade with sacking. Spray the cuttings daily with water during hot weather. Remove the cloche when new growth indicates rooting.

If not already carried out in mid summer, take cuttings of callicarpa, cistus, cotinus, escallonia, euonymus, honeysuckle, hypericum, *Jasminum officinale*, pyracantha, spiraea and viburnum. Root them in a cold frame in pots filled with a proprietary cuttings compost and leave them until the following late spring.

In a shaded greenhouse or in a cold frame, also root 10-15cm (4-6in) long half-ripe cuttings from the current year's growth of bay *(Laurus nobilis), Buddleia davidii*, caryopteris, fuchsia, heathers, hebe, holly (*Ilex*), ivy (*Hedera*), lilac (*Syringa*), pernettya, pieris, senecio and skimmia. And take 7.5-10cm (3-4in) long half-ripe heel cuttings of broom (*Cytisus*), ceanothus and genista.

Propagate rhododendrons and azaleas in late summer by layering *in situ*. The pinned-down shoots should be growing strongly on their own roots after two or three years, when they can be severed from the parent for planting out separately.

Continue to trim all fast-growing hedges, such as privet and *Lonicera nitida*. Remove all weeds growing at the base of a hedge by hoeing or applying a contact weedkiller.

The fruit garden

Early top fruit varieties are beginning to ripen in late summer, and most soft fruits come to an end. Protect ripening fruit from birds by netting the trees, and lure wasps away from the trees with traps consisting of a spoonful of jam mixed with water in a jam jar. Protect late-fruiting raspberries from attack by birds by covering the canes with fine-mesh netting.

Watch early-maturing apples and pears carefully and pick them while slightly under-ripe – they retain their best flavour for only a short period. Test fruit for near-ripeness by lifting and twisting gently. When it is ready it parts easily from the spur.

Continue to summer-prune restricted apple and pear trees – cordons, and espaliers, for instance – as in mid summer. Also complete the summer pruning of any plums and damsons.

In the middle of late summer, spray sweet and sour/acid cherries with a copper fungicide to control bacterial canker.

RIPENING MARROWS

To assist the ripening of marrows for storage in autumn, rest the fruits on platforms of glass or wood, supported on bricks. This will raise them above the leaves where they will get more sun.

Hardy species fuchsias (*Fuchsia magellanica* varieties) flower for a long period, beginning in mid summer and continuing right through until the first hard frost of autumn, but they are especially showy in late summer. Growing up to 2.5m (8ft) tall with age, they can be used for informal hedging or as specimens in a mixed border or shrubbery. 'Riccartonii' has slender scarlet-and-purple flowers.

Other late summer flowers, making good partners for fuchsias, include shrubby blue, mauve, red or white hibiscus, pink, blue or white hydrangeas and bright yellow hypericums.

Among the wide range of herbaceous perennials and bedding annuals still providing rich colours are dahlias, white Shasta daisies (*Chrysanthemum maximum*), golden rudbeckias, orange or yellow African marigolds (*Tagetes erecta*), red or pink nicotianas, and pink, mauve or purple petunias. Blue agapanthus and white summer hyacinth (*Galtonia*) are real gems.

When the fruit from wall-trained peaches, nectarines and sour/acid cherries has been picked, prune the shoots that have borne fruit, leaving the current season's growth that has been selected to replace them. Re-tie new shoots where necessary to make the best use of space and to encourage the growth to ripen.

Pick blackberries, loganberries and hybrid berries when fully ripe. Continue to train new shoots. When harvesting has finished, cut out all shoots that have fruited.

With black currant bushes, try to keep the leaves as healthy as possible so that they continue to feed the present season's shoots as long as possible. Control leaf spot disease, which is the most likely to cause premature leaf fall, and also rust disease, by spraying with mancozeb, benomyl or carbendazim after fruit picking is over.

Plant rooted strawberry runners in late summer to ensure a good crop the following year. Runners rooted in pots in early summer are the most successful and are ideal for cloches.

The vegetable garden

At the beginning of late summer sow seeds of spring cabbage, first dressing the drills with calomel powder as a precaution against club root. Make the seedbed in ground that has not been manured since the previous autumn.

Until the middle of late summer, sow batches of 'All The Year Round' lettuces for cutting in early winter.

Pick cobs of sweet corn when the tassels on the ends have withered and the seeds are firm but exude 'milk' when pressed with your thumb nail. Harvest the cobs by breaking them off the stems.

Start to harvest self-blanching celery as soon as there are sizeable plants. The crop should be cleared before the first hard frost.

Herbs Every four years chives should be divided in late summer. Lift the clumps and cut them into segments with a sharp knife, taking care that each segment retains a number of roots. Replant the clumps 30cm (1ft) apart.

Take cuttings of bay, hyssop, lavender, mint, rosemary, rue and sage, inserting them in well-drained soil in open ground. For the first two weeks, protect the cuttings from sun and winds with a cloche, and water in the evenings until the roots have formed. Alternatively, put the cuttings in pots filled with sand and place in a cold frame.

Collect and dry the seeds of dill and fennel. Cut and prepare foliage herbs for drying. Store dried herbs before they have had time to re-absorb moisture from the air. Rub them between your hands, discarding stems and other chaff, and store in tightly sealed jars or plastic bags.

EARLY AUTUMN

As fruit is harvested and dahlias and chrysanthemums blaze with colour, shortening days spell the onset of autumn.

As the last days of summer draw to a close and the sun's rays weaken, the difference in climate between north and south increases. There may still be spells of warm, dry weather with temperatures in the south often reaching 21°C (70°F), but the north is much cooler. Nights become colder and can be humid, making mildew more likely.

Early morning frosts can be expected in most inland areas, while sporadic frost is likely in valley bottoms and sheltered pockets in northern areas, even when surrounding hillsides and higher garden slopes remain well above freezing point.

Cool, wet, windy weather is common in the west, with sunnier, drier weather in the east. Towards the end of early autumn, the weather may be more unsettled, with strong winds and rain in all areas. To protect plants from gale damage, check that stakes and ties are secure and be ready to move tender plants under cover if frost is forecast. Control mildew – especially on Michaelmas daisies – by spraying with fungicide.

Garden borders

For the first two or three weeks continue dead-heading and cutting back. Hoe new beds prepared in mid or late summer, particularly if deep digging was followed soon afterwards by rain.

Continue to harden-off rooted cuttings of garden pinks (*Dianthus*) and plant them out when growing strongly. Towards the

LAWN MAINTENANCE

Scarify or rake the lawn vigorously in both directions to remove debris and open up the turf surface. This lets air and water into the soil, and 'prunes' leaves and roots. If the lawn is compacted, spike it with a fork or hollow tine aerator. Dress poor draining or clay soils with sharp sand; on light or sandy soils use compost. Brush in well.

Apply a proprietary granular autumn fertilizer, sprinkling it in two directions at the rate of 60g (2oz) per sq m3yd. Continue to treat areas affected by disease and to control weeds and moss. Repair damaged areas by reseeding or by laying new turf if it is really bad.

▼ **Early autumn blaze** Sheltered by a brick wall, a multitude of dahlias, in their numerous different shapes and colours, jostle for space with brown-eyed, golden-orange rudbeckias and a cascade of mauve-cerise Michaelmas daisies (*Aster novi-belgii*). In the foreground, antirrhinums add their bright red spires.

REPAIRING A LAWN

1 In early autumn, repair damaged patches in the lawn by re-seeding. Use an edging iron to cut round the damaged area, and lift out the turf carefully with a spade. Loosen the soil beneath with a garden fork.

2 Fill the hole with a thin layer of sieved soil and firm gently. Repeat in layers until the surface of the soil in the patch is at the same level as the surrounding turf. Sow seed at the rate of 40-60g (1½-2oz) per sq m/yd.

3 Gently sift a mixture of soil and peat substitute over the seed to a depth of 12mm (½in). To protect the bed from birds, stick short pegs in the grass around the patch and criss-cross black cotton between them.

end of early autumn, stop pinks that start to run to flower without making good side-shoots. Do this in early morning during damp weather when the tops snap off most easily.

Continue frequent watering of plants in containers and remove faded flowers. Discard plants that are past their best and prepare empty containers for spring bulbs. Replenish the compost and plant the bulbs slightly deeper than normally recommended so that plants for winter colour can be placed on top. Empty containers that will not be used during the winter and store timber containers under cover.

Annuals Remove fading annuals to make room for spring bedding plants. In mild districts and on well drained soils, direct-sow the hardiest of the annuals – such as calendula, cornflower (*Centaurea*) and candytuft (*Iberis*) – to over-winter outdoors. Plants that are 5-7.5cm (2-3in) high by mid winter stand the best chance of coming through harsh weather.

Biennials Water hardy biennials growing in rows in a nursery bed, then plant out in their flowering positions the next day. Water the ground thoroughly beforehand if the weather is dry. Set the plants out with a trowel and water generously around their roots.

Chrysanthemums Outdoor types are now in full flower. Label the best for next year's stock. Cut fully open blooms for the house.

Bulbs and tubers Plant bulbs – preferably in groups – between shrubs or herbaceous plants, in rock gardens and in lawns. Bury each bulb twice as deep as its height. For instance, a 5cm (2in) tall daffodil bulb should be covered with 10cm (4in) of soil.

Pot up bulbs for indoor flowering during winter and spring. Towards the end of early autumn, use bulbs to replace unattractive summer bedding. Plant the bulbs on their own, or between wallflowers, forget-me-nots and polyanthus.

With dahlias, check stakes and ties to prevent gale damage. Give a fortnightly liquid feed to maintain good quality blooms and build up strong tubers.

ROSE CUTTINGS

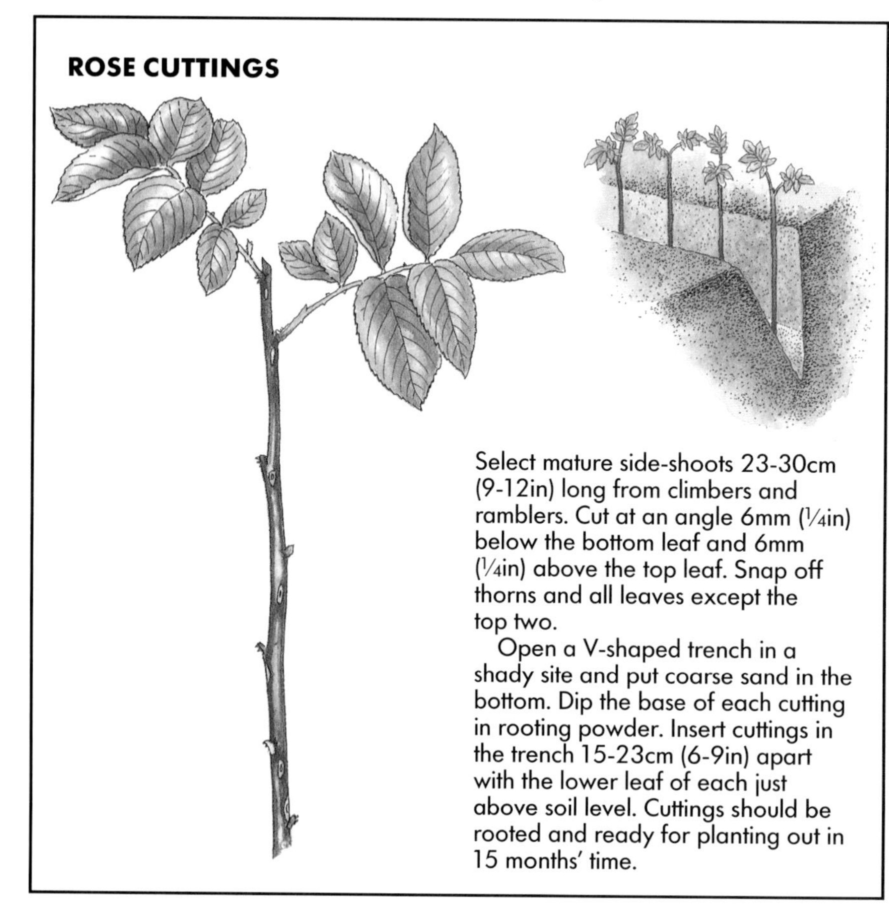

Select mature side-shoots 23-30cm (9-12in) long from climbers and ramblers. Cut at an angle 6mm (¼in) below the bottom leaf and 6mm (¼in) above the top leaf. Snap off thorns and all leaves except the top two.

Open a V-shaped trench in a shady site and put coarse sand in the bottom. Dip the base of each cutting in rooting powder. Insert cuttings in the trench 15-23cm (6-9in) apart with the lower leaf of each just above soil level. Cuttings should be rooted and ready for planting out in 15 months' time.

Roses

Continue to dead-head faded blooms. On weak plants, cut the stem above the first leaf; on vigorous plants cut off faded blooms with one or two leaves.

BULB PLANTERS

Planters save time and effort when dealing with large numbers of bulbs. They are particularly useful for planting bulbs in grass and among other plants where it is important to disturb the soil as little as possible.

Holding the planter by the handle, push the metal cylinder firmly into the soil. Withdraw the planter, which automatically brings the plug of soil with it. Place the bulb in the hole and replace the plug of soil by pressing the release catch on the tool's handle.

Disbud Hybrid Teas to maintain the quality of blooms. To encourage hardening of new wood before the first frost, feed with sulphate of potash by scattering a handful per sq m/yd over the surface of the bed, leaving a 15cm (6in) circle round each bush. Alternatively, use wood ash at the rate of two handfuls per sq m/yd. Hoe lightly into the surface soil.

Bend and tie in shoots of climbers to form a fan shape. This will encourage the sprouting of new side-shoots which will bear flowers. Make sure the ties are tight enough to hold the stems in place, but loose enough to allow for thickening of the stems.

Prune climbing and rambling roses which have only one flush of blooms, as well as weeping standards, removing old growth which has flowered this summer. Also take cuttings from strong side-shoots of mature wood. Floribundas and Hybrid Teas can sometimes be propagated successfully in the same way.

Spray regularly against mildew and continue to spray to prevent greenfly and black spot disease.

Shrubs and trees

At the beginning of early autumn, dig the ground thoroughly in preparation for the planting of trees and shrubs later on. Incorporate plenty of garden compost or well-rotted manure into the soil, but avoid quick-acting fertilizers.

Start planting evergreens – preferably during showery weather – at the end of early autumn. Use stakes to support upright shrubs until they are established. During dry spells, water freely and spray the foliage with water to prevent leaf drop.

Propagate berberis, griselinia, juniper, phlomis, potentilla, privet and yew from hardwood and half-ripe cuttings taken with a heel. Root in sandy soil in a shaded cold frame or in sheltered, shady, open ground. In cold weather, cover cuttings in open ground with cloches. Hardy species should be ready to plant out the following spring, while tender or semi-hardy species should be potted singly and kept in the cold frame before planting out in late spring to early summer.

Late-flowering shrubs, such as phlomis and senecio, need light pruning after flowering.

Hedges Clip new growth for the last time this season, but leave alone hedging plants which flower on new shoots in spring, such as berberis and forsythia.

Remove any remaining weeds around the base of a hedge before they set seed and either burn them or put them on the compost heap. Do not leave weeds on the surface at this time of year as they will take root again.

The fruit garden

Prepare storage places for apples and pears, checking that they are free from mice and that trays are clean. Pick fruit in cool conditions before it is fully mature. Exposed

HARVESTING PEARS

1 Harvest pears before they reach full maturity when the colour is changing from green to yellow. Fruits left on the tree too long become dry with a floury texture. Place one hand under the fruit and twist it gently.

2 The stalk should part from the spur easily. If the stalk is left attached to the tree the fruit will not store well. If the stalk brings leaves with it, it is not mature enough and will fail to ripen in storage.

3 Arrange pears on clean slatted racks – without touching each other – in a dry, moderately warm atmosphere. Fruit which is to be stored for a long time should be free from blemishes and not too large.

Sedums have dense, often flattened, heads of flowers which can almost completely cover the attractive fleshy foliage. The most familiar flower colours for autumn-flowering sedums are shades of pink, purple and red.

Sedum spectabile 'Carmen' (above) is an herbaceous plant up to 45cm (1½ft) high with pale grey-green leaves and fluffy bright carmine-pink flowers.

Other sedums in flower in early autumn are *S.* 'Autumn Joy' with pink flower heads deepening to copper-red, and *S. maximum* with flowers in shades of red and pink. *S. maximum* 'Atropurpureum' has purple-red tinted leaves and stems, and pink flowers.

Other early autumn flowers
Many perennials are still in full bloom at this time of year. For partnering with sedums, try Michaelmas daisies with starry flowers in shades of blue, purple, pink, red or lilac, or African lilies (*Agapanthus*), with long-stemmed, rounded clusters of funnel-shaped flowers in shades of blue or white.

Korean chrysanthemums have an enormous range of flower form and colour, including pink, white, yellow and orange.

Late season red-hot pokers (*Kniphofia*) have flowers in shades of red, orange and yellow, while golden rod (*Solidago*) has plumes of vivid yellow flowers.

Dahlias are an important plant for early autumn colour. There are also bulbs, such as pink autumn crocus (*Colchicum*), white or pink *Dierama* and deep pink *Nerine bowdenii.*

fruit at the tops of trees matures first, followed by fruit on the sides. Inside fruit matures last. Wrap apples which are to be stored for a long time in paper. Complete the summer pruning of apples and pears.

In the middle of early autumn, spray cherries again with a copper fungicide to control bacterial canker.

Continue to pick peaches and nectarines, prune old shoots and tie in new growth. Pick and use plums and damsons as they do not keep well. Prune the trees as soon as picking is over, protecting large wounds against disease spores.

Continue to pick blackberries, loganberries and hybrid berries when ripe. When harvesting is complete, cut out old growth and tie in new shoots.

Pick early autumn fruiting raspberries. Continue to protect autumn-fruiting strawberries against birds and slugs and cover fruit with cloches during cold weather.

The vegetable garden

In the south of Britain, sow spring crop lettuces at the beginning of early autumn for over-wintering without cloche protection.

In the north, plant spring cabbages if this was not done in late summer.

Lift maincrop carrots with a fork and cut off the tops. Use split roots as soon as possible but store surplus healthy ones in a dry shed. Put them in layers in deep boxes, packing 12mm (½in) of sand between each layer.

Harvest marrows for immediate use. If marrows are to be stored for use during the winter, leave them on the plants until mid autumn.

Use cloches to protect overwintering crops, including lettuces, spring cabbages, broad beans and carrots. This helps to cut down winter losses and speeds up maturity in spring.

Sow carrot seed on ground which was manured for the previous crop, and protect with cloches.

Herbs Sow parsley and chervil for a spring crop. Take cuttings of bay and rue, and root them in a shaded cold frame.

MID AUTUMN

Make the most of fine spells to dig the ground, clear fallen leaves and fading annuals, and divide perennials.

Mid autumn is usually wet, windy and cloudy, though the weather is often calmer and drier towards the middle of the season. Night fog is likely and frost can have a severe effect on more tender plants.

Widespread rain is particularly heavy in the west of Britain. Afternoon temperatures average 16-18°C (61-64°F) in south-east England but are considerably lower in northern England and Scotland. Scattered showers may follow with sunny periods in the east, where afternoon temperatures average 13°C (55°F).

The end of mid autumn is often stormy, so during good weather take every opportunity to carry out autumn digging. Soil dug over now gets the maximum benefit from the winter frosts, and will be broken down in time for spring planting. Tidy away fallen leaves and stack them in a heap until they have rotted down into leaf-mould – ideal for digging into the ground and for mulching.

LAWN MAINTENANCE

Apply autumn fertilizer to all lawns. To improve drainage on lawns prone to flooding or waterlogging – particularly where heavy soil has become compacted – first thoroughly rake or scarify the area. Use a hollow-tined fork to open up the surface, making holes about 10cm (4in) deep and 5-7.5cm (2-3in) apart. Apply a good quantity of sharp sand and gypsum, working them thoroughly into the surface of the turf. Do not walk on the turf during wet weather. In difficult cases, consult a drainage expert for specialist help.

Lay turf in mid autumn to give the grass time to root before winter. Prepare a weed-free turf bed in advance and allow it to settle for a few weeks. Apply fertilizer at the rate of 70g (2½oz) per sq m/yd and lightly rake it into the surface before laying the turf.

Large numbers of worm casts can make the lawn unsightly, smothering areas of grass and encouraging weeds and moss. Treat affected areas with carbaryl during dull, moist, warm weather.

Garden borders

Mid autumn is the best time for planting most herbaceous perennials, except in cold wet areas. If planting out during a wet spell, lay short boards over the ground and work from these to avoid trampling down the soil.

Plant out hardy perennials raised from seed as soon as possible so that they have time to become established before winter.

Tidy beds and borders, but cut back faded growth only if it looks unsightly. Continue dead-heading and keep down seedling weeds by hoeing in dry weather.

Divide and replant old clumps that finished flowering in early summer, but leave soft-leaved types such as pyrethrum and achillea until early spring.

◄ **Autumn tints** The flame-coloured foliage of a Virginia creeper (*Parthenocissus quinquefolia*) trails above the small golden and red leaves of a deciduous berberis. On the right, the sweet gum (*Liquidambar styraciflua*) has begun its transformation into a dome of brilliant orange and scarlet.

STORING DAHLIA TUBERS

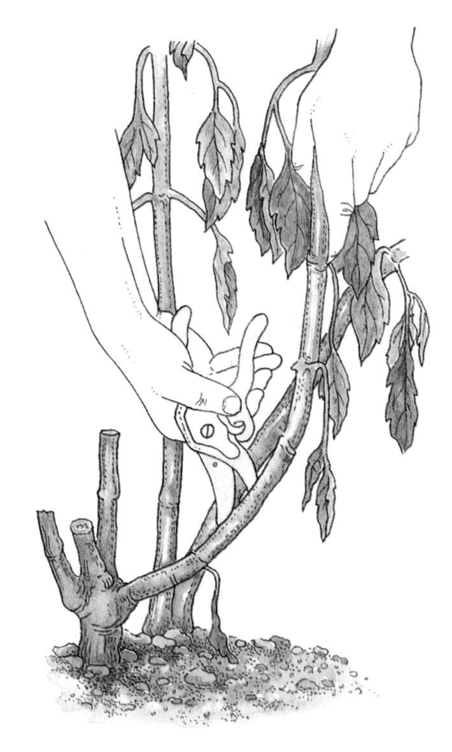

1 After the first frost, dahlia foliage becomes limp and black. As soon as this occurs, cut back the stems to 15cm (6in) and lift the tubers with a border fork. Stand them upside down to drain.

2 When the stems have dried out, put the tubers in shallow boxes. Cover with slightly damp compost, making sure that the crowns are above the surface. Store in a dry, frost-free shed.

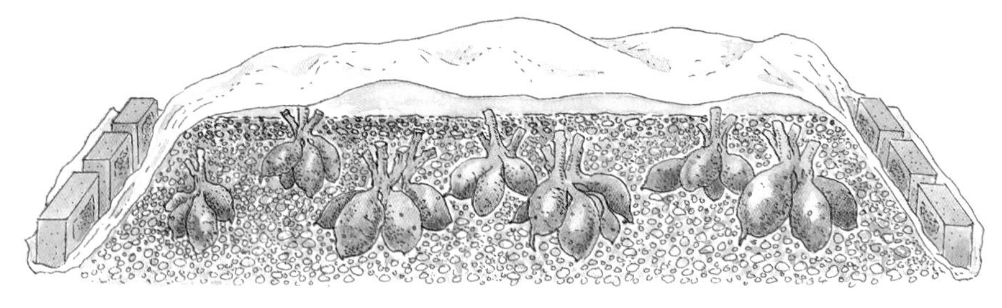

3 For outdoor storage, place the tubers on a 7.5cm (3in) layer of vermiculite. Use more vermiculite to cover the tubers to a depth of 7.5-10cm (3-4in) and cover with a layer of polythene held in place with bricks.

With new beds and borders planned for planting up in spring, dig the ground thoroughly now if not already done.

Dig over old borders which need a complete overhaul if this was not done in late summer. Dig up all growth and shake the earth off the roots. Discard all but healthy plants or any divisions which are to be replanted.

Then dig deeply and manure as for bare ground, making sure that all the roots of any perennial weeds are picked out and destroyed. Green annual weeds can be dug in, but turn them upside down and cover with at least 23cm (9in) of soil.

Chrysanthemums Prepare for over-wintering as the plants stop flowering. Many modern varieties – especially Koreans – will survive an average winter outdoors in southern England, provided the soil is well-drained and not infested with slugs. Clear away any surrounding debris and remove dead leaves and flowers, but leave the top growth intact until spring.

Elsewhere, cut the top woody growth down to about 15cm (6in) and remove any soft green shoots at ground level. Lift the stools and label them, then wash them thoroughly in cold water and bed them in a cold frame protected from frost, or in compost-filled boxes in a greenhouse.

Annuals and biennials If frosts arrive late and the weather is mild, leave summer bedding plants such as marigolds, begonias and pelargoniums until there are no more flowers on them. Otherwise, remove them as soon as possible.

Remove annuals from borders where biennials such as wallflowers and forget-me-nots are to provide a spring display. Plant these during mid autumn while the soil is still warm enough to prevent damage from severe frost or cold east winds.

Do not manure beds or borders for spring-flowering bedding plants. Instead, work bone-meal into the top 15cm (6in) of soil at the rate of about 100g (4oz) per sq m/yd at the time of planting.

If desired, sow sweet peas directly into the ground outdoors as soon as possible, but this method is suitable only for naturally-grown plants in mild districts with well-drained soil. Treat the seeds with a proprietary fungicidal dressing and sow at the rate of 10g(⅓oz) of seed for a row 3m (10ft) long. Alternatively, sow sweet peas in pots or boxes by the middle of mid autumn and place in a cold frame. Remove the frame lights when the seedlings appear.

Bulbs, corms and tubers Complete the planting of spring bulbs and start planting tulips and hyacinths. Hoe beds of newly planted daffodils, except in the mildest areas where shoot growth may have started. Alternatively, spray with a contact herbicide to destroy weed seedlings.

Lift tender summer-flowering bulbs, such as acidanthera, chincherinchee, schizostylis and spa-

PROTECTING ALPINES

Protect alpines with woolly or hairy leaves from winter wet. Fix a pane of glass over the plant using strips of metal or galvanized wire. Alternatively, stand the glass on four wooden pegs and weight with a stone.

raxis. In cold districts, take inside tubs of amaryllis, crinums and nerines for the winter.

After lifting bulbs, dry them as quickly as possible to prevent rotting. Place in shallow boxes in any warm spot. After a few days, separate the bulbs and corms from the debris and store them in a cool dry, frost-free place.

Cut down dahlias to about 15cm (6in) above the ground as soon as the first frost blackens the plants. Lift the tubers carefully, remove as much soil as possible and then stand them upside down in a frost-free place for about a week to allow the sap on the stems to dry out. Dust the crowns with sulphur before storing.

Lift gladioli corms when the leaves turn brown. Cut off all but 12mm (½in) of the main stem and leave the corms to dry for about a week. Store them in trays in a dry and frostproof place.

Plant lilies, staking late-flowering types which are prone to wind damage. Bury the bulbs to a depth of two and a half times their height. If the soil is alkaline or very heavy, plant less deeply.

Rock gardens

Plant alpine seedlings or rooted cuttings by the third week of mid autumn, except for pot-grown plants which can go in at almost any time. When moving established plants to a new site, retain plenty of soil on the roots.

Water the plants if the soil is dry. Protect woolly or hairy-leaved plants from winter wet by covering with small sheets of glass supported on wire or metal cleats.

Renew the writing on labels that are becoming difficult to read, otherwise winter rain will make them totally illegible.

Scatter slug pellets if the weather is damp, paying particular attention to the ground close to evergreen, trailing and shrubby plants, or rough grass.

Water gardens and pools

Spread a net over the pool to catch falling leaves, clearing up the debris every week or so. Towards the end of mid autumn, thin out underwater oxygenating plants and remove old water lily leaves.

If the water is dark green or brackish, drain off half the volume and replace with fresh water. While the pool is half drained, remove old foliage and debris but leave most of the mud, which contains aquatic insects and the resting buds of some plants.

Roses

Prepare the ground for new roses which are to be planted in late autumn. Double-dig new beds, incorporating plenty of organic matter into both spits (spade depths), plus bone-meal at the rate of 50-100g (2-4oz) per sq m/yd. On light soils use materials such as chopped turf, hop manure, leaf-mould and sawdust. Lighten medium or heavy soils by adding clinker, gravel, pulverized forest bark or straw. If the topsoil is less than two spits deep, add more topsoil or dig out a hole at each planting site and mix in the materials listed above.

If the soil is strongly acid, spread lime over the surface at the rate of a good handful per sq m/yd.

Spray roses with a systemic rose insecticide if greenfly appear. In areas prone to fungal diseases continue to spray fortnightly with rose fungicide.

Shrubs and trees

Towards the end of mid autumn start planting hardy deciduous shrubs and trees in well prepared ground. Firmly stake newly planted standard trees. Do not plant in frosty or wet weather or when a strong north or north-east wind is blowing. If shrubs are delivered during bad weather, unpack them and stand in a dry shed with straw or sacking around the roots until the weather improves.

If bad weather has set in or planting cannot be done for a few weeks for other reasons, insert the shrubs in a V-shaped trench so that their roots are covered, and firm down the soil. The plants should survive until spring.

When moving evergreens, try spraying the entire plant with a special aerosol moisture-retention spray – often sold for spraying Christmas trees to reduce needle-drop. This helps to prevent wilting and the coating washes off after a month or so. It can also be used for deciduous trees which have to be moved while still in leaf.

Take 30cm (1ft) long hardwood cuttings of *Aucuba japonica*, *Buddleia davidii*, deutzia, escallonia, spring-flowering honeysuckle, philadelphus, spiraea, tamarisk and weigela. Root in sandy soil in a cold frame or in the open.

WINTER PRODUCE

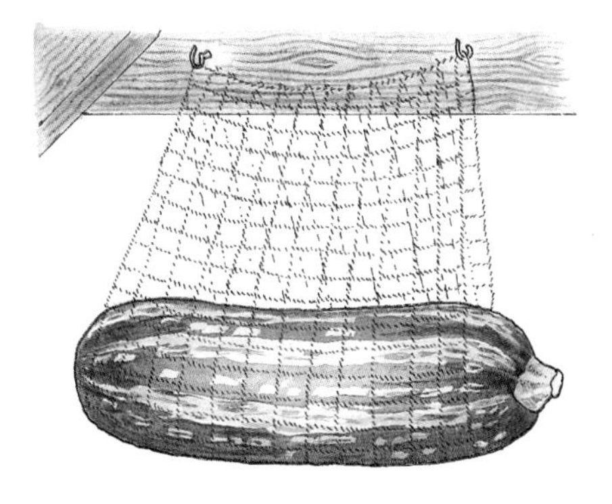

1 To store ripe marrows for winter use, hang them in nets suspended on hooks from the roof of a dry frost-free shed or a cool room. Alternatively, place on shelves in a well-ventilated position. Use by the end of early winter.

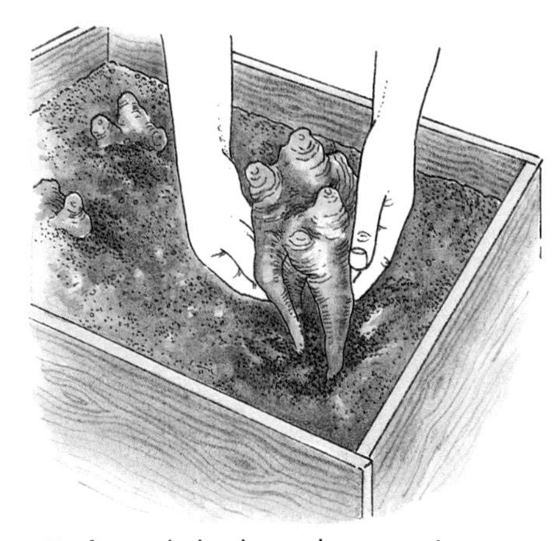

2 To force rhubarb, pack crowns in a large box and cover lightly with moist soil, leaving the growth buds exposed. Water well. Cover with black polythene or a bell jar to exclude light and keep at a temperature of 10-13°C (50-55°F). Young shoots will appear within about four weeks.

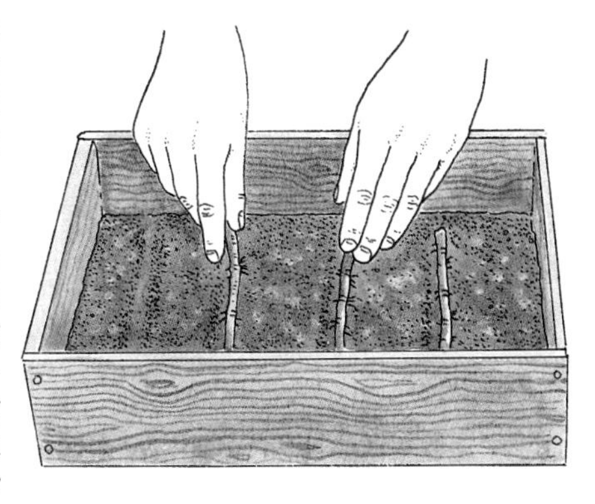

3 Force mint for use during the winter by planting a few lengths of root about 5cm (2in) deep in a box of damp soil. Place in a greenhouse or on a sunny window-sill and keep the soil moist. Fresh young shoots will be ready for use in a few weeks.

Propagate *Daphne cneorum* and fothergilla by layering young shoots in pots of compost, plunged around the parent plants.

Separate rooted suckers of celastrus, *Forsythia suspensa*, poplar, *Rhus typhina*, robinia and snowberry from their parent plants. Replant in their permanent growing positions, staking where necessary. Divide and replant overgrown *Euonymus fortunei* and spiraea.

The fruit garden

Order fruit trees and bushes for immediate delivery if this has not been done already. Begin to prepare the planting sites.

Apply bands of vegetable grease around the trunks of established apple and cherry trees to catch the wingless female winter moths as they climb up to lay eggs on twigs and fruit spurs.

Continue to pick apples and pears. Some of the longest-keeping varieties will not mature on the tree, but should be left as long as possible before they are picked. Store in polythene bags which are closed but not completely sealed and keep at an even temperature of 2-4°C (36-39°F).

In the middle of mid autumn, spray cherries with a copper fungicide against bacterial canker. Spray peach and nectarine trees at leaf-fall with Bordeaux mixture or another copper fungicide to help to control peach leaf curl in the following season.

With plums and damsons, root prune after leaf-fall any trees which regularly fruit badly. Sever vigorous roots but leave the fibrous feeding roots intact.

With blackberry, loganberry and hybrid berries, cut out canes that have fruited and train new shoots on to the supporting framework. Clear away weeds from the soil round the plants.

Propagate gooseberries by taking 25-30cm (10-12in) cuttings from well-ripened wood of the current season's growth.

Pick autumn strawberries and protect ripening fruit with cloches. Complete the replanting of runners for fruiting next year and tidy established beds.

The vegetable garden

Pick and take indoors the last of the tomatoes, including green ones which can continue ripening in a warm, light place.

Plant winter and spring lettuces early in mid autumn after raking in bone-meal at the rate of 100g (4oz) per sq m/yd. Space the plants 23cm (9in) apart in rows 30cm (1ft) apart.

Sow lettuces for growing under cloches 6mm (¼in) deep on well manured land in rows 30cm (1ft) apart. Apply a pre-emergence weedkiller. At the end of early autumn, thin out to 23-25cm (9-10in) apart and cover the ends of the cloches with glass.

Lift beetroot with a fork and twist off the tops. Store them outdoors on a base of brushwood or straw, covering them first with straw and then a layer of soil.

In mild areas, plant out spring cabbages early in mid autumn. As the weather gets colder, place cloches over spring cabbages and early carrots, closing the ends of the rows with glass.

In the north, set out in a nursery bed Brussels sprouts grown from a late summer sowing. Choose poorish soil and dust the dibber holes with calomel to discover club root disease. Allow 25-30cm (10-12in) between plants and rows.

Cut any remaining marrows and store in a dry, frost-proof place. Clear away the top-growth of peas and beans once harvesting is over. Start to dig vacant ground, digging in a good quantity of farmyard manure or garden compost. Leave the soil surface rough.

Stag's-horn sumach (*Rhus typhina*) provides brilliant autumn foliage interest when its large, toothed leaflets turn from mid green to vivid shades of orange, red, yellow and purple.

A small tree or large shrub with a spreading, rather gaunt frame, it grows up to 4.5m (15ft) high. In mid summer it bears upright greenish flower clusters, replaced in early autumn – on female trees only – by clusters of dark red felted fruits which last on the branches until early winter.

Stag's-horn sumach can be cut back to the ground each year from late winter to mid spring to obtain a coppice of lush foliage. The female variety 'Laciniata' has deeply cut leaflets giving a ferny effect and rich autumn tints.

Other mid autumn trees include maples (*Acer*) with an outstanding range of autumn tints in shades of red, orange and yellow. The multi-stemmed *Parrotia persica* develops beautiful amber, crimson and gold tints, while crab apples (*Malus*) have decorative fruits in shades of red and yellow, as well as autumn tints in a range of colours.

LATE AUTUMN

Use the last few mild days to plant shrubs and perennials and clear up the garden before winter sets in.

Late autumn is usually one of the wettest seasons, with shorter days and weaker sun bringing lower temperatures, though there may be a few warm, sunny days.

In the west of Britain, rainfall may increase, and gales are often more frequent than in mid autumn. Fog and mist are common, particularly in built-up areas of the Midlands and in south-east England, and especially after a drier spell of cold easterly winds. If no fog forms, hard frost can occur. Snow settles on northern hills, but on lower ground it usually melts quickly.

Take full advantage of the few days suitable for outdoor work in late autumn. Continue clearing up the ground, making sure that diseased leaves are burnt – good garden hygiene now can prevent disease the following summer.

Garden borders

Finish digging new beds and borders for winter weathering, and continue to tidy existing borders and cut down tall herbaceous plants. Cut plant tops into 15-30cm (6-12in) lengths for composting: use fallen leaves for leaf-mould or to protect the crowns of tender plants against frost.

Take precautions against slugs and snails in established borders, and pack away supporting canes in a dry place.

In the middle of late autumn, begin winter digging between plants on heavy soil. Do this when the weather is fine and the soil is not sticky. Winter frost will break up the soil, improving its texture in time for spring.

Use a flat-tined potato fork and insert it at an angle so that its wide tines turn over a neat wedge of surface soil, burying any annual weeds such as meadow grass, dead nettle and chickweed. Deep-rooted perennial weeds should be dug up completely and burnt.

New herbaceous perennials which have been delivered late, and hardy perennials raised from seed, can still be planted out in their permanent positions during fine weather as long as the soil does not form a hard compacted surface when trodden on. If the weather is too cold for planting or the soil is unsuitable, delay planting out until early spring.

LAWN MAINTENANCE

On established lawns, continue drainage work started in mid autumn, and aeration treatment started in early autumn. Apply an autumn fertilizer if this has not been done already.

Cut the grass for the last time before winter, and have the lawnmower overhauled.

Continue treatment against earthworms and water with HCH to control leatherjackets.

Prepare sites for new lawns to be sown next spring.

▼ **Last autumn colours** A waterside planting in autumn dress includes the browning fronds of the Royal fern (*Osmunda regalis*) beside the brilliant red of a deciduous euonymus. In the foreground, pale hostas, purple-leaved bugle and faded astilbe spires carpet the ground below a tall silver grass (*Miscanthus*) and yellow-variegated evergreen euonymus.

If chrysanthemums over-wintering outdoors show signs of waterlogging, improve drainage by piercing the soil round the roots deeply with a garden fork. Keep the beds clear of fallen leaves and weeds, which can conceal pests such as eelworms.

Bulbs Finish planting tulips and hyacinths as soon as possible

Examine dahlia tubers in storage. If they are shrivelling, plunge them in a bucket of tepid water and leave overnight before removing and drying carefully. Using a sharp knife, cut off any parts that show signs of rotting and dust the cuts with sulphur. Replace the tubers in vermiculite or slightly damp compost.

After gladioli corms have dried off, they can be cleaned at any time until just before planting out in spring. Remove the bulblets from around the base of the new corms and store them separately in paper bags if they are to be used for propagation. Break away and discard the old shrivelled corms and remove the tough outer skins from the new corms. If they are infested with thrips or they were attacked by thrips during the growing season, dust with malathion or HCH.

Annuals Dig the beds to be used next year for hardy and half-hardy annuals, incorporating a dressing of well-rotted manure or compost. Leave the land rough – winter weathering will break the soil down, leaving a fine tilth suitable for seed sowing. Autumn digging is particularly helpful where the soil is heavy with clay but it is important to complete this task before winter rain and snow make the soil too sticky to work on.

Send for seed catalogues to allow plenty of time to plan next year's bedding programme.

Rock garden plants

Finish trimming and dead-heading alpine and rock garden plants, saving any seeds wanted for propagation.

Clear away fallen leaves and mound beech or oak leaves over tender plants to protect them during the winter. Place sticks over the mounds to prevent the leaves blowing away.

Plant out shrubs, heathers and pot-grown alpines.

On clean, level ground between the plants, spread a 12mm-2.5cm (½-1in) deep layer of small shingle or stone chippings. This will supress most weed seedlings, making hoeing unnecessary.

Elsewhere, fork over the surface between plants, preferably using a small hand fork with flat tines. Carefully remove the roots of all perennial weeds.

Water gardens

Finish drastically thinning out underwater oxygenating plants and continue to remove dead leaves from the water. Leave the foliage on marginal plants such as reeds and rushes to provide some protection during severe weather.

If the pool is sited where leaves and plant debris are likely to fall or blow into the water, stretch small-gauge wire netting on to a frame and place over the pool. The netting catches the leaves and is easy to remove.

WEEPING STANDARD ROSES

To train a weeping standard rose with stiff growth, secure the stem to a stout stake about 15cm (6in) higher than the head of the rose. Fix a hoop-shaped wire training frame to the top of the stake. Pull the shoots through the top and tie them down carefully. Trim the ends of the shoots to shape.

Overhaul pumps used for waterfalls and fountains and store in a dry place. Remove submerged pumps from the water and clean and dry the working parts. With surface pumps, disconnect the suction line and run it for a few seconds only to empty the pump chamber. If possible, disconnect the pump from its fittings, clean and dry the metal parts and smear with grease.

Stop feeding the fish when the days become colder.

Shrubs and trees

In mild weather, continue to plant deciduous trees and shrubs as well as heathers. Examine heathers

PREPARING GLADIOLI CORMS FOR WINTER STORAGE

1 After gladioli corms have dried off, gently break off the bulblets. If the bulblets are to be used for propagation, store them separately in paper bags in a cool, dry place.

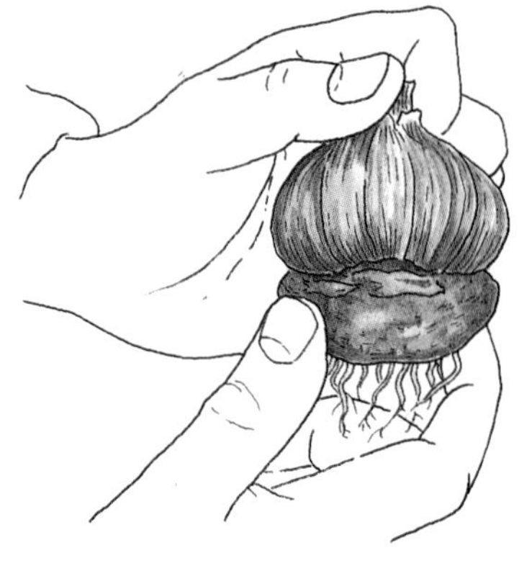

2 At the base of each new corm formed in the current year there will be the old shrivelled corm. Break off the old corm gently, using a slight twisting action, and discard it.

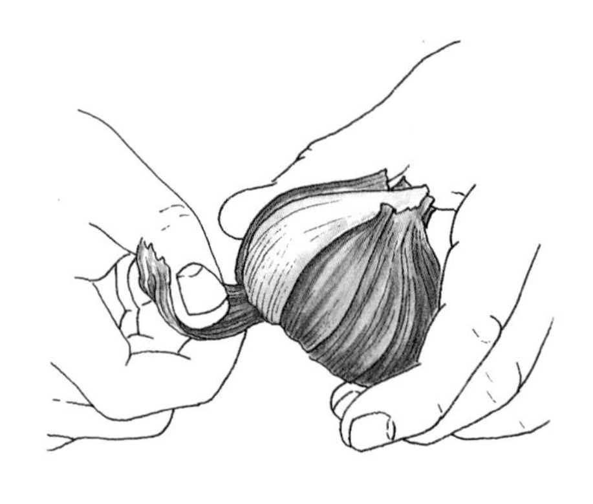

3 Peel away the tough outer skin of the new corm. If there are thrips on the corm, or if there has been an attack of thrips during the growing season, dust with malathion or HCH.

▲ **Autumn berries** Evergreens continue to provide welcome colour, and berrying trees and shrubs are at their finest in late autumn. Huge clusters of red and orange berries adorn a windbreak of tall-growing pyracanthas, interspersed with variegated hollies (*Ilex × altaclarensis*), backcloths for variegated euonymus.

planted during mid autumn and remove any weeds. Gently firm into place any plants which have been lifted and loosened by frost.

More tender trees and shrubs may need protection in severe weather – these include campsis, caryopteris, cistus, garrya, hydrangea, hypericum and spartium. For a windbreak, use a screen of wire netting which has old sacking woven or packed into it. Alternatively, place three or four stakes around the plant and wrap stout polythene round them, tying securely. To prevent snow damage, fix a polythene lid over the windbreak.

Take hardwood cuttings of *Elaeagnus pungens*, ivy, poplar, ribes and willow (*Salix*). Select strong, firm shoots about 30cm (1ft) long and insert them in sandy soil in a cold frame or in open ground. Plant out the cuttings in their permanent positions the following spring. Take hardwood cuttings of winter jasmine and root in a covered cold frame.

To propagate actinidia, layer firm young shoots in pots of compost sunk into the ground round the parent plant. The following spring, when the layers have made enough roots, sever them from the parents and plant out.

Examine cuttings in cold frames and in open ground, and firm in any that have been lifted or loosened by frost.

Hedges Prepare the sites where hedges are to be planted if this was not done in early or mid autumn, and complete planting as soon as possible.

If the site is not ready when the plants are delivered, separate the plants in the bundles and bury the roots in shallow trenches. Lay the plants at an angle so that they are not blown about too much while awaiting planting.

The fruit garden

Clear weeds from the soil around established fruit trees and bushes. On heavy soils, complete all work that involves treading on the ground.

Late autumn is the best time to plant fruit because the soil is still workable and is warm enough for the roots to establish themselves before winter. However, it is possible for fruit trees to be planted out at any time between autumn and spring during suitable, still weather, providing the soil is neither waterlogged nor frozen below the surface.

If planting cannot be done immediately, store the trees in a frost-free shed, covering the roots with sacks to prevent drying out or frosting. Alternatively, heel them in with the tops leaning over at an angle and tread the soil down firmly.

Prepare the holes immediately before planting. If the roots are dry, soak them for a few hours before planting. Cut off any broken roots with secateurs.

Provide vertical support for dwarfing rootstocks – many of which are poorly anchored – and for trained trees and bushes. Drive the stakes into the ground before planting to prevent damage to the roots. With short-stemmed trees, insert the stake at a slant to the trunk with its top towards the prevailing wind.

Plant fruit trees and bushes at the same depth as they were in the nursery. Spread out the roots in the prepared planting hole and refill with layers of topsoil, firming in each layer with your heel. Repeat until the level of the surrounding soil has been reached. Firm in thoroughly, unless the soil is wet and sticky, and then water in well to settle the soil.

Beauty berry makes a colourful late autumn feature with its profuse clusters of berries in shades of mauve and purple on leafless stems. In mid to late summer it bears small pink to lilac flowers and the leaves turn puplish pink in autumn. Plant several specimens close together to ensure a good show of berries.

If you have room, choose *Callicarpa bodinieri giraldii* 'Profusion', which grows up to 2.4m (8ft) high and 1.8m (6ft) across and bears rose-violet berries. For a smaller garden, plant *C. japonica* with lilac-mauve berries. The variety 'Leucocarpa' has unusual, decorative white fruits. All require sheltered sites.

Tie all trees and bushes firmly to stakes, using plastic ties. When planting trees on windy sites, set them with their best shoots growing into the prevailing wind to help the formation of a well balanced tree.

Prune fruit trees after planting: this can be done at any time from now until spring, except during hard frost. Prune only enough to shape the tree and form the framework. Cut just above a bud which points in the direction that a shoot is required to grow. With old trees which have been transplated, remove part of the top to make up for the loss of roots.

Start winter purning established trees, but do not prune cherries, peaches, nectarines, plums or damsons. If it is necessary to prune these fruits, for example to remove damaged branches, tidy up the ragged wounds with a pruning knife and protect them with butuminous paint.

When winter-pruning fruit trees, cut off the tips of leaders, or shoots which have been selected to extend the branch framework, and remove badly placed shoots. Thin out spur systems on older trees. Stop tip-pruning the leaders after four or five years. After this, restrict winter pruning to cutting out crossing and rubbing branches and dead or diseased wood.

If birds are attacking the fruit buds, do not prune until the spring. Check that ties are not cutting or chafing the bark. Scrape and cut out cankers and treat woolly aphid colonies with malathion if they cannot be removed by pruning.

Inspect stored fruit: to ripen pears, remove from storage and keep at room temperature until ready to eat.

With raspberries, cut out all fruiting shoots which have carried this season's crop as soon as possible. Tie new canes to the supporting framework. On windy sites, tie in growth above the top wire. Remove weak and surplus shoots at ground level.

Complete as soon as possible the pruning of blackberries, loganberries and hybrid berries. Train new growths on to the supporting framework.

Prune established back currant bushes by removing some of the old wood – leave in as much new growth as possible. Do not prune bushes at the end of their first season of growth after planting.

With established gooseberry, red currant and white currant bushes, shorten the leaders by a half and shorten the laterals to 5cm (2in). Prune cordons by shortening the leader by one-third and the laterals by a half. Remove all weak growth.

Plant strawberries so that the flowers will all face south – the end of the runner should point away from the sun.

The vegetable garden

In mild regions, sow broad beans outdoors for an early crop. Dust the seeds with pirimiphos-methyl and draw flat drills 23cm (9in) wide and 6-7.5cm (2½-3in) deep. Sow the seeds 15cm (6in) apart in two rows 18cm (7in) apart.

Apply a pre-emergence weedkiller where broad beans are sown under cloches and cover the ends of the rows with glass.

Also in mild regions, complete sowings of lettuces under cloches as early as possible.

Force chicory under the greenhouse staging at 10-13°C (50-55°F) for eating during winter. Cut off all but the bottom 2.5cm (1in) of the top growth, and pack the roots closely in large pans or boxes with a little moist soil between them. Cover with other pots, boxes or terracotta bell jars and then with a sheet of black polythene to exclude all light. Discard the roots after harvesting.

Trim the outer growths of globe artichokes and draw soil around the crowns. To increase stock, detach suckers from mature plants and grow on in pots in a cold frame or cool greenhouse and plant out in mid spring.

Herbs Clear away basil, chervil and dill. Also clear fennel and parsley which have grown for a second season.

Put cloches over parsley and chervil sown in early autumn.

EARLY WINTER

Use the short days to prune and spray fruit trees and protect tender plants against frost.

Early winter can be the coldest time of the year, except in severe years when temperatures drop lower still in mid to late winter. Gales and rain are common and there is usually little sunshine. When pressure rises and winds drop, fog and frost are likely.

South-westerly winds may bring showers and brighter intervals in England. At other times, north-east winds bring raw, cold weather. In the Midlands, afternoon temperatures average 7°C (45°F), with night temperatures falling below 2°C (35°F), but it is much colder in northern areas.

The most important general task in early winter is to tidy plots and complete the preparation of ground. Remember to eliminate draughts in the greenhouse.

Roses

Complete the planting of new stock, but not if the soil is wet and sticky or if there is frost or snow on the surface. If conditions are unsuitable, heel the roses in or keep them in a frost-free place.

Prepare established rose beds for winter. Shorten long growths to 75cm (2½ft) and collect and burn fallen leaves which show signs of black spot. On heavy or compacted soils, chop up the top 2.5cm (1in) to expose it to frost for winter weathering. Ensure that cuttings planted out in early autumn are still firm in their open trenches.

Garden borders

Continue tidying beds and borders and digging between plants. If beds are close to tall-growing trees, shrubs or hedges, cut back invasive roots, using a sharp, deep-bladed spade. Push it deeply into the edge of the bed to sever outgrowing roots. Cut large, thick roots with a chopper or axe. Also

LAWN MAINTENANCE

If you are planning to sow an area of new lawn next spring, prepare the site if this has not been done already. Dig over the ground and apply well-rotted farmyard manure. It is always a good idea to have a small area of turf specially sown to use for pacthing up any damaged areas of lawn.

Water with HCH to control leatherjackets if this was not done in late autumn.

Avoid treading on the lawn when it is wet or frozen. Lay down boards to prevent damage if heavy loads must be wheeled over the grass.

Clean and overhaul mowing machines and other lawn maintanence equipment. Oil them well before putting them away in a dry place until the spring. A small-nozzle oil dispenser is useful for getting at intricate parts of the machinery.

▼ **Early winter colour** Deciduous wall shrubs, such as yellow-flowered winter jasmine and red-berried cotoneasters bring cheer to dull days. At ground level, the frosty-grey carpeting foliage of cerastium and glossy bergenia leaves provide evergreen ground cover.

Holly is a handsome specimen tree or bush with dense growth and glossy, prickly leaves. Female hollies bear shiny berries, provided a male plant is nearby.

Favourite varieties include *Ilex* × *altaclarensis* 'Silver Sentinel' (*illustrated*), a red-berried female form. It has deep green, grey mottled leaves edged with creamy white or creamy yellow. *I. aquifolium* 'Fructuluteo' bears yellow fruits and *I. aquifolium* 'Pendula' has weeping branches and bright red berries.

prune overhanging branches of deciduous trees or bushes.

Replace worn turf beside beds and borders, and spread fresh gravel on paths if necessary.

After a frosty spell, re-firm the ground around chrysanthemums which are over-wintering outdoors and check for waterlogging.

Bulbs Hoe beds of late-planted tulips and hyacinths, or spray them with a contact herbicide to control weeds.

Discard any unhealthy stored gladioli corms. If stored dahlia tubers are shrivelling, plunge them in tepid water overnight. Cut off parts which have rotted and dust the cuts with sulphur.

Annuals Plan your seed requirements for the coming season and send off your mail-orders as soon as possible. Continue digging ground to be used for next year's hardy and half-hardy annuals, weather permitting.

Rock garden plants

Remove fallen leaves and fork over vacant spaces between the plants. Remove perennial weeds.

Sow slow-germinating seeds, and seeds needing exposure to frost to promote germination. Use clay pots or pans, or shallow wooden boxes. Put crocks or coarse gravel in the base and fill with a proprietary seed compost. Sprinkle shingle or coarse sand over the top if you are sowing very small seeds.

Distribute the seeds evenly and dust over with sand so that they are just covered. Put the containers outdoors and stand them on paving or a similar hard surface to prevent worms entering from below. Germination should start by the end of early spring, when the pans or boxes should be moved to a cold frame to prevent the seedlings from drying out.

Water gardens

Keep a small area of the pool free of ice to allow toxic gases to escape. Use a pool heater or place boards or rush matting over a small area of the pool to prevent ice from forming too quickly. Alternatively, stand a container of boiling water on the ice to melt a hole but be careful not to touch any fish.

Shrubs and trees

In mild weather continue to plant deciduous trees and shrubs, treading the soil around the roots. Re-firm soil loosened by frost around previously planted shrubs.

To prevent heavy snow breaking the branches of conifers, wind string round the branches and trunks to keep them together.

Gather fallen leaves into a heap to make leaf-mould for top-dressing the garden next spring.

In cold districts, bring tub-grown hydrangeas and fuchsias into a cold greenhouse or shed.

Rhododendrons and azaleas may be planted if the weather is fine. Spray the flower buds with a bird repellent.

Hedges Complete the planting of deciduous hedges. If plants arrive when the ground is frozen or wet, store them in a frost-free shed with straw around their roots until the weather improves.

The fruit garden

When fruit trees and bushes are fully dormant, spray with a tar-oil winter wash to kill pest eggs and remove algae. Also remove annual weeds at ground level.

Continue planting fruit trees and fruit bushes in suitable weather. Check stakes and ties on newly planted trees. Check framework supports and wires for trained trees and renew and tie in where necessary.

Continue winter pruning except when there is a hard night frost. Feed with nitrogen all trees and bushes grown in grass.

Every other year feed all apple and pear trees with sulphate of potash and every third year with superphosphate. Dress trained trees with farmyard manure.

Feed sweet cherry, plum and damson trees and peach and nectarine bushes in the same way as apples. With fan-trained 'Morello' cherry trees and fan-trained peach and nectarine trees, feed every year with hoof-and-horn. Every other year, feed with sulphate of potash.

Cut back newly planted apples, pears, blackberries, loganberries, currants, cherries, gooseberries and raspberries.

The vegetable garden

In the north of Britain, lift turnips and swedes and store any surplus. In the south, draw soil around the plants. Prepare the site for next year's runner beans.

Herbs Bring bay trees grown in tubs into the greenhouse or put them on a patio sheltered from cold winds. In cold districts, mulch marjoram and rosemary.

MID WINTER

Frost and snow prevent outdoor gardening activities, but equipment can be overhauled and plans made for spring.

Many of the coldest days of the year occur in mid winter, and this, combined with snow, rain, icy winds and continuous grey cloud, make outdoor gardening undesirable; nevertheless there are some tasks which must be carried out. However, many of these can be done in the shelter of a shed or greenhouse.

Routine jobs

Using a mild detergent, wash old pots and plastic seed trays to destroy fungal diseases. Treat wooden trays with wood preservative (but not creosote). Sharpen cutting tools – such as secateurs, shears, knives and lawnmowers – or take them to a service centre for sharpening or repair.

During fine weather, check all fences, gates, trellis, pergolas and other timber structures for rotting or breakages. If they are weak, repair them immediately – a heavy snowfall or high wind may bring them down. Treat all bare timber with wood preservative, applying several coats if necessary.

Paths and paving may also need attention. Heavy manual work is actually less exhausting on a fresh winter day than it is on a humid summer one, so dress up warmly and get on with the tasks you've been putting off.

Mail-order catalogues become available in mid winter and the dark evenings are a good time to plan your year's requirements. Order vegetable and flower seeds, gladioli corms, onion sets, shallots and other plants – varieties in short supply may be sold out unless you order in good time.

◄ In the deep mid winter
Snowdrops and golden winter aconites defy the coldest days, with the promise of better things to come, while clumps of nodding hellebores introduce more sombre purple tones to the pale winter scene.

LAWN MAINTENANCE

The lawn requires little attention in mid winter. Keep off it entirely if the ground is waterlogged or frozen. If water is not draining away quickly from part of the lawn, wait until it does eventually dry, then dress with coarse sand and aerate the surface with a hand fork, treading as lightly as possible. Although late, turfing is still possible in fine weather.

Garden borders

Regularly check all plants stakes and ties, especially after windy or snowy weather, securing or replacing them as necessary.

After hard frosts, check newly planted perennials, biennials and heathers – if they haven't grown good anchorage roots, frosts can lift them out of the ground and they will need re-firming.

Fork over the surface of the soil between the plants and turn in any annual weeds which may have appeared since the autumn clearance. Be careful not to tread on the dormant crowns of plants which have been cut right down.

Cut or snap off any remaining dead stems of herbaceous perennials. On light soils the tops pull away cleanly if the ground is frostbound and you may prefer to do all your border clearing at this time of year rather than in the autumn – although the dried out tops won't make good compost.

Shrubs and hedges

Roses, shrubs and deciduous hedging plants may be planted if the soil is fairly dry, but not if it is wet or frosty. If bare-root plants are delivered to you when the ground is unsuitable for planting, keep them temporarily in a frost-free shed with straw or sacking packed around the roots.

Thin out dead and diseased branches from established shrubs and trees. Winter prune wisteria by cutting back to within 7.5cm (3in) of the old wood all young shoots not needed to increase the plant size. Apply a generous mulch around rhododendrons.

Plants usually survive under a complete cover of snow, but heavy snow can break branches, so brush it off them with a soft broom.

Fruit and vegetables

Inspect stored fruit and discard any that have rotted. Spray fruit trees with a tar-oil winter wash. Carry out winter pruning of fruit trees and bushes as necessary.

Before the middle of mid winter, feed trees or bushes growing in grass with a high-nitrogen fertilizer. If not already done in early winter, feed apples, pears and other fruit trees, and complete the pruning of newly planted trees. Also cut back newly planted fruit bushes.

Plant rhubarb crowns in well-manured soil. Cover established rhubarb crowns with a generous layer of manure or garden compost to encourage early growth, or cover the crowns with upturned, light-proof containers.

In sheltered, mild areas sow peas and broad beans for an early crop. Shallots can be planted now on well-drained soil, though most gardeners prefer to wait for another month or two.

LOWEST TEMPERATURES

The map shows the minimum temperatures of the year, likely to be exceeded only one year in five.

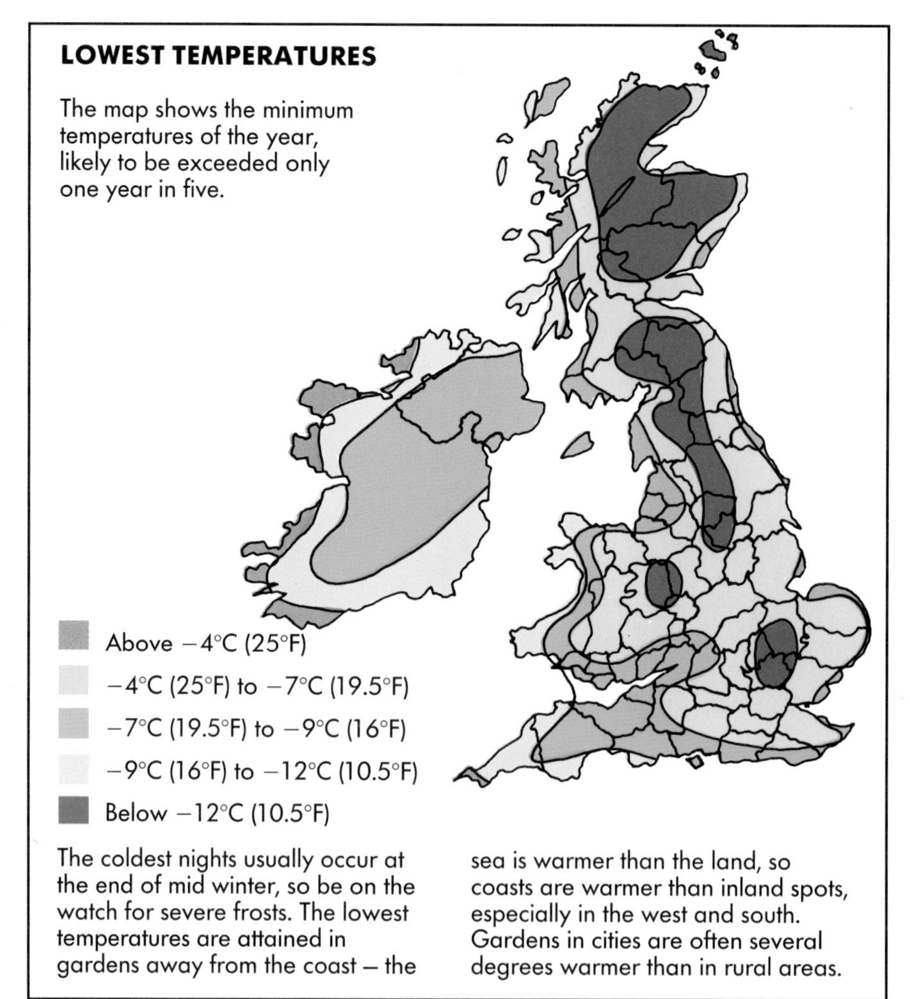

The coldest nights usually occur at the end of mid winter, so be on the watch for severe frosts. The lowest temperatures are attained in gardens away from the coast – the sea is warmer than the land, so coasts are warmer than inland spots, especially in the west and south. Gardens in cities are often several degrees warmer than in rural areas.

The Christmas rose (*Helleborus niger*), with its white or pink-tinged, 5-13cm (2-5in) wide flowers, is a real gem in mid winter. The flowers are long-lasting and cold-resistant, rarely being spoiled by bad weather. But in exposed gardens protect the opening buds with cloches from early winter if you want perfect blooms for cutting.

Other mid winter flowers There are several flowering shrubs which will enliven the mid winter garden. These deserve a position where they can be seen from indoors.

Chinese witch hazel (*Hamamelis mollis*) makes a large shrub, or small tree with age, and its leafless branches are decked with clusters of fragrant, golden or sulphur-yellow, spidery flowers. For a similar effect, try the fragrant, yellow wintersweet (*Chimonanthus*) or the cornelian cherry (*Cornus mas*) with clusters of tiny yellow flowers.

The silk tassel bush (*Garrya elliptica*) is an unusual wall shrub, producing masses of silver-grey catkins which are eye-catching after a white frost or sprinkling of snow. *Crocus tomasinianus* is one of the earliest crocuses, giving a pretty show of slender lavender blooms beneath the winter-flowering shrubs.

LATE WINTER

Early spring bulbs spell the end of winter, and preparations for spring can begin on mild days.

Late winter can bring some exceptionally cold days and nights, together with freezing winds, snow and poor light. The greatest possible use should be made of any available glass – a greenhouse, cloche or cold frame. Glass cover will not keep out frost in a severe winter, but in most years it gives reasonable protection against the night cold. Use cloches to warm up the soil so that outdoor sowing can take place a week or two earlier.

Garden borders

Late winter is the last opportunity for clearing the dead tops from last year's herbaceous perennials.

Preparation of the ground for spring planting among existing border plants can be carried out in late winter whenever the weather permits. Lightly hoe or fork over the top 5-7.5cm (2-3in) of soil. At the same time, work in bone-meal, hoof and horn or any organic fertilizer which is high in phosphates and potash but low in nitrogen.

Also, lightly fork over beds which have been previously winter-dug and reserved for sowing and planting annuals. If manure or compost has not been applied earlier, rake or hoe in a 100g/4oz per sq m/yd dressing of bone-meal.

If frost has loosened any border or rock garden plants, firm the soil around them. Remove small tufts of grass and the seedlings of annual weeds. These often germinate unnoticed during the autumn but become more prominent during a mild late winter. Scatter slug pellets during mild weather, especially if slime trails are seen.

LAWN MAINTENANCE

In dry periods, aerate, rake, and brush off worm casts. Apply sharp sand to lawns on heavy wet soils, and sieved loam and organic materials on light porous soils.

Apply lawn sand towards the end of late winter to control daisies and clover. Moss invasion may be serious now. Try to discover the cause – it may be bad drainage or impoverished turf. Correct poor physical conditions and treat with a mercury-based moss killer.

Roses, shrubs and hedges

Roses and other shrubs may be planted in late winter if the soil is dry or just moist, but not if it is wet and sticky, or if there is frost or snow on the surface.

Prune callicarpa, campsis, spiraea and *Tamarix pentandra* hard

▼ **Red against the snow** Dramatic in the shape of its curious flowers, the red witch hazel (*Hamamelis × intermedia* 'Ruby Glow') flames bright copper-red in late winter. Its autumn foliage is equally spectacular.

back by cutting away the previous year's growth to within a few centimetres of the old wood. This will encourage new, vigorous shoots to develop.

Prune summer-flowering clematis varieties hard back, either to 30cm (1ft) above ground, or to within two buds on young growth.

Cut back all the shoots that have completed flowering on chimonanthus and winter jasmine, but leave this until early spring if they are still in bloom. Thin out climbers such as celastrus and potato vine by removing any weak growths, and shorten or pinch out the tips of main shoots.

Cut back overgrown hedges towards the end of late winter so that they produce new growth in spring. Cut the top growth 30cm (1ft) or more lower than the height ultimately required, so that there will be space for new growth to hide the old skeleton.

Fruit and vegetables

Prune newly planted fan-trained peaches, nectarines, cherries, plums and damsons, cutting back shoots to 30-45cm (1-1½ft). Spray peaches with copper fungicide at bud-swelling stage against peach leaf curl.

Prune established autumn-fruiting varieties of raspberry close to the ground. In the second half of late winter place cloches over strawberry plants which have been planted for early fruit.

Sow early crops of peas and broad beans,if this was not done in mid winter, but wait until early spring in cold, northerly districts unless the seed-bed can be covered with cloches.

If you want to grow early potatoes, buy the tubers as soon as possible. Arrange them in one layer in shallow boxes, with the eyes – embryo shoots – uppermost. Put these in a light, frost-proof place to promote sprouting.

Carrots, such as 'Mokum F1' or 'Amsterdam Forcing', sown in late winter in light, fertile soil in a cold frame, should be ready for harvesting in early summer. Keep the frame lights on for a week or two to warm the soil, then sow the seed thinly. Keep the frame closed until the seed has germinated, then give some ventilation.

Plant shallots, drawing a little soil over the sets to anchor them. Dig the site in preparation for planting out asparagus.

Winter-flowering mahonia

(*Mahonia × media* 'Charity') is one of the most elegant of all shrubs, especially during late winter. Its upright branches carry huge evergreen leaves which are made up of holly-like leaflets. Tapering sprays of lily-of-the-valley-scented, yellow flowers crown the branches in late winter. Tassels of berries then develop, which ripen blue-black with a grey bloom. At maturity, this imposing shrub reaches 2.4-3m (8-10ft) in height.

Other late winter flowers

Winter jasmine (*Jasminum nudiflorum*) is a delightful wall shrub, its green stems being showered with bright yellow trumpet flowers over a long period in winter.

For rich purplish pink flowers on upright naked branches, choose *Daphne mezereum*. As the flowers mature, tufts of bright green leaves unfurl at the tips of the branches. For a low display of late winter blue or mauve flowers, grow chionodoxa and *Iris reticulata*.

Growing under glass

Greenhouse cultivation opens up a new dimension of gardening, where the growing season for certain crops and flowers is considerably extended, starting earlier and finishing later than in the open garden. A greenhouse allows both plants and people to be protected from the extremes of British weather, by maintaining a more or less constant atmosphere from spring until autumn or, in the case of a heated greenhouse, throughout the year.

Installing a greenhouse can be expensive (a conservatory even more so), but the benefits of higher and out-of-season yields and finer blooms can be enormous. Even a modest lean-to or grow-frame can dramatically extend the range of plants you can grow and will also provide a sheltered environment for sowing early seeds and rooting cuttings.

The greenhouse gardener is in control of growing conditions and can regulate temperature, humidity, ventilation and shading. Plants can be grown in the most suitable composts, watered and fed as and when necessary, and strict hygiene can be maintained. It is even possible to combat greenhouse pests biologically by introducing beneficial parasites.

In the winter months a frost-free greenhouse lets you enjoy crisp winter salads as well as early vegetables and fruit, and you can grow flowering plants such as freesias, carnations, early polyanthus and late-flowering chrysanthemums. With a little more heat the scope is greater still, and you could specialize in true exotics like orchids and tender flowering climbers.

Under glass Home-raised young tomatoes and trays of bedding seedlings represent considerable savings.

GREENHOUSE KNOW-HOW

In a well-equipped greenhouse, the choice of plants and produce extends from the half-hardy all the way to the near-exotic types.

Choosing the right site is vital to successful greenhouse cultivation. Even if space is so limited that the eventual choice of site is less than ideal, consider adapting the garden – by moving a border, for example – to counteract obvious drawbacks.

Light

Choose an open sunny site so that the greenhouse gets as much light and warmth as possible – ideally it should be in full sunlight for most of the day and artificial shading can be applied when it is wanted. If only a shaded place is available, it is still possible to grow a wide range of plants though the choice is more limited.

If possible, site the greenhouse well away from large buildings, tall hedges, screens, fences or big tres so that it is not overshadowed. Avoid also sites prone to waterlogging and frost pockets and any exposed to strong cold winds.

Remember that shadows cast in winter are much longer than summer shadows. Also, a wall or tree on the north side of the greenhouse will cast a smaller shadow than a similar plant or structure on the east, west or south side.

Even if a nearby tree does not directly overshadow the greenhouse, twigs and branches may break the glass during a gale, while the roots can damage the foundations. However, small trees up to about 3.5mm (12ft) high should cause little trouble and can help to provide shelter.

Orientation

The orientation of the greenhouse – the direction in which the ridge runs – affects the amount of light and heat available at different times of the year, and the types of plants which will grow in it.

East-west axis Most gardeners prefer the ridge of a free-standing greenhouse to run on an east-west axis. This provides the best light in winter, making it suitable for winter and early spring crops, and plants such as orchids, flowering annuals, winter bulbs and alpine plants. It is also useful for raising batches of half-hardy annuals from seed. However, temperatures may rise too high at midday during the summer.

North-south A free-standing greenhouse with the ridge running north-south is best for plants which crop in summer and

▼ Free standing greenhouse
Ideally, choose a site that gives maximum light and shelter, on a solid foundation. Here, shade is cast during the hottest part of the day over vegetables grown in the greenhouse border. Full light is thrown over flowering plants on the staging on the opposite side.

autumn. In summer, it heats up very quickly in the morning and remains warm well into the evening or night.

If space is scarce, consider a lean-to greenhouse against a wall of the house. It will get less light than a free-standing one, but bricks store heat, helping to keep the greenhouse warm after dark. It is also easier and cheaper to extend existing services, such as water, gas and electricity.

South-facing wall A lean-to greenhouse with an east-west ridge on a south-facing wall ensures maximum heat in summer and maximum light throughout the year, but it might be too hot for many plants. Tropical fruit, such as melons, and exotic vegetables like aubergines and peppers will do well.

North-facing wall A lean-to greenhouse running east-west on a north-facing wall will be in shade for much of the time, even in summer, making it a haven for many shade-loving foliage plants and ferns.

West-facing wall A north-south lean-to on a west-facing wall will be shaded in the morning, but warmth will linger after nightfall, making it useful between autumn and spring. However, on winter mornings it will be chilly and shaded.

East-facing wall With a north-south axis, a lean-to will receive morning light, but will otherwise be shaded for much of the day, especially in winter. It also retains little natural heat.

Shelter

Although an open site is important to let light and warmth into the greenhouse, shelter from winds – particularly north and east winds – is essential. Strong, cold winds lead to rapid heat loss and hence large heating bills, while even gentle breezes can cause chilling draughts. A gale may rip apart a plastic-sheet greenhouse, and break panes in a conventional one.

If the garden does not have a suitable sheltered site, plant a hedge or a row of shrubs to filter the wind, or build a wall or fence in its path to act as a windbreak. Site the windbreak at a sufficient distance so that it does not cast shade over the greenhouse.

Access

Plants grown under glass need to be inspected and cared for daily, so make sure that the greenhouse is easy to get to, especially in cold or wet weather when it is tempting to stay indoors.

Site it as close to the house as practicable, and provide a hard access path wide enough for a wheelbarrow or a person carrying heavy loads.

Water Greenhouse plants need constant watering, particularly at the height of the growing season, so site the house close to a source of mains water – automatic watering systems require mains pressure in order to operate successfully. Alternatively, install a standpipe. For easier watering, run a hose off the water source.

If the mains water is hard, consider installing a tank near the greenhouse to collect rain-water, or a water-softening system.

Electricity A supply of electricity close to the greenhouse can be used to provide heating – allowing the greenhouse to be used through the year – fan ventilation, and lighting for evening work or to supplement natural daylight.

SITING A GREENHOUSE

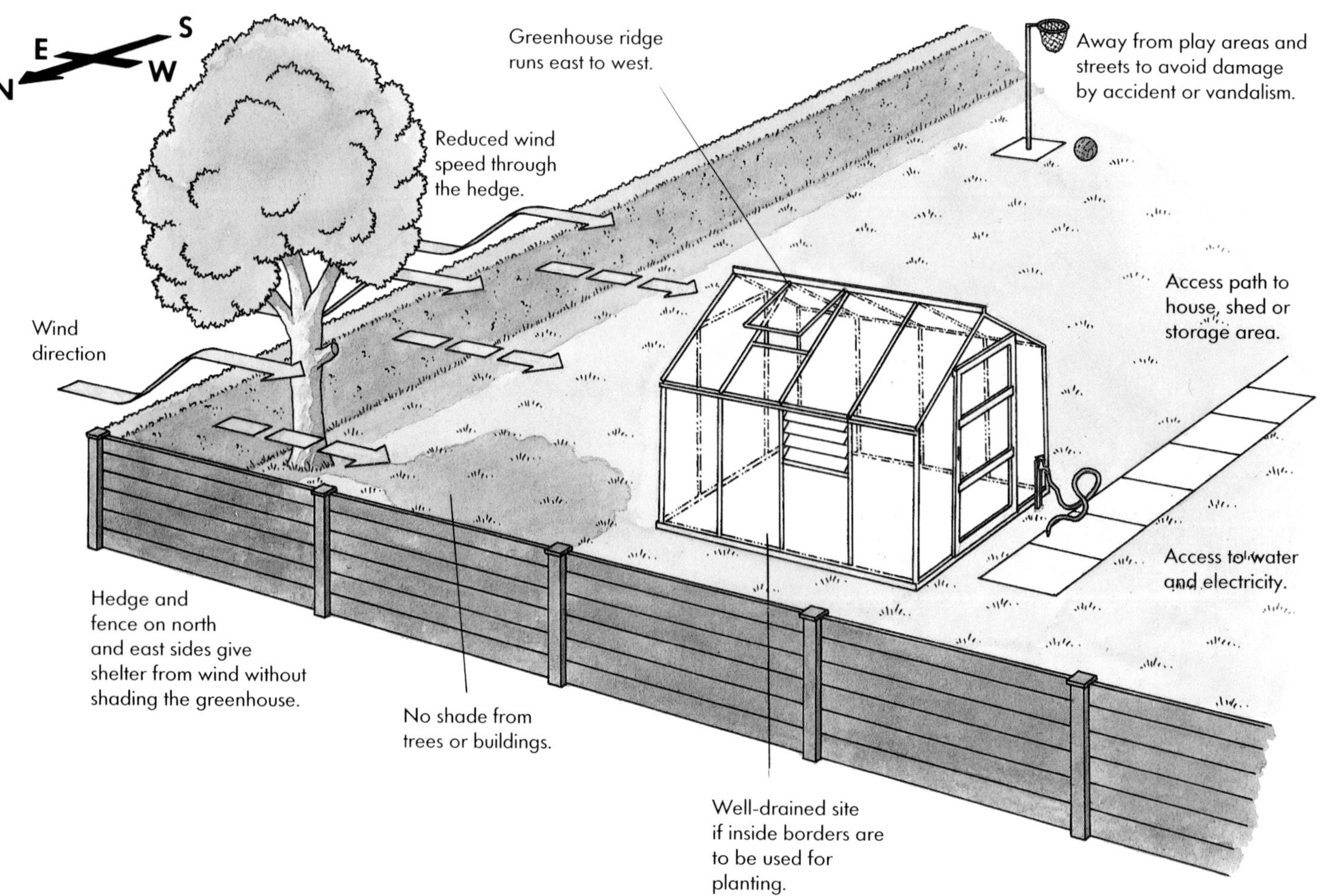

Sloping gardens

If your garden is on a sloping site, stand the greenhouse on a levelled foundation – it is impractical to have sloping benches inside, or doors which don't hang straight.

If plants are to be grown in containers, sloping sites provide no particular problem once construction is complete. But remember that if you want to grow plants directly in the greenhouse border, soil drainage on a sloping site will create problems. Take measures to impede the drainage of soil moisture down the slope before building the greenhouse. Remember also that frost pockets are likely at the base of a slope.

Unheated greenhouses

A greenhouse can free gardeners from the tyranny of the weather. Under cover of glass plants flourish that would suffer from cold, heavy rain and wind if they were grown in the open. A greenhouse also protects food plants from attacks by birds, animals and some other pests.

An unheated greenhouse will not keep out much winter frost, but it creates warmer conditions for plants in the growing season. This extra heat speeds up the ripening of crops, and improves the flowering of many decorative plants.

Perhaps the most valuable function of a greenhouse is to lengthen the growing season. Plants can be encouraged into growth early in the spring, and either kept under glass or planted out in the garden. In the greenhouse, plants will grow on well into the autumn.

This artificial growing season is achieved by the glass or plastic cladding trapping the heat of the sun, and retaining it in the soil, staging, any brickwork and in the plants themselves.

Unheated greenhouses are widely used to grow a crop of tomatoes during spring and summer, and then for growing late flowering chrysanthemums in autumn, when the tomato plants have been discarded. They can also be used for grapes and melons.

For the gardener who is interested in producing top-quality blooms, an unheated greenhouse is invaluable for growing a range of half-hardy shrubs, fruits, annuals, lilies, gladioli and many other bulbs.

All out-of-season vegetables normally grown under frames or cloches – lettuces, carrots, radishes, potatoes and French beans, for instance – can be grown just as well in an unheated greenhouse.

By installing equipment for ventilation, shading and watering, control of the growing environment can be quite precise – with some of the more expensive systems, control can be semi- or even fully automatic.

▼ **Greenhouse staging** Aluminium or wooden shelves along the greenhouse walls increase the growing space for pot plants and seedlings and provide a convenient working space. Ferns and other shade-lovers beneath the staging benefit from the humidity of an enclosed environment.

Staging and shelving

By installing staging and shelving in your greenhouse, you can at least double the growing area, and at the same time raise the plants to a more workable height. Sun-lovers, including seedlings and young plants, can be given the top-most spot while plants preferring some shade can be put under the staging or on low shelves. Similarly, trailing plants can be placed on high shelves to tumble to eye-level, and tall upright plants can be put at a low level. Where space allows, stepped or tiered staging is useful for displaying plants.

By cramming as many plants as possible into the greenhouse, you will also help to increase the humidity – essential to plant health when the temperature is high in summer.

The simplest form of staging is the slatted wooden type. Many timber greenhouses come complete with adequate wooden staging, or you can build your own. Manufacturers of aluminium greenhouses invariably offer a range of aluminium shelving and benching to match, which screws or bolts on to the framework. Some shelving has a surface top of stout wire-mesh.

To provide extra humidity in summer, cover the slats with a sheet of polythene, then spread a 2.5cm (1in) layer of moist sand, gravel or vermiculite over the top. Prevent the sand from falling over the edges by pinning a timber framework on to the staging, under the polythene. Alternatively, use special plastic or aluminium trays filled with a moisture-absorbing material.

Pot plants standing on moist sand will draw up water through their drainage holes by capillary action. Keep the sand moist – but not flooded – at all times. You can do this by manual watering or by an automatic system. In winter, when high humidity is not required, the sand should be cleared to allow good air circulation around the plants and better distribution of artificial heat.

Whenever staging or shelving consists of two or more tiers, always use drip trays, sand trays or polythene sheeting to prevent drainage water from splashing on to the plants below.

STAGING AND SHELVING TYPES

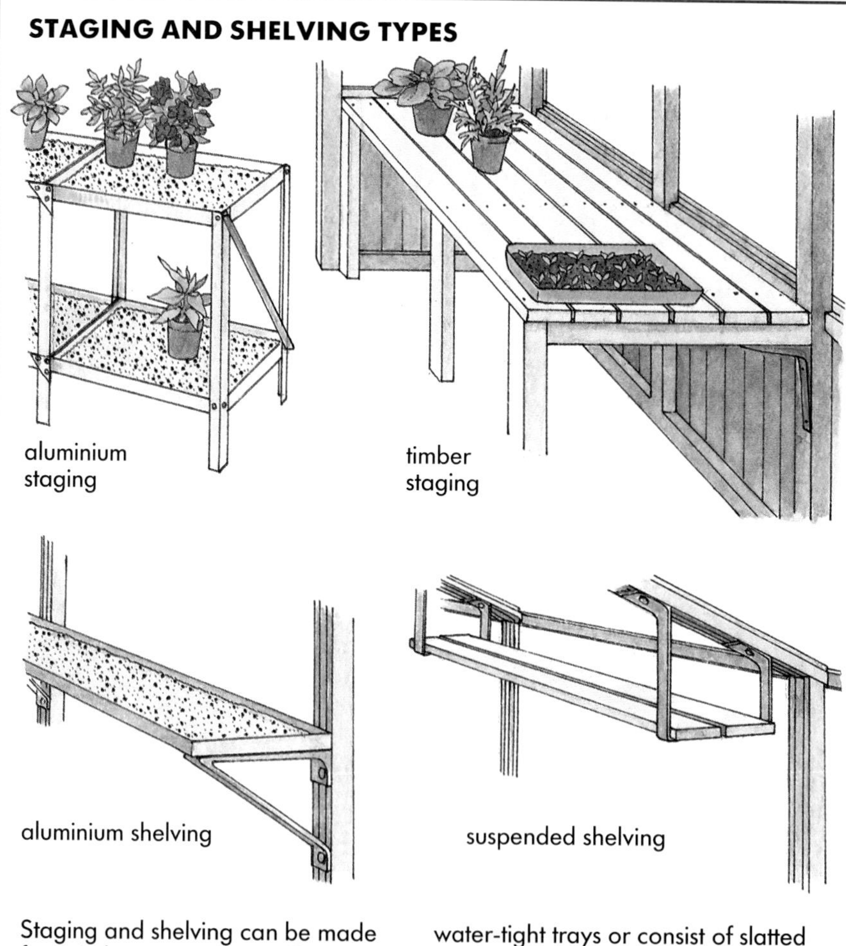

Staging and shelving can be made from timber or metal (usually aluminium). Manufacturers invariably supply staging and shelving to fit each of their greenhouse models, or you can construct your own. Staging can be free-standing or fixed permanently to the greenhouse framework, and can incorporate water-tight trays or consist of slatted shelves.

Aluminium shelf brackets can be secured easily to aluminium glazing bars using bolts or self-tapping metalwork screws. Specially shaped brackets are even available to secure high-level shelves to the sloping roof glazing bars.

Ventilation

A greenhouse – whatever its design or size – should have at least two ventilators in the roof and some low-positioned ventilators at opposite sides, staggered so as to avoid through draughts, otherwise it is very likely to become too hot in summer. As a general rule, the total surface area of the roof vents should be at least equal to one-sixth of the floor area – hot air rises, so the roof vents are of prime importance.

Fungus diseases flourish in a warm stagnant atmosphere. When top vents and side vents are open at the same time a rapid change of air takes place, keeping the air as fresh as possible – hot air escaping through the roof vents pulls cooler air in through the low side vents. Additional ventilation can be achieved as necessary simply by propping the door open.

Sliding side vents at ground level allow access to the area under the staging, for cultivation and the addition or removal of pots and boxes.

Top vents, and most hinged side vents, can be fitted with automatic openers in glass greenhouses. A special liquid compound inside the unit expands or contracts with temperature changes and motivates a piston system of levers. These units are quite expensive, but once installed you can leave the greenhouse unattended even in the most extreme of weather conditions while you are away.

An alternative form of ventilation is by an electric extractor fan controlled by a thermostat. A supply of mains electricity in the greenhouse is, of course, necessary. The fan is best placed in the apex of the roof, at the end of the greenhouse opposite the door. Various sizes of fan are available. As the fan sucks air out of the greenhouse, sufficient air will usually come in under the door

THERMOMETERS

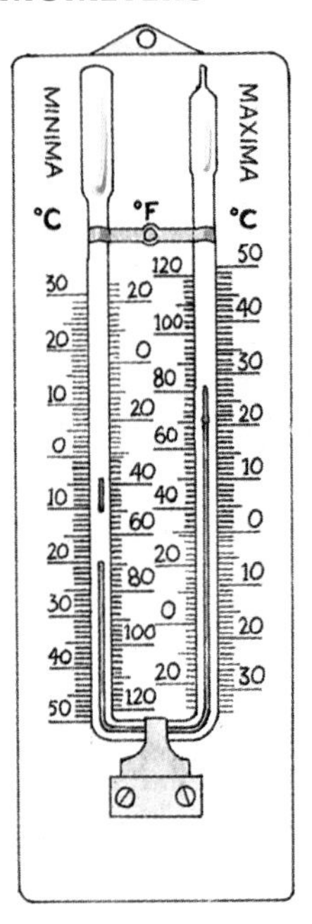

Keep a check on the temperature in a greenhouse and take action to regulate it within an acceptable range by adjusting the ventilation and shading. Ventilation should usually be provided when the inside temperature reaches 21°C (70°F).

Hang a thermometer in the greenhouse out of direct sunlight and away from the door or vents. The type which gives a minimum and maximum reading within any one time interval is the most useful – you can see at a glance how low the temperature falls at night. Reset the floats daily.

and through gaps under the glass. But during very hot weather the door or vents at a distant point from the fan should be left open to give maximum ventilation.

Shading

The most efficient method of shading the greenhouse is to use one of the proprietary roller blinds, usually made of wood, cane or aluminium slats, or woven material such as hessian. They can be lowered on sunny days and rolled back on dull days. They can be fitted to the inside or outside of the roof, and should be set on rails 2.5-5cm (1-2in) from the glass.

Automatic blinds are also available but are expensive. These are operated by photo-electric cells which respond to light intensity.

Blinds are usually used only across the greenhouse roof, although they are available to cover the sides as well. A greenhouse where the ends face east and west should be shaded on the south side of the roof. A greenhouse running north and south should be shaded on both sides of the roof.

An effective, and also cheaper, alternative to blinds is electrostatic shading paint. This type of paint is bought in a concentrated form and must be diluted with water before use. Use either a brush or sprayer to apply the paint to the outside of the glass. If you cannot reach all parts of the roof area easily from a step-ladder, attach the brush to a long pole, or use an old soft broom to apply the paint. Never attempt to climb on a greenhouse roof – you may break the glass, buckle an aluminium frame, or even fall through the glass and suffer severe injury.

Shading paint is waterproof so will not be washed off by rain, but is easily wiped off with a dry cloth at the end of the season. It can be applied to the sides of the greenhouse as well as to the roof. If the house runs north-south paint the south, east and west sides, and both sides of the roof.

Shading – whether blinds or paint – should be used only where plants need to be protected from strong, direct sunlight. Ferns, orchids and tropical jungle plants will definitely need such protection, but other plants generally do not, provided the ventilation is adequate. For a cheap, temporary shade during spells of unusually hot weather, you can pin an ordinary cotton or nylon sheet across the glass rather than using proprietary shading materials.

Water supply

Unless a greenhouse is being built alongside an existing garden tap,

VENTILATION SYSTEMS

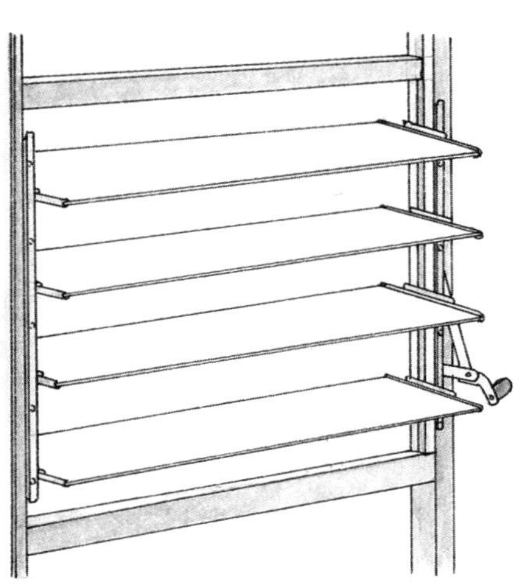

1 Side louvre vents can be opened fully and occupy little space on a horizontal plane. They are usually designed to replace a standard 60 × 60cm (2 × 2 ft) pane of glass.

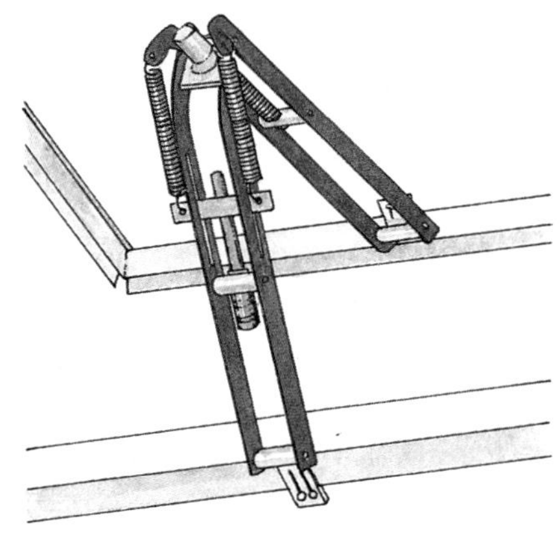

2 An automatic opener can be fitted to almost any type of hinged vent. A special piston operates via levers to open or close the vent, expanding or contracting with temperature changes.

3 Ordinary window stays provide the simplest and cheapest means of supporting a hinged vent in a fully open or partially open position. Ensure they are secure to prevent wind damage.

4 An electric extractor fan can be set into a pane of glass or mounted on to hardboard or exterior-quality plywood. It is controlled by thermostat and gives draught-free ventilation.

SHADING SYSTEMS

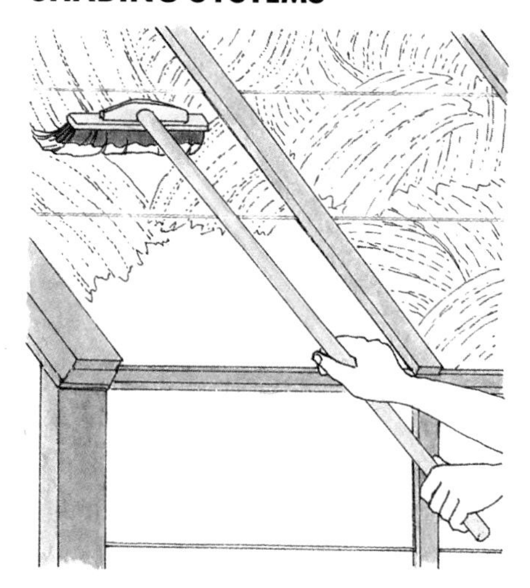

1 White electrostatic shading paint is the simplest and cheapest means of shading a greenhouse during the summer months – it can be wiped off easily when no longer needed.

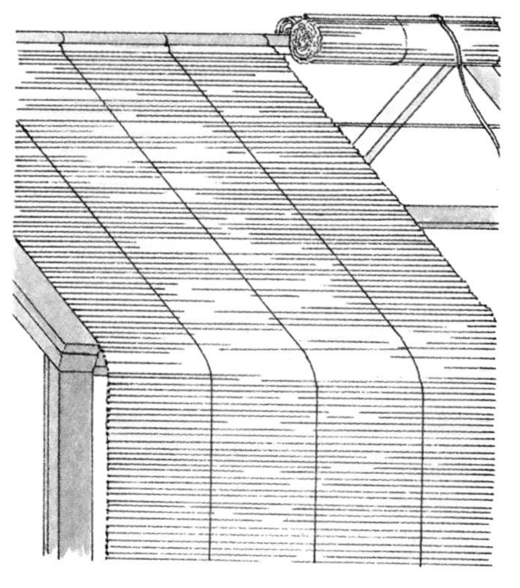

2 Roller-type wooden or plastic slat blinds can be bought for use inside or outside the greenhouse. Those for outside are the easiest to put up, but may be damaged by winds.

3 Roller blinds, with an aluminium frame, are made from a strong polyester and cotton fabric. Extra rollers can be obtained to allow blinds to be pulled over the side panes as well.

a permanent water supply should be installed. This is work for a plumber, but the expense is justified by the saving in work and time later. You may need to pay an additional water rate for the use of an extra supply point – check with your local water authority.

Once a tap has been installed, plants can be watered either by hand, with a long-spouted can, a hosepipe or automatically. The amount of water depends on the plants, time of year and the temperature and must be guided by common sense. During active growth, more water is obviously needed than during dormancy. The aim is to keep the compost just moist, never waterlogged or desiccated – on a hot summer's day, tomatoes, for example, may need watering several times.

Automatic watering has several advantages. It can be more reliable than hand-watering, especially where plants are crammed in and difficult to get at, and it promotes steady growth of plants. It also saves time and enables you to leave the greenhouse unattended for days, or even weeks provided ventilation is controlled automatically.

Capillary sand benches are a popular method of automatic watering. Small units are avilable that can be extended. A unit consists of a plastic tray, a tank or reservoir, and a constant-level float valve.

Place a layer of sand mixed with a proprietary non-toxic algicide to prevent the growth of algae in the tray. An alternative to sand is a proprietary absorbent mat – capillary matting.

The float valve regulates the level of water in the tray and hence the degree of wetness of the sand or matting. Use plastic pots with large drainage holes for capillary-bench work. Do not put crocks in when potting. Press the pots down firmly on the moist sand or matting, so that the compost makes contact with it thorugh the pots' drainage holes.

Water the pots well. This will ensure continued uptake of water from the capillary bench.

Trickle irrigation is a more sophisticated system of watering which consists of a plastic pipeline with nozzles at intervals which drip water into the pots. The flow of water is controlled from a water tank that siphons automatically. The frequency and amount of water supplied can be controlled by a valve. Water flow can also be regulated by adjusting the nozzle aperture. Nozzles can be held over the pots by wire staples, or by proprietary clip-pegs.

TRICKLE-FEED WATERING

A regular supply of water is essential at all stages of plant growth, but watering by hand is not always possible.

Trickle irrigation, in which a pipe fed from a tank or cistern is laid near the plants and drip nozzles release a steady supply of water, is an ideal system for plants of all sizes. The nozzles can be adjusted to regulate the flow of water to suit each plant's needs.

Provided the tank is higher than the supply nozzles – the system is gravity-fed – plants can be watered on several levels of staging at once. Liquid fertilizer can be added to the tank so that plants are watered and fed at the same time.

HEATED GREENHOUSES

Artificial heat is needed to guide tender shrubs, young seedlings and exotic house plants through the average British winter.

Greenhouses provide some protection for overwintered plants even if they are not heated, shielding them from rain, snow and freezing winds. However, glass does little to protect plants from the effects of low winter temperatures – at best, an unheated greenhouse of all-glass or glass and timber construction is two or three degrees centigrade higher inside than outside. If the outside air temperature falls dramatically below freezing point, so too will the temperature inside the greenhouse.

With a polythene-clad greenhouse or tunnel, the protection against low temperatures is even less.

An unheated greenhouse will serve you adequately for growing most plants from spring to late autumn. Many gardeners shut down their greenhouses for the winter although they are useful for overwintering more delicate plants or for enjoying blooms unspoilt by cold weather – ericas, camellias, winter pansies, polyanthus and primroses. Certain lettuce varieties can also be grown in an unheated greenhouse.

However, heating a greenhouse, even just to keep it frost-free, widens the range of plants that can be grown enormously. Seeds can be sown early to produce sturdy seedlings and bedding plants by spring, and many tender shrubs, climbers and house plants will flourish in the controlled environment of a heated greenhouse or conservatory.

Unfortunately, both glass and plastic allow heat to escape very easily, so heating a greenhouse, however small, is a wasteful and costly business. Consider whether it is worth heating the entire greenhouse or just part of it – it may be possible to divide the structure into two or more compartments, heating just one small area in the middle.

Makeshift double-glazing may be installed by securing sheets of clear polythene across the inside edges of the glazing bars during the winter. This will reduce heat loss, but remember that it will also cut down the light transmission greatly and often create problems with condensation and ventilation. Repair any broken panes of glass and fit draught-excluders to doors and ventilators if necessary in autumn.

In an open position, the winter sun can provide free warmth. A lean-to greenhouse may be against a wall that will store outside warmth or warmth from the house, and maintain frost-free conditions overnight in all but the very coldest spells. Cold winds carry away heat, so in an exposed garden a windbreak of trees or tall shrubs may cut down the fuel bills.

Calculating heat

The cost of most greenhouse heaters is quite high so evaluate their usefulness before buying them. There is no point in choosing the smallest, cheapest model in the hope that it will suffice – unless it is able to raise the temperature constantly above freezing, plants will die just as surely as if they hadn't been given any heat at all. On the other hand, an excessively large and elaborate heater will be expensive to buy and run.

Most manufacturers of greenhouse heaters give recommenda-

◄ **Paraffin heaters** The cheapest heaters to install and invaluable in emergencies, paraffin heaters equal the running costs of electricity. Buy a type designed for greenhouse use, with a proven heat output and provide good ventilation for combustion.

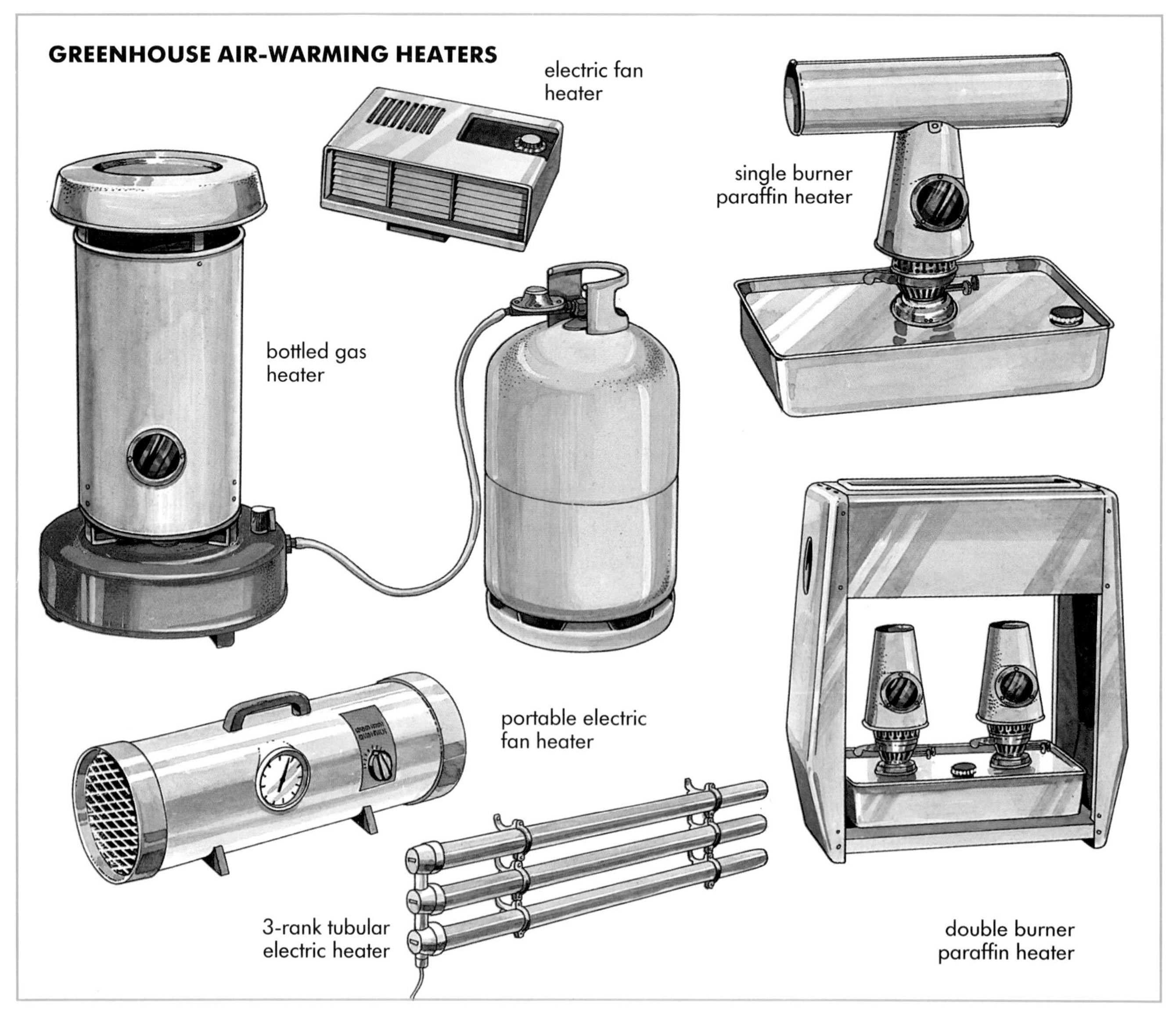

tions with their products regarding the size of the greenhouse for which each model is suited – usually quoted according to the floor area or total surface area of glass – and on the fuel consumption rate in watts or kilowatts (electric) or thermal units (oil and gas). Your local electricity board or oil/gas supplier will be able to give you quotes for the cost of these fuel units and may be able to give you an off-peak tariff to reduce night-time running costs.

For most amateur greenhouse gardeners, a minimum air temperature of about 7°C (45°F) should be adequate. In these conditions, a wide range of tender garden plants can be overwintered successfully and many house plants will also survive, provided you do not over-water them. Higher temperatures can be created in small compartments for propagation purposes.

To calculate the heater output requirements to maintain a winter temperature of 7°C (45°F), first measure the total surface area of the greenhouse – all sides plus the roof. The multiplication factor then required to calculate the heater output in British Termal units (BTUs) per hour of oil or gas, or watts (W) of electricty, depends on whether you measure the surface area in sq m or sq ft:

□ (area in sq m) × 355 = BTUs
□ (area in sq m) × 108 = Watts
□ (area in sq ft) × 33 = BTUs
□ (area in sq ft) × 10 = Watts

For example, a greenhouse with a total surface area of 20 sq m will need 20 × 355 = 7100 BTUs per hour, or 20 × 108 = 2160 watts (2.16kW) of heat output.

By maintaining a minimum temperature of 13°C (55°F) you will be able to grow a much wider range of plants during the winter, but the fuel costs will be very high. Again, calculate the required BTUs per hour or watts as above, but use a further multiplication factor of 1.4. Hence, a greenhouse with a total surface area of 20 sq m will require 20 × 355 × 1.4 = 9940 BTUs per hour, or 20 × 108 × 1.4 = 3024 watts (3.024kW) to maintain a temperature of 13°C (55°F).

These calculations give only very approximate heat requirements – individual greenhouses vary enormously according to site, construction and climate. Buy a heater which will give slightly more heat than required, rather than less.

Commercial growers often maintain temperatures of 18°C (64°F) or more throughout winter, but this is beyond the scope of the amateur gardener.

Types of heaters

In practice there is little difference between the costs of the various fuels, though prices do vary from year to year and from region to region. Some fuels are also more efficient than others.

It is often more economical to

ELECTRICAL SAFETY

Electricity can be lethal in a greenhouse, especially where water is used, though if precautions are taken it is the most efficient energy source.

Have a permanent mains supply installed by a qualified electrician. Ensure that permanent cables are run in conduit and that weatherproof sockets are used which incorporate a screw-on faceplate to shield the terminals when not in use. Screw-lock shielded plugs prevent moisture from touching the terminals when equipment is in use. A residual current circuit breaker at the main consumer unit will protect you against serious electric shocks.

Always use electrical equipment designed for the greenhouse. Domestic equipment can be dangerous.

use two fuels rather than one for heating. The cheaper, such as paraffin, can be used for background warmth, and the dearer, such as electricity, can be used to attain maximum heat with thermostatic control.

Electricity is most likely to be trouble free, gives excellent automatic control, produces no harmful fumes and does not raise humidity in winter. There is no need to transport or store fuel, and electrical equipment is usually compact.

For a small greenhouse, an electric fan heater is ideal. These are cheap to install – they plug into a 13 amp waterproof socket – and are portable. Fan heaters usually incorporate a thermostat which controls the fan and the heat output simultaneously. The air circulation is good for the plants and minimizes fungal diseases. A disadvantage is that if the fan breaks down, heat loss is total.

Tubular electric heaters – aluminium tubes sealed at both ends and containing a heating element – are also highly efficient. They are screwed to the uprights around the sides of the greenhouse about 15cm (6in) clear of the floor.

If they are mounted in banks, there should be 2.5cm (1in) space between each tube. Tubular heaters are often sold in banks of three or four, but the heat distribution is usually better if they are fitted singly all round the greenhouse. They respond well to thermostatic control, and if one fails, the others should keep out the frost.

Convector heaters, which produce a current of warm air without a fan, are fairly inexpensive and easy to install, but heat distribution is not as good as with fan or tubular heaters. If you are using convector heaters, have one at each end of the greenhouse.

Electric storage heaters, using off-peak electricity, are not really suitable because the heat output cannot be efficiently controlled – it is not possible to link them to a thermostat.

Soil-warming cables Cuttings root slowly if the soil is cold, and seeds are slow to germinate in cold composts. To heat the soil or compost in a propagator or frame by air warmth would be slow and costly. And a high air temperature in winter or spring would produce unwanted top growth in plants being propagated. The simple and economic answer is to use electric soil-warming cables. These are inexpensive and easy to install.

Cables are made in lengths to fit any area and give the correct amount of heat – follow the manufacturer's instructions carefully. They are available with a thermostat fitted. The wire is fully insulated and usually has a braided metal earthed sleeve for safety. The heating section is usually a distinctive colour and must never be cut.

Soil-warming cables can be connected direct to the mains supply, or special low-voltage cables can be operated via a transformer – safer if there is a risk of damage to cables from garden tools.

Paraffin heaters are somewhat cheaper to buy than electrical heaters, but the running costs are about the same. The best kind to use are those that burn with a blue flame. They produce a certain amount of carbon dioxide and

SOIL-WARMING CABLES

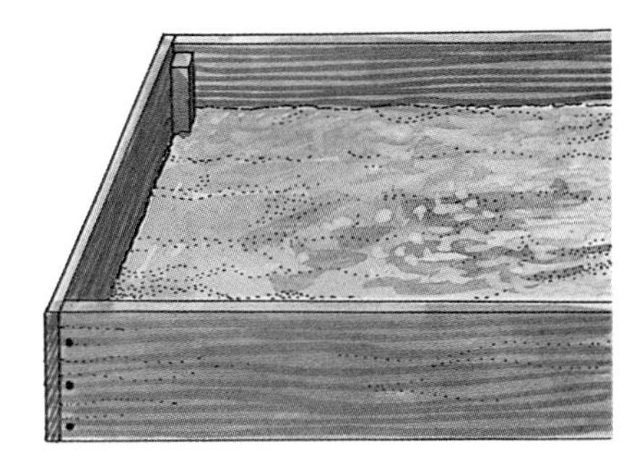

1 For a bottom-heated propagating frame, begin by spreading a 5cm (2in) layer of sand in the base of the wooden tray – there should be several drainage holes in the bottom.

2 Lay the heating cable backwards and forwards over the sand. Avoid sharp bends and lay it not less than 10cm (4in) and not more than 20cm (8in) apart. It must never cross itself.

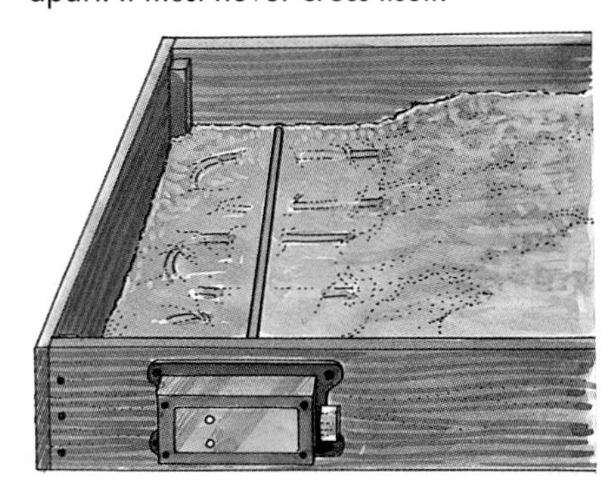

3 Cover the cable with a further 2.5cm (1in) of sand and 7.5cm (3in) of moist compost. Fit a thermostatic control unit, positioning it so that the sensor rod lies 2.5cm (1in) above the cable.

4 Cuttings can be planted directly into the compost, and pots can be sunk in it so that each base is in contact with the sand. Ensure that the compost remains evenly moist at all times.

water vapour, which increases the humidity and can be beneficial to plants if ventilation is adequate.

It is important to use good-quality paraffin oil because low-grade oil, when burnt, can give off sulphur fumes which may damage plants. However, with larger and more sophisticated paraffin heaters there is a flue which takes the fumes outside the greenhouse. Condensation is reduced by the heated flue, creating a drier atmosphere in winter.

Paraffin heaters are probably most useful as emergency heating during cold spells to supplement electrical heating, or during power cuts.

Bottled gas heaters can give a high heat output and are controlled by a sensitive manual valve. The gas bottle is connected to the heater unit by a neoprene hose. This is an economical heating system, but the gas bottles, which are cumbersome and heavy to handle, need refilling or replacing regularly. Gas heaters also produce water vapours and require free ventilation.

Hot-water pipes heated by an oil or gas boiler can be used for heating a greenhouse, but they are costly to install, if the greenhouse is some way from the house.

However, hot-water pipes can be installed in a lean-to greenhouse or conservatory, where they form an extension to the main house central heating system. Thermostatic control is possible, but the pipes retain the heat and do not respond quickly to temperature changes.

Thermostatic control

Thermostats for use with a greenhouse heating system should be easily adjustable, graduated in degrees and be able to regulate the temperature to one or two degrees.

Set the thermostat according to readings taken from a minimum/maximum thermometer in the greenhouse. This records the highest and lowest temperatures since the previous day. Adjust the thermostat so that the minimum temperature does not drop below the desired level.

With an electrically heated greenhouse with thermostatic heat control, it is possible to wire fan ventilators into the system so that humidity and air flow can be continually adjusted automatically to suit the temperature.

HEATED PROPAGATORS

An electrically heated propagating frame provides adequate warmth for rooting cuttings or raising seeds at a much lower running cost than heating an entire greenhouse, though most types are fairly expensive to buy.

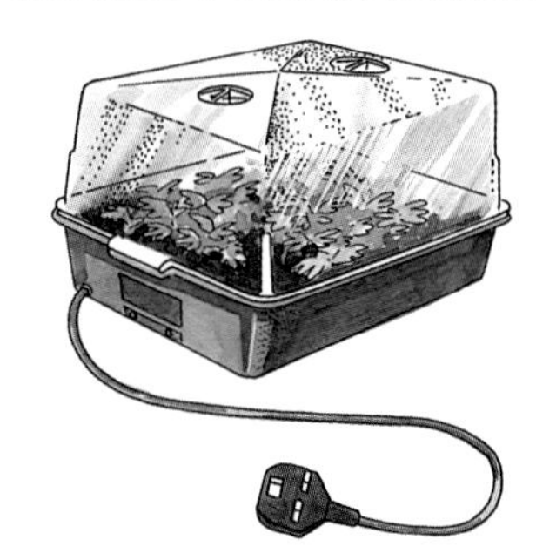

Single compartment propagators with a fixed temperature thermostatic cut-out are the cheapest and suitable for raising small quantities of seedlings or cuttings. Adjustable vents in the top allow some regulation of humidity.

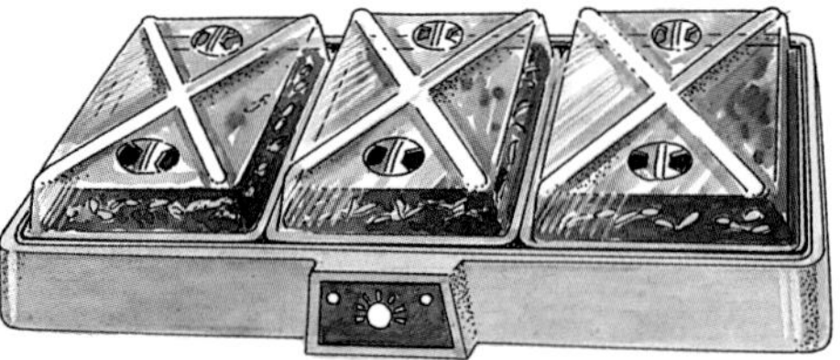

Triple top propagators designed for use with three full-size or six half-size seed trays are useful for raising larger numbers of seedlings. Each lid can be removed separately. An adjustable thermostat gives good temperature control.

High-framed single compartment propagators are better for rooting cuttings or protecting tender pot plants. The cover may be framed with aluminium and glazed with shatterproof perspex.

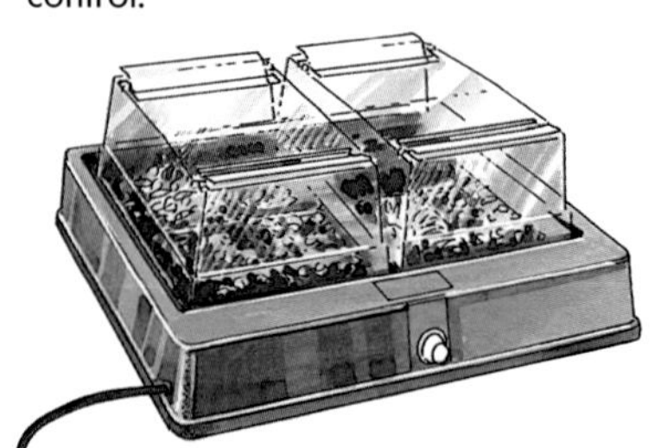

Twin compartment propagators are a good mid-range choice. As with many models, this type comes complete with trays.

GROWING FRAMES

Growing frames are cheaper than a heated greenhouse for raising seedlings and cuttings, and can be installed inside an unheated greenhouse or in the open. They consist of an aluminium framework with removable trays, covered with clear polythene which can be rolled up and down. The roof can be lowered to adjust the size of the tent. Some incorporate a built-in soil-warming unit.

THE GREENHOUSE YEAR

With careful planning and good hygiene, flowering pot plants and many food crops can fill the greenhouse the year round.

The greenhouse adds an extra dimension to gardening, enabling tender plants to be grown which would not survive in the garden, and providing an all-weather retreat for the dedicated gardener. The greenhouse is also invaluable for raising bedding annuals and propagating plants.

It is important to plan how you propose to use the greenhouse. A year-round growing programme is possible provided suitable plants and crops are chosen and a meticulous care routine is followed. For obvious reasons, avoid plants with widely differing needs although it is easy to lodge shade and sun lovers within the same greenhouse and to create an micro-climate on capillary matting for plants requiring moist growing conditions.

Mid winter

Stocking a greenhouse with crops and ornamental plants is easier if a plan is made every year. With few other tasks in the garden, mid winter is a good time to do this.

During mid winter, regularly examine plants that are in flower – such as primulas and cyclamen – removing any faded flowers or discoloured leaves.

Take care when watering not to splash the flowers or to leave water lodging in the crowns of the plants, as this may lead to rotting. Avoid over-watering tender or young plants, or the fine roots may be damaged.

Examine cuttings of zonal pelargoniums inserted in autumn. Remove any leaves showing signs of mildew and discard cuttings which have diseased stems. Water these plants only when the soil in the pots shows signs of drying out.

If you have a propagating case and can maintain a temperature of 16-18°C (61-64°F) during germination, sow florist's carnations, wax begonias, gloxinias and streptocarpus towards the end of mid winter. Otherwise delay sowing for another month. Sow sweet peas in slight heat – about 4°C (39°F).

Late winter

Move dormant fuchsias, heliotropes and hydrangeas on to the greenhouse staging, if possible in a warm spot where a temperature of 10°C (50°F) can be maintained. Spray the plants with water on sunny days, and give them increasing amounts of water as growth becomes active.

Sow seeds of coleus, tuberous and fibrous begonias, celosias and streptocarpus. Place the seed boxes in a propagating frame heated to 16-18°C (61-64°F). When the seedlings are large enough to handle, prick them out and grow them on at normal greenhouse temperatures.

Stop florist's carnations when they have made nine or ten pairs of fully developed leaves.

If you want to plant tomatoes in a cool greenhouse during mid spring, sow the seeds in late winter at 16°C (61°F).

Prune greenhouse climbers, such as plumbago and passion flowers, by cutting back the growths made last summer to within one or two buds of their point of origin. Keep watering to a minimum and ventilate freely on mild days.

Increase your stock of ferns by dividing old plants. Use the vigorous pieces from the outsides of the old plants and discard the old wooden centre. Pot on any other pot-bound ferns.

Early spring

Tomato plants grown from a late winter sowing now need extra space to encourage sturdy growth. If you aim to plant tomatoes in late spring, sow the seeds now in a heated propagating frame.

► **Greenhouse summer** A glazed aluminium-framed greenhouse is fairly easy to erect. With good planning it will support a wide range of tender and semi-hardy ornamental plants and food crops. It also offers the gardener a warm and sheltered workplace.

GREENHOUSE PLANTS MONTH BY MONTH

Mid winter
Azalea (*Rhododendron simsii* hybrids)
Cineraria (*Senecio cruentus*)
Narcissus (*Narcissus* Tazetta varieties)
Poinsettia (*Euphorbia pulcherrima*)
Primrose (*Primula obconica*)

Late winter
Azalea (*Rhododendron simsii* hybrids)
Cineraria (*Senecio cruentus*)
Florist's cyclamen (*Cyclamen persicum* varieties)
Hippeastrum/amaryllis (*Hippeastrum* hybrids)
Hyacinth (*Hyacinthus orientalis*)
Narcissus (*Narcissus* varieties)
Primrose (*Primula obconica*)

Early spring
Cineraria (*Senecio cruentus*)
Freesia (*Freesia* × *hybrida*)
Hippeastrum/amaryllis (*Hippeastrum* hybrids)
Kaffir lily (*Clivia miniata*)
Mimosa (*Acacia* species)
Primrose/primula (*Primula kewensis, P. malacoides, P. obconica*)

Mid spring
Cineraria (*Senecio cruentus*)
Hippeastrum/amaryllis (*Hippeastrum* hybrids)
Mimosa (*Acacia* species)
Primrose/primula (*Primula kewensis, P. malacoides*)
Slipper flower (*Calceolaria* × *herbeohybrida*)

Late spring
Butterfly flower (*Schizanthus hybrida*)
Cineraria (*Senecio cruentus*)
Primula (*Primula obconica*)
Regal and zonal pelargonium (*Pelargonium* varieties)
Slipper flower (*Calceolaria* × *herbeohybrida*)

Early summer
Begonia (*Begonia* species and varieties)
Hot water plant (*Achimenes* varieties)
Slipper flower (*Calceolaria* × *herbeohybrida*)
Gloxinia (*Sinningia speciosa*)
Regal and zonal pelargonium (*Pelargonium* varieties)
Streptocarpus/Cape primrose (*Streptocarpus* hybrids)

Mid summer
Begonia (*Begonia* species and varieties)
Black-eyed Susan (*Thunbergia alata*)
Busy Lizzie (*Impatiens* varieties)
Fuchsia (*Fuchsia hybrida*)
Glory bush (*Tibouchina semidecandra*)
Gloxinia (*Sinningia speciosa*)
Heliotrope (*Heliotropium hybridum*)
Hot water plant (*Achimenes* varieties)
Italian bellflower (*Campanula isophylla*)
Lily (*Lilium* species and varieties)
Paper flower (*Bougainvillea* species)
Plume flower (*Celosia plumosa*)
Slipper flower (*Calceolaria* × *herbeohybrida*)
Streptocarpus/Cape primrose (*Streptocarpus* hybrids)
Zonal and ivy-leaved pelargonium (*Pelargonium* varieties)

Late summer
Begonia (*Begonia* species and varieties)
Columnea (*Columnea* species)
Flowering maple (*Abutilon* species)
Fuchsia (*Fuchsia hybrida, F. triphylla*)
Glory bush (*Tibouchina semidecandra*)
Gloxinia (*Sinningia speciosa*)
Heliotrope (*Heliotropium hybridum*)
Hot water plant (*Achimenes* varieties)
Italian bellflower (*Campanula isophylla*)
Passion flower (*Passiflora caerulea*)
Plume flower (*Celosia plumosa* varieties)
Smithiantha (*Smithiantha* species and varieties)
Streptocarpus/Cape primrose (*Streptocarpus* hybrids)
Zonal and ivy-leaved pelargonium (*Pelargonium* varieties)

Early autumn
Begonia (*Begonia* species and varieties)
Canna (*Canna* hybrids)
Columnea (*Columnea* species)
Flowering maple (*Abutilon* species)
Fuchsia (*Fuchsia hybrida, F. triphylla*)
Glory bush (*Tibouchina semidecandra*)
Heliotrope (*Heliotropium hybridum*)
Italian bellflower (*Campanula isophylla*)
Zonal pelargonium (*Pelargonium* varieties)
Plumbago/Cape leadwort (*Plumbago capensis*)
Scarborough Lily (*Vallota speciosa*)

Mid autumn
Flowering maple (*Abutilon* species)
Fuchsia (*Fuchsia hybrida, F. triphylla*)
Glory bush (*Tibouchina semidecandra*)
Italian bellflower (*Campanula isophylla*)
Plumbago/Cape leadwort (*Plumbago capensis*)
Zonal pelargonium (*Pelargonium* varieties)

Late autumn
Capsicum/pepper (*Capsicum annuum*)
Cineraria (*Senecio cruentus*)
Florist's cyclamen (*Cyclamen persicum* varieties)
Florist's/pot chrysanthemum
Flowering maple (*Abutilon* species)

Early winter
Azalea (*Rhododendron simsii* hybrids)
Cineraria (*Senecio cruentus*)
Florist's carnation (*Dianthus* species)
Florist's/pot chrysanthemum
Florist's cyclamen (*Cyclamen persicum* varieties)
Poinsettia (*Euphorbia pulcherrima*)
Primrose/primula (*Primula kewensis, P. obconica*)

In a cool greenhouse, prepare the bed for planting tomatoes in mid spring. Dig in plenty of well-rotted manure or compost and apply a dressing of tomato base fertilizer at 100g (4oz) per sq m/yd.

Sow seeds of many half-hardy annuals in trays of seedling compost at temperatures of 10-18°C (50-64°F). Sow seeds of *Campanula isophylla* at a temperature of 13°C (55°F) or take cuttings from overwintered plants. Sow seeds of primulas in trays on the staging at normal greenhouse temperatures.

Take cuttings of fuchsias and coleus, rooting them in compost at a temperature of 10-16°C (50-61°F). Take cuttings of chrysanthemums, and also of zonal pelargoniums to produce plants for flowering next winter.

Plant hippeastrum bulbs in 15cm (6in) pots. Provide a temperature of 10-13°C (50-55°F) and water sparingly until buds appear.

Apply liquid fertilizer every ten days to pelargoniums, heliotropes, fuchsias and overwintered annuals.

Prick out carnation seedlings and pot on and stop florist's carnations. Disbud flower stems.

Mid spring

Complete the greenhouse sowings of half-hardy annuals. During sunny weather, shade the seedlings and newly potted plants – the changeable weather often experienced at this time of year can cause violent fluctuations in temperatures. Keep the greenhouse well ventilated. Move established half-hardy annuals into a cold frame for hardening off.

Give increasing amounts of water to plants repotted in early spring. Continue to liquid feed established plants, such as pelargoniums. Hydrangeas in pots are now in active growth and need a temperature of 10°C (50°F) and generous watering.

► **Glass protection** Unaffected by rain and wind, tender ivy-leaved pelargoniums and trailing fuchsias tumble from baskets in a riot of colour. Potted half-hardy annuals – black-eyed Susans and petunias – occupy the staging.

In a cool greenhouse, plant tomatoes in the bed prepared last month and provide suitable supports. Sow seeds of winter cherry (*Solanum*) and outdoor tomatoes at a temperature of 16°C (61°F).

Sow melons and cucumbers at 16-18°C (61-64°F), setting them individually, about 2.5cm (1in) deep in 7.5cm (3in) pots.

Late spring

Move boxes of annuals sown in mid spring to a cold frame for hardening off. Apply a liquid fertilizer to boxed plants if the leaves show signs of yellowing.

Sow cineraria seeds at a temperature of 10-13°C (50-55°F) to produce plants that will flower in early winter. Sow cucumbers and melons if not done already.

On warm days, provide shade for plants now in flower, such as calceolarias, pelargoniums, cinerarias, primulas and hydrangeas. Increase the humidity by damping down the staging and floor. Provide adequate ventilation. Give plenty of water and a weekly liquid feed to vigorous plants.

When fuchsias are 10-13cm (4-5in) tall, pinch out the growing point of each plant to encourage bushy growth. Later, pinch out the side shoots as necessary.

Pot carnations on to 15cm (6in) pots. Stop side-shoots when they are about 15cm (6in) long; stopping until the middle of early summer results in autumn flowers, from early to late mid summer produces winter blooms and stopping up to the end of late summer gives early spring flowers.

Stop laterals growing from the main stems of cucumbers at two leaves beyond the first or second developing fruit. Pinch out subsequent sub-laterals as soon as they have made two leaves beyond their first fruit. Remove tendrils and all male flowers – those without an embryo fruit behind them on old varieties; modern varieties are all-female plants.

Twist the stems of tomato plants round the support strings, or tie them to the canes, and remove side-shoots regularly. Feed the plants every week or ten days from the time the fruits on the first trusses begin to swell. In an unheated greenhouse, plant tomatoes in the border.

Plant out into cold frames melons which have been raised from a mid spring sowing, one plant to each light.

Early summer

Plants which have finished flowering – such as azaleas – can be put into the open garden for the rest of the summer to make more room in the greenhouse. Young cyclamen, seedling cinerarias, calceolarias, primulas and solanums can also be moved to a cold frame.

Pay particular attention to watering – plants in earthenware pots may need two or more applications daily during hot weather. Maintain a humid atmosphere by frequently damping down the staging and floor.

Sow cineraria seeds if this was not done in late spring, and also sow *Primula malacoides*.

Pot on streptocarpus plants, raised from a winter sowing, to 13-15cm (5-6in) pots. Make a further sowing at 16°-18°C (61-64°F) to provide flowering plants next year.

Plants such as pelargoniums and fuchsias which are now flowering must be dead-headed regularly and given liquid fertilizer every ten days.

When young polyanthus primroses for growing outdoors are being set out in nursery rows, pot a few strong specimens in to 7.5cm (3in) pots to provide greenhouse flowers next winter.

Propagate African violets (*Saintpaulia*) and *Begonia rex* from leaf cuttings, rooting them in a propagating frame at a temperature of 16-18°C (61-64°F).

Continue to pot on young carnations into 15cm (6in) pots and move year-old plants into 20cm (8in) pots. Continue stopping side-shoots.

Examine the stems of tomato plants. If they are becoming thin, change to a liquid fertilizer containing extra nitrogen. Harvest the first cucumbers when they are about 30cm (1ft) long.

Towards the end of early summer artificial heat can be dispensed with and more ventilation given in a cool greenhouse. If the weather becomes very warm, leave the top ventilators on the sheltered side of the greenhouse open a little way at night.

▲ Dual-purpose greenhouse A well-organized house can support ornamental plants as well as food crops. Here the border along one side is occupied by tomatoes while the staging opposite houses pot plants such as coleus, begonias, fuchsias and pelargoniums.

A closed small room at the far end can be closed off from the main house by a glazed door. It is heated in winter to accommodate delicate plants.

Mid summer
Damp down the borders, path and staging at least once a day during warm weather, but do not spray overhead, as the water droplets may mark the flowers. Unless the plants are standing on self-watering capillary matting, most require watering daily and possibly two to three times a day during hot spells.

Tomato plants should be in full cropping, with a few fruits requiring picking almost every day. Continue to feed and twist the stems round the supporting strings, or tie them to canes, and remove side-shoots regularly.

Continue picking cucumber fruits and removing any male flowers as soon as they show. If white roots appear on the surface of the bed, apply a 5cm (2in) deep dressing of well-rotted manure or leaf-mould.

To encourage prolonged blooming of pot plants now in full flower, shade the plants during sunny weather and give ample ventilation, especially in the early morning. Except during unusually cold or windy weather, leave the roof ventilators on the shelterd side of the greenhouse open a little way all night.

Take 10cm (4in) cuttings from non-flowering shoots of regal pelargoniums – the best material will come from stock plants which were cut down by about half in early summer and are now producing lots of fresh growth. Root them in a propagating frame.

Late summer
Renew shading if necessary and damp down during hot weather. Continue to feed plants and watch out for pests and diseases.

This is a good time to repair and paint the greenhouse in readiness for the winter. Wooden greenhouses must be painted before heavy autumn dews soak into the timber. Mastic tapes are ideal for sticking over glazing bars to cure stubborn leaks. Also check over the heating system if you have one before you need to turn it on.

Hippeastrums should have died down by now and can be stored just as they are in their pots under the greenhouse staging, until required again in early spring.

Continue to take cuttings of regal pelargoniums. Zonal pelargoniums should also be propagated by cuttings at this time – choose firm, medium-sized, non-flowering growths, with 7.5cm (3in) of stem, from healthy plants.

Take 7.5cm (3in) cuttings of *Campanula isophylla*, setting three or four to a 5cm (2in) pot. As soon as rooted, pot on the whole clump to the next pot size.

During the second half of late summer take 7.5cm (3in) fuchsia cuttings from sturdy young growths if young plants are required for growing on as standards next summer. Sow cyclamen seeds at a temperature of 16°C (61°F) for flowering the winter after next.

YEAR-ROUND GREENHOUSE HYGIENE

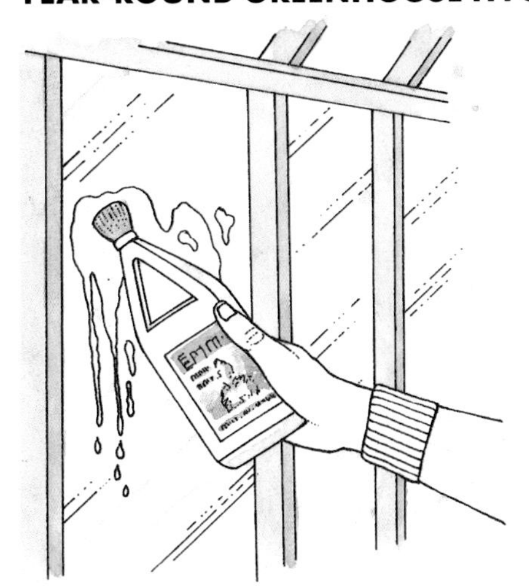

1 Keep the glass or plastic cladding clean at all times, especially at the onset of autumn when natural daylight lessens. Wash off algae and dirt with mild detergent or use a proprietary greenhouse glass cleaner.

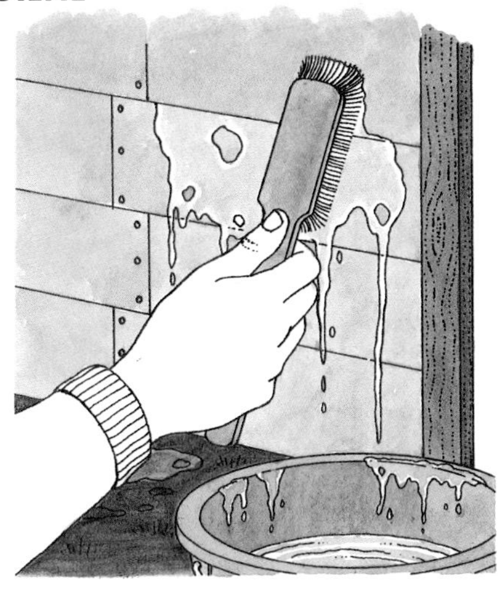

2 Using a scrubbing brush and a mild detergent, remove dirt from any solid walls or timber cladding and from the staging, doors and framework of the greenhouse – dirt may harbour fungal disease spores.

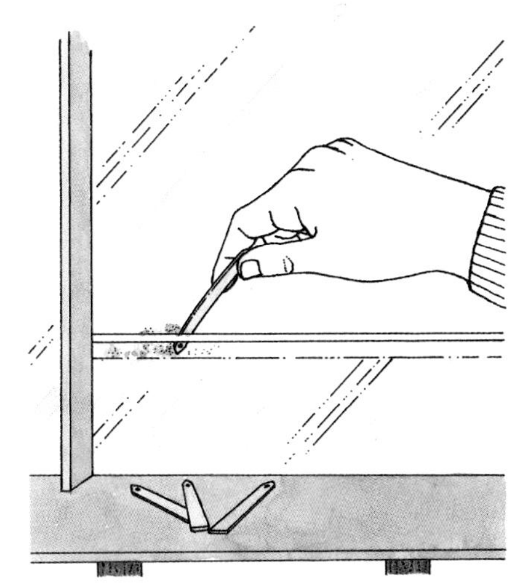

3 Scrape out algae and dirt which accumulate in gaps between overlapping panes of glass and so reduce the light transmission; don't scratch the glass. A plastic plant label makes an ideal tool for this purpose.

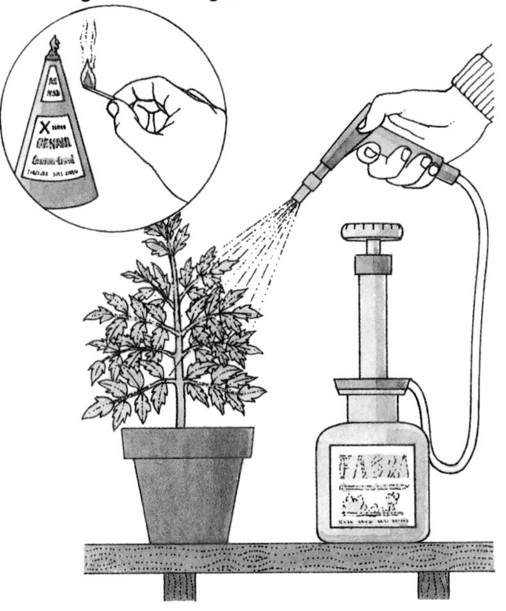

4 Maintain a regular spray programme against greenhouse pests and diseases – prevention is far easier than cure. Proprietary smoke canisters – like cone-shaped fireworks – can be used to fumigate an empty greenhouse.

5 Sterilize any soil in greenhouse borders or below the staging in autumn or winter when there are no plants growing in it. Jeyes Fluid is a good general soil sterilizer, and it can be used for cleansing paths and staging.

6 Empty old compost out of pots and boxes and scrub the containers with mild detergent before storage or re-use – dirty containers harbour diseases and defeat the object of using sterile potting or seedling composts.

Remove the growing points of tomato plants to encourage rapid development of the fruits on the top trusses. A couple of weeks later, discontinue feeding and reduce watering. This helps to prevent splitting of the fruits. If the nights turn chilly, close the vents early in the evening.

Early autumn

Annuals such as clarkias, cornflowers, nemesias, schizanthus, godetias, antirrhinums and pot marigolds, sown in early autumn and grown in pots in a cool greenhouse, make a colourful display during spring and early summer. Sow the seeds in trays of seedling compost at a temperature of 13-16°C (55-61°F).

Continue to take cuttings of regal and zonal pelargoniums, and also fuchsias. Other greenhouse plants to propagate from cuttings in early autumn include coleus, busy Lizzies, heliotropes, shrubby calceolarias and *Plumbago capensis*. They will root in pots standing on the staging, but speedier and more certain results can be obtained by using a propagator.

Disbud florist's carnations as they become ready; remove all buds except the top or crown bud.

Towards the end of early autumn remove any permanent shading from the glass. In sunny weather provide local shading for seedlings and cuttings. Before the nights turn cold, bring into the greenhouse cinerarias, primulas, cyclamen, solanums, regal pelargoniums and begonias which have been standing out in frames.

▲ **Greenhouse spring** Pots of forced narcissi, eye-catching multi-coloured cinerarias and dainty, yellow-flowered *Primula kewensis* announce the arrival of spring while it is still winter in the garden outside.

Mid autumn

Bring into the greenhouse without delay any tender plants still standing outdoors in cold frames.

In the greenhouse, reduce syringing, damping down and watering as the days get shorter and the nights colder. Where possible, carry out any watering and damping down before midday.

Thin out the shoots of climbing ornamentals, such as plumbago, passion flower and *Tibouchina semidecandra*, to admit more light and air during the coming winter.

Maintain a temperature of 7°C (45°F) for carnations and continue disbudding and cutting stems. Water and feed sparingly.

Clean the glass inside and out, then line the greenhouse with clear polythene sheeting, to within 30cm (1ft) of the ridge, to conserve heat during the winter. Cover the ventilators separately so that they can still be opened.

Check heating systems during the evening to make sure that they are working properly and that the thermostats are operating at the required temperature.

Late autumn

Ventilate the greenhouse freely on all sunny days, but avoid cold draughts and close the ventilators fairly early in the afternoon to trap some of the daytime warmth. Keep the greenhouse closed during damp, foggy weather.

Complete any outstanding potting as early as possible. Annuals raised from seeds sown in early autumn will now be ready for moving to 7.5cm (3in) pots.

Cuttings of pelargoniums, fuchsias, heliotropes and campanulas will now be rooted and also ready for potting up into 7.5cm (3in) pots of a proprietary compost.

Dry off fuchsias, begonias, heliotropes and hydrangeas which have flowered during the summer and early autumn. Store the pots under the staging in a cool greenhouse or in a frost-free shed, but do not allow the compost to become dust dry at any time.

Pinch back new growths on solanums, which may otherwise hide the berries. When the earliest cinerarias begin developing their flower heads, give the plants extra space to allow them to grow freely and ensure that they get as much light as possible.

Early winter

Plants grow very slowly or remain dormant in early winter due to the brief hours of daylight. Don't try to make them grow more rapidly by raising the temperature – you will just encourage soft, weak and straggly growth.

At the beginning of early winter give extra attention to plants that you hope to have in flower in the next few weeks. Select the warmest spot for any cinerarias, cyclamen or primulas which are a little backward. Move to a cooler spot any plants that are too forward.

Propagate carnations from cuttings of side-shoots with four or five pairs of leaves. Ideally, root them in a mist propagator.

Open ventilators a little on sunny days but close them again quite early in the afternoon. Most plants – except those actually in flower – must be kept fairly dry. But do not allow them to dry out so much that the soil begins to shrink from the sides of the pot.

If the floors and paths need damping down to increase humidity, do this during the early part of the day. Discontinue overhead spraying of the plants.

USING GREENHOUSE BORDERS

Pots are the obvious choice for greenhouse growing, but the roots of large or heavy-cropping plants are less restricted when grown in open border soil.

Most amateur gardeners who own a greenhouse will want to grow a variety of plants, both ornamental types and food crops. Most ornamental plants do well in containers where their individual needs can be monitored and regulated carefully, and for these you will need shelving or staging, pehaps with capillary matting. Growing plants in containers also allows you to move them around the greenhouse as light or temperature conditions demand.

The single biggest limitation of growing plants in containers, however, is the restriction imposed on root growth and hence water and nutrient uptake. It is vital to attend to watering and feeding during the growing season to avoid loss of vigour. Some fruit and vegetable crops, however, can suffer badly from restricted root growth – they may run to seed, give reduced yields or produce tough-textured crops. It is common practice, therefore, to grow crops and large plants in an open greenhouse border. Ideally, you should use a crop rotation system, with free-standing, moveable staging, so that tomatoes, for example, are grown in the east border one year and in the west border the following year.

Greenhouse borders are suitable for growing tomatoes, cucumbers, melons, lettuces, sweet peppers, aubergines, radishes, spring onions, French beans, strawberries, vines, peaches and nectarines and all climbing or shrubby ornamentals.

◀ Greenhouse tomatoes For high-yield crops, tomatoes need a constant supply of water and nutrients. These are easily applied when the plants are grown in the greenhouse border. An edging of marigolds helps to ward off harmful whiteflies.

Preparing the soil

When starting with a newly erected greenhouse which has not been put on a solid concrete plinth, you may be lucky enough to have good quality soil already on the floor. In this case, all that is needed for the first season is the normal routine digging and the same application of a base dressing which would be carried out on an outside plot.

It is unlikely that the foundations for the outer walls of the greenhouse will be deep enough to impede the natural drainage of the soil inside, but on very poorly drained sites it is advisable to incorporate a drainage layer of coarse grit while double-digging.

Plants grown under the protection of glass or plastic tend to respond by growing more quickly than in the garden. In so doing, they take up nutrients rapidly from the soil – often depleting ordinary soils well before the end of the growing season. You must take special care to keep the greenhouse border soil enriched. Well-decayed manure, garden compost or leaf-mould should be dug into the soil at a rate of one bucketful per sq m/yd at few weeks before planting.

Before planting, water the border thoroughly with a hosepipe and when completely drained through, scatter a general-purpose fertilizer over the surface at a rate of one generous handful per sq m/yd and rake it in.

If the greenhouse has been built on poor soil, dig out the soil entirely to one spade's depth and replace with fertile garden soil. Better still, use sterilized compost, such as John Innes or a similar

BORDER SOIL PREPARATION AND AFTERCARE

1 If your greenhouse border soil is of poor quality, prone to waterlogging or infested with pests and diseases, dig it out entirely to one spade's depth and discard it.

2 Where the site is poorly drained, add a layer of coarse sand or grit across the bottom of the excavated ground. Or, install a proper soil-drainage system with ceramic pipes.

3 Infill the site with good-quality sterilized garden soil or bought top soil, incorporating one bucketful per sq m/yd of well-rotted manure, garden compost or leaf-mould.

4 Leave the border to settle for a few weeks before planting. Just before planting, soak it through, sprinkle on a general-purpose fertilizer and rake it into the top 2.5cm (1in) of soil.

5 Throughout the growing season, apply liquid fertilizer to the soil around plants using a watering can, or apply granular fertilizer by hand. Follow the manufacturer's instructions for rates.

6 Once a year, after the plants have been cleared, sterilize the border soil using a suitable liquid pesticide, fungicide or disinfectant, or dig out and replace the soil.

potting compost available from most garden centres and nurseries – delivery can usually be arranged within a reasonable radius, often without charge.

Raised beds

On a site where the greenhouse border soil is poorly drained, an alternative to digging the soil out and replacing it is to construct a raised bed over the broken-up subsoil. Build an outer framework of wooden planks – well treated with a proprietary wood preserver – or use brick or concrete to form the sides. A height of about 23-30cm (9-12in) should be adequate for most plants.

Infill the bed with sterilized garden soil to within about 2.5-5cm (1-2in) of the top. You can fill a small bed with potting compost – John Innes No.2 or No.3 potting compost, for instance.

Planting and aftercare

The principles of growing plants in a greenhouse border are identical to those for growing outdoors, except that you must take extra care with watering and feeding – regulation of the greenhouse environment relies entirely on your constant attention. Soil dries out very quickly under glass and it may be a good idea to install some form of automatic watering system, especially when growing salad crops which tend to run to seed when they are hot and dry.

Pests and diseases must be kept under strict control – minor outbreaks can turn rapidly into a major epidemic in a confined environment. Many of the chemical pesticides and fungicides recommended for garden use can be used in the greenhouse (check the manufacturer's instructions), but be careful not to breathe them in when spraying or dusting. It is best to wear a face mask and to leave the greenhouse afterwards until the chemical has settled.

House plant pesticides can also be used, and these tend to be much safer, though they may not be as efficient in controlling the more persistent pests. For a thorough clearance of above-ground pests, use a proprietary greenhouse fumigant smoke. These are sold in a canister like a firework and give good control of aphids, whitefly, red spider mites, mealy bugs, leaf miners and many other pests. You must follow the safety instructions on the container to the letter – close all windows and vents to contain the smoke, then evacuate the greenhouse immediately after lighting the touch paper and do not return until after the manufacturer's specified time.

Biological pest control is more

environmentally friendly than chemical sprays and is often a better remedy as some greenhouse pests, notably red spider mite and whitefly, have become resistant to pesticides available to the amateur gardener.

Control of soil-borne pests and diseases can be more of a problem in the greenhouse border, since they build up unnoticed and the few chemicals which are effective against them are not recommended for use by amateurs – they are far too dangerous. For this reason, it is important to use only sterilized soil in the greenhouse border and to maintain scrupulous hygiene at all times throughout the house.

Tar acids formulated as an emulsion are used to clear moss and slime from paths and can also be applied to the glass, framework and border soil as a sterilizer. Soil disinfectants like Jeyes fluid give some control of soil pests and are relatively safe to use.

Ring culture

Ring culture is a specialized growing system which is best suited to tomatoes. The growing medium is free from pest and disease problems (as with plants grown in sterilized compost in a pot) yet allows roots to extend without any restriction.

Plants are grown in bottomless fibre cylinders filled with sterilized potting compost and roots grow into an inert medium which holds plenty of water and also provides stability. The system combines the advantages of growing plants in open border soil with those of growing in sterilized potting compost.

Begin preparations for ring culture by digging a trench to one spade's depth. The soil can be removed from the greenhouse – it won't be used. Line the trench with a single sheet of heavy-duty polythene. This will act as a watertight membrane and isolate the plant roots from the garden soil underneath (which may contain pests or disease organisms). Fill the trench with coarse washed gravel.

Transplant seedling tomatoes singly into 20cm (8in) fibre ring pots – or any suitably sized bottomless container – filled with a proprietary loam-based potting compost. Stand each container on the gravel bed, sinking them in to a depth of about 2.5cm (1in) to aid stability.

Fibrous feeding roots will eventually fill the container while anchorage and water-absorbing roots will grow into the gravel. Water plants via the gravel, but feed them by applying liquid tomato fertilizer to the compost in the container. Since the gravel bed has an open structure with plenty of air trapped in tiny pockets, the plant roots can be kept permanently moist without fear of waterlogging – tomatoes are qucikly checked by periods of water shortage in normal all-soil growing systems in a greenhouse.

Grow bags

Plastic grow bags, pre-filled with a peat-based compost together

RAISED BEDS

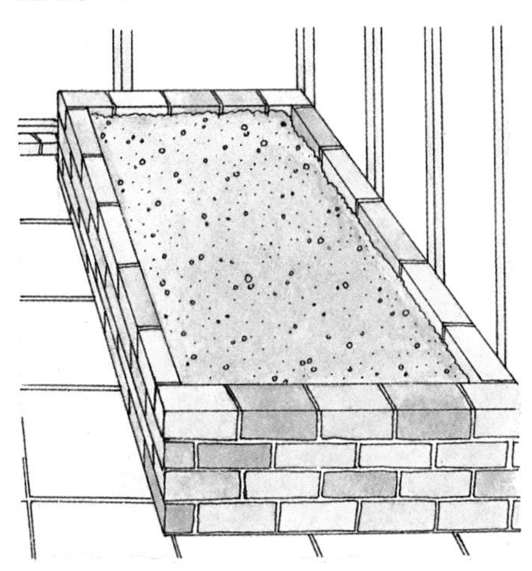

1 A raised bed, constructed from bricks, timber or concrete, provides an ideal means of growing plants where border soil is poorly drained, or where low walls of the greenhouse framework shade the floor.

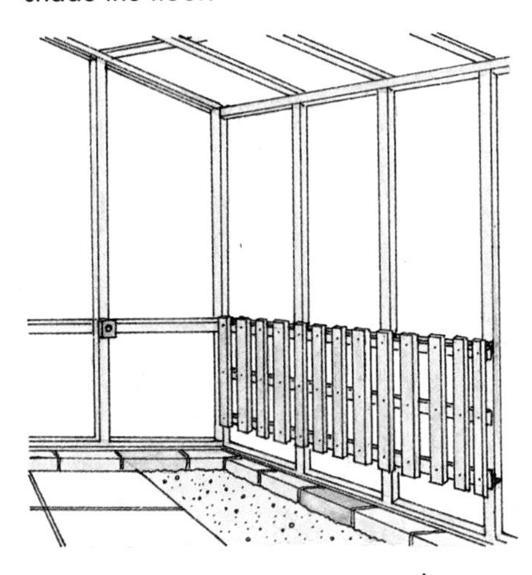

2 With a little ingenuity you can hinge slatted timber or aluminium shelving so that it can be lowered during summer leaving the border soil available for use, but secured horizontally for pots at the other times.

RING CULTURE

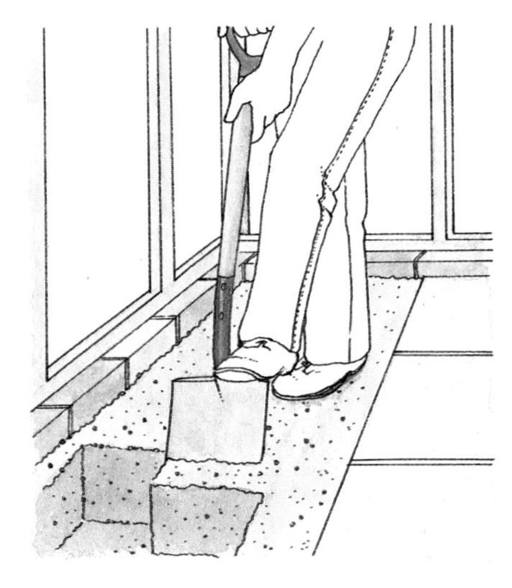

1 The natural border soil is not used for ring culture. Dig a trench the full length of the greenhouse, or to whatever size you have allocated for the greenhouse border – there are no rules for size.

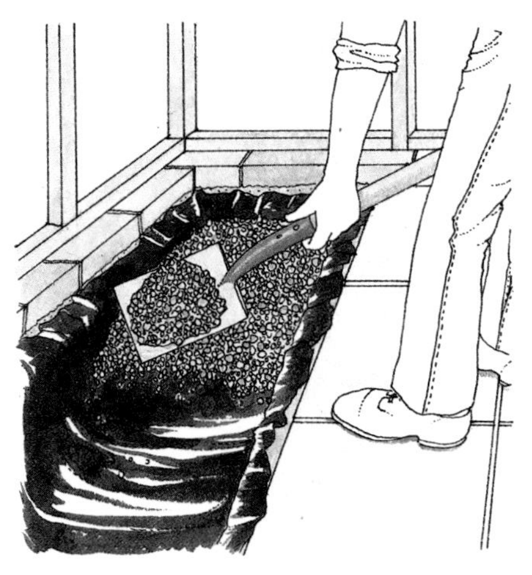

2 Discard the soil dug from the trench. Line the trench with a single sheet of heavy-gauge polythene, then infill with washed gravel. This will form a water reservoir and anchorage medium for the plants.

3 Tomatoes are suited to this form of culture. Plant them singly in 20cm (8in) bottomless pots filled with good-quality potting compost. Stand each pot on the gravel. Water via the gravel, but liquid feed via the pots.

USING GROW BAGS

1 Lay grow bags on any flat surface. It's cheaper to cultivate border soil than to buy grow bags, so use them only where the soil is unworkable or on a solid floor. Cut three holes in the top of each bag.

with a base fertilizer, provide a simple though expensive means of growing tomatoes, aubergines, cucumbers, sweet peppers and other high-value, high-cropping vegetables and fruits.

Grow bags can be laid directly on a concrete or paving floor, or on uncultivated soil in the greenhouse border. The bag is sufficiently large to give a long root-run for large plants, and the growing medium is sterile – useful where soil-borne pests and diseases are known to be a major problem. Unfortunately, they can be used only for one growing season, after which the compost is suitable only for mixing with fresh soil as a texture conditioner or as a garden mulch.

Support systems must be chosen carefully. Deep rooting is not possible and the growing medium has little substance, so plants fall over easily unless they are tied in. Do not push garden canes through the bottom of the bag – you will reduce its water-holding capacity. You can insert tall canes into a grow bag, however, and prevent them from falling over by securing the top end to a fixed structure within the greenhouse, such as roof glazing bar.

Tie tall plants to wires, strings or netting secured to the framework of the greenhouse, or use proprietary support frames specially designed for use with grow bags.

Alternatively, canes may be inserted around a grow bag and strings tied between.

2 When bought, the compost in all grow bags is dehydrated, making it light to handle. Before planting, fully moisten the compost with water, following the instructions on the bag – each bag needs thorough soaking.

3 Water carefully – never over-water, but ensure that the compost remains moist at all times. New bags contain enough nutrients for a couple of weeks, but liquid fertilizer must be added regularly from then on.

SUPPORT SYSTEMS

1 Ordinary bamboo canes or wooden stakes make adequate supports for tall border-grown greenhouse plants such as tomatoes. Loosely tie plants to the canes or stakes using soft garden string or synthetic raffia.

2 Tomatoes can be supported on strings hung from the greenhouse roof – nylon string is the strongest. Simply tie the bottom end of the string loosely around the tomato base. Twist the stem around the string as it grows.

3 Cucumbers are heavy crops so need careful support to prevent the stems from breaking. Fix wires across the glazing bars for the side branches, and vertical strings or wires for the main stem. Tie in each fruit's stalk.

4 For climbing ornamental plants, or cucumbers, grown against a vertical wall, use nylon netting secured to wooden battens or spacing blocks. Alternatively, mount wooden or plastic trellis on battens.

POT-GROWN PLANTS

Greenhouse plants that spend their entire life in containers must be correctly potted and repotted to maintain health and vigour.

The concept of potting seems a simple one – merely bedding a plant in some sort of soil in a pot. To be successful, however, you must use the correct type and size of pot, choose an appropriate compost type, and pay attention to the season, spacing and cultural demands of each plant.

There are three basic methods of potting:

□ Potting up – moving a seedling, rooted cutting or divided section of a plant into its first pot.

□ Potting-on – moving a plant which has outgrown its container into a slightly larger one.

□ Repotting – providing a mature plant which is not required to grow any bigger with new soil without increasing the pot size.

Choosing the pot

Plastic pots have generally replaced clay ones, especially for pot plants bought in shops and nurseries. They have a number of advantages, but also several disadvantages, over unglazed clay, glazed ceramic and china pots.

Plastic pots are generally quite cheap, easily cleaned and light to handle and store. They come in a vast range of sizes, colours and patterns. Apart from clay-coloured types, plastic pots may be green, black, white, buff, red and many other colours besides. Though useful for modern interiors, garish colours are best avoided in the greenhouse.

The porosity of clay versus plastic is also important. Plastic pots are non-porous so the compost can easily become waterlogged. Where the pots stand in a bed of moist gravel or capillary matting to provide constant moisture and extra humidity, plastic pots are essential – porous types would soak up the water and defeat the process.

Plastic pots have smooth surfaces so roots don't cling to them – making the removal of plants from their pots much easier. If the root ball does get a grip, the walls of a plastic pot are usually flexible so the bond can be eased apart. At the same time, plastic pots become brittle, especially when exposed to sun and break easily.

Clay pots allow water to evaporate from the side walls as well as the top, so soil dries out quickly. They are good for plants which enjoy dry conditions, such as cacti, but less suitable for moisture-lovers, such as ferns. If you are unsure of how much water a plant needs, however, there's less chance of waterlogged soil in a clay pot. In hard water areas, lime deposits build up on the outsides of clay pots as water evaporates and these can look unsightly.

Clay is much heavier than plastic so pots are less likely to fall over, especially when tall, unstable plants are grown in a lightweight compost. Obviously, this also makes larger sizes more difficult to move around. Cost, too, can be restrictive – clay types are often at least twice the price of plastic, and glazed ones ten times or more.

Pot sizes

A standard pot can be measured by the diameter of its rim or by its

► **Potting up** The process of moving young seedlings and rooted cuttings to their first pot size is known as potting up. Avoid handling seedlings by the fragile roots, but hold them gently by the leaves.

POTTING UP

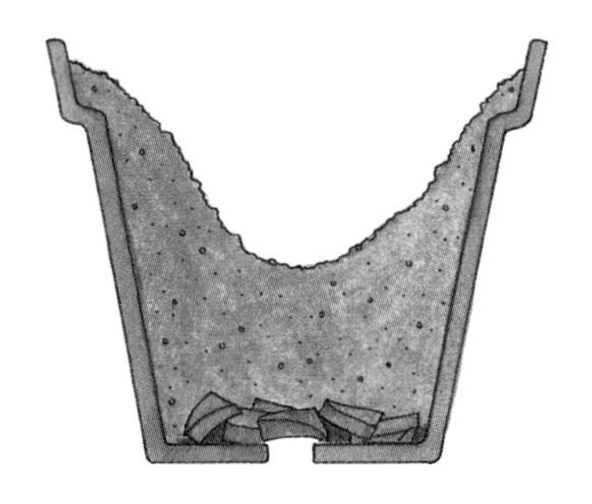

1 Make sure the pot is thoroughly clean – scrub in soapy water or mild detergent to remove old soil and lime deposits which could be harbouring disease. Add a few crocks if necessary to stop compost falling out through large drainage holes, then part-fill with potting compost.

2 Settle the compost by gently bumping the pot on a solid surface, but don't compress it too much or you may encourage waterlogging. Hold the plant in the pot with its neck level with the rim of the pot, then fill with compost around the roots. Try to keep the roots well spread out so that the plant is stable and grows upright.

3 Firm the compost by gently bumping the pot – don't use your fingers to firm the compost as you can damage the roots of young plants (though with spongy composts this is less of a problem). Fill the pot to within 1-2.5cm (½-1in) of the rim. Water in well, but don't saturate.

height – both are the same. So-called half-pots, however, are half as deep as they are broad, making them ideal for plants with shallow roots and those with a low habit – they give a better-balanced appearance to the potted plant and use less compost.

Standard pots range from 5cm (2in) right up to the size of a bucket or even larger. It is possible to buy all sizes at about 1cm (½in) step-ups, but popular sizes for house plants are 9cm (3½in), 12cm (5in) and 18cm (7in). Large plants, shrubs and climbers may need correspondingly larger pots. Ensure that all pots have adequate drainage holes. (Containers with no drainage holes *can* be used but you will have to water very carefully to avoid waterlogging; ideally put a drainage layer of pebbles or crocks in the bottom.)

Round shapes are the most common, but plastic pots in particular come in several other shapes as well, including square. Saucers and drip trays are usually available to match – some plastic pots and hanging baskets even have built-in or clip-on drip trays.

Potting up

Before use, clean all pots thoroughly in warm, soapy water. Scrub off encrustations of lime, especially from clay pots. It's best to soak clay pots thoroughly before use, since they absorb a lot of water and quickly dry out.

In general, plastic pots need no drainage material in the bottom – they have several small drainage holes which allow free passage of water without loosing compost. Clay pots usually have only one drainage hole, but it's quite large so compost can fall through. First cover the drainage hole of a clay pot with a few crocks (pieces of broken clay pot) or clean pebbles. If you plan to stand the pot on a capillary watering mat or sand bed, never add crocks – they impede the intake of water.

Begin potting by placing moist potting compost in the bottom of the pot. Firm it down gently. Hold the plant in the pot so that its roots are resting on the compost, and the base of the plant comes to about 2.5cm (1in) below the rim of the pot. (Add or remove compost if the level isn't correct.)

Position the plant carefully and sprinkle more compost around it, topping the pot up to about 2.5cm (1in) from the rim – tiny pots can be filled a little fuller. Settle the compost by gently tapping the pot on the table or bench. Loam-based

POTTING COMPOSTS

Loam/soil-based composts have substance and weight – ideal for large, top-heavy plants. They retain water and nutrients well. The John Innes formulations are most popular. J.I. No.1 is a mix of loam, sphagnum peat, coarse sand and lime/chalk, suitable for young plants. J.I. No.2 has double the loam and lime, and extra fertilizer – for most mature pot plants. J.I. No.3 has treble the loam and lime – for vigorous, bulky mature plants. Good loam is difficult to obtain, so quality of all proprietary loam composts may be variable. Use lime-free composts for acid-loving plants, such as azaleas and rhododendrons.
Soil-less composts were formerly based on peat, but as use of this scarce material is being discouraged, composts based on peat alternatives are now common. Coconut fibre – or coir – is readily available and suitable as seedling, cuttings and potting composts, on its own or mixed with composted bark, farm waste, vermiculite or perlite. They are clean and light to handle, blended with nutrients and water-absorbent.

Multi-purpose composts are a cross between loam-based and other types.

Bulb fibre is based on coir, with oyster shells to reduce acidity, and charcoal to keep it 'sweet'. It's clean and free-draining, but as it contains no nutrients, the bulbs deplete themselves and cannot be used again.
Bromeliad compost is spongy, very porous and free of lime.
Cactus compost should be free-draining. Add grit, coarse sand or perlite to any proprietary potting compost.
Fern compost should generally be acid, with sand or perlite for drainage and charcoal to keep it sweet.
Orchid compost (formerly made of osmunda fibre, peat and sphagnum moss) should be obtained from orchid nurseries.

Perlite is a heat-expanded volcanic mineral which holds water very well and is also free-draining.
Vermiculite is a pale, spongy, granular material manufactured from a silicate mineral. It retains a lot of water and air.

POTTING-ON

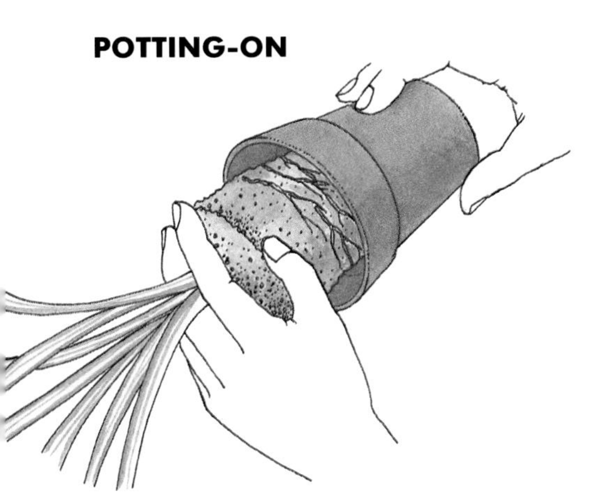

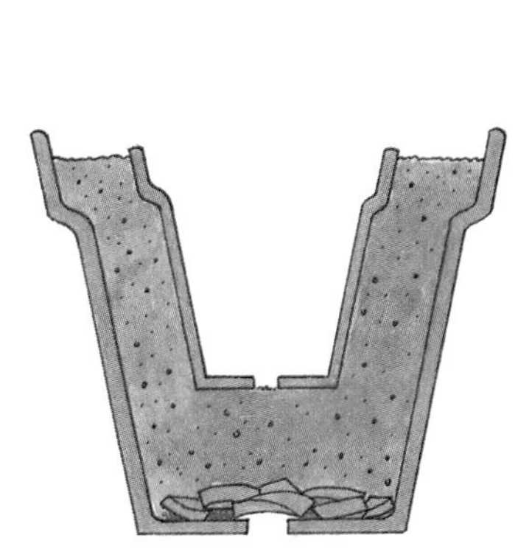

1 Gently remove the plant from its pot; cover the soil with the palm of one hand, turn the plant over and then lift off the pot with the other hand. Stubborn pots can be loosened by tapping against a table or by running a knife around the rim.

2 Part-fill the new, slightly larger pot with moist compost as for potting up. Prepare an exact-sixed hole for the rootball by using the old pot as a mould, gently firming the compost down around the mould by hand. Add more compost until the pot is full.

3 Carefully lift out the empty pot – the compost should stay in place if sufficiently moist. Then insert the plant into the hole and firm in by tapping the pot down on the table. Top up with more compost if necessary and water the plant well.

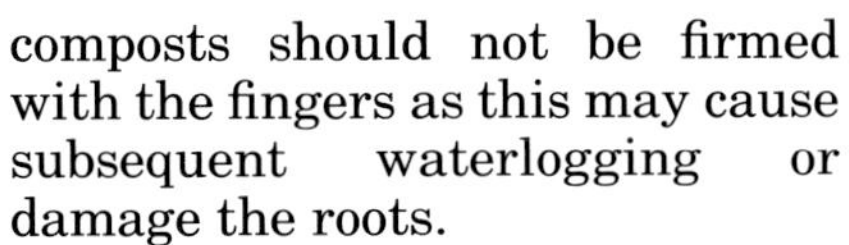

composts should not be firmed with the fingers as this may cause subsequent waterlogging or damage the roots.

Once potted, water the plant, but don't give it too much – any damaged roots quickly rot if the compost is very wet.

POT-BOUND PLANTS

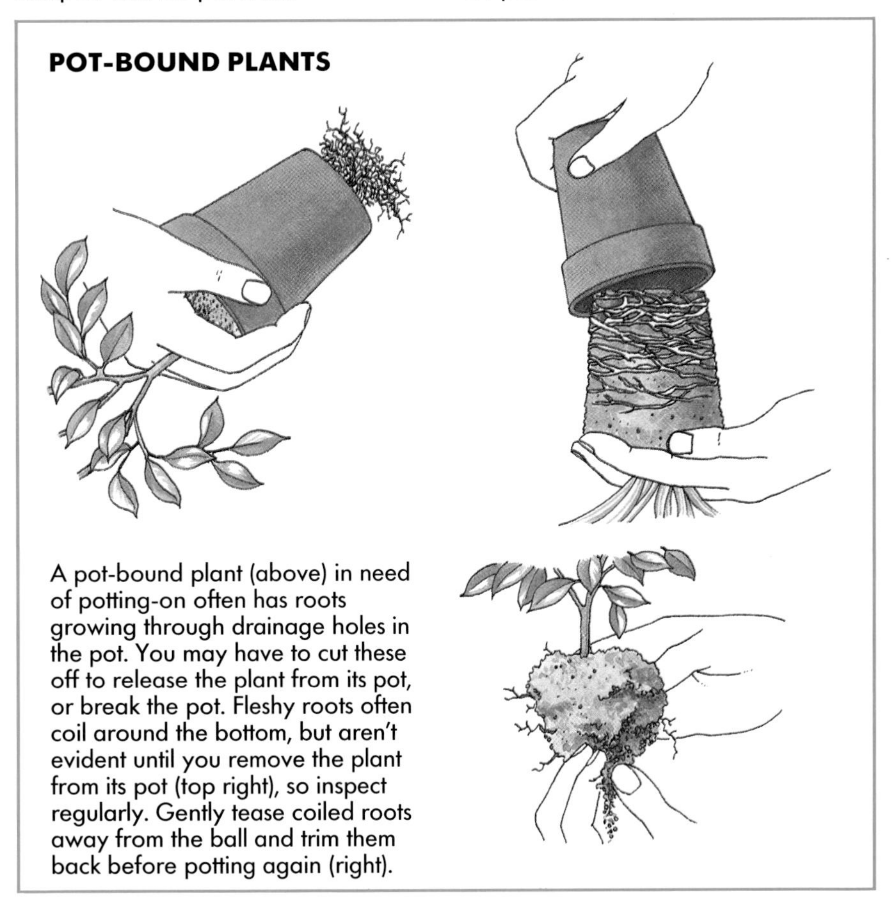

A pot-bound plant (above) in need of potting-on often has roots growing through drainage holes in the pot. You may have to cut these off to release the plant from its pot, or break the pot. Fleshy roots often coil around the bottom, but aren't evident until you remove the plant from its pot (top right), so inspect regularly. Gently tease coiled roots away from the ball and trim them back before potting again (right).

Potting-on

Pot plants must be potted-on when they become pot-bound (or repotted if you don't want them to increase in size). A plant is pot-bound when it has filled its pot with roots and exhausted the soil. Under such conditions it makes little or no new growth and dries out rapidly, even when watered frequently. Roots often grow through the drainage holes in the bottom of the pot, giving an obvious indication of being pot-bound.

Young plants, and those which you wish to increase in size, should be potted-on into larger pots every year, preferably in spring or early summer, and when the compost is just moist.

To dislodge a pot-bound plant, place one hand over the compost with the fingers either side of the main stem. Lifting it from the table, turn the pot over carefully and tap it firmly on the base with the other hand to shake out the soil ball. If it won't come free, tap the upturned rim of the pot against the edge of the table.

If the soil ball still sticks as can happen with clay pots, use a knife with a long, thin blade – such as an old kitchen knife – to slice carefully around the edge of the soil. Poke a stick through the drainage hole to apply extra pressure if necessary.

Select a new pot slightly larger than the last – about 2cm/1in larger for small to medium sized plants, or up to 8cm/3in larger for bulkier ones. Depending on the depth of the root ball, put a 2.5-5cm (1-2in) layer of potting compost over the base of the pot.

Set the root ball on the compost so that the top is about 1cm (½in) below the base of the broader rim of the pot. Hold the plant in the centre and sprinkle more compost into the space between the root ball and pot. It is possible at this stage to correct plants which have developed a list to one side.

Cover the top of the ball with compost. Gently bump the pot down on the table to settle the compost, then top up to within 1-2.5cm (½-1in) of the top with more compost. Water the plant well and leave it to drain.

When potting-on fragile plants or those with a spreading habit, it may be difficult to infill the new compost without damaging the foliage or stems. To avoid this problem, prepare a mould of compost by firstly 'potting' the old, empty pot in the new one.

Repotting

Established plants which have reached their required size still need new compost every year or so if they are to remain healthy, but pot size need not be increased.

First remove the plant from its pot as before and thoroughly clean the pot. If the soil ball and roots are fairly loose, gently tease away some of the spent compost and sever a few old roots completely. This allows space for new compost to be added. Return the plant to its pot using the same principles as already described.

If the soil ball is hard and crammed with matted roots, simply slice some of the ball off with a sharp knife – an old bread knife is ideal. Root pruning, however, does weaken the plant somewhat and renewed growth will be quite slow.

Top-dressing

This is a simpler method of revitalizing an established plant and suitable for mature plants in heavy, unwieldy containers. Instead of removing the plant from its pot, tilt the pot and scrape the top surface of the old soil out – a small fork or spoon will help. Be careful not to damage the stem or any large, essential roots. Then, top up with fresh compost and firm it down gently. Water in as before.

Incorporating a moss pole

Moss poles are long plastic tubes bound with moss – held in place with nylon thread – suitable for supporting climbing plants with aerial roots such as Swiss cheese plant (*Monstera*), devil's ivy (*Syngonium*) and certain philodendrons. Unlike other forms of support for pot plants, they are bulky in cross-section and cannot simply be pushed into the compost. Instead, they must be incorporated at the same time as the plant is potted.

Position the root ball off-centre in the new pot and stand the moss pole in place behind the plant before filling the pot with the new compost. Ensure that it is upright and securely firmed in. Tie stems to the pole with soft thread or fine raffia at first – aerial roots will eventually grow into the moss and support the plant.

Finishing touches

An additional top-dressing of gravel or limestone chips improves the appearance of the pot plant and also helps to reduce water evaporation from the compost. This is particularly beneficial to cacti and many hairy-leaved plants which dislike having moist compost in contact with their leaves.

Gravel and chippings are available in many different colours and sizes to suit all purposes.

Outdoor pots can be given a top-dressing of wood bark chips to reduce water loss, improve appearance and deter weeds.

REPOTTING

1 Reduce the size of the root ball by teasing away loose soil and severing some old roots. Slice solid, matted root balls with a knife if necessary.

2 Part-fill the original pot – or a new one of the same size – with fresh compost. Position the plant and fill in around the root ball. Water in.

TOP-DRESSING

1 Without removing the plant from its pot, scrape the old surface soil away, taking care not to damage the base of the stem or major roots. An old kitchen fork is an ideal tool.

2 Clean away loose scale from the rim of the pot then refill with fresh potting compost up to the original level. Firm it in gently and water well. Restake and trim the plant if necessary.

HANDLING PRICKLY CACTI

The spines of many cacti are very sharp, making handling during potting difficult and dangerous – some are barbed and cause infection if lodged in flesh.

Make a strap from a piece of rolled up paper or thin card. Pinch it firmly around the base of the cactus and you will be able to manoeuvre it quite easily.

GREENHOUSE PROPAGATION

A greenhouse is the ideal laboratory in which to raise new plants – from seed, cuttings, divisions and offsets.

A small unheated greenhouse can provide ideal conditions for rooting cuttings, germinating seeds and carrying out most other types of plant propagation. If you can afford to install some form of heating – even if it is only a small heated frame – within the greenhouse, the scope for raising new plants is even wider.

In order to germinate or root well, most seeds or pieces of plant material taken from indoor plants and soft-stemmed garden plants need warmth. And although many hardy, woody garden plants will germinate or root at lower temperatures – easily provided in a cold frame or outdoor nursery bed – a constant, controlled greenhouse environment will ensure much better results.

It is usually possible to keep plant material suitably warm and moist in an inexpensive plastic-topped propagating case or improvised unit placed on an indoor window-sill. But space is invariably a limiting factor indoors, so if you want to propagate large numbers of plants – especially if you enjoy growing annual bedding plants – you will need to set aside a part of the greenhouse especially for this purpose.

Another problem associated with raising new plants indoors is lack of light. Although a window-sill may be very bright, the light comes from one direction only and seedlings in particular are drawn towards it, producing leggy, thin-stemmed plants. Devices can be set up to reflect light back on to the young plants – using aluminium foil reflecting screens, for instance – but such methods are cumbersome and unsightly.

Heat passing through glass when the sun strikes it is a real problem with plants raised on window-sills. If seedlings and cuttings are not shaded from direct sun they soon dry out, wilt and die.

A greenhouse eliminates these problems. If properly sited, natural sunshine keeps the plants well lit throughout the day and from all angles, so new growth is even, compact and upright.

The air temperature increase caused by sunlight through the greenhouse glass or plastic cladding is used to beneficial effect. With better air circulation and the means to maintain much higher humidity, high temperatures no longer dry out the soil and kill the plants. Instead, high and constant temperatures encourage better plant metabolism and hence improved germination, rooting and subsequent growth.

Essential conditions

Taking cuttings or sowing seeds and merely placing the trays or pots in a greenhouse will not ensure success – you must get all the growing conditions right and make appropriate allowances for different types of plants.

Humidity A humid atmosphere is essential for vegetative propagation – using cut sections of shoot, stem or leaf – of most plants. Humidity helps to prevent water loss from a cutting, which is temporarily unable to take up moisture readily because it has been severed from its roots.

Loss of moisture is greatest where leaves are included in the cutting material, because the leaves continue to transpire – give off moisture from their pores – as long as they live.

Leafless stem-section cuttings, on the other hand, don't transpire very much, or not all. But if the rooting compost in which they are planted dries out, they will soon wither and eventually die.

Maintaining high humidity in the air is more effective than watering as a means of maintaining the optimum amount of moisture in the rooting compost. This is because watering – even if carried out on a very regular basis – is intermittent and so there are fluctuations in the water content of the compost. Where frequent regular watering is not possible, the compost can go through severe fluctuations of wetness and dry-

◄ **Vegetative propagation** By planning and timing softwood cuttings, flowering and foliage plants can be kept at a continuous stage of growth. The light shade cast by flowering begonias and fuchsias are beneficial to young pelargoniums and trays of rooted cuttings waiting to be potted up.

PROPAGATING CASES

1 An improvised single-pot case can be made simply by inserting a wire hoop in the compost and covering it with a clear polythene bag. Use string or an elastic band to secure the bag and punch a few holes for aeration.

2 Unheated purpose-made propagators have a rigid plastic cover over an ordinary seed tray. They come in a range of sizes and have ventilators in the top. Individual pots or small trays are placed beneath the cover.

3 Elaborate heated cases have thermostatically controlled electric heating cables buried in the base below the rooting compost. This allows the temperature to be regulated to suit the special needs of each batch.

ness, doing great damage to the emerging roots or discouraging rooting in the first place.

However, humid air is not a requirement for the rooting of cuttings taken from fleshy-stemmed plants, such as cacti and other succulents and certain perennials and sub-shrubs, including pelargoniums. In fact, humid air can encourage the growth of fungal spores, resulting in various rot diseases.

Even where high humidity is required, the secondary effect of encouraging fungal diseases can be a major problem unless good ventilation is maintained. Always ensure that fresh air circulates around cuttings or seedlings, at least from time to time.

Temperature Most cuttings and seeds start growth best at a temperature of at least 18°C (64°F). Tropical plants generally require higher temperatures – above 24°C (75°F). Use a minimum-maximum thermometer to monitor the day and night temperatures and take steps to ensure that the heating remains as constant as possible.

Rooting powder contains a synthetic plant rooting hormone, identical to the one normally possessed by plants. Soft-stemmed plants usually root swiftly without the assistance of extra hormones, and a thick coating of powder on the base of the stem or leaf can actually form a barrier against successful rooting. If you want to use a rooting powder on soft-stemmed cuttings, make sure the dusting is light.

Woody stems root more slowly and the process can be speeded up by dusting the base of the cutting with hormone rooting powder. Buy fresh powder every year – it becomes less effective with age.

Rooting mixtures Standard potting composts are not suitable for cuttings or seeds. The texture of such mixtures is too heavy and they contain too much nutrient, which will scorch delicate young roots. All that is required of the compost is that it holds moisture well, yet prevents waterlogging.

Use a proprietary seedling/cuttings compost or a general purpose compost. Several are readily available, including organic com-

CREATING THE RIGHT ENVIRONMENT

1 Maintain humidity around newly sown seeds by covering the tray with glass, rigid transparent plastic or clear polythene sheeting. For surface-sown seeds needing darkness to germinate, sandwich newspaper under the glass.

2 During direct hot sunshine, shade cuttings or seedlings in a propagating case by covering with a semi-opaque fabric. The fine-mesh netting or sacking often used to contain supermarket root vegetables is ideal.

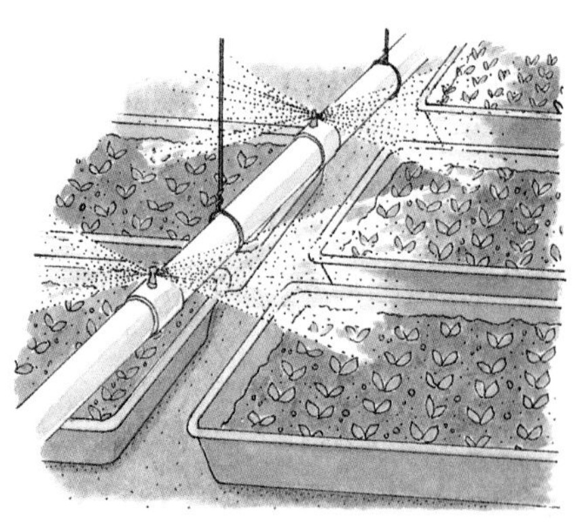

3 A spray tube fitted with mist nozzles at intervals and connected to a mains water supply is the ideal means of maintaining high humidity around seedlings or cuttings. The system can be manually operated or automated.

MIST PROPAGATION UNIT

The specially constructed mist unit provides a fine spray of water in the air above the cuttings or seedlings. An electronic humidity sensor monitors evaporation from an artificial leaf to assess when to switch on the mist nozzle automatically, and a time-switch or light/moisture sensor controls a cut-off valve in the water supply pipe. In this way, the real plant material never dries out; nor does it get too wet.

A rod thermostat controls electric heating cables buried in the sand in the base of the unit. Cuttings can be rooted directly in compost laid on top of the sand; seedlings can be raised in trays bedded in the compost. Shade the mist unit from hot, direct sun.

posts, multi-purpose or coir mixtures which are recommended for sowing seeds and rooting cuttings.

All rooting mixtures must be sterile – the presence of fungal spores leads to damping-off and other rot diseases. Use compost taken directly from a sealed bag. Never use garden soil or old compost, however good it may look.

Germinated seeds and rooted cuttings soon need more food than is provided by seedling/cuttings composts. They should be transplanted into potting compost, which contains fertilizer, as soon as they are large enough to handle, although liquid feeding with a weak solution of ordinary house plant fertilizer provides a good temporary alternative if transplanting has to be delayed for a short while.

Propagating cases

The simplest way to maintain high humidity for greenhouse propagation is by means of a plastic-topped case or frame. These can be bought from any garden centre and come in a range of sizes and shapes. Some cover just one seed tray or pot; others cover several trays. And for potted cuttings, there are deep cases in the form of miniature greenhouses.

It may seem odd to put a miniature greenhouse within a greenhouse, but unless you are prepared to hose down the floor and staging every few hours, or invest in a more sophisticated humidifying system, this is the best method, especially for small amounts of cuttings or seeds.

As a money-saving compromise, you can use ordinary plastic boxes designed for packing sandwiches or for presenting and storing food. Those with transparent lids are excellent for raising seedlings.

For individual pots of cuttings or seeds, the simplest covering is a transparent plastic bag. This must be large enough to fit over the top of the pot without touching the plant leaves. A few sticks or hoops of wire inserted in the compost will hold the bag upright.

Once rooting has occurred, high humidity is less essential, so remove the cover to let more air reach the leaves and prevent fungal diseases getting a hold. With the more elaborate propagating cases, this can be done in easy stages with the aid of one or more adjustable vents in the cover. If you are using a plastic bag as a cover, slice open one side of the bag at first, and remove the bag entirely only after a few days of acclimatization.

Heated cases have a heating element incorporated in the plastic base or in separate heating trays.

LABOUR-SAVING UNITS

1 Special multiple dibber plates can be bought to speed up and simplify the sowing of large seeds and the spacing out of seedlings. Level the compost in the tray, then firm the dibber plate into the surface to make equally spaced holes. Press lightly to make shallow holes for small seeds.

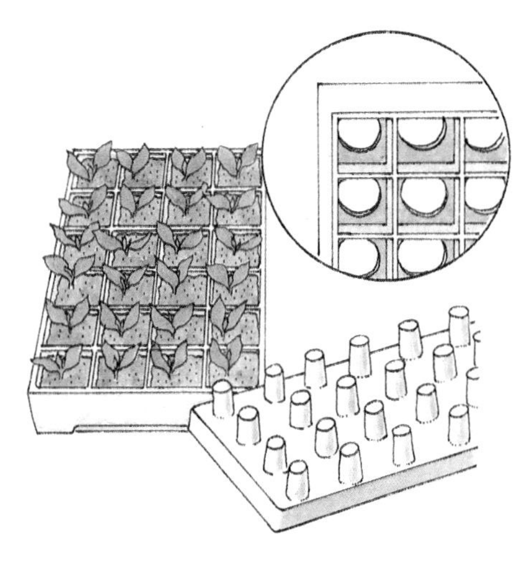

2 Special polystyrene slabs with pot shaped insulated cells are ideal for bedding plants. By putting seedlings one to a cell, the roots of adjacent plants don't knot together. A studded drip tray serves as a compost compressing tool, and is used to push the plants out of their cells.

3 Miniature grow bags can be obtained for rooting cuttings. Simply lay the bag flat, cut holes in the top and moisten the compost inside as recommended. Insert the cuttings through the holes and into the compost. Being enclosed, the compost remains more constantly moist than in a pot.

SUMMARY OF PROPAGATION TECHNIQUES

Vegetative propagation
Methods which involve cutting and growing on sections of plants:
Division Used to propagate plants that grow in clumps. Having removed the clump from its container, break apart or cut the clump into pieces, each with roots and top growth attached, and replant them.
Layering Roots and shoots are encouraged to develop on stems still attached to the parent. Air layering is a special technique where roots are encouraged to sprout from a stem above ground.
Leaf cuttings are taken by detaching individual leaves and inserting their stalks in compost. In a few cases, the leaf can be cut into segments without the stalk, each of which is inserted cut edge down in compost. Or a whole leaf can be pegged down flat on compost and shoots encouraged to sprout from slices made across the veins.
Offsets Small replicas of the parent plant may spring directly from the base of the stem of the parent plant and these can be detached and potted up. Many bulbs also produce offsets which can be grown on.
Plantlets Some plants naturally produce replicas of themselves. These can be detached and potted up individually.
Shoot tip cuttings are taken by cutting off the tips of shoots, with two or more leaves attached, and inserting them in compost.
Stem-section cuttings are similar to tip cuttings, but older stem material from lower down the plant is used. The soft tip growth is trimmed away and discarded.

Propagation from seed
Large numbers of new plants can be raised from seed, and this is the most common way to propagate annuals.

HANDLING SEEDLINGS

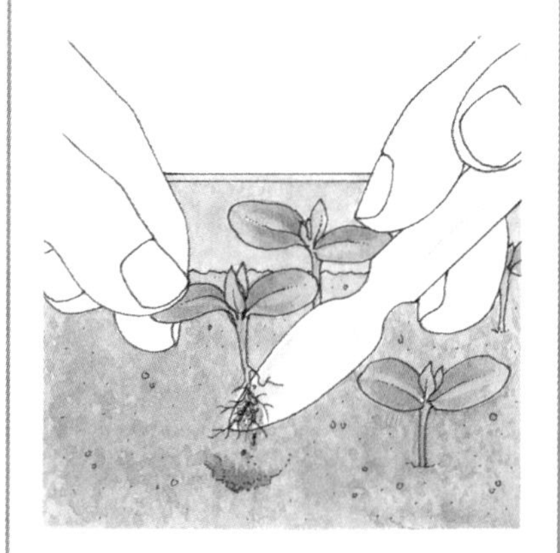

When pricking out seedlings, always handle them gently by a leaf – either a seed leaf or a true leaf. Never hold them by the stem, because if you injure the stem the seedling may rot and die. Though you may slightly damage the leaf by holding it, the growing tip and stem will not be affected so the seedling survives.

You will need a safely installed supply of mains electricity in the greenhouse if you choose this type.

Small electrically heated cases have a built-in pre-set thermostat which is set to a moderate temperature suitable for the propagation of most plants. Larger cases have an adjustable thermostat. Consider carefully your needs before you buy – the larger cases often give more value for money and provide much more scope for raising a selection of plants.

There is no need to operate the case at high heat. Most seeds will germinate at a maximum temperature of 18°C (64°F) and cuttings root readily at around 21°C (70°F). Excessive temperatures may even inhibit seed germination.

To prevent scorching of the plant material, all propagating cases should be shaded lightly during periods of direct sunlight.

Mist propagation
Intermittent mist spraying is an expensive but more efficient alternative to keeping cuttings or seedlings in a closed case or in a bag. A thin film of moisture is maintained over the leaf surfaces using a water jet controlled automatically by an electronic sensor.

With this method, propagation can be carried out in full sunlight or with just very light shading, and the normal processes of plant growth and food production within the leaves can take place at maximum efficiency.

Heat from underneath the cuttings or seedlings – known as bottom heat – is usually needed to balance the cooling effect of moisture passing constantly through the compost and to encourage healing, callus formation and rooting of cuttings.

With mist propagation, rooting is more rapid and certain – especially with species that are difficult by other means. Also there is less risk of disease because spores of grey mould and other fungal organisms are washed away before they do any damage.

However, cuttings rooted by mist propagation need to be weaned gradually to drier air if they are to grow vigorously without a check.

Small mist units, with a transparent surrounding screen to keep the mist within bounds, are available, but cost more than a heated propagator.

Alternatively, you can build your own mist unit. In addition to basic materials for making the case, you will need water pipes, mist nozzles, heating cables, a thermostat and humidity sensor, and a control unit. Seek advice from a specialist supplier and from a qualified electrician before starting such a project.

PREVENTING FUNGAL DISEASES

1 When sowing seeds under glass, always use sterile compost. Unless you can steam-sterilize your own compost, buy sealed bags of ready-made compost. Prepare a fine surface for tiny seeds by sieving the compost.

2 Spray seedlings with Cheshunt compound – powdered copper sulphate and ammonium carbonate which has to be dissolved in water. This should prevent fatal damping-off which causes seedlings to keel over and die.

GREENHOUSE PESTS

The warmth and humidity of a greenhouse promote growth, but also encourage pests and diseases.

The best way to keep greenhouse plants healthy is to give them the right growing conditions. Most troubles are due to inadequate care and attention.

Many diseases result from poor cultivation – periods of excessive dryness or unduly humid air, lack of air movement among crowded plants, and overwatering. It is generally easy to deal with such problems once they are spotted.

Pests are harder to guard against. Some live all year in the greenhouse, and others come in through windows and doors or are introduced on new stock.

Try to keep newly acquired plants in isolation until you are sure they are healthy – if there are eggs or spores concealed on the plant the problem can soon spread to other plants close by.

Examine all plants regularly for signs of trouble – turn leaves back to check the undersides as well as the top surfaces. The shoot tips, which are the most succulent, are usually the first to be attacked by sap-sucking pests. Fungal diseases often appear on mature leaves. Any unusual leaf or flower disfigurement or discoloration is likely to be a sign of trouble.

There are number of liquid, wettable powder and smoke cone formulations for greenhouse insecticides and fungicides. Follow the maker's instructions exactly for handling and applying these chemicals – fumigant smokes are especially dangerous if used incorrectly in an enclosed space.

Also check the pots and potting compost. A white crust on the surface of the compost or around the rim of clay pots may simply indicate that you are using very hard water, but it can also result from over-feeding. Collected rain-water, provided it is clean, is softer and more suitable than tap-water for watering pot plants. A green scum of algal growth on the compost or around the rim of the pot indicates over-watering or poor drainage.

▲ **Glasshouse greenfly** This and other aphids are among the most common and troublesome pests. They make shoot tips and flowers sticky, deplete the plants' energy and frequently transmit virus diseases.

Biological control

Some pests have become resistant to chemical pesticides, but can be treated by biological control. This technique introduces a pest's natural enemies – predators, parasites or diseases – to the greenhouse in order to control it. Predators and parasites must be put on to host plants before these become too heavily infested, and they need a temperature of 21°C (70°F) for at least part of the day if they are to breed fast enough to overcome the pests. The most effective season is mid spring to mid autumn, though the vine weevil nematode should be applied in late summer when young grubs are present. The caterpillar bacterium can be used at any time and also on some outdoor plants such as cabbages.

Most insecticides are harmful to natural pest enemies and should not be used in the greenhouse. Pirimicarb is a selective aphicide and can be used safely against greenfly and other aphids.

◄ **Tomato blight** This fungal disease can eventually lead to rotting of the fruit. Spray greenhouse and outdoor tomato plants with Bordeaux mixture as a preventative measure.

APHIDS

Plants affected Most plants.
Symptoms Colonies of small, round-bodied, green, pink, reddish, yellow or black insects, mostly wingless but often with some winged individuals present. Sticky excretions foul leaves.
Danger period Any time.
Treatment Spray with permethrin or pirimicarb, or fumigate the greenhouse with a pirimiphos-methyl or permethrin smoke cone. Alternatively, use biological control.

BLACK LEG

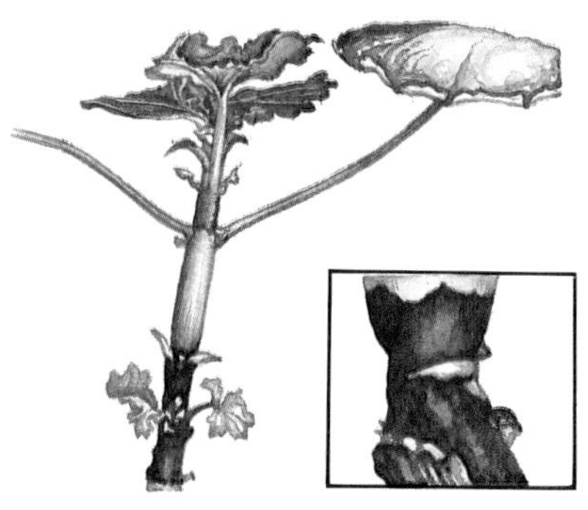

Plants affected Pelargoniums.
Symptoms A black rot develops at the base of cuttings or at the stem base, and the affected tissues become soft. Leaves turn yellow and the whole cutting or stem dies.
Danger period Soon after cuttings are taken.
Treatment Destroy badly affected plants. Use sterilized compost, maintain strict greenhouse hygiene.

CATERPILLARS

Plants affected Chrysanthemums, carnations and many greenhouse plants.
Symptoms Petals eaten; caterpillars often inside the blooms. Irregular holes in leaves.
Danger period Any time.
Treatment If relatively few plants are affected, remove the caterpillars by hand. Spray larger infestations with permethrin or pyrethrum, or fumigate with a permethrin smoke cone. Or use biological control.

DAMPING OFF

Plants affected Any seedlings, especially fast-growing species, which tend to have the softest stems. Bedding plants are susceptible.
Symptoms Seedlings rot and collapse at soil level. The disease may affect a small group of seedlings or spread rapidly through an entire tray or pot of seedlings.
Danger period Soon after germinating seedlings emerge.
Treatment Water seedlings with Cheshunt compound (copper sulphate and ammonium carbonate formulated as a soluble powder) or copper oxychloride as a preventative measure. Remove all totally collapsed seedlings as soon as they are seen. Maintain good greenhouse ventilation.

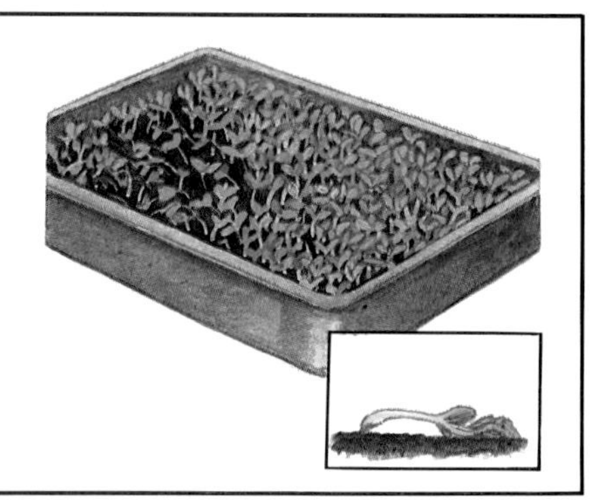

BIOLOGICAL PEST CONTROL

The following biological controls are commercially available from specialist suppliers. Best used from mid spring to mid autumn.
Aphids
Predatory midge larva, *Aphiodoletes aphidimyza.*
Caterpillars
Bacterium, *Bacillus thuringiensis.*
Glasshouse red spider mite
Predatory mite, *Phytoseiulus persimilis.*
Glasshouse whitefly
Parasitic wasp, *Encarsia formosa.*
Mealybugs
Ladybird predator, *Cryptolaemus montrouzeri*
Scale insects (soft scale, hemispherical scale)
Parasitic wasp, *Metaphycus helvolus.*
Vine weevil grubs
Pathogenic nematode, *Heterorhabditis megidis* (apply in late summer).

GREY MOULD (botrytis)

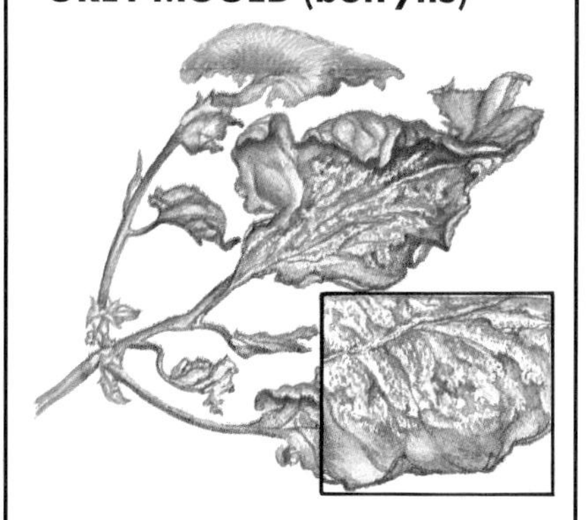

Plants affected All types, especially tomatoes, chrysanthemums and lettuces.
Symptoms Grey, velvety mould on rotting leaves.
Danger period Growing season.
Treatment Remove and burn infected parts. Ventilate well, and spray with benomyl, carbendazim or thiopanate-methyl. Disinfect greenhouse at end of season with dichlorophen, phenols or similar.

LEAFHOPPERS

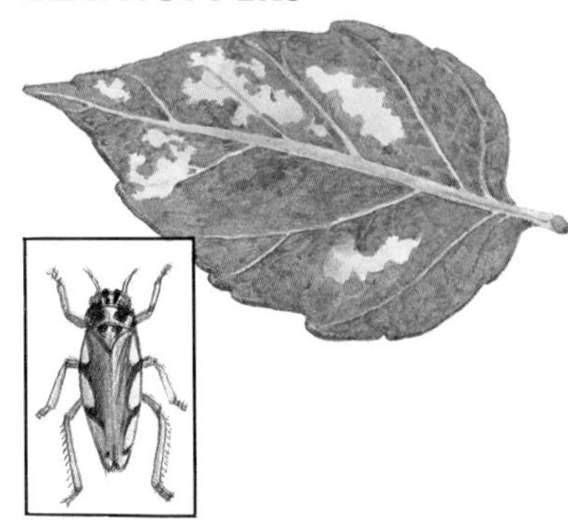

Plants affected Many types, especially pelargoniums, primulas and tomatoes.
Symptoms Coarse white flecks on leaves; insect skins present on the undersides. Small yellowish-green insects leap from leaves.
Danger period Any time.
Treatment Spray thoroughly with malathion, permethrin or pyrethrum, repeating at fortnightly intervals if necessary.

LEAF MINERS

Plants affected Many types, especially chrysanthemums.
Symptoms Whitish-brown twisting lines on leaves trace the path of tunnels mined in the inner tissues by small fly maggots. Growth is weakened.
Danger period Any time.
Treatment If numbers are few, pick off and burn each affected leaf. Spray more serious outbreaks with gamma-HCH or pirimiphos-methyl.

LEAF MOULD

Plants affected Tomatoes.
Symptoms Purple-brown mould on the under surfaces of leaves; yellow blotches on upper.
Danger period Summer.
Treatment Grow resistant varieties. Ventilate well. Spray with benomyl, carbendazim, thiophanate-methyl or mancozeb. Disinfect with phenols or dichlorophen.

MEALYBUGS

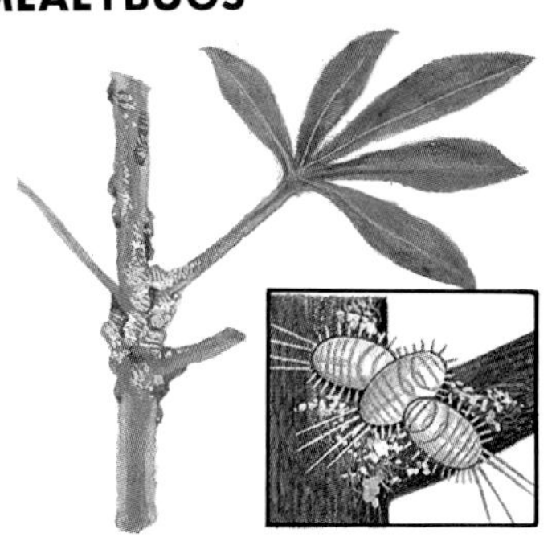

Plants affected Many types, especially cacti and succulents, vines, camellias and orchids.
Symptoms Colonies of pink bugs covered with white mealy or waxy wool, usually concentrated around buds and leaf axils.
Danger period All year.
Treatment Spray forcibly with malathion (or paint it on infested areas), or spray with a systemic insecticide such as dimethoate. Or use biological control.

RED SPIDER MITES

Plants affected Many types, especially busy Lizzies, fuchsias, vines, cucumbers and tomatoes.
Symptoms Fine, light mottling of upper leaf surfaces, yellow discoloration and silk webbing between leaves.
Danger period Any time.
Treatment Maintain high humidity. Spray with malathion or pirimiphos-methyl or control biologically.

SCALE INSECTS

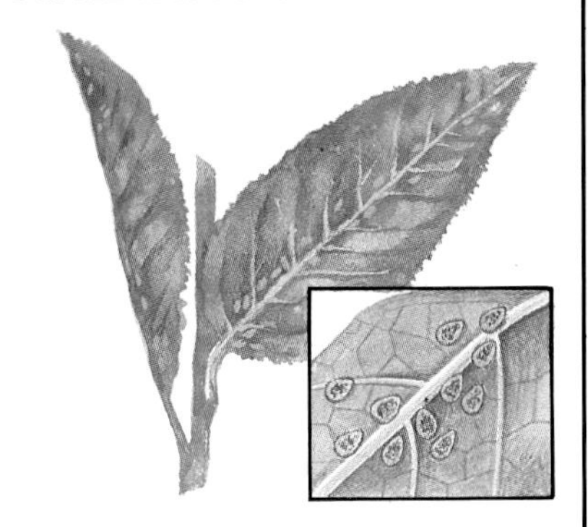

Plants affected Many types, especially camellias, bays, citrus, stephanotis and ferns.
Symptoms Flat or rounded, yellow or whitish-brown scales, mainly on the undersides of the leaves and lying alongside veins.
Danger period Any time.
Treatment Spray with malathion, pirimiphos-methyl or dimethoate when first seen, repeating three weeks later. Or control biologically.

SCORCH

Plants affected Most plants growing under glass.
Symptoms Pale brown spots appear on the leaves or affected plants, but sometimes whole leaves become papery.
Danger period Mainly summer, during prolonged spells of hot sunshine.
Treatment Shade the greenhouse with blinds or shading paint. Ensure that the potting compost does not dry out.

TARSONEMID MITES

Plants affected Begonias, fuchsias, gerberas, cyclamen, amaryllis and hippeastrums, ferns and many other greenhouse plants.
Symptoms Very small, slow-moving mites, similar to red spider mites, but feeding in more concealed parts of the plants – protected in buds or in the crevice of a sheathing leaf, for instance. New growths are checked and distorted by severe infestations, and leaves are slightly curled at the edges, often becoming thickened and brittle. Flower buds may be killed; those which open are discoloured and often very distorted.
Danger period Any time.
Treatment No chemical treatment gives effective control. Destroy and burn infected plants.

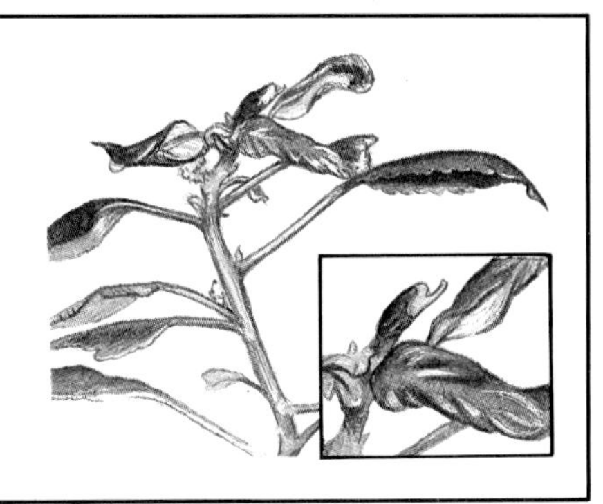

TOMATO GREENBACK AND BLOTCHY RIPENING

Plants affected Tomatoes.
Symptoms A hard green or yellow patch develops on the shoulder of the ripening fruit near the stalk, and similar patches may develop on other parts of the fruit. Greenback may be associated with scorch (see page 87).
Danger period As the tomato fruit swells and ripens.
Treatment Grow resistant tomato varieties, such as 'Eurocross BB', 'Shirley', 'Alicante', 'Tigrella' and 'Moneymaker'. Never allow the soil or compost to dry out, in order to maintain even growth of the fruit. Shade the greenhouse when the weather is hot and maintain good ventilation. Don't allow the greenhouse temperature to rise excessively, but maintain steady warmth.

VINE WEEVILS

Plants affected Cyclamen, begonias, gloxinias and others.
Symptoms Legless white grubs, up to 8mm (1/3in) long, eat roots, tubers and corms. Leaves wilt. Adult weevils eat notches from leaf margins.
Danger period Any time.
Treatment Remove dead leaves and debris from around the base of pot plants. Fumigate or dust with gamma-HCH. Use biological control against larvae.

VIRUSES

Plants affected Pelargoniums and many other plants.
Symptoms Variable, according to plant affected – colour changes in leaves and stems, wilting, crinkling and stunting of leaves.
Danger period Any time.
Treatment No chemical treatment available. Destroy and burn affected plants. Maintain good greenhouse hygiene. Control aphids.

WHITEFLY

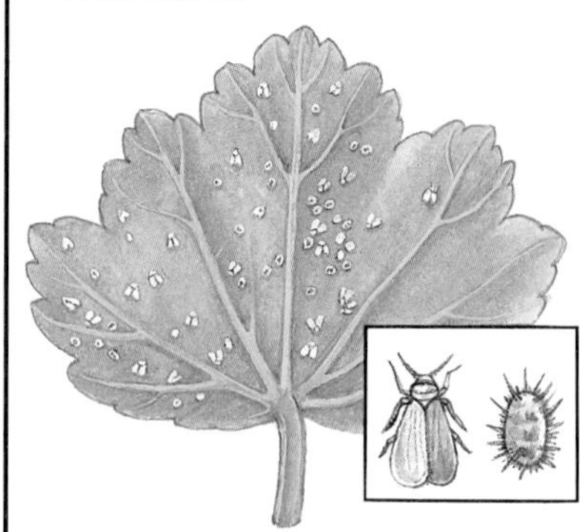

Plants affected Many, chiefly fuchsias, pelargoniums, tomatoes and cucumbers.
Symptoms Small moth-like white flies take off from the undersides of leaves when disturbed. Leaves are discoloured and sticky.
Danger period All year.
Treatment Spray with pirimiphos-methyl or permethrin or fumigate with permethrin or pirimiphos-methyl smoke cone. Or control biologically.

OTHER TROUBLES

Earwigs eat irregular, tattered holes in the leaves of many plants, or may bite flower petals. They are active at night from late spring to mid autumn. These small brown insects hide during the day under pots and among debris on the floor or staging. Spray or dust with malathion or gamma-HCH.
Rust disease affects many plant types. Brown, orange or yellow powdery masses of fungal spores develop on affected leaves and stems during the growing season. Remove and burn all diseased leaves. Ventilate the greenhouse to reduce humidity. Apply a liquid copper fungicide.
Sciarid/mushroom fly larvae feed on fungal growth in potting compost and on rotting plant debris. They also eat the young roots of seedlings and cuttings. Adult flies are midge-like, up to 5mm (3/16in) long, often seen swarming over the surface of moist compost. Don't overwater plants. Dust with gamma-HCH, water in spray-strength pirimiphos-methyl or fumigate the greenhouse with a smoke cone.
Slugs and snails may crawl into the greenhouse, eating irregular holes in the leaves of many plant types in summer and autumn. Characteristic slime trails mark their path. Maintain good greenhouse hygiene. Sprinkle proprietary slug baits around the floor.
Thrips attack tomatoes and many ornamental plants, causing fine, light-coloured mottling on leaves, giving them a silvery appearance. Avoid underwatering and overheating the plants – hot, dry conditions encourage these small insects. Spray with permethrin or pyrethrum as soon as symptoms appear.
Tomato blight is a serious fungal disease of outdoor tomatoes, but may also occur in cool greenhouses. Brownish black blotches develop on the leaves; dark streaks and spots develop on green fruits, and brown discoloration spreads over ripening fruits until they shrivel and rot completely. Spray with Bordeaux mixture at fortnightly intervals as a preventative measure even if the blight has not appeared.
Tomato leaf mould occurs in early to mid summer. Pale yellowish patches develop on the leaves. These patches become covered with a greyish or brownish velvety mould. Leaves eventually wither and die, but don't drop. Plant growth is checked and fruit is slow to develop. Remove and burn infected leaves or entire plants. Maintain good ventilation, and avoid simultaneous high temperatures and high humidity. Spray with benomyl carbendazim, copper, mancozeb or thiophanate-methyl as a preventative measure where the disease has occurred in previous years. Disinfect the greenhouse thoroughly at the end of the season with phenols, dichlorophen or a quaternary ammonium compound.

GROWING ORCHIDS

Many orchids will grow well in a cool greenhouse or conservatory, and with a little extra care and heat, some tropical ones can also be tried.

Though several of the more popular orchids will survive in the home, conditions are rarely ideal, so if you want to grow a wide range of these exquisite plants you really need a cool greenhouse or conservatory. To widen the scope to include tropical types, a heated glass frame is an essential piece of equipment.

Orchids are members of the *Orchidaceae* family. There are some 30,000 species, coming from almost every country in the world, making this one of the largest families of flowering plants. Their natural habitats vary from high up among the leafy canopies of tropical forests, through woodland floors to heathland, grassland, marshes and even semi-deserts.

Some species are terrestrial (ground-dwelling) with swollen stems called pseudobulbs, some have climbing stems, others live epiphytically (without damaging the host) on branches and trunks of trees. Epiphytes have specially adapted roots.

Orchid flowers are wide-ranging in size, shape and colour. Most of them are specially adapted for pollination by insects and other animals, and often there is a very specific relationship with just one type of pollinating creature.

The seeds are dust-like and are produced in vast numbers – in the wild, seed is wind-dispersed – but they may not germinate under artificial conditions, so gardeners mostly use vegetative methods of propagation, such as taking cuttings or division of the bulbs. Commercially, orchids are often increased by a special micro-propagation technique under laboratory conditions – this is known as meristem tissue culture.

Choosing orchids

Hundreds of modern hybrids and a wide range of natural species suitable for amateur gardeners are available from specialist nurseries. Beginners should choose between *Angraecum, Brassia,* × *Brassolaeliocattleya, Cattleya, Coelogyne, Cymbidium, Dendrobium, Laelia,* × *Laeliocattleya, Lycaste, Miltonia,* × *Odontioda, Odontoglossum, Oncidium, Paphiopedilum, Phalaenopsis, Pleione, Vanda* and × *Vuylstekeara.*

See plant descriptions on pages 95-98.

Growing conditions

The ideal growing conditions for orchids are provided by a conservatory built against a house wall. It will draw some heat from the wall, and if the house has central heating an extra radiator could be fixed inside the conservatory to provide cheap winter heating.

A small greenhouse is quite adequate for growing orchids, provided it can be maintained at a winter temperature of 7°C (45°F), is clean and free from fungal diseases, which can wipe out a valuable collection very rapidly. An electric extractor fan, 25-30cm (10-12in) in diameter, is the best way of ventilating the greenhouse. Install this in the wall opposite the entrance door, about 1.8m (6ft) from the ground.

There should also be a bottom ventilator in the base of the entrance door. It will need a sliding or hinged shutter to help control air flow and humidity.

A small number of tropical orchids, which need very warm conditions, can be grown economically in a cool greenhouse by keeping them in a fairly tall glass frame on the staging. A frame with bottom heating should provide enough heat, but if necessary it can be lined on the inside with plastic sheeting for extra insulation during winter.

Fix the plastic sheeting to

◄ **Slipper orchids** The numerous species and hybrids of *Paphiopedilum* are characterized by their exotic, waxy-textured flowers with a pronounced slipper-shaped pouch. The colours vary from yellow, green and brown to violet, purple and deep crimson, striped, speckled or marbled. Some slipper orchids (*P. insigne*) can be grown as house plants.

Dendrobium wardianum

Cymbidium 'Rincon Clarisse'

Cattleya 'Pink Debutante'

pansy orchid
Miltonia 'Hamburg Stonehurst'

tiger orchid
Odontoglossum 'Natrium Mont Millais'

wooden supports around the sides and top of the frame, leaving a 2.5cm (1in) space between plastic and glass. In summer, remove the plants from the frame and keep them in the warmest part of the greenhouse. At least six tropical orchids would fit into a frame 60 × 60cm (2 × 2ft) wide and 90cm (3ft) tall.

An alternative is to construct a glazed partition at the end of the greenhouse, forming a cubicle which can be kept warmer and more humid. This can provide quite a large area for tropical orchids. During the winter, line the area with plastic sheeting mounted on wooden frames. Remove the plastic in spring when maximum sunlight is needed.

Another place to grow tropical orchids is indoors, in a miniature greenhouse. The 'greenhouse' is a small glazed frame standing on a large window-sill over a central-heating radiator. If possible, keep the frame in a north or east-facing window in summer, and in a south or west-facing window in winter. Cultural requirements are the same as for greenhouses, but ventilation is crucial as temperature changes are more rapid in a small space.

Providing heat

Most orchids can be divided into either cool greenhouse types, such as *Coelogyne, Cymbidium* and *Pleione*, or warm greenhouse (tropical) types, such as *Miltonia* and *Phalaenopsis*.

The cool greenhouse plants need a minimum temperature of 7°C (45°F) in winter and 14°C (57°F) in summer. Tropical orchids need a minimum temperature of 16°C (61°F) in winter – although they will tolerate brief, cooler periods – and 22°C (72°F) in summer. However, many commonly grown orchids, such as *Cattleya, Dendrobium, Odontoglossum* and some

slipper orchid
Paphiopedilum 'Chipmunk Vermont'

moth orchid
Phalaenopsis scilleriana

Vanda 'Rose Davis'

TYPICAL ORCHID FLOWER STRUCTURE

petal
sepal (dorsal)
column
petal
anther cap with pollen sac (pollinia) beneath
sepal (lateral)
sepal (lateral)
lip or labellum (modified lower petal)

Orchid flowers comprise three outer sepals, which are often coloured to match the petals, alternating with three inner petals. The lower petal (lip or labellum) is modified in shape and contrastingly coloured or marked. The lip serves as a showy landing stage for pollinating insects. The finger-like column carries the reproductive organs.

Paphiopedilum species tolerate temperatures intermediate between these two ranges.

To provide the heat, an electric fan heater with a thermostatic control is ideal as it keeps the air moving. A 3kW heater will keep a 3 × 2.4m (10 × 8ft) greenhouse warm enough for cool-house orchids. A 4½kW heater is needed in the same size greenhouse for tropical orchids.

To grow tropical orchids in a separate section of a 3 × 2.4m (10 × 8ft) cool greenhouse, you would need an additional smaller heater in this section.

Keep a paraffin heater as a safeguard against power failure.

Providing humidity

In their natural habitat, many orchids grow in areas where water vapour rises from the damp ground or foliage around them. They absorb moisture through their leaves and roots.

This humidity is produced in the greenhouse by spraying water frequently on the flooring and on the staging where the plants stand. Light but frequent damping down is more effective than occasional flooding.

In summer, damp down the orchid house at least once a day – in the morning – and preferably again in the late afternoon or evening. If the weather is particularly hot, three or four dampings may be necessary, as well as mist spraying of the foliage.

In winter, two or three dampings a week are sufficient, before midday. Do not damp down if the outside temperature drops below freezing.

The easiest method of damping down the staging is to use tap-water applied through a hose with a fine-spray nozzle. Do not spray the water on the flowers or bulb bases. This can be avoided by standing the plants permanently on up-turned flower-pots. When tropical orchids are grown in a frame, damp down with a syringe filled with collected disease and pest-free rainwater.

Automatic damping down systems can be installed, which provide a fine mist at intervals from a spray line according to instructions received from computerized humidity sensors, but these are expensive to install.

Providing ventilation

Fresh air is essential to all orchids, but it must be provided without causing a draught or lowering the temperature or the humidity. A close, muggy atmosphere encourages fungal diseases.

A 25-30cm (10-12in) extractor fan will draw in enough air through gaps around the door to ensure adequate ventilation, and a ventilator at the bottom of the greenhouse can be opened to increase air flow in hot weather.

Fans can be connected to a thermostat, so that they come on automatically when the temperature of the house becomes too high.

The cheapest form of ventilation is by the traditional ventilators fitted to the top and bottom of the greenhouse on both sides. It is preferable to have one top vent and one bottom vent on each side of the orchid house for every 1.2m (4ft) of its length. Bottom ventilators should be at least 30 × 60cm (1 × 2ft), and covered with fine-mesh wire netting to keep out pests.

During summer, open the top vents on the leeward side by 10-

TWO TYPES OF PSEUDOBULB

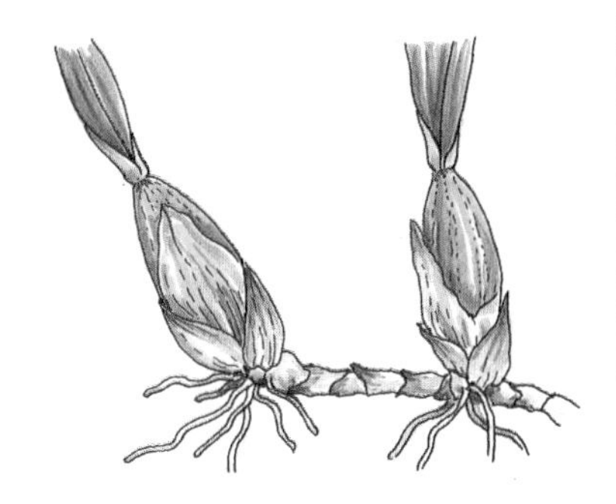

Pseudobulbs are thickened portions of the stem adapted to storing water and food – they are not true bulbs. Cymbidiums (*above*) have stout pseudobulbs, measuring 7.5-10cm (3-4in) long and covered with leaves. The old, leafless bulbs are called back-bulbs. The pseudobulbs of *Coelogyne* (*above*) grow along a creeping, horizontal rhizome.

SUPPORTING STEMS AND FLOWERS

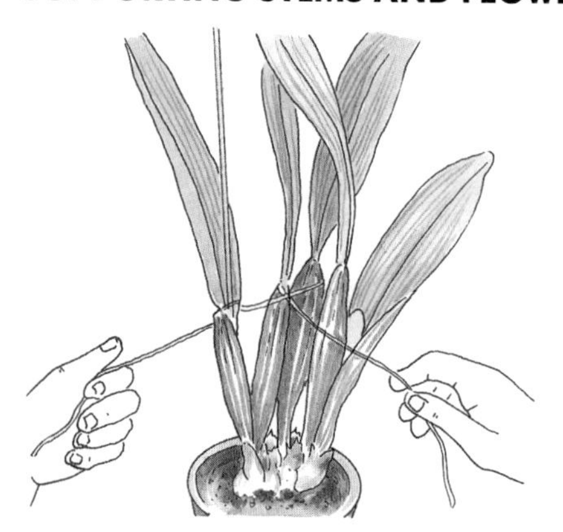

1 With cattleyas and other top-heavy orchids, provide support after potting or repotting. Wind garden string around the upright growths and tie to a thin cane or stake.

2 Upright stems and slender flower stalks, such as those of slipper orchids, can be supported with a piece of galvanized wire shaped into a U and pushed into the compost.

3 For a very long, arching flower spike, insert a cane at an angle and tie the spike to it with raffia. This will maintain the plant's natural curves and grace, but prevent breakage.

15cm (4-6in) day and night. On very hot days, also open the bottom ventilators on the same side. With below average temperatures, close all ventilators.

In winter, close the top ventilators to retain the warm air, and open the bottom vents on the leeward side to allow fresh air into the greenhouse.

Providing shade

To prevent the temperature inside the greenhouse from rising too high in summer, the greenhouse must be shaded.

The best – but most expensive – form of shading is provided by roller blinds made of wooden or plastic laths. Plastic fabric roller blinds, which are run up and down the roof, provide cheaper shading.

Leave an air space between the glass and the blinds to allow air to circulate over the surface of the glass and so keep an even temperature in the greenhouse. Unroll the blinds on the sunny side of the greenhouse whenever the sun shines brightly during late spring and summer.

A less satisfactory method of shading is to paint the greenhouse glass with whitewash or special electrostatic shading paint. Apply a thin coat in late winter and then another coat on top in mid spring. Wipe off the whitewash in early autumn.

Composts and containers

Compost for growing orchids was formerly made from the root fibres of osmunda ferns, with sphagnum moss and leaf-mould. However, the formulations today are quite different, often organic and chemical-free; some contain pine bark chippings or plastic shavings.

If you want the best-quality compost in large quantities, it is cheaper to make it yourself than to buy it ready-made. The ingredients can be bought from specialist orchid

ORCHID CONTAINERS

1 Upright orchids grow well in perforated clay pots. These provide good drainage – which is essential for all indoor orchids – and their weight helps to prevent top-heavy plants from toppling over.

2 Orchids with trailing flowers grow best in hanging wooden-slat baskets. These can be hung from the greenhouse framework and positioned at an appropriate height so that the flowers open at eye-level.

3 Pieces of tree bark or cork are ideal for mounting epiphytic orchids. The aerial roots of these plants eventually gain anchorage between the bark fissures, but must be tied in place to begin with.

nurseries and some garden centres or shops.

The simplest compost is made by mixing two parts of sphagnum moss peat, one part of coarse horticultural sand or fine gravel, and one part of perlite.

A more complex compost is made from ten parts of medium-grade pine bark, five parts of fine-grade pine bark, one-and-a-half parts of horticultural perlag and one-quarter part of crumbled charcoal.

With both types of compost, bring the pH value up to 5.5-6.0 by adding lime. For slipper orchids, raise the pH to 6.5.

Orchids can be grown in ordinary pots, but these must have a good layer of crocks at the bottom to allow for rapid drainage.

Special orchid pots or pans – obtainable from some garden centres and specialist nurseries – are perforated around the sides as well as the bottom, so need no drainage material.

Wooden baskets are more suitable for pendent plants. When planted, they are hung up in the greenhouse using wires or slender chains, allowing the stems to droop downwards.

Alternatively, pendent epiphytic orchids can be grown on sections of rough tree bark or cork. Sections of tree fern stems – if available – are also ideal. Bind the orchid roots to the raft of bark using nylon fishing line or fine plastic-covered wire.

To prevent the orchid drying out unduly until new roots develop and get a firm hold on the bark, pack some compost under the roots before you tie them in. Hang the bark and attached orchid from the greenhouse framework.

SHORTENING SINGLE-STEMMED ORCHIDS

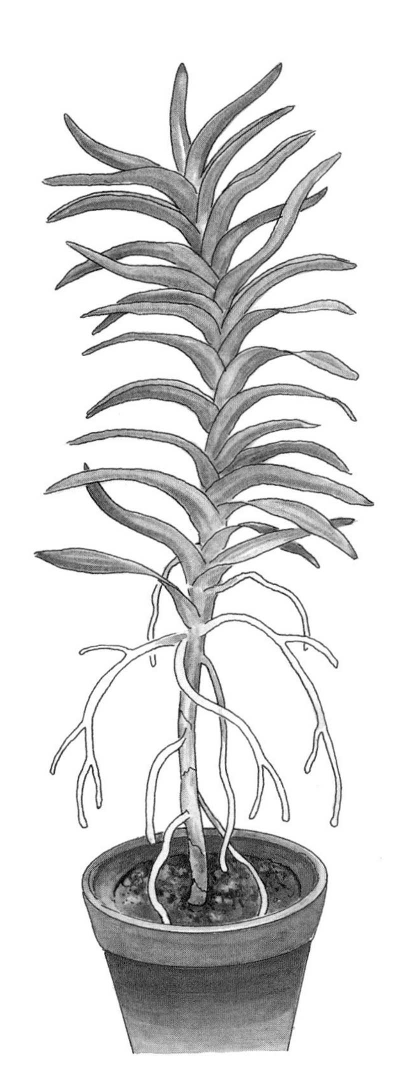

1 The slender, upright stems of *Vanda* orchids eventually become too tall and must be shortened by half to prevent collapse. Line a 13-15cm (5-6in) pot with crocks and add a 2.5cm (1in) layer of orchid compost.

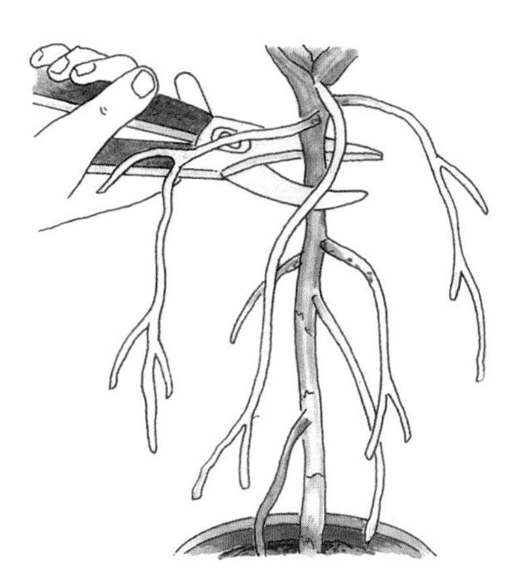

2 With secateurs, sever the stem beneath a group of aerial roots. Remove any dead leaf bases from the severed section. Save the base of the original stem – it will produce new shoots suitable for propagation.

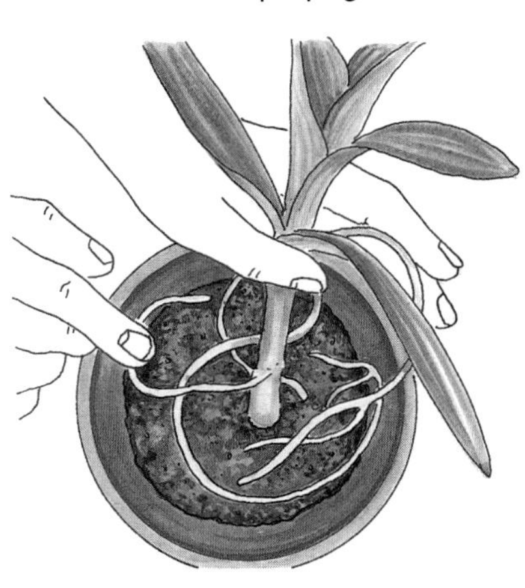

3 Twirl the severed uppermost section into the pot so that the roots coil around the inside. Fill the pot with more orchid compost, tamping it down gently with a dibber and making sure no pockets of air remain. Water well.

Providing support

Some orchids, such as *Cattleya* and *Dendrobium*, can be top-heavy, and need support after potting until they have produced strong new roots. Insert a cane at the back of each plant. This should stand as tall as the eventual height of the plant.

Pass a piece of green string around two or three of the rear growths, halfway up, and tie it to the stake. Repeat with the other growths.

Flowers that grow on tall thin stems – such as those of some slipper orchids (*Paphiopedilum*) – can be supported by means of galvanized wire. Bend the wire into a U-shape at the end, and then bend the U over at right angles. The U-shape then holds the stem upright. Support long, arching flower spikes by inserting a cane at an angle, and fixing the stem to it with pieces of raffia.

Watering and feeding

Don't water orchids with very cold or limy (hard) water. Preferably keep a tank of rainwater inside the greenhouse, where it will remain tepid. Don't use rainwater from an outside water butt; it can contain small pests and disease spores. When rainwater is not available, use tapwater. But if your tap-water is limy, first boil it and let it cool.

Whenever the compost has become reasonably dry, water thoroughly until it is saturated. Do not water if the compost is already moist. If humidity is high, weekly watering is enough.

To water hanging plants, take them down and immerse them in a bowl of water until bubbles stop rising from the compost.

After orchids have been in the same compost for over a year, feed them with a liquid fertilizer about once a fortnight during the growing season – late spring to late summer. Water the plants first, as fertilizer can damage dry roots.

The resting period

Many orchids require a resting period, usually from late summer

REJUVENATING OLD PSEUDOBULBS

1 Many orchids can be propagated successfully from the old pseudobulbs – called back-bulbs. In autumn, or when a plant needs repotting, gently knock it out of its pot or basket.

2 Using a sharp knife, carefully cut off the largest back-bulbs, trying not to sever their roots. Leave at least four pseudobulbs – either old or new – on the parent plant.

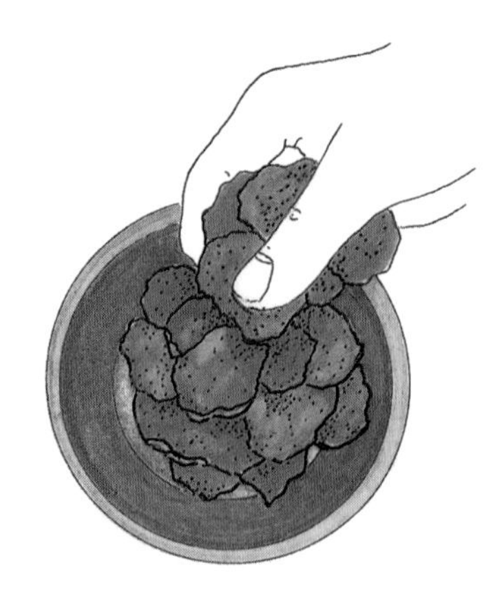

3 Back-bulbs with few roots should be rooted in compost before potting up. Put a layer of crocks or gravel in the bottom of a 7.5cm (3in) pot and fill with moist orchid compost.

4 Cushion the base of the back-bulb in compost and stand it in the pot. Infill with more compost and insert a label with the name of the plant – non-flowering orchids are easily confused.

5 Stand the pot in a propagating frame lined with moist sand, preferably with bottom heat of 16-18°C (61-64°F). Put the propagator in a shaded, warm part of the greenhouse.

6 When shoots begin to grow from the base of the back-bulb, remove it from the propagator and stand it on the greenhouse staging – still in its pot. Pot on within a year.

to mid autumn. During this time they may lose their leaves so that only the pseudobulbs remain.

When the leaves have fallen, or when the pseudobulbs have grown stout and healthy, move the plant to a shelf in better light and in a cooler part of the greenhouse. Reduce the humidity to a minimum.

During the resting period, orchids with pseudobulbs need no water unless the compost dries out completely; then drench thoroughly. Orchids without pseudobulbs need occasional watering. When growth begins again, return the plant to its normal place and resume watering.

Propagation

Some upright, slender-stemmed orchids – such as vandas – eventually become too tall and floppy for the greenhouse and should be cut down and left to grow on.

These orchids have aerial roots growing out of the stem. Every year the roots develop laterals, which begin to grow green points. When the laterals start to grow in the spring, the plant can be cut up and repotted.

The most common method of propagating orchids which grow from pseudobulbs is by division of the pseudobulbs, making sure each division contains three bulbs. Alternatively, separate and pot up the back-bulbs. These are the old pseudobulbs that have lost their leaves and are found behind the new leafy bulbs.

Remove back-bulbs in autumn, at the end of the resting period, or when an overlarge plant is being divided and repotted in summer.

A PESTICIDE BATH

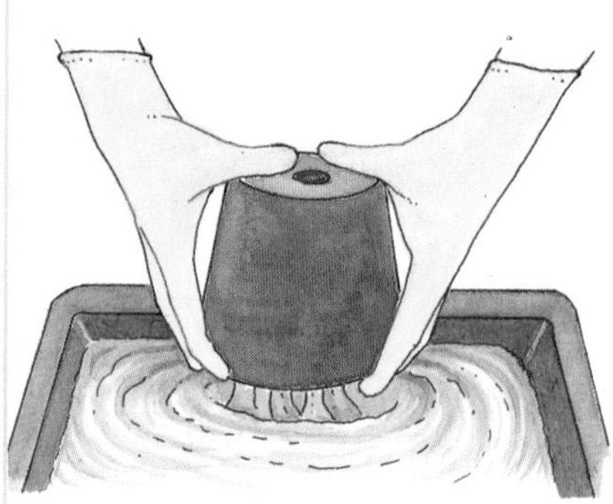

To cure scale insects, red spider mite and thrip infestations on orchid leaves – which cause yellow or brown mottling and weaken the growth – invert the entire plant and dip it in a bowl of spray-strength permethrin. Wear gloves to protect your hands.

ORCHID PORTRAITS

The exquisite orchids, in spite of their reputation, are remarkably tolerant and will flourish in the greenhouse, given a little warmth.

The orchid family contains hundreds of genera and thousands of species from all over the world. In addition, there are numerous man-made varieties and hybrids. But not all orchids make ideal greenhouse plants for the beginner; the following pages describe the easiest and most rewarding types.

Orchids are perennials with often bizarre flowers. Almost half are terrestrial (growing on the ground), but the rest are epiphytic (living on branches of trees or on rocks). The epiphytes obtain food from air and rain-water and from humus in bark crevices by means of special roots – these orchids are generally the easiest to grow.

Most epiphytic orchids consist of a horizontal rhizome from which arise upright and usually swollen bulbous stems, known as pseudobulbs. Fleshy aerial roots may grow from the stems. The leaves are strap-shaped or lance-shaped and are carried singly or in rigid tufts or fans.

Terrestrial orchids have either a tuft of fleshy roots at the base or underground tubers. The leaves – which are in tufts – are usually strap-shaped and more floppy than those of the epiphytic orchids; they are pale yellow or dark green, sometimes spotted with maroon.

Orchid flowers are composed of three sepals and three petals. The third petal is shaped into a lip.

General care

Orchids vary in their needs, but the following should be catered for, unless stated otherwise.

□Grow terrestrial orchids in ordinary pots, but preferably grow epiphytes in specially perforated orchid pots or wooden baskets, or grow them directly on a piece of wood bark or tree trunk – fix the plants with wire or staples.

□Potting compost should be specially formulated for orchids; some nurserymen supply ready-mix packs.

□Minimum temperature depends on the plant's country of origin - cool types require at least 14°C (57°F) in summer and 7°C (45°F) in winter; intermediate types require at least 18°C (64°F) in summer and 10°C (50°F) in winter; and warm, tropical types require at least 22°C (72°F) in summer and 14°C (57°F) in winter. However, they will all tolerate temperatures of up to 11°C (20°F) above these minimum levels.

□Good ventilation is essential when the temperature is high.

□Shade the greenhouse during the summer, ideally with wooden slatted or plastic blinds.

□Maintain high humidity at all times, especially when the temperature is at a maximum. Spray orchids with water at least once a day and damp down the floor and staging in the greenhouse. Stand container-grown plants in bowls of moist pebbles.

□Keep all orchids moist during the growing season – mid spring to early autumn. Let the compost dry out between watering; excessive moisture leads to root rot.

□Follow specific advice on feeding – some orchids are sensitive to fertilizers. Newly potted orchids need no feeding as the compost contains enough nutrients for one season.

□Allow a period of rest after flowering – plants may lose their leaves at this time. Stop watering and reduce the humidity.

◄ **Exotic orchids** Epiphytic orchids revel in the controlled atmosphere of a greenhouse. The magnificent blooms last for weeks, on the plants and as cut flowers for the house.

Brassia verrucosa
Spider orchid

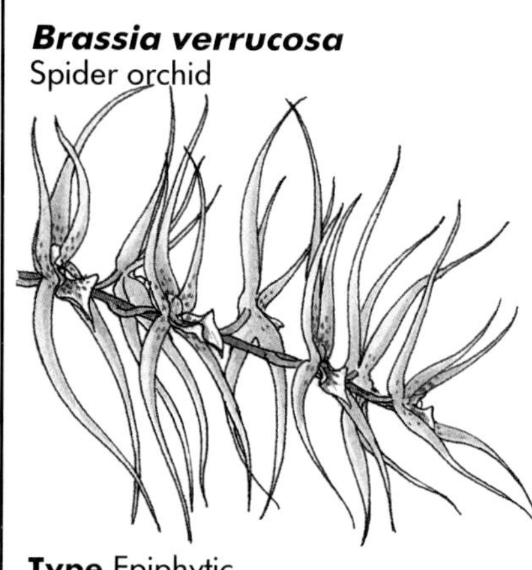

Type Epiphytic.
Features Upright egg-shaped pseudobulb topped with a pair of dark green leathery leaves. Arching flower stems, arising from the base of the pseudobulb, carry close-set 10-15cm (4-6in) long spidery flowers. The slender sepals and petals are pale green spotted with dark green, red or brown-purple; the lip is white with green spots.
Size Arching flower stem up to 90cm (3ft) long.
Special needs Bright but filtered light; intermediate to cool temperatures; apply a weak foliar fertilizer fortnightly during active growth; allow three weeks rest after flowering.

× *Brassolaeliocattleya*
(Trigeneric orchid)

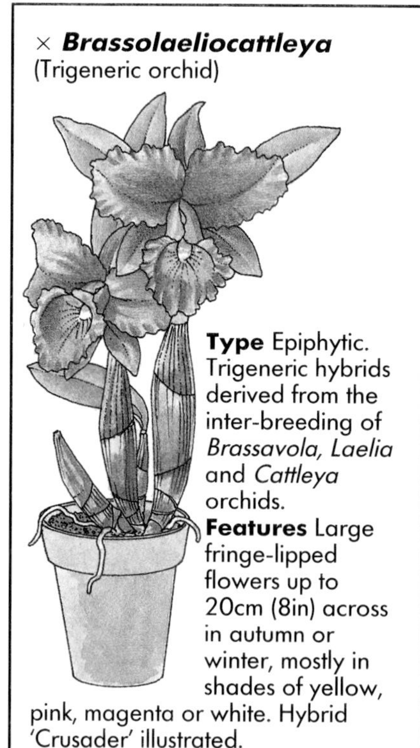

Type Epiphytic. Trigeneric hybrids derived from the inter-breeding of *Brassavola, Laelia* and *Cattleya* orchids.
Features Large fringe-lipped flowers up to 20cm (8in) across in autumn or winter, mostly in shades of yellow, pink, magenta or white. Hybrid 'Crusader' illustrated.
Size Up to 45 × 30cm (1½ × 1ft) long.
Special needs Bright light but no direct sun; intermediate and constant temperatures; water plentifully and foliar feed fortnightly during active growth; allow six weeks rest period.

Cattleya
Cattleya

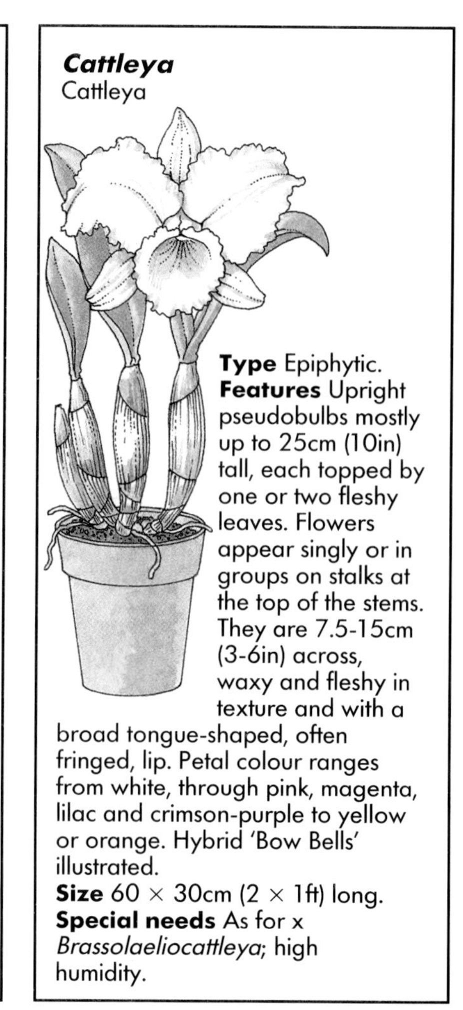

Type Epiphytic.
Features Upright pseudobulbs mostly up to 25cm (10in) tall, each topped by one or two fleshy leaves. Flowers appear singly or in groups on stalks at the top of the stems. They are 7.5-15cm (3-6in) across, waxy and fleshy in texture and with a broad tongue-shaped, often fringed, lip. Petal colour ranges from white, through pink, magenta, lilac and crimson-purple to yellow or orange. Hybrid 'Bow Bells' illustrated.
Size 60 × 30cm (2 × 1ft) long.
Special needs As for x *Brassolaeliocattleya*; high humidity.

Coelogyne
Coelogyne

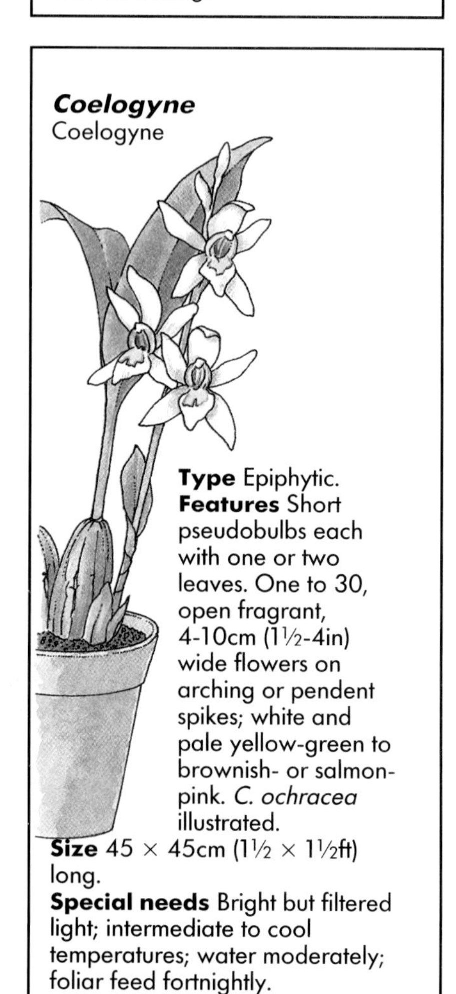

Type Epiphytic.
Features Short pseudobulbs each with one or two leaves. One to 30, open fragrant, 4-10cm (1½-4in) wide flowers on arching or pendent spikes; white and pale yellow-green to brownish- or salmon-pink. *C. ochracea* illustrated.
Size 45 × 45cm (1½ × 1½ft) long.
Special needs Bright but filtered light; intermediate to cool temperatures; water moderately; foliar feed fortnightly.

Cymbidium
Cymbidium

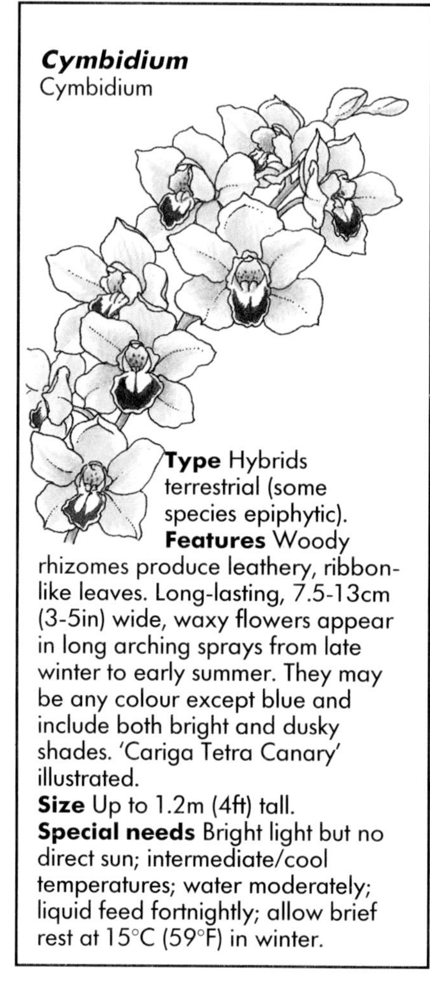

Type Hybrids terrestrial (some species epiphytic).
Features Woody rhizomes produce leathery, ribbon-like leaves. Long-lasting, 7.5-13cm (3-5in) wide, waxy flowers appear in long arching sprays from late winter to early summer. They may be any colour except blue and include both bright and dusky shades. 'Cariga Tetra Canary' illustrated.
Size Up to 1.2m (4ft) tall.
Special needs Bright light but no direct sun; intermediate/cool temperatures; water moderately; liquid feed fortnightly; allow brief rest at 15°C (59°F) in winter.

Dendrobium
Dendrobium

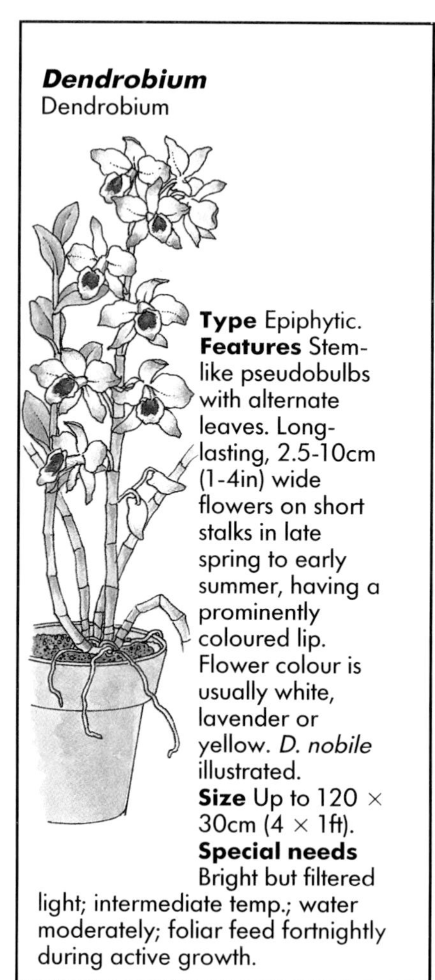

Type Epiphytic.
Features Stem-like pseudobulbs with alternate leaves. Long-lasting, 2.5-10cm (1-4in) wide flowers on short stalks in late spring to early summer, having a prominently coloured lip. Flower colour is usually white, lavender or yellow. *D. nobile* illustrated.
Size Up to 120 × 30cm (4 × 1ft).
Special needs Bright but filtered light; intermediate temp.; water moderately; foliar feed fortnightly during active growth.

Laelia
Laelia

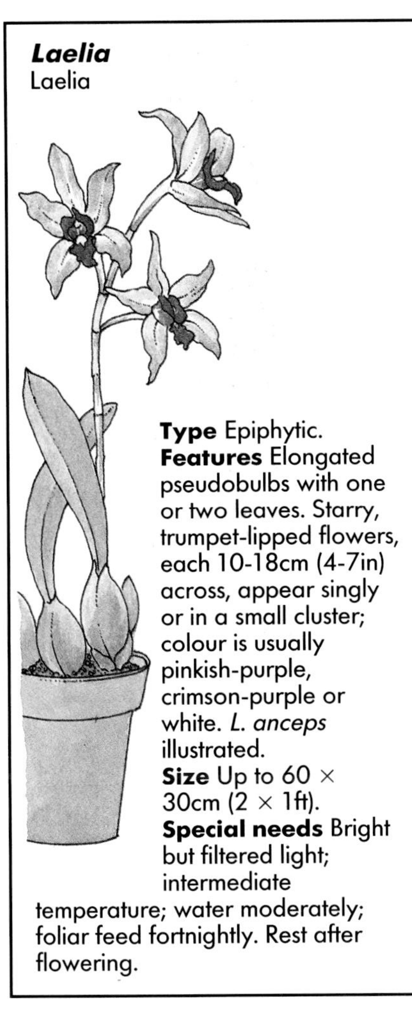

Type Epiphytic.
Features Elongated pseudobulbs with one or two leaves. Starry, trumpet-lipped flowers, each 10-18cm (4-7in) across, appear singly or in a small cluster; colour is usually pinkish-purple, crimson-purple or white. *L. anceps* illustrated.
Size Up to 60 × 30cm (2 × 1ft).
Special needs Bright but filtered light; intermediate temperature; water moderately; foliar feed fortnightly. Rest after flowering.

× ***Laeliocattleya***
Laeliocattleya

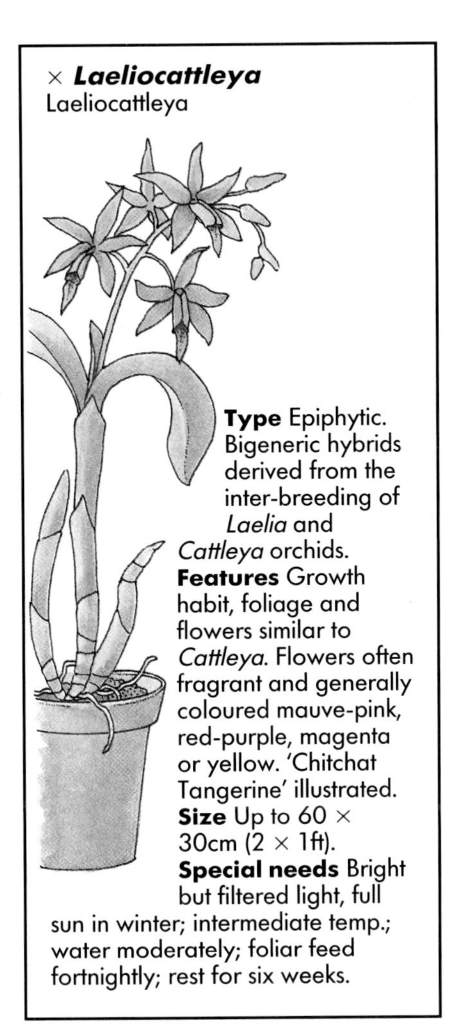

Type Epiphytic. Bigeneric hybrids derived from the inter-breeding of *Laelia* and *Cattleya* orchids.
Features Growth habit, foliage and flowers similar to *Cattleya*. Flowers often fragrant and generally coloured mauve-pink, red-purple, magenta or yellow. 'Chitchat Tangerine' illustrated.
Size Up to 60 × 30cm (2 × 1ft).
Special needs Bright but filtered light, full sun in winter; intermediate temp.; water moderately; foliar feed fortnightly; rest for six weeks.

Lycaste
Lycaste

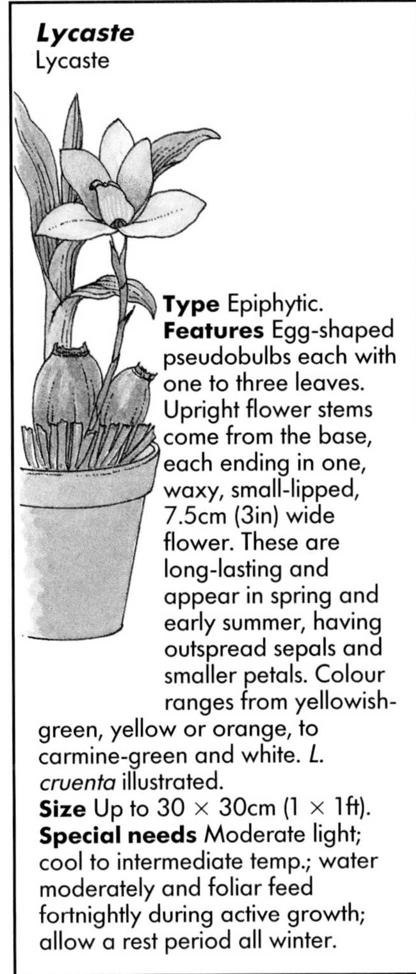

Type Epiphytic.
Features Egg-shaped pseudobulbs each with one to three leaves. Upright flower stems come from the base, each ending in one, waxy, small-lipped, 7.5cm (3in) wide flower. These are long-lasting and appear in spring and early summer, having outspread sepals and smaller petals. Colour ranges from yellowish-green, yellow or orange, to carmine-green and white. *L. cruenta* illustrated.
Size Up to 30 × 30cm (1 × 1ft).
Special needs Moderate light; cool to intermediate temp.; water moderately and foliar feed fortnightly during active growth; allow a rest period all winter.

Miltonia
Pansy orchid

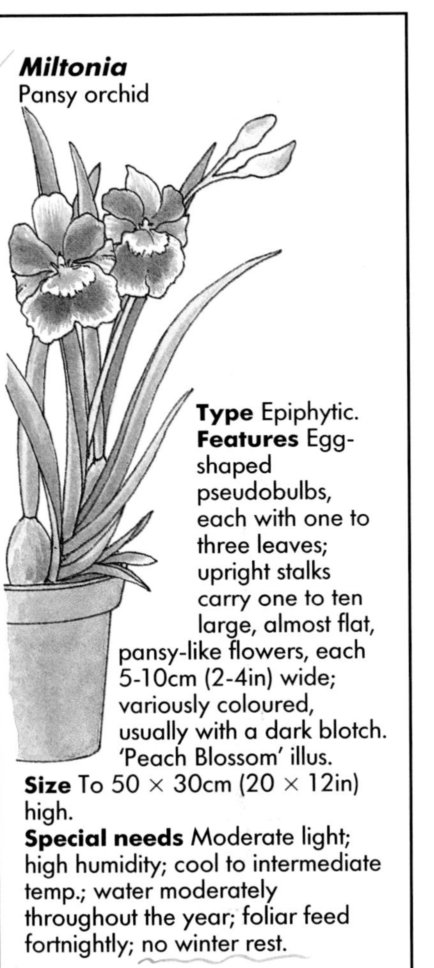

Type Epiphytic.
Features Egg-shaped pseudobulbs, each with one to three leaves; upright stalks carry one to ten large, almost flat, pansy-like flowers, each 5-10cm (2-4in) wide; variously coloured, usually with a dark blotch. 'Peach Blossom' illus.
Size To 50 × 30cm (20 × 12in) high.
Special needs Moderate light; high humidity; cool to intermediate temp.; water moderately throughout the year; foliar feed fortnightly; no winter rest.

× ***Odontioda***
Odontioda

Type Epiphytic. Hybrids derived from inter-breeding *Odontoglossum* and *Cochlioda* orchids.
Features Growth habit and flower shape similar to *Odontoglossum*, but flower colour is influenced by the brighter *Cochlioda*. Flowers are 9-10cm (3½-4in) wide and are carried in long, arching sprays. 'Dalmar Lyoth Bachus' illustrated.
Size Up to 60 × 45cm (2 × 1½ft).
Special needs As for *Odontoglossum*, but cool temp.

Odontoglossum
Tiger orchid

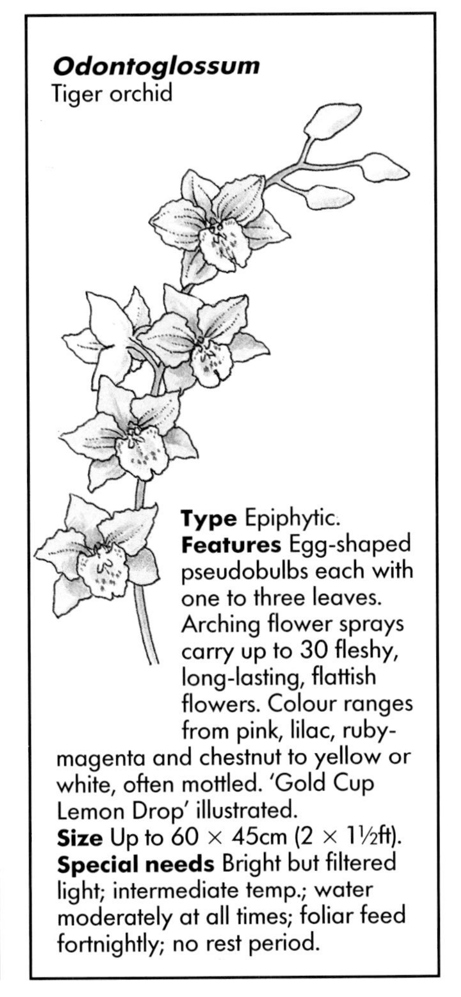

Type Epiphytic.
Features Egg-shaped pseudobulbs each with one to three leaves. Arching flower sprays carry up to 30 fleshy, long-lasting, flattish flowers. Colour ranges from pink, lilac, ruby-magenta and chestnut to yellow or white, often mottled. 'Gold Cup Lemon Drop' illustrated.
Size Up to 60 × 45cm (2 × 1½ft).
Special needs Bright but filtered light; intermediate temp.; water moderately at all times; foliar feed fortnightly; no rest period.

Oncidium
Dancing-lady orchid

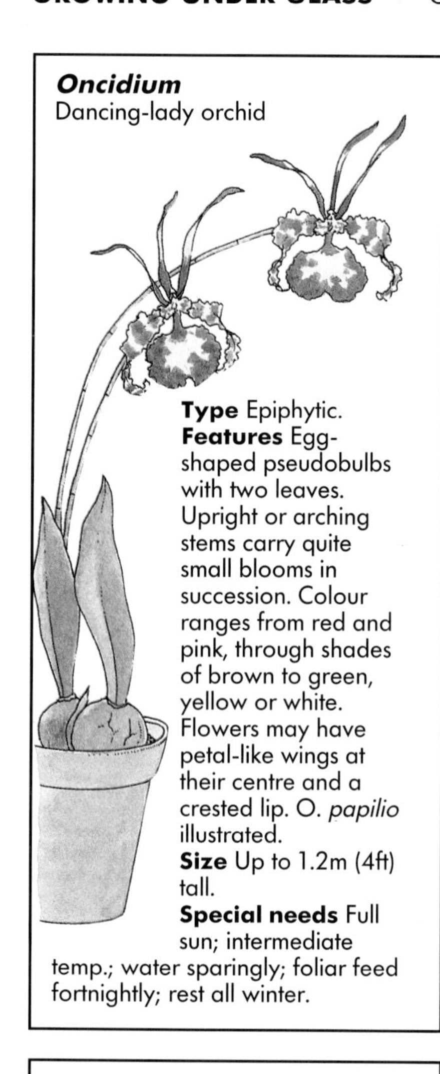

Type Epiphytic.
Features Egg-shaped pseudobulbs with two leaves. Upright or arching stems carry quite small blooms in succession. Colour ranges from red and pink, through shades of brown to green, yellow or white. Flowers may have petal-like wings at their centre and a crested lip. *O. papilio* illustrated.
Size Up to 1.2m (4ft) tall.
Special needs Full sun; intermediate temp.; water sparingly; foliar feed fortnightly; rest all winter.

Paphiopedilum
Slipper orchid

Type Terrestrial.
Features Stemless with short leaves growing from the rhizome. Upright flower stalk topped with one long-lasting flower any time of year, depending on type. They are 5-9cm (2-3½in) across with a waxy sheen. The uppermost sepal is usually in a contrasting colour to the petals, and the lip is pouched. 'Winston Churchill' illustrated.
Size 15-30cm (6-12in) tall.
Special needs Moderate light; high humidity; intermediate to cool temp.; water moderately; foliar feed fortnightly.

Phalaenopsis
Moth orchid

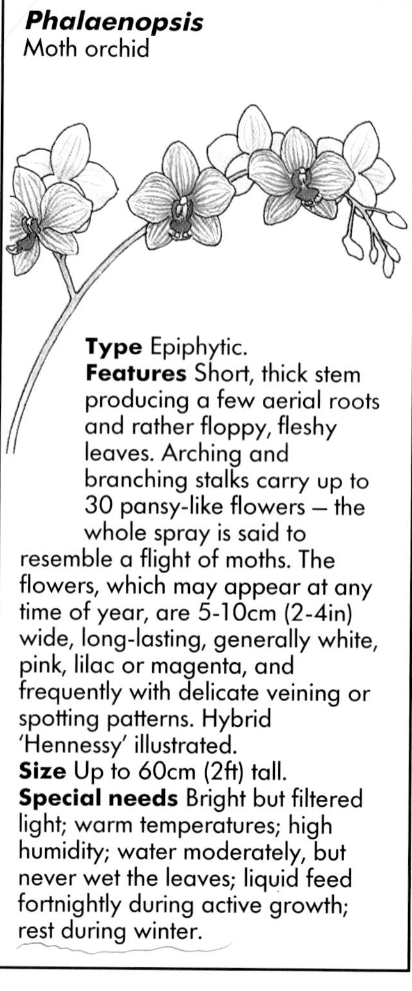

Type Epiphytic.
Features Short, thick stem producing a few aerial roots and rather floppy, fleshy leaves. Arching and branching stalks carry up to 30 pansy-like flowers – the whole spray is said to resemble a flight of moths. The flowers, which may appear at any time of year, are 5-10cm (2-4in) wide, long-lasting, generally white, pink, lilac or magenta, and frequently with delicate veining or spotting patterns. Hybrid 'Hennessy' illustrated.
Size Up to 60cm (2ft) tall.
Special needs Bright but filtered light; warm temperatures; high humidity; water moderately, but never wet the leaves; liquid feed fortnightly during active growth; rest during winter.

Pleione formosana
Pleione

Type Semi-epiphytic or terrestrial.
Features Short, squat pseudobulbs with ribbed leaves – produced only after flowering. Trumpet-shaped 7.5-10cm (3-4in) wide flowers with lance-shaped spreading petals, in shades of pink, mauve, creamy yellow or white. The flower lip is fringed or crested and often distinctly marbled.
Size Up to 15cm (6in) tall.
Special needs Bright but indirect light; cool temperatures; water moderately; liquid feed fortnightly; plunge in a cold frame outdoors during the dormant winter period.

Vanda
Vanda

Type Epiphytic.
Features Single stem with fleshy aerial roots and leaves in two ranks – no pseudobulb. Upright or pendent stalks carry several 7.5-12cm (3-5in) wide flowers with equally sized sepals and petals, in shades of mauve, blue, pink or cream, often with netted markings. 'Rothschildiana' illustrated.
Size 30-60cm (1-2ft) high, often much taller.
Special needs Bright but filtered light; warm to intermediate temp.; water plentifully during growth; rest all winter.

× *Vuylstekeara*
Vuylstekeara

Type Epiphytic. Hybrids derived from inter-breeding *Miltonia* and *Odontioda* orchids.
Features Egg-shaped pseudobulb with two or three upright or arching strap-shaped leaves. Slender flower stalks carry several showy richly coloured flowers, each generally about 9cm (3½in) wide and with a large ornate lip. Hybrid 'Cambria Plush' illustrated.
Size Generally up to 60 × 45cm (2 × 1½ft).
Special needs Bright but filtered light; intermediate to cool temperatures (even tolerant of fluctuating temperatures); water moderately; foliar feed fortnightly during active growth; no rest period required.

CONSERVATORY MANAGEMENT

Unlike greenhouses, conservatories must be managed in such a way that they provide comfortable living conditions for people and for plants.

The environment achieved inside a conservatory or sun-room is generally something of a compromise. While you probably wish to grow rather exotic 'hot-house' or tender greenhouse plants, there is also a need to maintain clean and pleasant conditions in which you can sit and relax – a conservatory usually forms an extension to the main living area of the home.

For example, watering, spraying and damping down can be a relatively haphazard process in a purely functional greenhouse, but in a conservatory laid with decorative flooring and furnished with fabric-covered chairs you must be much more careful.

Display systems

To use just single level staging for displaying plants would make the conservatory or sun-room look like a greenhouse. Although this system makes quite good use of space and available sunlight, it gives little scope for decorative arrangements and the plants are too high to be appreciated from a low, seated view-point.

If you choose to use aluminium or timber staging, opt for a multi-level, tiered design which will provide surfaces for displaying all types of plants in the most imaginative way possible.

A conservatory is an expensive luxury and, as such, should be put to the maximum use. Don't just grow bushy and compact pot

▼ Conservatory accessories
Bamboo plant stands and screens, together with planting bed edgings of wood bark, create a natural frame for a veritable jungle of luxuriant foliage and trailing plants.

plants of the type popularly grown indoors. Try tall climbers, cascading trailers, spreading ground covers, exotic flowers, luxuriant foliage – even unusual edible fruits and vegetables, such as melons, lemons, passion fruits and sweet peppers.

To grow this range of plants successfully and attractively you will need a variety of containers and support systems.

As in a greenhouse, one of the best places to grow climbers, tall perennial plants and food crops in a conservatory is in a floor-level bed or border. However, since the foundations of a conservatory are more substantial and there may be a solid concrete floor comprising a damp-proof membrane, such a bed will have to be specially constructed. It can be sunk in the floor with drainage pipes leading to the outside, or it can be in the form of a raised bed with brick, concrete or timber retaining walls.

Alternatively, grow tall plants and climbers in tubs or other large containers placed on the floor. Smaller plants can be grown individually in conventional pots or interplanted with the larger ones.

There are many ways of displaying pots besides standing them on benches or on the floor. Special pot holders can be bought or made, which support standard sized pots on a wall, post or vertical glazing bar. If you don't want drainage water to drip on the floor – where it is carpeted, for instance – use plastic pots with clip-on saucers.

Plant stands made of bamboo, metal or plastic are another decorative type of pot holder, usually taking four or more plants. Many of these have the advantage of being portable, so you can change the display arrangement as frequently as you wish.

Hanging baskets and wall-mounted troughs make additional use of space without cluttering the floor area and are ideal for arching and trailing species, especially those with pendent flowers which are best viewed from below. Again, these can be obtained with clip-on or built-in drip trays.

Heating

Temperature is a major consideration in a conservatory and the provision of artificial heating creates the most expensive running cost. If your budget is limited you will not be able to raise the

DISPLAYING PLANTS

1 Wall-mounted pot holders, such as this spring-loaded metal device which grips the rim of an ordinary plastic pot, allow you to secure plants to any vertical surface – even a glazing bar.

2 Planter poles, adjustable to any height up to 2.7m (9ft), or free-standing plant stands, give height to a conservatory or sun-room and are ideal for displaying arching or trailing plants.

3 Hanging baskets are particularly suitable for growing flowers which are best viewed from below, such as trailing fuchsias. Buy the plastic type with clip-on or built-in drip trays if the floor is carpeted.

4 Tiered and staggered staging gives depth and height to your display. Plants which need maximum light can be put on the top shelves and those which prefer shade can go on the lower tiers.

WATERING SYSTEMS

1 All plants must be watered and some like to be mist-sprayed regularly with tepid water. A long-spouted watering can and a hand sprayer are therefore essential equipment – dual function spray/watering cans are available.

2 Pump-action watering cans with a slimline nozzle on a long tube allow an average height person to water a hanging basket or container up to 2.7m (9ft) above ground without stretching. The nozzle swivels in all directions.

3 Water-retentive clay aggregate pebbles laid on the staging are a useful aid to watering. Drainage water from the pots is soaked up, later evaporating to increase humidity.

4 Mist-spray nozzles mounted on tall stems can be positioned between groups of plants that require extra humidity or regular damping down. The water supply must be under pressure.

5 Drip-irrigation nozzles pegged into each pot, linked to a network of hoses, are excellent labour-saving devices for regular watering. An auto-control module can be incorporated.

6 Radiator humidifiers help to improve the atmosphere for moisture-loving plants in a small sun-room. Humid air reduces the need to water plants frequently during hot weather.

winter day and night temperature to a level suitable for sustaining tender plants or, indeed, comfortable for living in – the conservatory will have to be primarily a warm weather retreat.

Even without artificial heating, conservatories which are built against a house wall retain more heat from the sun than an all-glass greenhouse of equivalent size – the brickwork acts as a huge storage radiator. For this reason, summer evenings and even mild spells in spring and autumn can be spent comfortably in an unheated conservatory. Plants also benefit from this free heat, but you will still be limited to growing only hardy species out of season – as in an unheated greenhouse.

By installing add-on radiators from the domestic central-heating system, or some other form of independent heating, the choice of plants becomes much larger and the conservatory forms an all-year live-in extension to your home. Seek expert advice before spurring off the central-heating pipes – the room thermostats and time clock are unlikely to give suitable responses for a conservatory heat regulation.

The amount of heat required to maintain sufficiently high autumn to spring temperatures for growing tender plants all year round is roughly the same as for a heated greenhouse (see pages 63-66), but remember that some supplementary heat may be derived passively from the house, especially when adjoining doors are left open.

Ventilation and humidity

Most conservatories tend to get too hot in summer and too cold in winter. These factors also influence the amount of moisture held in the air – the humidity level and the condensation rate. Ensure that the structure has adequate opening windows or ventilators so that excessively hot air can be continually replaced by cooler outside air in summer.

In winter, ventilation is just as important as a means of eliminating stagnant, humid air – a common cause of both fungal rot disease and excessive condensation, neither of which are welcome in a living area. Local building regulations usually demand a certain minimum level of ventilation in a conservatory where it is built against existing house windows, but extra vents are always worth installing.

The level of humidity required in a conservatory depends very much on the type of plants being grown. In general, high humidity is advantageous when the air temperature is high – hot, dry air is invariably fatal and encourages serious pests such as red spider mites. Tropical plants like the highest humidity, whereas cacti and other arid region plants prefer drier air.

The frequency and quantity of watering carried out is the main regulator of humidity. To increase humidity in a greenhouse, the simple answer is to hose down the floor and staging. However, in a furnished conservatory this is not possible. Instead, provide localized humidity around each plant by standing its pot in a saucer filled with gravel or clay pebbles which can be kept constantly moist without waterlogging.

Where staging is employed, spread a layer of gravel or clay pebbles across the entire surface, preventing water damage to timber structures by lining these with polythene sheeting or made-to-measure zinc trays. This layer can be kept moist either by watering from a hosepipe or can, or by drip-irrigation pipes connected to a mains water or tank supply. Capillary matting beds provide an alternative solution.

Groups of plants which demand higher humidity than is desirable for the rest of the conservatory can be catered for by installing a mist-irrigation system. Connected via pipework to a mains water supply, perhaps with some form of automatic regulation, mist nozzles emit a fine spray of water over the plants when necessary.

Shading

During spells of hot sunshine in summer, ventilation alone will not be sufficient to reduce the inside temperature to an acceptable level, either for human comfort or plant health – some form of shading is essential. Scorched leaves and flowers rapidly turn brown and will not recover. High humidity will alleviate the scorching effect of high temperatures under glass, but it is uncomfortable for people so you must strike a balance between the two.

There are many types of blinds to choose from. Ideally, they should be adjustable, so that the amount of light passing through them can be regulated, and they should also be capable of being raised and lowered. Reeded or slatted types, whether made from natural wood or artificial materials, are therefore the best.

Fabric roller blinds can be used, but the quantity of shading which they provide is not adjustable – they are either up or down. In their favour is the fact that they can double as heat insulators during the night.

If you grow a lot of climbing or tall plants near the glass, it is much more convenient to put the blinds on the outside of the conservatory where they can be adjusted with ease, but be sure to choose weather-proof materials and secure them well, especially in exposed areas.

Lighting

Unlike a greenhouse, it is generally desirable to have some form of lighting in a conservatory so that it can be used at night. Ordinary household units with tungsten filament bulbs provide all the light that is necessary for human activity, but be careful where you position them.

▲ **Multi-level shelving** Pre-treated wooden shelves and staging erected along a timber-framed conservatory are ideal for displaying a variety of pot plants. A rich green carpet of mind-your-own-business (*Helxine soleirolii*) hides the edge of the benching and makes a superb foil for the bright flowers of kalanchoe, hibiscus and Indian shot (*Canna*).

Spotlamps get very hot and can scorch plants if they are too close. However, if they are mounted on tracks, they can be re-directed with ease – a useful feature where plant displays and seating positions are frequently changed in the conservatory.

Also make sure that unprotected lamps are nowhere near an automatic mist nozzle or other watering device – if they are splashed when alight they are likely to explode. For safety reasons, it is better to choose shielded lamp fittings of the type used outdoors. Fluorescent lighting is also suitable, but again make sure the tubes are enclosed in a plastic casing.

Wall-mounted coach lamps, festoon lights and coloured flood lamps give a garden feel to the conservatory and can create a party atmosphere.

USING GARDEN FRAMES

Cold frames are an important greenhouse adjunct. They can bring on vegetables, harden off bedding plants, strike cuttings and overwinter rootstocks.

A garden frame is a low, generally oblong box designed for a variety of garden purposes – mainly associated with raising or protecting plants in a similar though smaller-scale way to a greenhouse. It invariably has a sloping roof to allow rain-water to run off and is glazed to allow sunlight in. The sides may be glazed or solid.

Traditionally, a frame has no artificial heating and the soil and air temperature are increased by warmth from the sun alone – the 'greenhouse effect'. Hence, it is known as a cold frame.

However, with the increasing availability of easy-to-install electric heating cables, such frames need not be cold and can serve as small extension to, or replacement for, a heated greenhouse. In small gardens a frame is invaluable.

Types of frames

Three main types of frames are in use in gardens – each has its advantages and disadvantages.

Timber frames fitted with glass tops – known as lights – and with solid sides are the most efficient in conserving heat.

Until recent years, most frames were built from timber and glass. Nowadays, however, there are very few suppliers of timber kit-form frames, so if you do choose timber you may have to build your own frame, buying materials from a timber merchant.

Cedar is the best wood to choose since its copious resin provides

▼ Twin-light cold frame
Invaluable for the intermediate stage between greenhouse and the open garden, a cold frame should be easily accessible, with lights that prop open.

HARDENING OFF ANNUALS

1 Seedlings which have been raised indoors or in a greenhouse must be acclimatized gradually to outdoor temperatures. Two to four weeks before planting out, put them into the frame.

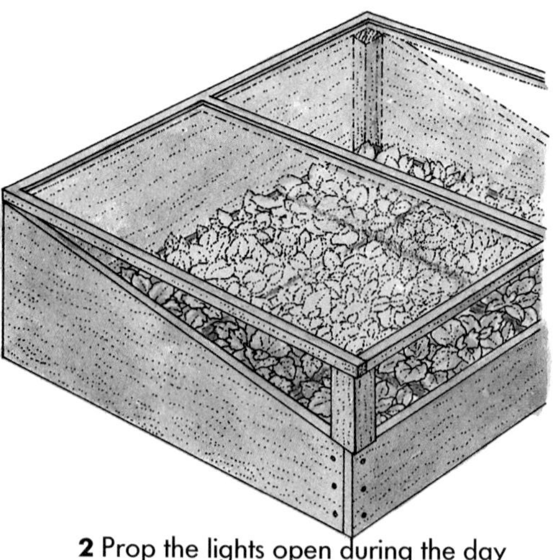

2 Prop the lights open during the day for the first week – provided it is not too cold or windy – but close them at night. During the second week, leave the lights partially open at night.

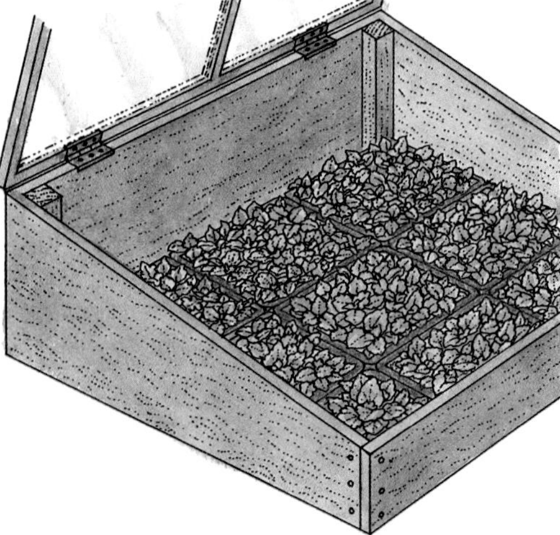

3 At the end of the second week open the lights fully at all times unless it is very windy. Water the plants as necessary – they may dry out quickly. Plant out about a week later.

good resistance to rotting and wood-boring insects. Alternatively, use exterior quality (marine) plywood and apply a wood preservative to the structure.

A useful size is 75cm × 1.5m (2½ × 5ft) with an internal headroom of 30-60cm (1-2ft). However, a frame can be built to any size to suit your particular requirements, but the distance from front to back should never exceed your reach – you must work from outside the frame at all times.

The glass lights can be designed to slide on runners or hinge from the back wall or the sides to provide ventilation and give access to the plants. The walls of a timber frame can be built with bricks or breeze-blocks, though it is difficult to construct the required sloping side edges.

A well-constructed timber frame should last for many years. However, timber is quite expensive and requires some routine care and attention to prolong its life. You can protect a timber frame from rising damp by setting it on a footing of concrete or bricks laid dry.

Aluminium frames need no routine maintenance and are lightweight, making them easy to move from one part of the garden to another if necessary. For those gardeners with little carpentry skill, aluminium frames sold in kit form are the best choice.

They can be fitted with glass or clear plastic (rigid uPVC) lights. Glass lets the maximum sunlight pass through it, whereas plastic filters out a small amount of sunlight, though this is not generally a problem. Plastic does not shatter easily so it is safer to use than glass where children play in the garden. But plastic can be scratched easily and damaged panes are difficult to keep clean, since algae builds up on the roughened surface.

Most aluminium frames have glazed sides, making them ideal for growing plants which demand a lot of light, such as melons. But they are less efficient than timber frames at keeping in the heat during cold weather. They have a very modern, architectural look and may appear out of place in an old-fashioned garden.

Galvanized iron/steel frames are similar in construction to aluminium types. Years ago, they would have been sturdy and heavy, but modern types comprise more slender structural members to minimise the price – iron and steel are now expensive. For this reason, modern galvanized frames may be less robust than aluminium ones.

Siting the frame

For general purposes, position the frame in a sunny, south-facing spot sheltered from cold winds. If you already have a greenhouse with solid side walls, position the frame against it so that some of the heat escaping from the greenhouse will help to heat the frame during the winter months.

If you intend to use the frame mainly for rooting cuttings, choose a lightly shaded position. However, cuttings can be rooted successfully in a sunny frame provided some form of temporary shading is used during the hottest sunshine – shading paint or sacking, for instance.

A non-slip path around the frame will improve ease of access and reduce the risk of accidents – especially if you have to lean over to reach plants in the centre or at the back of the frame.

Using a cold frame

There are two main ways of growing plants in a frame – whether it is unheated or heated. You can grow them directly in the soil in the base of the frame or grow them in containers. The first method is best for plants which will spend their entire life in the frame, while the second is appropriate for short-stay plants.

Raising seeds An unheated cold frame can be used to raise seeds of all types of plants which would normally be sown directly in the garden, such as many half-hardy annual and hardy biennial bedding plants and hardy perennials – even shrubs and trees. Cold frame protection means that the seeds can be sown a few weeks earlier than in the open garden so that young plants have more time to develop before being planted out in their permanent sites.

Seeds are best sown in pots or trays of a proprietary seedling compost and set out on a bed of gravel in the frame to provide good drainage. Water them regularly – the compost will dry out very quickly in warm weather.

Hardening off greenhouse-raised plants before planting them outdoors is another valuable function of a cold frame – young plants must be acclimatized gradually to the lower outdoor temperature. By adjusting the ventilation in the frame, the day and night temperature can be modified as needed over the course of several days or weeks.

Growing vegetables in a cold frame produces earlier crops than outdoors. Ridge cucumbers, marrows, courgettes and melons are ideal for this type of cultivation and should be grown in the soil in the base of the frame rather than in containers. However, they are best raised from seeds sown in a greenhouse at about 21°C (70°F), then planted into the frame at the beginning of late spring.

Prepare the cold frame soil some weeks before planting by digging in well-rotted manure or compost at the rate of a bucketful per sq m/yd. Just before planting, rake into the top a general fertilizer at 75g/3oz per sq m/yd.

▼ Aluminium frames Virtually maintenance-free, aluminium frames are durable and easy to move around. They admit plenty of light but are less good than timber frames at preserving heat.

GROWING EARLY CARROTS

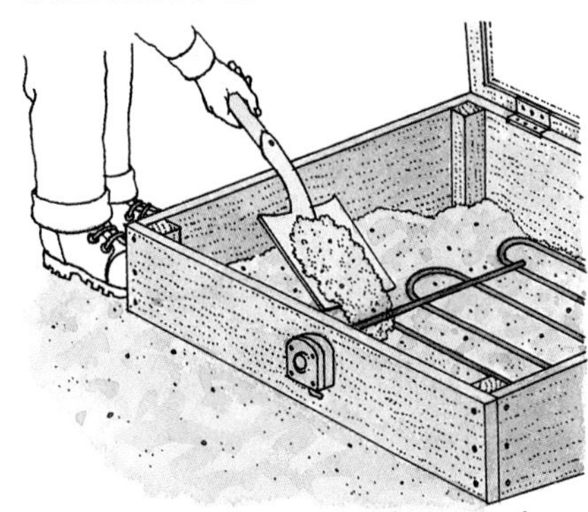

1 You will need a heated frame with under-soil electric cables and a thermostat. Well before sowing, cover the cables with a 15cm (6in) layer of good soil, but don't add manure.

2 Mix in a dressing of a general fertilizer at the rate of about one handful per sq m/yd and rake the surface level. Water the soil and close the lights, letting the soil settle.

3 One week later, turn on the heating with the thermostat set at 18°C (64°F). Sow carrot seeds thinly the next day, either in rows or broadcast. Keep the lights closed.

4 Thin seedlings to 4cm (1½in) apart. Water to firm the soil. Open the lights during warm days, but close them at night. When danger of frost is past, open the lights fully all the time.

Grow on the vegetables in the frame, ventilating it as necessary during the day. Always close the lights at night until the plants are fully established. In early summer, remove the lights completely, or hinge them wide open, during the day and night.

Shrub cuttings can be rooted successfully in a shaded cold frame – softwood cuttings in early summer; semi-hardwood cuttings in mid to late summer. Again, insert them directly into the soil in the bottom of the frame or into pots of a proprietary compost.

Overwintering tender plants A cold frame provides just enough protection from winter frosts to sustain slightly tender plants such as border chrysanthemums.

Cut back the plants after flowering, lift them and box the stools up in potting compost. Place the boxes in the cold frame and provide some ventilation – except in extreme weather – to reduce the risk of fungal infection.

Forcing bulbs Instead of forcing hyacinths, narcissi and tulips in an airing cupboard, shed or cellar, try starting them off in a cold frame – the cooler conditions will promote more sturdy growth. Plant the bulbs in pots or bowls and bury them under a 15cm (6in) layer of soil or cold ashes. Eight weeks later they can be uncovered and brought indoors for flowering.

Using a heated frame

By providing supplementary heat you can expand the use of a garden frame considerably – it then becomes a mini hot-house. Electric soil-warming cables laid under the surface of the soil in the bottom of the frame will hasten early vegetable crops.

Air-warming cables or tubes can be fitted on the inside walls of the frame above soil level to provide extra protection against cold temperatures in winter. Follow the manufacturer's instructions for the installation of heating cables or tubes.

Pre-warm the soil for early crops – such as carrots, lettuces, spring onions and radishes – and ornamental plants by switching on the heating two days before sowing. Hardy species can be sown as early as mid to late winter in a heated frame; or late winter to early spring for half-hardy types. Set the thermostat at around 18°C (64°F) for most vegetable crops.

Ventilate the heated frame during mild days. On cold nights cover the frame lights with sacking, sheets of newspaper or some other insulating material anchored with bricks – soil-heating won't be able to compensate for extremes of weather. Open the lights progressively during the day as the weather warms up, but close them again at night and during spells of windy weather.

When all danger of frost is over, remove the lights or open them fully and switch off the heating.

As with chrysanthemum stools, the more tender rootstocks of fuchsias and pelargoniums can be overwintered in a frame provided it is heated. In early autumn, cut down the plants and lift them from the ground. Transfer them to boxes of compost and stand them in the bottom of the frame.

USING A COLD FRAME

1 A plunge bed helps to reduce drying out and maintain an even soil temperature for germinating seeds of alpines, shrubs and trees. Spread a 10-15cm (4-6in) layer of sand in a solid-sided frame – if it is a timber frame, line the sides with a damp-proof membrane of polythene. Bury the pots of seeds up to their rims in the sand.

2 Semi-hardwood and hardwood shrub cuttings can be rooted directly in prepared soil in the bottom of a cold frame or inserted in pots or trays of potting compost. They require no supplementary heating. To reduce the risk from disease, those rooted in unsterilized garden soil should be taken with a heel of older wood at the base.

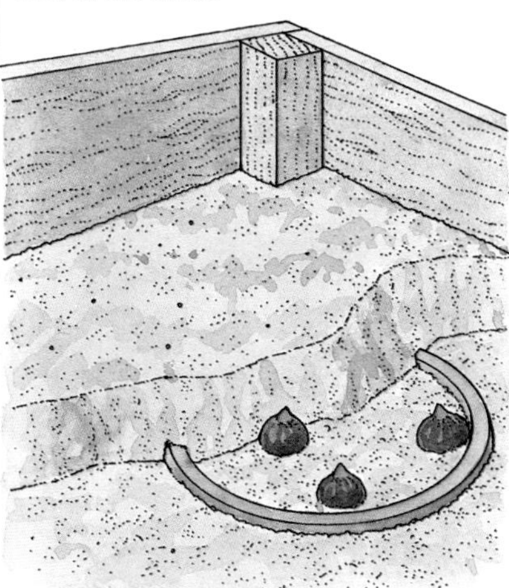

3 Bulbs for early indoor flowering can be started off in a cold frame. Pot them in bowls of potting compost or bulb fibre. Bury each bowl to its rim in a plunge bed of soil and then cover it with 15cm (6in) of soil. Ventilate the frame slightly. Eight weeks later, uncover the bowls and bring them indoors to a cool room. Flower buds will soon appear.

4 Lifted stools of frost-tender perennials, such as chrysanthemums, can be stored during the winter months in a cold frame. Dust the stools with sulphur to prevent mildew, place them in boxes and cover with potting compost. Water them very sparingly. Ventilate the frame slightly. Take cuttings as new shoots emerge in spring.

USING CLOCHES

Glass or plastic tunnels placed over crops or other plants to keep out frost and cold winds will speed up growth and extend the growing season.

Gardeners discovered long ago that a plant could be forced into early growth by protecting it with a glass cover. A Frenchman – whose name has escaped the history books – evolved a practical and efficient shape for protecting and forcing individual plants. This was a bell-shaped glass dome and it became known as a cloche, the French for bell.

The name has persisted to the present day, but cloches are no longer bell-shaped and they are more often used to protect whole rows of plants instead of individual ones. The final change from the original concept has come about with glass – because of its relatively high cost – being largely replaced with plastic.

Since most vegetables are grown in straight rows, a number of cloches set in a line, with the ends closed to exclude draughts, are ideal for producing early crops and for protecting tender plants. Generally, sowing and planting are possible two weeks earlier than in the open ground.

This earlier start – resulting in earlier harvesting – makes it possible for more than one crop to be grown on the same ground in a single growing season.

As an example of a cropping programme, lettuces sown in mid autumn may be cut in mid spring, to be followed by early-fruiting dwarf tomatoes. These, in turn, may be succeeded by spring cabbages planted in the open. The cloches, meanwhile, are transferred to another part of the garden to restart the cycle.

This mobility enables a gardener to use a cropping technique whereby cloches are moved from one row to another as the season progresses.

Early carrots, for example, may be given a good start by being covered in early and mid spring. They then go on to mature in the open and the cloches are moved in the middle of late spring to enable newly planted tomatoes to become established. Three or four weeks later the cloches are again moved, this time to protect tender, heat-loving plants – such as aubergines, melons, ridge cucumbers and sweet peppers – for the rest of the summer.

◀ **Barn cloches** Plastic-covered cloches, clad in 600 gauge PVC coated with an ultraviolet inhibitor for long life, vary in width from 30cm (1ft) to 1.2m (4ft) and in height from 20cm (8in) to 60cm (2ft). Their use extends the growing season by several weeks, in spring and in autumn.

Cloche types

A variety of shapes and sizes of cloches is available from most garden centres and from specialist manufacturers. They may be made from several materials. Alternatively, you can construct your own custom-designed cloches.

Obviously, costs are related to the size of the cloche, so decide what plants you intend growing before buying them. If you plant or grow only early lettuces, for instance, a cloche 30cm (1ft) wide and 23cm (9in) high is adequate. For growing melons to the fruiting stage, however, you will need cloches about 45cm (1½ft) wide and 30cm (1ft) high.

Each type of material used for cloches has advantages and disadvantages so choose carefully to suit your particular needs.

Glass cloches have proved their worth for many years, but the cost of glass and delivery has made them an expensive investment.

Many garden centres now carry only a restricted stock, while firms that sell by mail order advertise only the wire supports – you have to buy the glass from a local glazier. If you want glass, order horticultural quality which is cheaper than window glass.

Inevitable breakages also add to costs, but glass has some advantages over other forms of cladding. When kept clean, glass cloches let in the maximum amount of sunlight, and on cold, clear nights they retain heat better than polythene. Adjustable locking devices make for good ventilation and on exposed, windy sites their weight makes them more secure than lighter materials

There are two main types of glass cloches – tents and barns. A tent cloche consists of two 60 × 30cm (2 × 1ft) sheets of glass fixed at the top by a galvanized-iron clip to form a pitched roof or tent. This type is useful for raising seedlings or for single rows of low-growing crops such as lettuces, carrots, beetroots and strawberries.

Barn cloches generally have four panes of glass, two forming sides and two forming the roof. A low barn cloche is 60cm (2ft) long and 30cm (1ft) high. With a width of about 60cm (2ft), it is possible to grow a central row of lettuces and outer rows of carrots or beetroots, for instance. The lettuces will be harvested first, leaving the others space to mature.

A high barn cloche is as wide and long as a low barn cloche, but the height is about 49cm (19in). A row of high barn cloches is useful for getting plants such as dwarf tomatoes, sweet peppers and aubergines to a fairly advanced stage before protection is no longer necessary in summer.

Solid plastic cloches are cheaper than those made from glass but, initially, are more expensive than polythene sheeting types. Solid plastic lasts longer than glass, which is easily broken, or sheet polythene, which must be replaced every few years. They trap less heat than glass cloches.

Plastic cloches can be made of corrugated PVC, moulded or twin-walled polypropylene or twin-walled polycarbonate. The manufacturers have taken advantage of the flexibility and lightness of plastic. Some cloches, for example, are 1.8m (6ft) long – a size that would be excessively heavy and cumbersome to handle in glass. Also, the longer the cloches the simpler the task of moving them from crop to crop.

Widths of cloches vary from 30cm (1ft) for growing seedlings, to 1.2m (4ft), in which two or three rows of vegetables can be grown to maturity. Heights vary from 20cm (8in) for seedlings to 60cm (2ft) for fully grown plants.

Solid plastic cloches are available with straight sides or curved into hooped tunnels. Both types are equally effective, but many straight-sided models have the added refinement of ventilation flaps to reduce condensation and get air flowing. Condensation in solid plastic cloches is not, however, as serious as in various types of polythene cloches.

GLASS AND PLASTIC CLOCHES

▲ **Glass bell cloches** were very popular in Victorian times for protecting individual garden plants or crops from harsh winter weather, but they are rarely available nowadays.

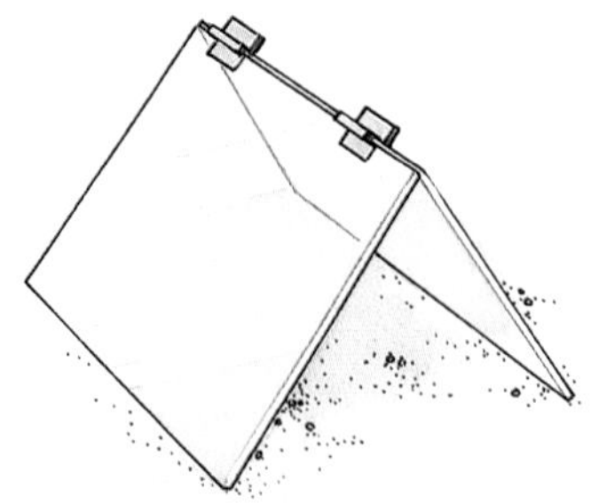

▲ **Glass tent cloches** comprise two panes of glass held together by proprietary clips.

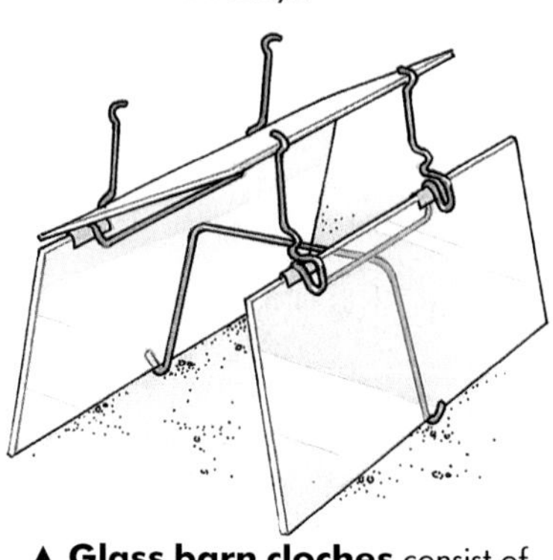

▲ **Glass barn cloches** consist of panes of horticultural-quality glass secured in a barn-like fashion with galvanized steel wire clips. An integral handle allows easy carriage from one part of the garden to another. The top section of this three-pane type can be hinged upwards to give good ventilation.

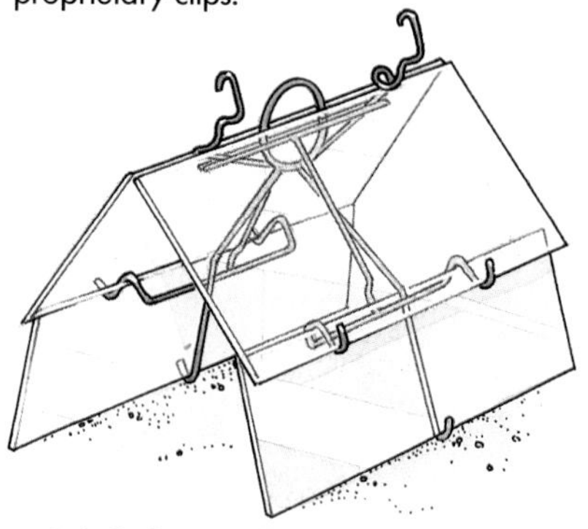

▲ **High-barn glass cloches** have four panes. Close each end with a separate pane.

▲ **An improvised cloche** can be made by cutting the bottom off a clear pastic bottle. Leave the screw cap off to provide ventilation, or cut some vent holes.

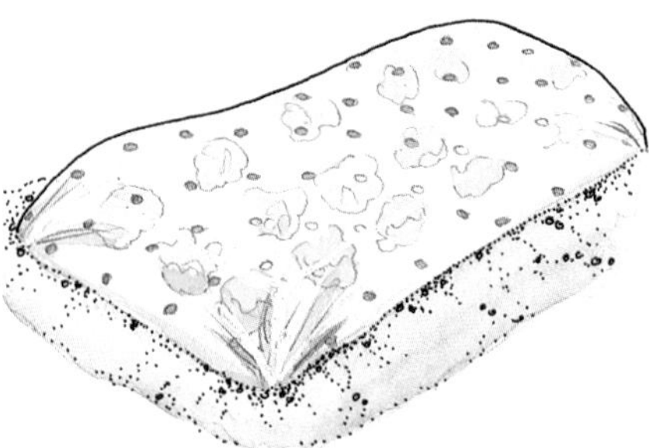

▲ **Floating cloches** are a recent idea. Germinating seeds and even mature crops can be grown under a single sheet of polythene, anchored by simply burying the edges. No support is required – the polythene can lie on the plants, but it must be perforated to allow air in. A light-weight woven material called agryl fleece can also be bought, which allows light, water and air to penetrate freely.

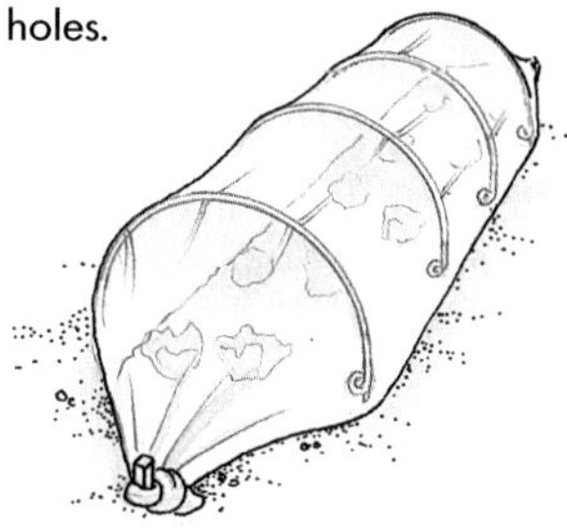

▲ **Polythene tunnels** provide cover for rows of plants. Polythene is stretched over wire hoops and knotted round anchor pegs. More hoops lash the polythene. Tunnels are cheap, but not portable. The polythene can be rolled back for ventilation and access.

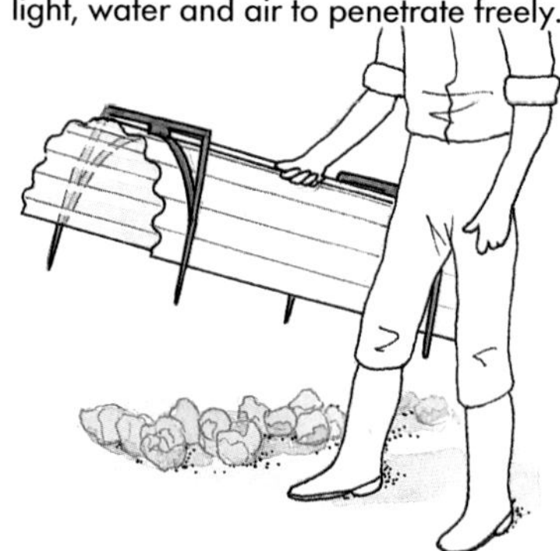

▲ **Segmented tunnel cloches,** made from corrugated PVC or moulded polypropylene, are long-lasting, but ventilation comes only from the ends.

GROWING VEGETABLES UNDER CLOCHES

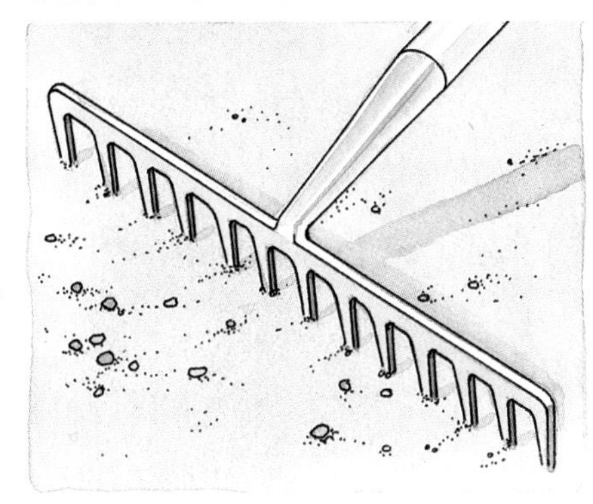

1 Dig the soil thoroughly several weeks before sowing or planting, allowing it plenty of time to settle. A fortnight before sowing, level the surface and rake in a moderate dressing of general-purpose fertilizer.

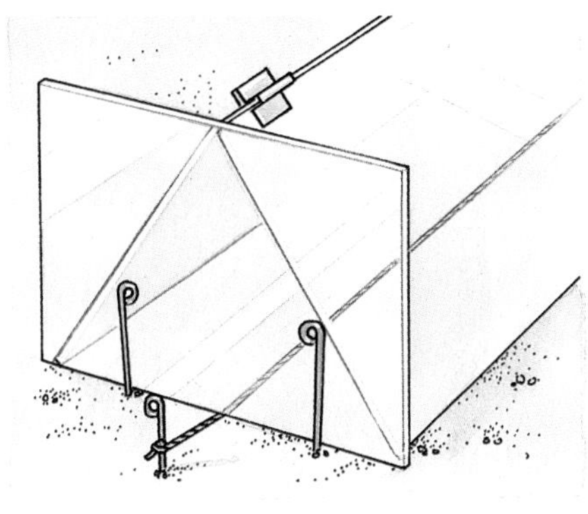

2 Immediately after raking, place the cloches centrally over a string line. If you are using tent, barn or segmented tunnel cloches, close each end of the run with a separate pane of glass or plastic.

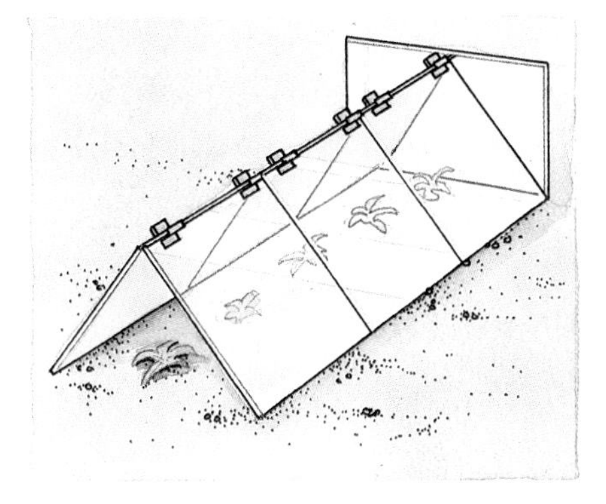

3 When the soil has had time to warm up, set the plants – or sow the seeds – along the string line. Scatter slug pellets on the ground, then replace the cloches as soon as possible. Also replace the end panes.

4 On clear evenings in mid to late spring place newspaper over the cloches – four or five sheets at a time. This should provide adequate protection against frost damage. Be sure to remove them the next morning.

Plastic equivalents of the old-fashioned bell cloche may be obtained from some suppliers for protecting individual plants – they are ideal for protecting the developing blooms of Christmas roses from harsh winter weather.

Polythene cloches are obtainable either as separate units, which are then put end to end, or as a complete tunnel cloche made from a length of polythene sheeting draped over wire hoops.

Polythene is obtainable in various thicknesses. The thinnest - 150 gauge – is the cheapest form of cladding but it will last for only a year or two. Heavier duty polythene – 250-300 gauge – is more expensive but it will last three or four years with care. Polythene treated with an ultraviolet inhibitor to slow down deterioration is also available. This lasts longer, than untreated material of the same gauge.

Condensation is a problem with polythene. It can provide conditions for the spread of disease, so it is important to ventilate the cloches to clear the condensation and to get air circulating.

As polythene is light and unbreakable, it has a big advantage over glass when being moved from one crop to another. Its lightness can be a disadvantage, however, in areas affected by high winds. If gales are forecast, anchor cloches with bricks, or form an inverted 'V' over them with canes driven into the ground. Tunnel cloches are satisfactorily anchored by their method of construction.

The simplest and cheapest of all plastic cloches is the modern floating cloche, which has no support members and consists entirely of a single sheet of perforated polythene anchored across the top of the plants by burying the edges in the soil. A special woven agryl fleece can be used in the same way.

Growing under cloches

If possible, prepare the ground a month before sowing or planting to give the soil time to settle. Dig in one bucketful of well-rotted manure or compost per sq m/yd.

Two weeks before sowing or planting, rake in a dressing of general fertilizer at about 50g (2oz) per sq m/yd. Mark a central row with a string line, leave this in position, and cover the row with the cloches to warm up the soil. Secure the end panels.

Remove the cloches at sowing time – the purpose of leaving the string line is to centre the row where the developing plants will get most headroom.

Sow small seeds about 6mm (¼in) deeper than in the open ground because the surface dries out during the warming-up period. Do not water until the seeds germinate – enough moisture will filter up from the soil beneath the seeds to begin with. However, water immediately after setting out young plants.

After sowing or planting, scatter slug pellets and replace the cloches in exactly the same position as when the ground was being warmed. Subsequent cultivation is the same as for plants growing in the open. Although the surface may look dry, a few centimetres down it will have the same moisture content as the uncovered soil alongside and water will reach the plants' roots by capillary action.

If spring days are unusually warm, open up some continuous cloches or slide back the polythene of a tunnel cloche to allow air to circulate. Replace or close the cloches an hour before sunset.

If late spring frosts are forecast, cover the cloches over tender crops with four or five sheets of newspaper in the evening and remove them in the morning.

A week before moving cloches from one row to another, harden off the plants that are about to be left in the open. Leave off some cloches – or slide back the polythene – during the day and replace them in the evening.

When using cloches to cover strawberries, they serve a dual purpose – it will be unnecessary to net the plants against bird attacks and, if put in position in late autumn, will provide an earlier crop than in the open garden.

A CROPPING PROGRAMME FOR CLOCHES

SOW EARLY SEEDS — **PROTECT YOUNG PLANTS** — **GROW ON CROPS** — **OVERWINTER PLANTS**

This programme is for average growing conditions – adjust it by one or two weeks as necessary in cold or mild regions.

SEASON	WEEK									
MID WINTER	1 2 3 4	Sow very early crops: beetroots broad beans carrots radishes salad onions	Overwinter seedlings of crops sown in autumn until planting-out time	Overwinter sweet peas and other hardy annuals sown in autumn	Grow on lettuces		Overwinter peas sown in autumn	Overwinter onions sown in late summer	Protect alpine plants and Christmas roses from winter wet	
LATE WINTER	1 2 3 4				Sow lettuces at two-week intervals	Sow hardy vegetables for trans-planting later: brassicas onions peas				Protect straw-berries for early harvest
EARLY SPRING	1 2 3 4		Sow hardy annuals for early flowers for cutting	Sow early crops: beetroots Brussels sprouts cabbages carrots cauli-flowers onions						
MID SPRING	1 2 3 4	Protect newly planted hardy vegetables raised under glass: Brussels sprouts cauli-flowers	Protect tender vegetables raised early under glass		Sow celeriac French beans sweet corn					
LATE SPRING	1 2 3 4					Sow half-hardy bedding annuals	Grow on borderline crops usually grown in a green-house: aubergines dwarf tomatoes melons ridge cucumbers sweet peppers			
EARLY SUMMER	1 2 3 4									
MID SUMMER	1 2 3 4							Shield ripening onions from rain		
LATE SUMMER	1 2 3 4									
EARLY AUTUMN	1 2 3 4		Overwinter seedlings of crops sown in autumn until planting-out time: e.g. cauli-flowers		Sow lettuces at two-week intervals					Extend harvest period for straw-berries
MID AUTUMN	1 2 3 4			Overwinter sweet peas and other hardy annuals sown in autumn			Overwinter peas sown in autumn			
LATE AUTUMN	1 2 3 4				Grow on lettuces			Overwinter onions sown in late autumn	Protect alpine plants and Christmas roses from winter wet	
EARLY WINTER	1 2 3 4									

Weeds and weed control

Any plant growing where it is not wanted can theoretically be described as a weed. In practice, though, a weed is any plant that thrives in a wide range of conditions and soils, grows rapidly, competes with other plants and reproduces itself with ease. Although weeds often have colourful flowers and can be attractive in hedgerows and on waste ground, they are unsightly among garden plants. However, they should be removed for other than aesthetic reasons, since they fight with cultivated plants for water, nutrients, light and space and can damage slow-growing annuals and vegetable crops. In addition they play host to a number of insect pests and viruses harmful to cultivated plants and infection can be carried over from season to season.

For all these reasons the gardener is engaged in a constant war against weeds, which often have the advantage of being native to the soil being cultivated. Annual weeds inhabit the surface soil and scatter literally thousands of seeds before they die off. These can remain viable in the soil for decades. Perennial weeds often have deep, wide-spreading roots which are difficult to eradicate.

Regular work with a hoe or weeding by hand are by far the best and safest ways of dealing with weeds near cultivated plants. Weedkillers should be handled with extreme caution; many are dangerous to humans, pets and wildlife, and sprays can easily drift to damage cultivated plants beyond recovery.

Perennial weeds Unchecked, deep-rooted perennial weeds spread quickly to strangle cultivated plants and food crops.

KNOW YOUR WEEDS

Learn to recognise some of the more persistent and troublesome weeds in the garden and you're half-way to eradicating them.

A weed is simply any plant growing where it's not wanted. Native wild flowers and grasses are generally regarded as weeds whenever they appear among cultivated plants, though some gardeners may actively encourage them in a 'wild garden'. Blackberries are welcome in the fruit garden, but are enemies in the flower border. Equally, some cultivated plants become weeds when they grow too vigorously for their allocated site – snow-in-summer (*Cerastium tomentosum*) is a charming rock garden plant, but will quickly smother its neighbours if left untrimmed.

Weeds become a problem when they compete with ornamental plants or food crops, reducing the available nutrients, light, water and space, and interfering with the garden's visual appeal. They may even harbour pests and diseases.

Most common weeds have one distinct advantage over garden plants – they are native to the country, rather than introduced from worldwide locations, and are best adapted to the local environment. They often germinate and establish faster than introduced species, so you must get rid of them quickly.

A predominance of certain weeds can be an indicator of soil type – for example, sheeps sorrel and field woodrush on acid soils; corn marigold, small nettle and ironweed on sandy soils; cornflower and wild carrot on chalk soils. But the most troublesome and commonly encountered weeds, such as ground elder and couch grass, will be found on all types of soil.

Annual weeds live for just one year. They produce seeds that lie dormant over winter then germinate in spring or summer. Some can even produce two or three generations a year – in fact, the main problem gardeners have with annual weeds is their capacity for shedding seeds. One of the worst of all, fat hen, produces around 3000 seeds on an average plant, while a chickweed seed may remain alive buried in the soil for more than a quarter of a century before germinating on being brought to the surface by cultivation. They may be spread around the garden in mud on your shoes, by wind, on animals' fur, in bird droppings or in composts.

Perennial weeds are often the most difficult to get rid of. Many multiply by creeping stems, either above ground or below, as well as by seed. New plants are also produced from tiny pieces of roots or underground stems which become severed during digging or hoeing. When turned over with the soil, they remain unnoticed until vigorous well-rooted shoots spring up everywhere.

Docks and dandelions are able to withstand longer periods of drought than most cultivated plants since their long tap roots penetrate the soil deeply to obtain water. Some plants, such as bindweed, may send down roots as deep as 3m (10ft), but others have relatively shallow rooting systems.

◄ **Troublesome weeds** Perennial weeds and tough-rooted grasses, being native plants, often grow better than cultivated plants. They usurp space, nutrients, water and light.

Annual meadowgrass
(Poa annua)

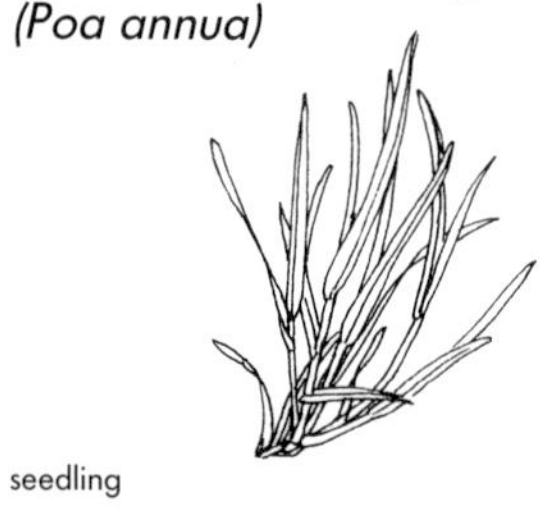

Height × spread 5-30 × 30cm (2-12 × 12in)
Leaves Bright green, ribbon-like, often wrinkled, in tufts or on creeping stems.
Flowers Greenish to buff, in triangular upright spikes, 1-8cm (½-3in) tall, all year.
Other features Continuously re-seeds itself. Annual.

Annual sow-thistle
(Sonchus oleraceus)

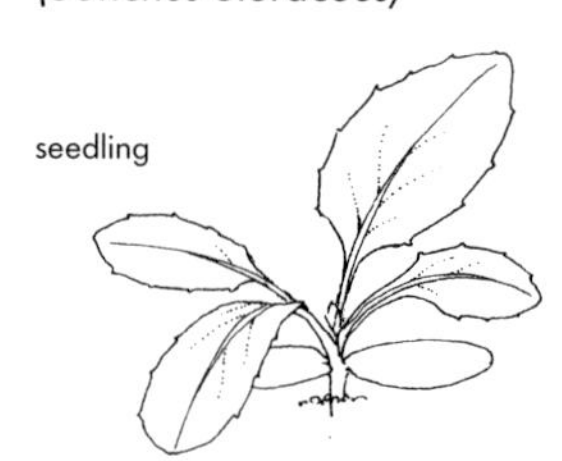

Height × spread 20-150 × 10-20cm (8-60 × 4-8in).
Leaves Dull blue-green, variable in shape with lobed and serrated edges.
Flowers Pale yellow, somewhat dandelion-like, 2-2.5cm (¾-1in) across in small clusters, summer.
Other features Seed heads fluffy. Annual.

Broad-leaved dock
(Rumex obtusifolius)

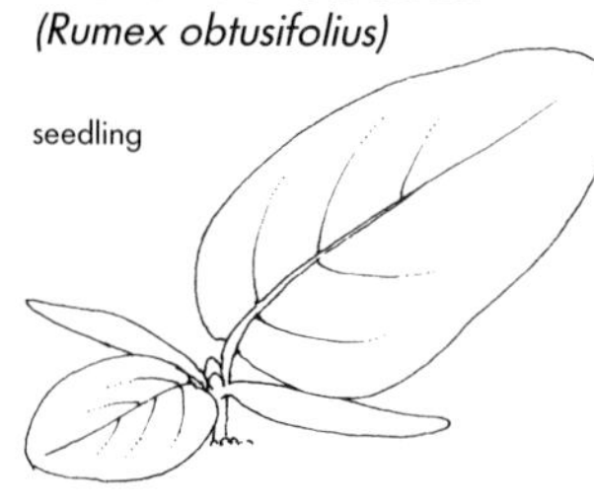

Height × spread 50-100 × 60cm (20-40 × 24in).
Leaves Large, wavy, broad, coarse-textured, underside hairy, to 25cm (10in) long.
Flowers Green to reddish, tiny but in large, branched spikes, late spring to autumn.
Other features Seedlings often crimson. Resistant to most weedkillers. Perennial.

Chickweed
(Stellaria media)

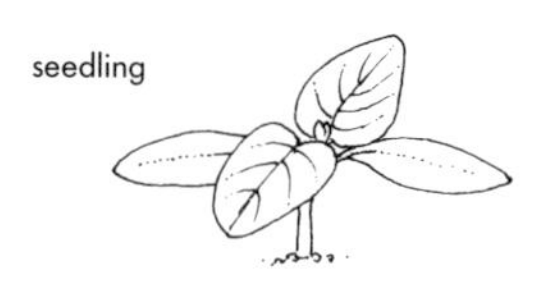

Height × spread 5-35 × 20cm (2-14 × 8in).
Leaves Bright green, oval, 3-20mm (⅛-¾in) long, hairy at the base.
Flowers Tiny, white, esp. spring and autumn.
Other features Sprawls along the ground, but can scramble up through other plants. Annual.

Cleavers (goosegrass)
(Galium aparine)

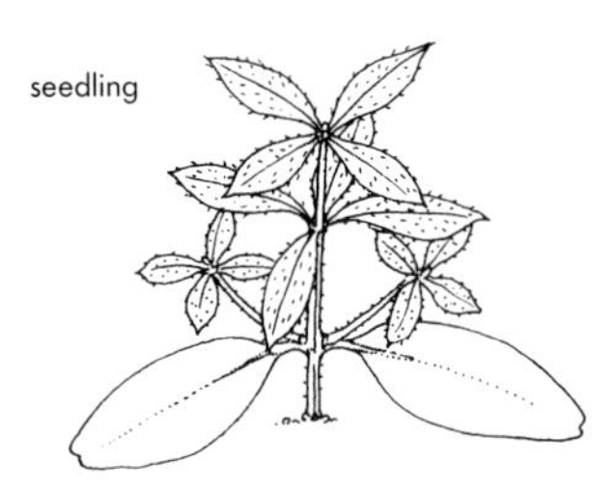

Height × spread 15-120 × 15-120cm (6-48 × 6-48in).
Leaves Soft green, narrow, 'sticky', 1-5cm (½-2in) long.
Flowers Insignificant.
Other features Scrambling habit; can smother others, clinging by hooks on stems and leaves. Fruits are bristly, globular burrs – stick to clothing and fur. Annual.

Couch grass (twitch)
(Elytrigia repens)

Height × spread 30-75 × 30-60cm (1-1½ × 1-2ft).
Leaves Dull green, slender blades forming large tufts.
Flowers Upright buff-green spikes, summer to autumn.
Other features Rhizomes spread vigorously; these often break during cultivation and produce new plants. Perennial.

Creeping buttercup
(Ranunculus repens)

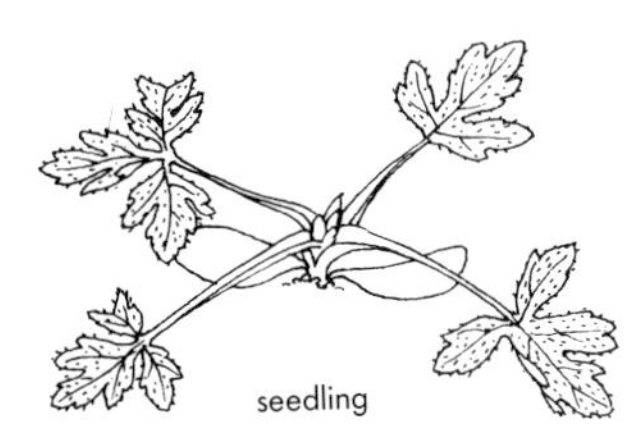

Height × spread Up to 30 × 50cm (12 × 20in).
Leaves Divided into three lobes, coarse-toothed, hairy, covered with pale spots.
Flowers Bright yellow, cup-shaped, 2-3cm (1-1¼in) across, spring and summer.
Other features Spreads by stout runners. Common on heavy, damp soils. Perennial.

Creeping cinquefoil
(Potentilla reptans)

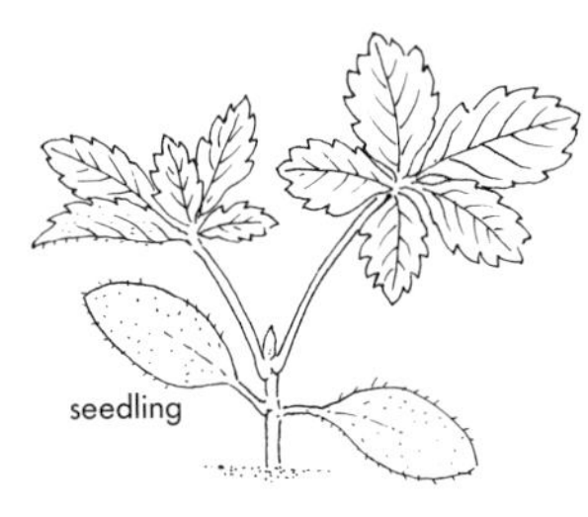

Height × spread Prostrate × 1m (40in).
Leaves Divided into five, finely serrated leaflets.
Flowers Yellow, strawberry-like, 1.5-2.5cm (⅝-1in) across, early summer to early autumn.
Other features Creeping stems root at leaf joints. Common. Perennial.

Creeping thistle
(Cirsium arvense)

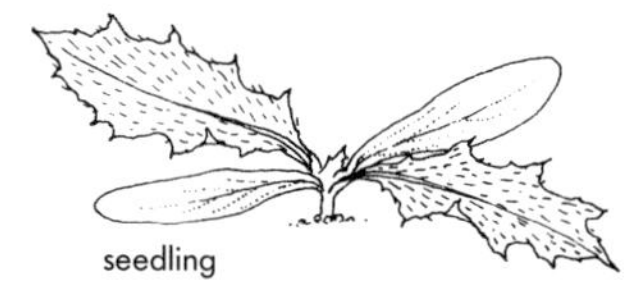

Height × spread 30-120 × 45cm (1-4 × 1½ft).
Leaves Dark green, long, narrow and wavy, triangular teeth and prickly spines.
Flowers Pale purple, fading whitish; heads 1.5-2.5cm (⅝-1in), summer to early autumn.
Other features Creeping roots. Resistant to most herbicides. Perennial.

Dandelion
(Taraxacum officinale)

Height × spread Up to 35 × 35cm (14 × 14in).
Leaves Dark green, glossy, lobed with toothed edges.
Flowers Yellow, 3.5-5cm (1½-2in) across, spring to late summer, open in sun.
Other features Fluffy, globular seed heads – seeds dispersed by wind. Roots deep and tough. Perennial.

Fat hen (white goosefoot)
(Chenopodium album)

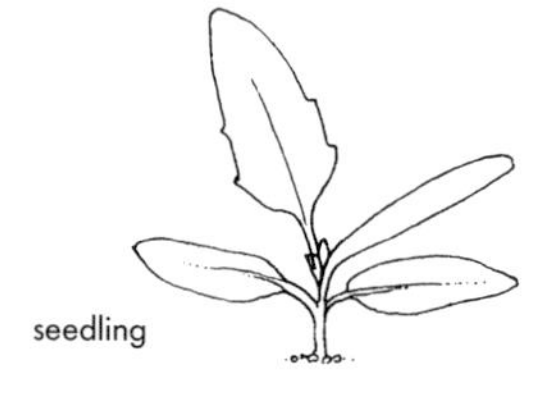

Height × spread Up to 90 × 30cm (3 × 1ft).
Leaves Grey-green with a whitish coating, mostly lance-shaped, lower ones broader and toothed, 8cm (3in) long.
Flowers Tiny, greenish, in upright spikes, mid summer to mid autumn.
Other features Thousands of fatty, edible seeds. Annual.

Field bindweed
(Convolvulus arvensis)

Height × spread 20-75 × 75cm (8-30 × 30in).
Leaves Arrow-shaped, mid green, 2-5cm (1-2in) long.
Flowers Pink and white striped, funnel-shaped, up to 3cm (1¼in) wide, long stalks, early summer to autumn.
Other features Roots deep, fragment easily. Twining stems. Perennial.

Field speedwell
(Veronica persica)

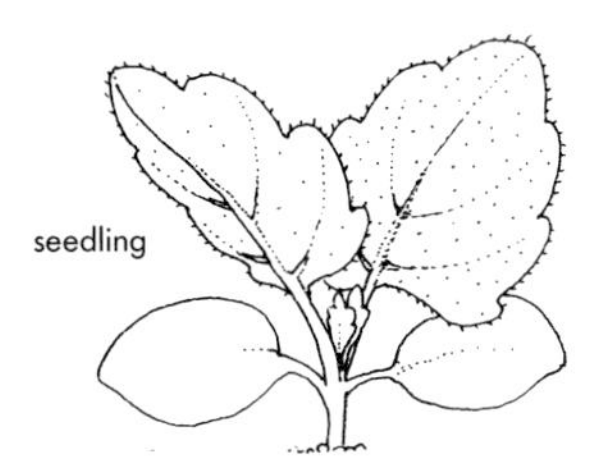

Height × spread Up to 30 × 40cm (12 × 16in).
Leaves Pale green, oval, toothed, 1-3cm (½-1¼in) long.
Flowers Bright blue, often paler or white in the centre, 8mm (⅓in) across, late winter to late autumn.
Other features Stems hairy and spreading. Annual.

Field woodrush
(Luzula campestris)

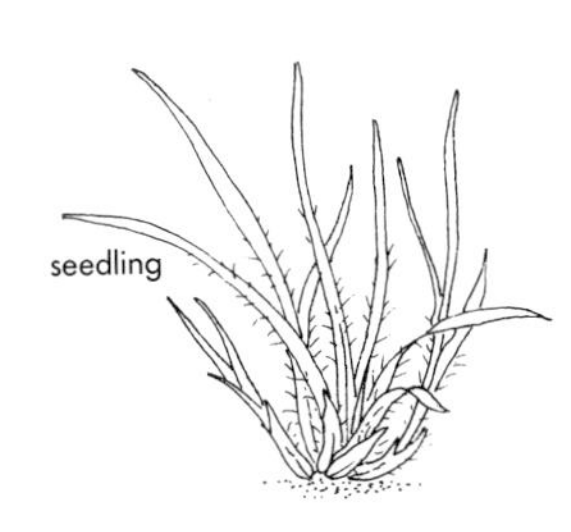

Height × spread 10-20 × 20cm (4-8 × 8in).
Leaves Grass-like tussocks, hairy, light green.
Flowers Close, brownish-green spikes, yellow anthers, early to late spring.
Other features Creeping rootstock, also spreads freely by seed.
Perennial.

Ground elder
(Aegopodium podagraria)

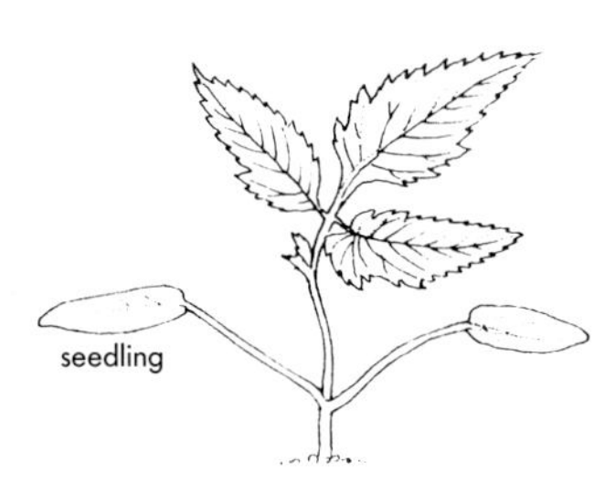

Height × spread 40-90 × 90cm (16-36 × 36in).
Leaves Divided into sprays of three, each toothed, 5-10cm (2-4in) long.
Flowers Umbrella-like heads up to 6cm (2½in) of tiny white flowers, early summer.
Other features Fruits oval, 4mm (⅜in) long, ridged. Hard to control. Perennial.

Groundsel
(Senecio vulgaris)

Height × spread 8-45 × 20cm (3-18 × 8in).
Leaves Dark green, long and fairly narrow, irregularly lobed and toothed.
Flowers Rich yellow, 4mm (⅜in) across, like tiny thistles in shape, any time of year.
Other features Germinate any time of year. Stems succulent. Fruits fluffy. Annual.

Horsetail, common
(Equisetum arvense)

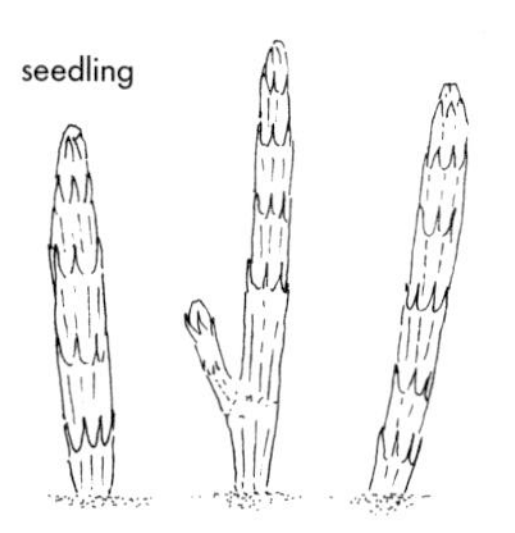

Height × spread Up to 60 × 90cm (2 × 3ft).
Leaves Evergreen plants allied to ferns. Jointed stems, whorls of scale-like sheaths at stem joints.
Flowers Non-flowering; spores in terminal heads, summer.
Other features Creeping deep rootstock. Perennial.

Knotgrass (irongrass)
(Polygonum aviculare)

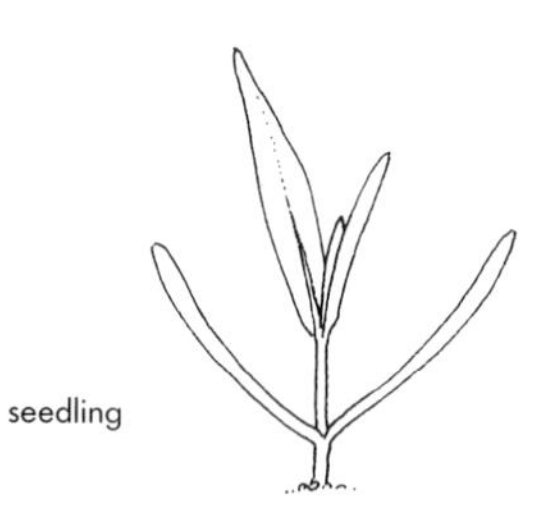

Height × spread Up to 60 × 150cm (2 × 5ft).
Leaves Lance-shaped; silver sheath around stalk base.
Flowers Small, pink and white, in clusters at base of leaves, summer to autumn.
Other features Germination mainly in early spring. Branching stems trail or scramble. Annual.

Oxalis
(Oxalis sp.)

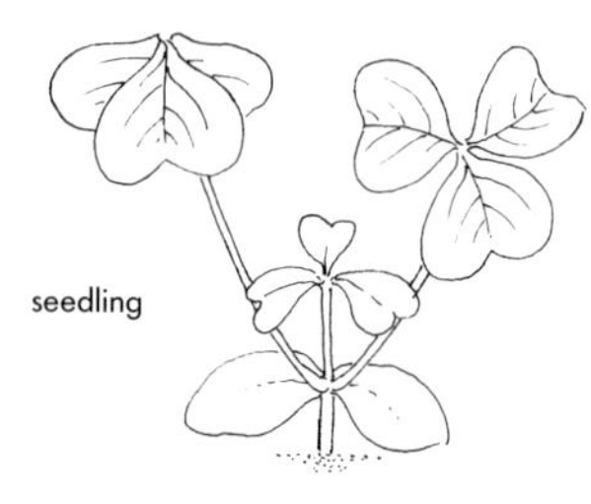

Height × spread 5 × 30cm (2 × 12in).
Leaves Trefoil, pale green spotted pale orange.
Flowers White, purple or pink clusters, late spring to early autumn.
Other features Reproduces by bulbils and seed; member of the wood sorrels. Invasive perennial.

Persicaria, common
(Polygonum persicaria)

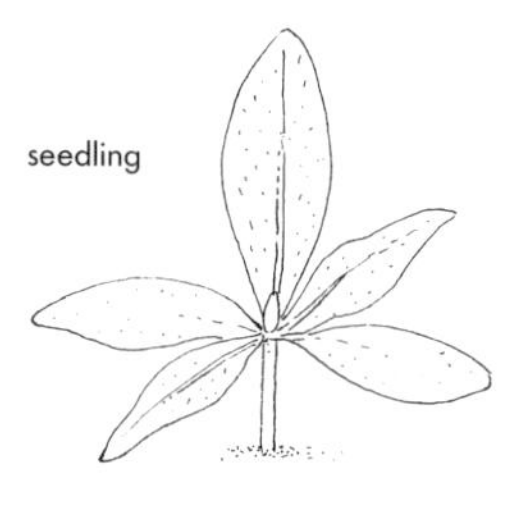

Height × spread 30-60cm (1-2ft).
Leaves Lance-shaped, dark green, often with purple blotches, on branching stems.
Flowers Dense pink or whitish spikes, early summer to mid autumn.
Other features Annual. Self-seeds freely. Common on damp soils.

Pineapple weed
(Matricaria matricarioides)

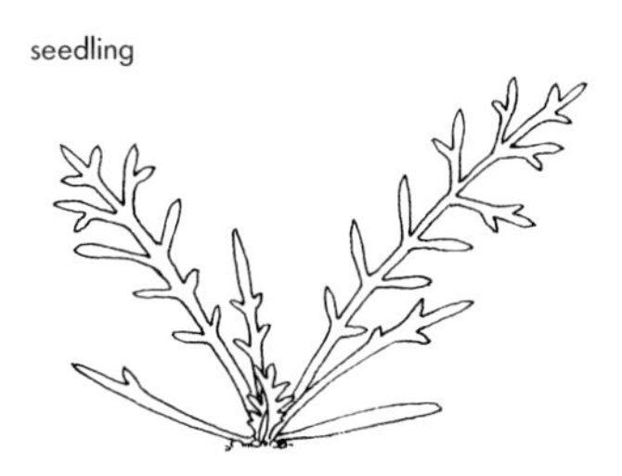
seedling

Height × spread 5-25 × 15cm (2-10 × 6in).
Leaves Finely divided, feathery, strongly aromatic.
Flowers Yellow-green, resembling a pineapple in shape, 5-8mm (¼-⅜in) across, early to mid summer.
Other features Particularly common along paths and well-trodden ground. Annual.

Red deadnettle
(Lamium purpureum)

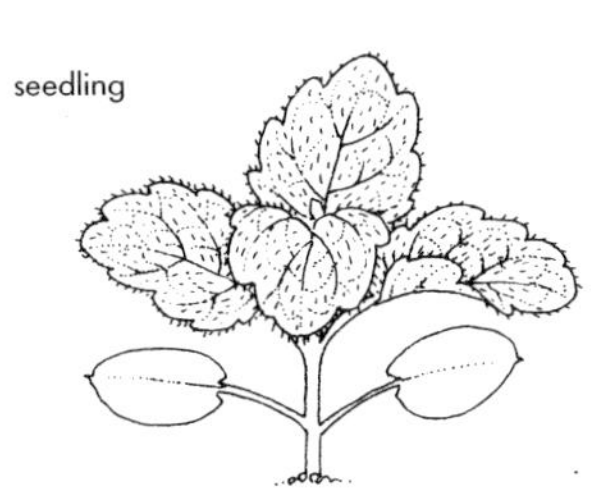
seedling

Height × spread 15-30 × 15cm (6-12 × 6in).
Leaves Oval, edges serrated, often tinged purple, up to 5cm (2in) long.
Flowers Pinkish purple, hooded, 1-1.5cm (⅜-⅝in) long, in rings at upper leaf joints, spring to mid autumn.
Other features Stems hairy, square in section. Annual.

Rosebay willowherb
(Epilobium/Chamaenerion angustifolium)

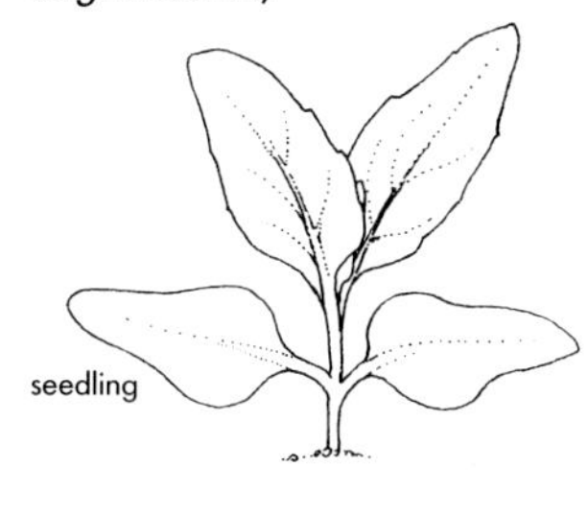
seedling

Height × spread Up to 150 × 30cm (5 × 1ft).
Leaves Dark green, narrow, veins reddish, edges wavy.
Flowers Rose-purple, 2-3cm (1-1¼in) across, in a tall spire, summer to early autumn.
Other features Slender pods release white fluffy seeds in autumn. Germinates on burnt ground. Perennial.

Shepherd's purse
(Capsella bursa-pastoris)

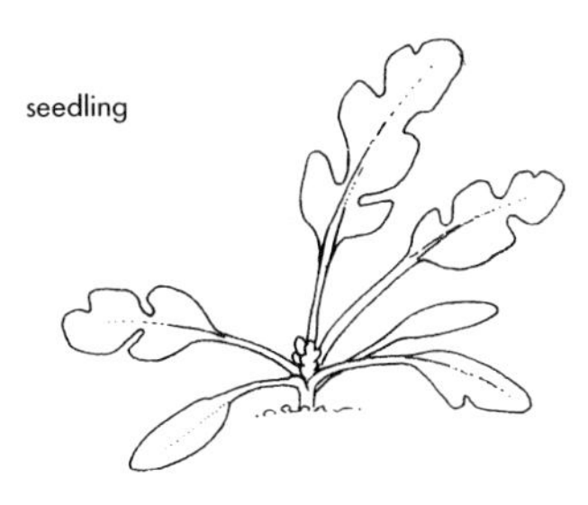
seedling

Height × spread Up to 35 × 25cm (14 × 10in).
Leaves Grey-green, long and narrow, variably toothed or lobed along the edges, all in a ground-level rosette.
Flowers Tiny, white, in a tall upright spike, all year.
Other features Small purse-shaped seed pods. Can carry club root disease. Annual.

Stinging nettle
(Urtica dioica)

Height × spread 30-120 × 30cm (1-4 × 1ft).
Leaves Deep green, toothed, hairy, 4-8cm (1½-3in) long.
Flowers Yellow green tassels, 10cm (4in) long, late spring to early autumn.
Other features Gives painful stings. Roots yellow, very tough. Perennial.

Sun spurge
(Euphorbia helioscopia)

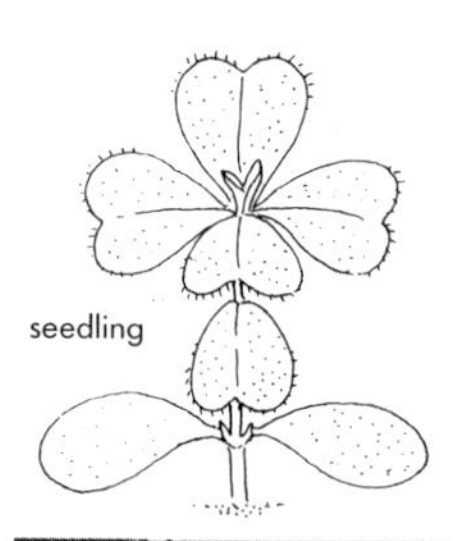

Height × spread Up to 50 × 20cm (20 × 8in).
Leaves Oval and finely toothed, pale green.
Flowers Yellow-green bracts in broad clusters, mid spring to mid autumn, often into winter.
Other features Milky stem sap. Common annual on cultivated ground.

Canadian pondweed
(Elodea canadensis)

Height × spread Submerged, wide-spreading oxygenator.
Leaves Dark green and lance-shaped, in groups of three.
Flowers Scarce, minute, purple-tinged white, late spring to early autumn.
Other features Spreads by water-borne seed. Perennial.

Duckweed
(Lemna minor)

Height × spread Prostrate, indefinite spread.
Leaves Stemless and rootless, tiny modified pale green leaves.
Flowers Minute and rarely seen, summer.
Other features Common annual, covering water surface with floating leaf carpet.

CONTROLLING WEEDS

Dig out perennial weeds during deep cultivation and attack annual weeds with a hoe. Use chemicals only in dire cases.

Weeds must be controlled in the garden for a number of important reasons. Obviously, they are unsightly, especially among flower beds and borders, but they also threaten the health and vigour of cultivated plants. During hot spells they compete for valuable water, and, throughout the year, tap nutrients and shade out sunlight. Many weeds also harbour pests and diseases which can easily spread to ornamental plants and food crops.

The old saying 'one year seeding means seven years weeding' is very apt. Both annual and perennial weeds, if left uncontrolled, shed seeds which often germinate when conditions suit – particularly when brought to the surface by soil cultivation. Many even flourish during cold weather, when other plants lie dormant.

Never allow weeds to flower and produce seed, even though some, such as the red deadnettle, dandelion, field speedwell and rosebay willowherb, may be attractive in their own right. Only by taking prompt action whenever seedling weeds first appear, can a long-term war on weeds be avoided.

Learn to distinguish between weed seedlings and cultivated seedlings. Sowing in orderly rows, especially in the kitchen garden, makes this task easier.

Manual weeding

The thought of hand-weeding is daunting to many people, but if you set to promptly and don't let weeds take over the garden, this can be a relatively painless task. Indeed, old-fashioned hand-weeding is still the most effective and safe deterrent against perennial weeds.

Individual weeds can be pulled up directly by hand. This technique is best where a few large weeds have grown up between ornamental or crop plants, since, with care, the neighbouring plants are not disturbed. Wear gloves for protection, especially when dealing with stinging nettles or thistles. Pull them gently but firmly, holding the main stem as close to the soil as possible, to remove the whole root system intact. Many perennial weeds can regrow from severed root sections left in the soil.

For dealing with more widespread weeds, a hoe – either a draw hoe or a Dutch hoe – and a small border fork will be needed. A hand fork, trowel and onion hoe may also be useful. Use an onion hoe, a short-handled version of the draw hoe, where plants are growing close together – in seed beds and rock gardens, for example. Drawing the hoe towards you, cut off the weeds at soil level with a chopping action. Be careful not to damage the tops of young ornamental plants.

Use a Dutch hoe for general surface hoeing or between crop rows, working with a skimming action back and forth through the soil to sever weeds and remove their roots. A border fork should be used only to loosen deep-rooted weeds around the base of a plant – remove the weeds by hand to avoid disturbing the soil round the roots of ornamental plants.

◀ **Annual weeds** Left unchecked, rampant weeds like red deadnettles can quickly swamp bedding plants. Apart from their unsightliness, such weeds can encourage fungal diseases as air and light are excluded.

USING A HOE

1 A Dutch hoe has a forward-pointing cutting edge – use with a skimming action to slice small weeds.

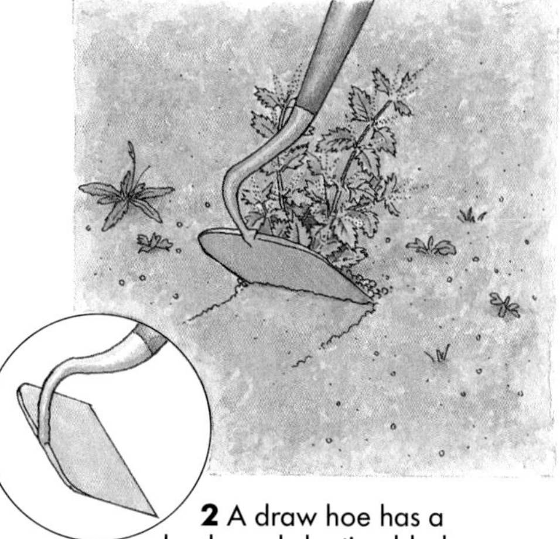

2 A draw hoe has a backward-slanting blade – use with a chopping action to cut down larger weeds at soil level.

Sometimes perennial weeds such as couch grass and ground elder become entangled with the roots of ornamental plants. The only manual solution is to dig up both, separate them by hand and replant the ornamentals.

Collect weeds to make sure they don't re-root. They can be put on the compost heap unless they bear seed heads, in which case burn them.

Choosing weedkillers

Chemical weedkillers – herbicides – take much of the physical effort out of weeding, but they need careful handling and application. Some gardeners prefer not to use them for ecological reasons, but they can be very effective against difficult weeds. There are several types of weedkiller, classified by their mode of action.

Chemicals referred to below are the active ingredient, not the trade name – read the contents label on weedkillers carefully if you are unsure.

Selective foliage-applied types kill only certain plants, leaving others unharmed. These are commonly used on lawns – for example 2,4-D, which selects all broad-leaved weeds among narrow-leaved grasses. Here, the selective principle relies on most of the weedkiller running off the narrow, channelled grass leaves, but wetting the broader weed leaves. Similarly, alloxydim-sodium selectively kills most grass weeds growing among broad-leaved ornamentals.

Non-selective foliage-applied types kill most plants they touch. Some have a contact action, killing only the parts above ground which are directly touched by the chemical, for instance glufosinate ammonium and paraquat with diquat mixtures. Others are translocated – absorbed into the plant's circulatory system – and kill the entire plant including roots and bulbs. These include glyphosate which takes several weeks to act thoroughly, but is very effective. Some non-selective types can be applied selectively by spraying or painting on to individual plants.

Soil-applied residual types, such as dichlobenil, remain active in the soil for some time and are taken up by the roots. They are effective against existing weeds and subsequent germinating weed seeds – they act in fact as weed preventers – so are useful for clearing land which won't be used for several months.

Some soil-applied weedkillers have a selective action when used in low concentrations, or a non-selective action at higher doses, so follow manufacturer's instructions carefully.

Total weedkillers, for example sodium chlorate (nowadays sold with a fire depressant), are used for clearing scrub-land. Since they can remain active in the soil for up to one year or more, do not use them among ornamentals or crops or on land soon to be used for crops, ornamentals or lawns.

Weeds near a pond
These pose a special problem. Never use a weedkiller to spray close to the edge since it could drift on to the water and kill fish and water plants. Avoid soil-applied chemicals with a residual action – especially near an unlined pond – since they can leach down into the water. Instead, weed by hand or use a paint-on gel type.

Applying weedkillers

Weedkillers may be sold as liquids which need dilution, as dry granules for direct application, or as wettable powders or soluble granules. According to the type, they are applied by watering can, sprayer or sprinkled over the soil. Check the manufacturer's instructions for application.

Where foliage-applied types are suitable for sprayer application, this is the most effective method, giving an even coating of fine droplets which do not run off the leaves. Choose a calm day when the spray won't drift on to ornamental or food plants. Spray systematically to avoid overdosing some and under-treating others.

You can make an effective spray drift guard for a pressurized sprayer. Cut the tube off an old plastic funnel so that the funnel will fit snugly over the tip of the spray nozzle. Secure it tightly with a Jubilee clip. When spraying weedkillers do not pump up the sprayer as much as you would for an insecticide or fungicide – you should be able to get very close to the weeds.

When applying liquid weedkillers to bare or open ground, use a watering can. The standard watering rose can be fitted, but for more even distribution replace it with a dribble bar. Walk across the area systematically and at a constant speed.

Granular types need careful application. First calculate the total area to be treated and weigh out the appropriate total quantity of the chemical. Then square off the bed into small segments and take enough chemical to treat one segment at a time.

Where individual weeds are growing too closely among garden plants for any kind of weedkiller treatment to be practical, a paint-on formulation of glyphosate can be used. In lawns, isolated weeds, such as scattered plaintains, can be treated individually with an aerosol-type of lawn weedkiller.

Whichever type of weedkiller you use, it is important to wear rubber gloves while mixing and applying it. If any chemical does get on to the skin or eyes, wash it off immediately and check the manufacturer's recommendations regarding accidental contact.

Weed suppressors

Systematic and continuous hand weeding, or the use of preventative herbicides as recommended here, will keep your garden clear of most weeds. However, there are other, almost labour-saving solutions that can solve the problem even before it arises. Prevention is better than a cure and several measures can be taken to suppress weed growth.

Ground-cover plants are ideal for covering every inch of soil in shrub and mixed border. By their very nature, they deprive emerging weed seedlings of light and space and colonize rapidly to form tight clumps. Some will spread

HOW WEEDKILLERS WORK

1 Contact weedkillers are absorbed into leaves and stems, quickly killing tissue directly under the surface. But, any part not wetted, including roots, may survive – the poison doesn't travel through the plant.

2 Translocated weedkillers are absorbed into the circulation, killing the entire weed, including roots and suckers, even if only part is wetted.

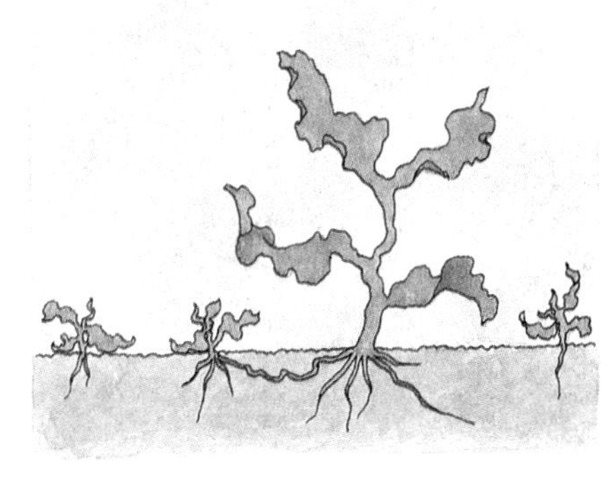

3 Soil-acting weedkillers are also absorbed into the weed's circulation, but via the roots. They, too, kill the entire plant. In addition, they remain active in the soil, killing any weed seeds as they germinate later on.

WEEDKILLER DO'S & DON'TS

- ☐ Do follow manufacturers' instructions regarding application method, dilution and dosage.
- ☐ Do keep out of reach of children – regard all as toxic.
- ☐ Do keep pets away from treated weeds.
- ☐ Do mix up only as much liquid chemical as you need – don't store diluted solutions.
- ☐ Don't apply chemicals to flowering plants – you may also kill pollinating insects such as bees.
- ☐ Don't mix up solutions stronger than recommended – you may scorch and kill some leaves but in so doing prevent translocated types from reaching and killing the root system.
- ☐ Don't get chemicals on your skin or eyes – if you do, wash it off immediately; wash your hands thoroughly after use.
- ☐ Don't allow spray to drift on to wanted plants – keep nozzles or trickle bars close to the ground and don't spray on a windy day.

WEEDKILLER APPLICATORS

1 Watering can with a dribble bar – enables uniform liquid application.

2 Pressurized sprayer with a fine spray drift guard – applies fine droplets.

3 Ready-mixed weedkiller applicators – liquid gun and gel brush types.

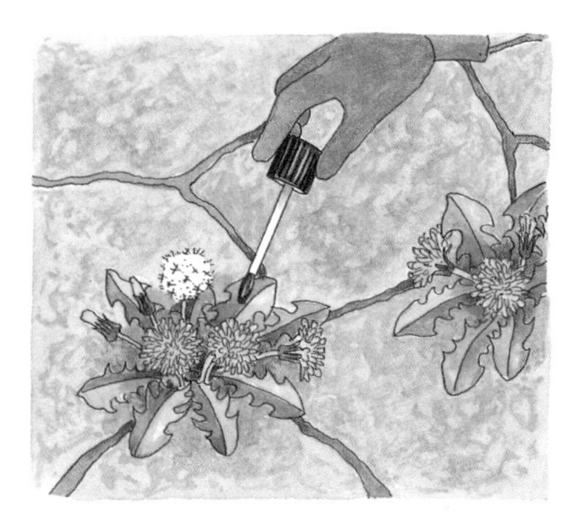

SPECIAL WEED PROBLEMS

Weeds in paths, drives and patios are perhaps the easiest to deal with, since they are not growing among decorative plants. The simplest method is to slice them off with an old knife or trowel. Perennial weeds with deep tap roots are best pulled out by hand.

Weedkillers provide the longest lasting cure. Choose non-selective or total foliage-applied weedkillers, such as ammonium sulphamate, atrazine or amitrole formulations, paraquat and diquat, or dichlobenil.

Proprietary mixtures for use on paths and paving usually contain a foliage-acting chemical to kill existing weeds, and a residual soil-acting one for preventing subsequent weed germination. Most are effective for several months and may on occasion persist for up to one year or more.

Mosses, algae and lichen are a nuisance on paving and steps, often making the surface slippery in wet weather. Dichlorophen or a tar oil emulsion will control these weeds effectively. Dichlorophen can be bought ready-diluted in a hand-held, gun-type spray canister, making spot treatment of a dangerous patch of moss very simple.

Weeds in flower beds are more of a problem. In established beds it's often difficult to use weedkillers. There are no chemicals which can select the weeds from wanted plants. Unlike the typical weed problem in a lawn where the wanted grass has narrow leaves in contrast to the broad leaves of the weeds, here most weeds and ornamentals have broad leaves.

Non-selective weedkillers can, however, be applied selectively by painting them on with a brush or special spot-treatment applicator. Glyphosate gels are ideal for dabbing on problem weeds. Alloxydium-sodium can be used where couch grass or other perennial grass weeds are troublesome. Apply it as an overall spray – except near ornamental grasses – although it will not control all grass weeds.

Hand weeding is the most effective method in a flower bed, either using a hoe or pulling out individual weeds, but be careful not to uproot or disturb the cultivated plants.

Weeds in rosebeds and shrubberies can be treated with paraquat and diquat mixtures. Use them around rose bushes, shrubs and ornamental trees but be careful to keep the chemical well clear of young green bark.

Dichlobenil can be applied well before spring growth starts if the plants have been established for at least two years. Hoeing is easy, but may accidentally damage roots and induce suckering in roses.

Weeds in lawns can to some extent be controlled through regular mowing. Isolated weeds should be removed by hand, with a daisy grubber, small hand fork, or a spot weedkiller. Selective weedkiller can be applied from late spring until early autumn. They can be bought as combined formulations with lawn fertilizers. Treat moss with a proprietary moss killer or with lawn sand in spring.

Where bulbs are naturalized in grass, do not apply weedkiller until the bulb foliage has died down and do not use chemicals on newly seeded or turfed lawns; hand-weed only for the first six months.

Weeds among fruit crops can be treated as for rosebeds and shrubberies. Paraquat and diquat mixtures and glufosinate ammonium – which have a contact action – can be applied around fruit trees and soft fruit bushes. Dichlobenil can be used around apple and pear trees and soft fruit bushes – but not around cane fruits – well before growth starts in the spring, but only when they have been established for at least two years.

Do not use weedkillers among strawberries. Hand weeding is the only safe solution.

Weeds among vegetable crops must be eradicated – they compete strongly for nutrients, water and light, significantly reducing the vegetable yield.

Hoe lightly between all vegetable rows regularly to get rid of as many germinating annual weeds as possible. Choose a warm day when the uprooted seedlings will collapse, otherwise they may re-root in the loose soil. Where weeds are growing in crop rows, handweed carefully.

Brushwood and coarse weeds on neglected areas can be treated with liquid weedkillers containing mecoprop, dicamba and 2,4-D, or with ammonium sulphamate. They are unsuitable for clearing a site just before planting as both leave residues in the soil.

Glyphosate applied from mid summer onwards will kill or strongly check most perennial weeds. It takes three or four weeks to be fully effective. The site can then be cleared and planted or sown at once.

to form flowering carpets, like the shade-loving London pride (*Saxifraga × urbium*), lungwort (*Pulmonaria* sp.), the red-flowered deadnettles (*Lamium maculatum*) and the almost-invasive evergreen, blue or white-flowered periwinkles (*Vinca* sp.).

Better in sun, but equally good as defenders of the soil, are the evergreen, blue-flowered and bronze-leaved bugles (*Ajuga reptans*), the blue catmints (*Nepeta × faassenii*) with their grey-green foliage and a long flowering season, the semi-evergreen *Viola labradorica* and several ground-hugging roses.

Low-growing shrubs give excellent ground cover over large areas, notably the evergreen spindles such as *Euonymus fortunei* 'Coloratus', tinged rose-purple in winter and 'Emerald 'n Gold', with green, gold and pink leaves. Prostrate junipers (*Juniperus horizontalis*), the evergreen Californian lilac (*Ceanothus thyrsiflorus repens*) and the hummocky rock rose (*Helianthemum* hybrids), in a range of bright colours, are other good choices. In smaller gardens, ericas spread their lush foliage beneath bell spikes, particularly valuable with the winter-flowering *Erica carnea* which, unlike other heathers, tolerates alkaline soil.

Ivies smother the ground closely in almost any situation, providing an all year-round, rich green cover as a fine backcloth for early spring bulbs underneath trees and shrubs.

▲ **Polythene mulches** Polythene, laid in spring when the ground has warmed up, helps to suppress weed growth and conserve soil moisture. They are particularly effective for thirsty crops such as Swiss chard, with its handsome ruby-red stalks.

Mulch covers

Another effective preventative measure is to cover the bare soil with a mulch. You can use straw, polythene sheeting, tree spats of bituminous felt or synthetic whalehide strawberry mats in the vegetable and fruit garden. Among ornamental plants, organic mulches are visually more pleasing and are good soil conditioners. Well-rotted leafmould, compost and stable manure can be spread in a 5-7.5cm (2-3in) deep layer over the soil, though these materials often harbour weed seeds.

Wood bark chippings make a decorative and long-lasting mulch, that withstands winds and keeps rain splashes off plants. Composted forest bark is finer in texture and a preferred peat substitute for acid-loving plants.

Small pebbles, stone chippings and coarse gravel look natural round alpine plants in the rock garden and raised beds. They keep the collars of plants dry and rot-free in winter and keep down weeds. They also act as a good obstacle to slugs and snails.

◄ **Mulch types**
Organic: (*top left*) coir; cocoa bean shells; (far right) coarse and fine bark. **Stone:** (*from top*) potting grit; horticultural grit; small pebbles; gravel; coloured and white chippings; washed pebbles; (*left*) cobbles and white pebbles.

WEEDKILLERS FOR ALL SITUATIONS

SITUATION	TYPES OF WEEDS	CHEMICAL	NOTES
Uncultivated areas, waste ground	All types, including grass weeds, woody weeds	Ammonium sulphamate	Persists for two to three months
	Woody weeds, ivy, sucker growths from old tree stumps	Ammonium sulphamate Mecoprop or dicamba with 2, 4-D	Persists for two to three months Persists for about three months
	Perennial weeds, including grasses	Glyphosate	Apply from mid summer onwards; fully effective after three to four weeks. Non-persistent
Paths and drives	Algae, moss	Dichlorophen, tar oil	Apply at any time of year
	Liverworts	Dichlorophen	Apply at any time of year
	All types, including germinating weed seeds, established annuals and perennials	Atrazine or simazine, with amitrole	Apply early spring. All path preparations control germinating weed seedlings for several months
	Mare's tail	Dichlobenil	Apply in early spring before weed emergence
Lawns	Clovers and other creeping weeds, pearlwort	Mecoprop or dicamba	Apply in spring, as grass becomes vigorous. Feed, top-dress and water lawns regularly
	Daisies and other rosette-type weeds	2, 4-D mixtures	
	Most weeds of both preceding types	Mecoprop or dicamba with 2,4-D	
	Speedwell	None effective	Rake and feed regularly to strengthen grasses
	Moss	Dichlorophen, ferrous sulphate	Give temporary control. Cultural attention needed including improved drainage, aeration and feeding
New lawns	Annual weeds	None	Avoid weedkillers for the first six months after germination of grass
Tree and shrub borders	Established annuals and perennials	Diquat with paraquat, glufosinate ammonium	Only kill green top growth of perennial weeds. Inactivated on contact with soil
	Established perennials	Glyphosate gel	Dab on individual weeds from early summer onwards
	Couch and most other grass weeds	Alloxydim-sodium	Apply as overhead spray when weeds are growing strongly
Roses	Germinating weeds, established perennials, established and seedling annuals	Dichlobenil	Apply early spring. Persists for several months
	Couch grass, perennial grasses	Alloxydim-sodium	Apply when weeds are growing strongly
Bulbs in borders	Established annuals and perennials	Diquat with paraquat	Use only after bulb foliage has been removed and the point of emergence covered with soil. Checks perennials only
Herbaceous borders	Established perennials	Glyphosate	Paint on to persistent weeds from mid summer onwards
	Couch grass and most perennial grasses	Alloxydim-sodium	Apply as overhead spray when weed grasses are growing strongly. Not with ornamental grasses
Fruit	Established annuals	Diquat with paraquat	Apply as growth starts
	Germinating weeds, established annuals and perennials	Dichlobenil	Apply in early spring around apple and pear trees and soft fruit bushes, but not cane fruits
	Grass weeds, including couch grass	Dalapon	Use in winter only
Vegetables	Germinating weeds	None	Hand-weed or hoe carefully
Pools, new	Green algae and blanket weeds	Proprietary algicides	No safe chemical control. Establish a balance of water plants and fish

Troubles in the flower garden

The gardener's foes include a number of insect pests as well as various disorders and diseases (often encouraged by unchecked weed growth). The following pages describe the range of troubles that can afflict ornamental plants, from herbaceous perennials and bulbs to shrubs and trees. Don't be too daunted – although they present a formidable picture seen together, only a small proportion is likely to be found in any one garden.

The best defence is to ensure plants are well cared for since strong-growing plants are generally healthy and able to withstand pest attacks. Plants weakened by such sap-sucking pests as aphids, slugs and snails are more likely to succumb to disease. Keep a constant eye on all plants to check whether leaves, stems or flowers look in any way sickly, distorted or discoloured. If you keep weeds down, and scrupulously remove accumulated garden debris, you will deprive common pests of their favourite hiding places. You can also discourage infestations by avoiding certain troublesome plants – honeysuckle and nasturtiums, for example, attract blackfly in large numbers, and certain rose varieties are especially prone to mildew and black spot.

A range of pesticides and fungicides can be sprayed or dusted on to infested plants once you have identified the cause of any symptoms. Make sure you use only approved chemical controls and avoid repeatedly using a particular insecticide, since many pests develop resistance to some chemicals.

Viridiflora tulips The beautiful "broken" colours of some tulips are caused by natural mutation and by a virus disease.

BULB PESTS AND DISEASES

Bulbs from reputable sources are usually healthy, but poor garden hygiene can encourage pests and diseases.

Garden plants grown from bulbs, corms, tubers and rhizomes are not especially vulnerable to pests and diseases. It's important, however, to be aware of the symptoms and causes of a number of problems so you can take early measures to eradicate them or avoid trouble from the outset. Always start with healthy stock – buy dormant bulbs from a reputable supplier – and give them the appropriate growing conditions. Never plant a sun-loving species in shade, or one which likes well-drained soil in a damp corner – it won't grow vigorously and will be more vulnerable to attack.

To get the right conditions you will need to prepare the gound before planting. If the soil is heavy, work in plenty of coarse sand or sharp, fine grit to suit bulbs requiring free-draining conditions. At the same time dig out all perennial weeds.

Fungal rots cause most problems – they attack the leaves and underground parts. Tulip fire, for instance, can cause considerable losses, spreading rapidly in wet weather from a single bulb to many others close by – especially where the bulbs are crowded. Other bulbs, lilies in particular, are susceptible to basal rot, which leads to plant collapse. Stored bulbs are particularly vulnerable to fungal diseases, so check them carefully and often.

Of the other diseases, viruses are the most damaging, although individual plants may take a long time to succumb. Sucking insects, such as aphids, are mainly responsible for transmitting viruses from one plant to another – so make sure these pests are kept in check, even when their direct damage seems of little consequence.

Inevitably, the food supply so neatly packaged in a bulb, corm or tuber is attractive to a number of pests, including mice, eelworms and the grubs of several insects. Leaves and flowers are less frequently attacked, although thrips can disfigure gladioli and birds mutilate crocus flowers.

In addition to pests and diseases, bulbs may be affected by disorders from other sources. Blindness, for example, is a disorder of narcissi and tulips, especially when container-grown, in which the flower bud actually ceases to develop. The causes are quite varied – pest and disease attack may be responsible, and perhaps waterlogged soil, very dry conditions, nutrient deficiency, or exposure of the bulbs to high temperatures after lifting.

Secondary diseases may also infect bulbs which have already succumbed to pest or disease damage. Bacterial soft rot, for example, usually invades cut or bruised tissues. Preventative measures are more effective than cures – maintain a balanced soil nutrient content, avoid waterlogging, eliminate wound-forming pests and diseases and handle lifted bulbs carefully.

Chemical treatment

Pesticides and other chemicals for disease control can be expensive, and you may prefer not to use them for ecological reasons. Chemicals referred to here are the active ingredients, not the proprietary names – read the contents label of each package carefully and follow manufacturers' instructions meticulously. If you adopt a wait-and-see policy, be vigilant and take quick action to limit damage if it occurs. Always destroy diseased bulbs – preferably burn them – and never put them on the compost heap.

◄ **Bulbs and tubers** Firm in texture, dry to the touch and with visible growth buds, these bulbs and corms are in prime condition. They include crocus corms, narcissi, tulip, lily and hyacinth bulbs as well as the fleshy roots of the foxtail lily (*Eremurus* sp.). Store in cool, dry conditions until planting time.

BASAL ROT

Plants affected Crocuses, lilies and narcissi.
Symptoms Roots and corm bases show dark strands from the base, or brown rot spreading through the inner scales.
Danger period All year, including storage.
Treatment Destroy rotten bulbs. Dip newly lifted bulbs in a solution of carbendazim or thiophanate-methyl. In early stages, cut out affected roots and scales of lily bulbs.

BULB SCALE MITES

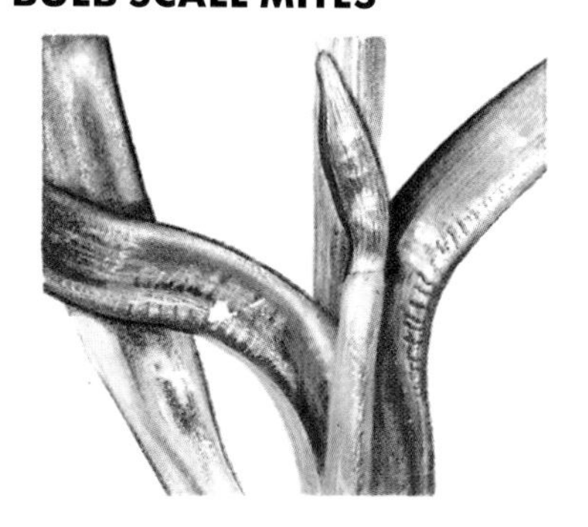

Plants affected Narcissi, amaryllis
Symptoms Deformed leaves and stems, especially on forced plants. Damaged tissue often covered with russet-brown scars.
Danger period Mid winter to mid spring.
Treatment Destroy severely damaged plants. No chemical treatment available. Expose bulbs for forcing to frost for two to three nights one week before planting.

CORE ROT

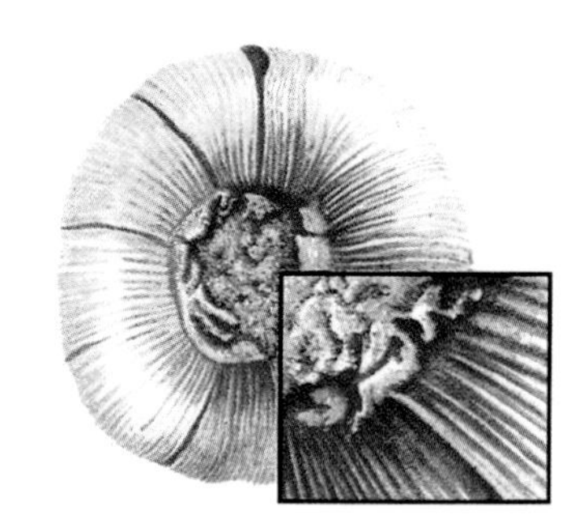

Plants affected Acidantheras, freesias and gladioli.
Symptoms Corms become spongy and dark brown or black, rotting from the centre outwards (often unnoticed until too late).
Danger period During storage.
Treatment Dip corms in a solution of carbendazim or thiophanate-methyl. Store in a dry atmosphere at a temperature of 7-10°C (45-50°F). Destroy affected corms by burning.

DRY ROT

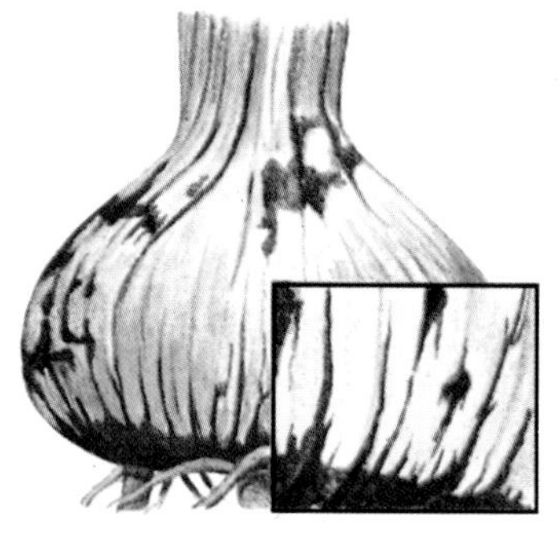

Plants affected Gladioli; also related plants such as acidantheras, crocuses and freesias.
Symptoms Top growth turns yellow, then brown and finally topples over, caused by rot of the leaf sheaths. Affected leaves are covered with tiny black clusters. Many small, dark lesions also develop on corms, which eventually merge to form larger black areas; finally, the corms shrivel completely and die.
Danger period Top growth affected during growing season; corms affected in storage.
Treatment Remove and destroy affected corms as soon as first symptoms appear. Dip corms in carbendazim or thiophanate-methyl solution, before storing or replanting them.

Plant corms in a fresh site each year – the fungus causing dry rot is soil borne. Improved soil cultivation helps to prevent spread of the disease.

GLADIOLUS THRIPS

Plants affected Gladioli and related species, such as acidantheras.
Symptoms Fine silvery flecks on petals and foliage; in severe cases, flowers discolour completely and may die.
Danger period Early summer to early autumn.
Treatment Dust corms with HCH powder before storage and planting. Treat affected plants with HCH, malathion or dimethoate.

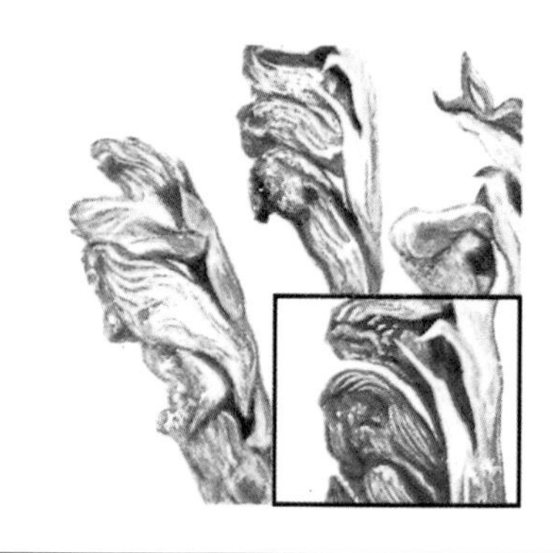

GREY BULB ROT

Plants affected Hyacinths, tulips; also sometimes crocuses, fritillaries, gladioli, irises and narcissi.
Symptoms Dry, grey rot at the bulb neck, soon developing into large areas of black fungal clusters which cause the bulb to disintegrate. Emergence of plants in an infected bed is patchy, those that do appear usually being stunted and discoloured; they eventually die.
Danger period Soon after bulbs are planted.
Treatment Remove and destroy debris from diseased plants, and replace surrounding soil with sterilized compost. No chemical treatment available to amateur gardeners. Grow bulbs on a different site each year.

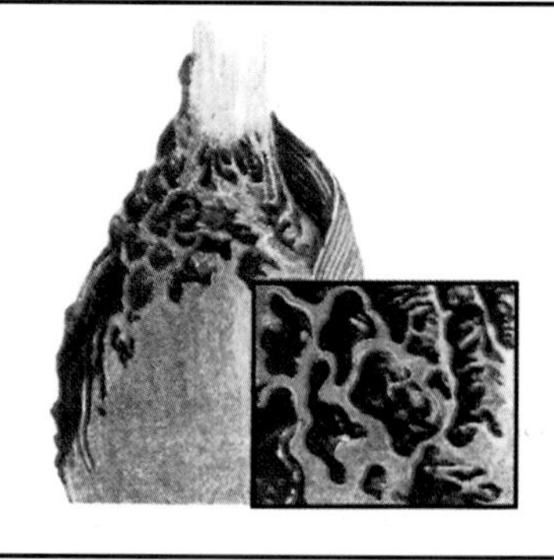

HARD ROT

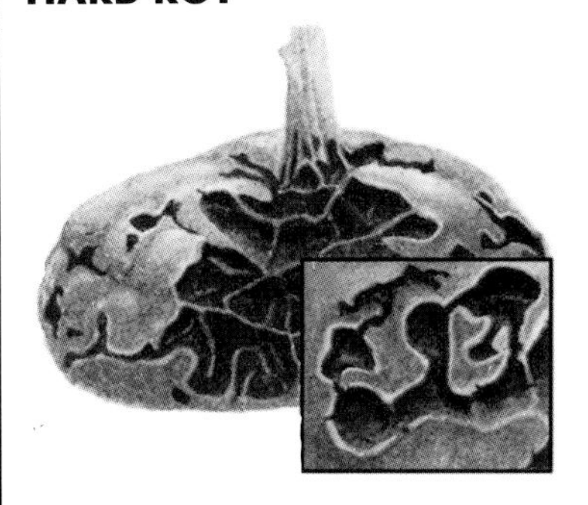

Plants affected Gladioli and acidantheras.
Symptoms Brown spots on leaves, which develop small black fungi. Black-brown, sunken spots on corms; may become hard and shrivelled.
Danger period Infection in summer; symptoms may appear during storage.
Treatment Dip corms in a solution of carbendazim or thiophanate-methyl before storing. Destroy affected corms.

NARCISSUS FLIES

Plants affected Narcissi, snowdrops and amaryllis.
Symptoms Leaves deformed, narrow and yellow; no flowers. Bulbs rotten, grey-brown larvae inside.
Danger period Late spring to early summer; symptoms usually spotted too late at planting time.
Treatment Destroy soft bulbs at planting time. Cultivate soil around plants in early summer – preventing flies entering the soil to lay eggs.

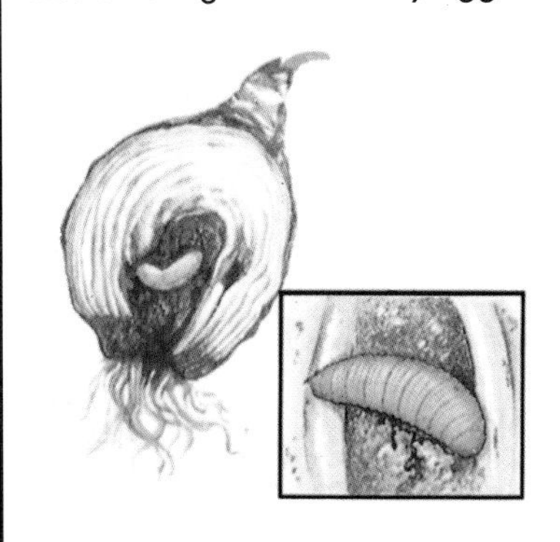

RHIZOME ROT

Plants affected Rhizomatous irises.
Symptoms Soft, yellow, acrid-smelling rot at the growing point; leaf fan collapses at ground level.
Danger period Any time; most prevalent in wet weather.
Treatment Improve soil drainage. Control slugs and other pests. Cut out rotting parts and dip leaf fringes repeatedly in disinfectant; destroy seriously affected plants.

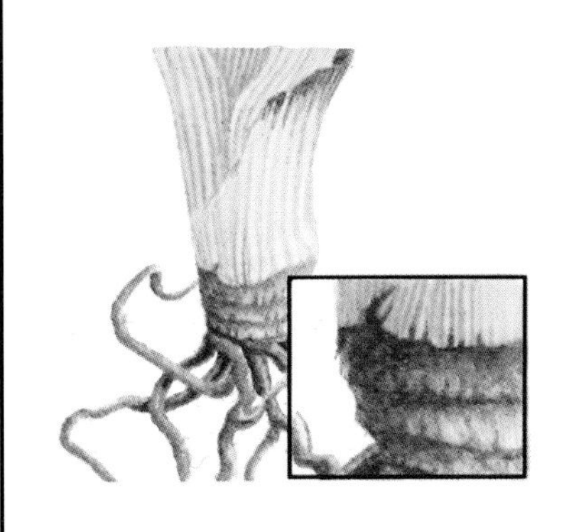

SCAB

Plants affected Gladioli species and varieties.
Symptoms Red-brown specks on leaves, enlarging to form dark brown spots. Stems may decay and keel over at ground level in wet weather. Round, sunken craters appear in the corm base, each with a prominent raised rim.
Danger period Infection occurs during summer, but symptoms may not be noticed until corms are lifted for storage.
Treatment Destroy affected corms. Dip remaining healthy corms in a solution of carbendazim or thiophanate-methyl.

Grow corms in a fresh site each year to prevent re-occurrence of the disease.

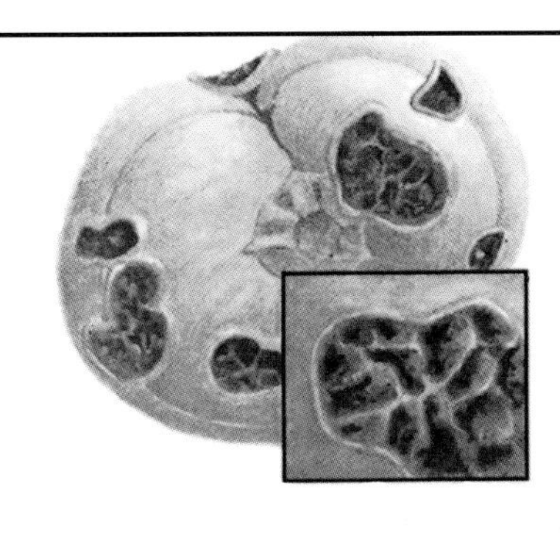

SLUGS AND SNAILS

Plants affected Acidantheras, alliums, alstroemerias, chionodoxas, daffodils and narcissi, dahlias, hyacinths, irises, lilies, puschkinias and tulips.
Symptoms Irregular holes eaten in leaves, stems, buds and flowers; sometimes also in bulbs and roots. Tell-tale slime tracks on damaged plants and surrounding soil.
Danger period Mainly warm and humid spells during spring and autumn. Slugs and snails generally feed at night.
Treatment Cultivate soil thoroughly and remove accumulations of decaying plant material. Avoid heavy dressings of organic manures and mulches. Scatter methiocarb or metaldehyde slug baits or use aluminium sulphate-based slug killers. A broad ring of grit scattered on the soil around each plant is also some deterrent.

SMOULDER

Plants affected Narcissi.
Symptoms Leaves rot; covered with grey, velvety mould. Bulbs decay.
Danger period During storage; foliage symptoms appear in spring.
Treatment Store cool and dry. Destroy affected bulbs immediately. Spray nearby plants with carbendazim or thiophanate-methyl.

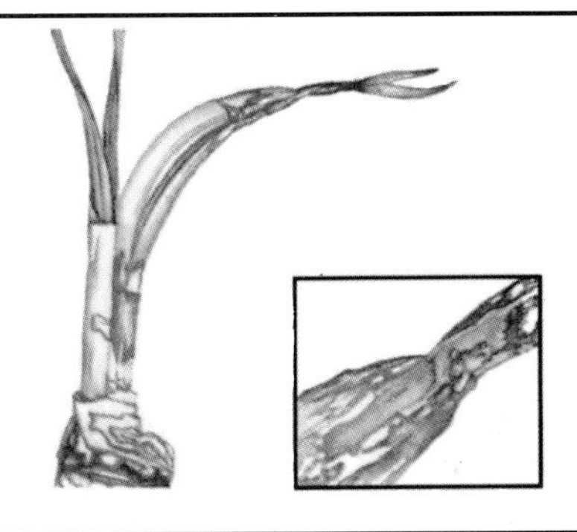

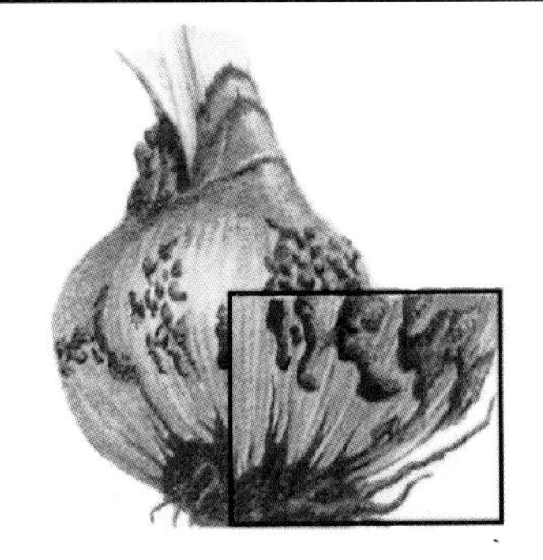

STEM AND BULB EELWORMS

Plants affected Narcissi, sometimes hyacinths, irises, scillas, snowdrops and tulips.
Symptoms Leaves stunted and deformed. Small, rough, yellowish-brown bumps on daffodil leaves; longitudinal splits in leaves and bending of flower stalks in tulips. Bulbs discoloured internally, eventually rotting away.
Danger period Growing plants mainly affected in spring; dormant bulbs show symptoms in late summer and autumn.
Treatment Dig up and burn affected plants. Do not replant bulbs in the affected area for at least three years.

Eelworms multiply rapidly within plant tissues and chemical control is difficult. Effective pesticides are not available for small-scale use.

TULIP BULB APHIDS

Plants affected Crocuses, gladioli, irises and tulips.
Symptoms Pale brown or green aphids infest stored bulbs; also damage growth after planting.
Danger period Winter/spring.
Treatment Dust bulbs with HCH. Malathion or HCH sprays may be effective, but dry bulbs thoroughly afterwards or plant out.

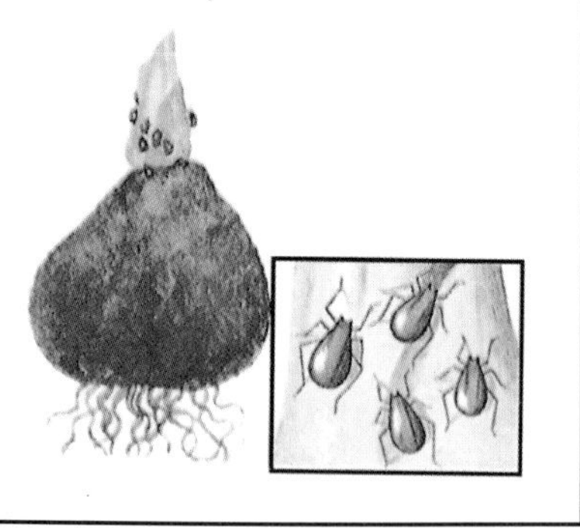

TULIP FIRE

Plants affected Tulips.
Symptoms Young shoots are stunted and rot above ground, becoming covered with grey, velvety mould. Small, brown spots on flower petals, later becoming covered in mould. Bulbs rot and bear small, black fungal growths.
Danger period Bulbs affected shortly before or after planting; shoots and flowers in spring.
Treatment Destroy rotting bulbs as soon as detected – spread is very rapid. Plant on a fresh site each year, particularly after the disease has appeared. Spray with mancozeb when leaves are about 5cm (2in) tall; repeat at 10-day intervals until flowering.

Within 24 hours of lifting, dip bulbs in a solution of carbendazim or thiophanate-methyl.

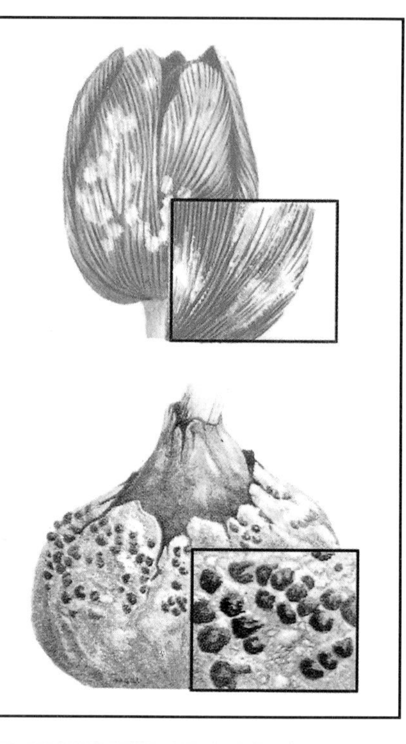

OTHER PESTS AND DISEASES

A number of other pests, diseases and disorders may occasionally affect bulbs, corms and tubers.

Bacterial soft rot Quite common among bulbs, both in the garden and in store. Invades tissues already damaged. Watery lesions appear around a wound, which enlarge quickly to form bad-smelling, slimy patches, or the tissues may totally disintegrate. Growing leaves may be affected, as may stored bulbs. Chemical control is rarely successful, though small infections may be cut out of the bulbs, which should then be dusted with Bordeaux mixture powder. Eliminate wound-forming pests, and maintain good cultural conditions – unhealthy tissues are most susceptible. Burn infected material.

Botrytis/grey mould Common on flowers and buds, and may be associated with stem and leaf rots. Greyish mould covers the affected surface – it spreads rapidly by air currents. Avoid overcrowding bulbs, don't plant in damp, shady sites, dead-head frequently and spray diseased plants with benomyl, carbendazim or thiophanate-methyl fungicide.

Cutworms Noctuid moth caterpillars which cut through stems at ground level, cause wilting and top-growth death. Hoe out weeds regularly since they attract egg-laying adults. Dig over soil in winter to expose caterpillars to their predators. Treat surrounding soil with diazinon + chlorpyrifos or HCH.

Iris leaf spot Affects irises and other members of the iris family, such as acidantheras, forming yellow-edged brown spots in spring which later enlarge into oval patches with a grey central mould and a reddish edge (on bulbous irises the blotches don't have the distinct edging and are greyer). Outbreaks are worse in wet seasons. Dress the soil with lime, spray with Bordeaux mixture or other copper fungicide or with mancozeb.

Leatherjackets Cranefly (daddy-long-legs) larvae cause symptoms similar to those of cutworms, mainly in spring. Hoe HCH powder or diazinon + chlorpyrifos into the soil to protect plants. Cultivate soil thoroughly, well before planting.

Mice Eat almost anything, but juicy bulbs – especially crocus, narcissi, lilies and tulips – are often favoured, both in store and in the open ground. Set traps in storage buildings. Animal repellant dusts applied at planting time may deter mice.

Powdery mildew Forms a white coating on leaves and stems, especially on begonias. Plants may droop and leaves turn yellow. Spray regularly with benomyl, propiconazole or triforine with bupirimate or spray or dust with sulphur.

Smut A fungal disease forming black, sooty patches. Some forms spread through the plant's veins, reproducing in the roots or bulbs. Burn infected plants and replant on a new site.

Swift moth caterpillars Similar to cutworms, but live below ground.

BORDER PLANT TROUBLES

Annual, biennial and perennial plants can be liable to attack by several pests and diseases, but they are rarely fatal.

Border and bedding plants are mostly quite quick-growing plants with soft, relatively succulent leaves and stems. This often makes them particularly attractive to sap-sucking, chewing and biting pests such as aphids, caterpillars, slugs and snails.

Fungal diseases and rots are also able to infest the soft tissues of annuals and perennials more easily than the woody stems of shrubs and trees.

The following pages will help you to recognize and control these pests and diseases. Although they present a formidable picture when seen all together, only a small number are likely to attack a single plant or infest a garden.

Keep a constant eye on all your plants to see whether the leaves, stems or flowers are in any way unhealthy. Distorted or discoloured tissues, for example, are sure signs of a problem. Practise good garden hygiene at all times, weeding, mulching and feeding regularly – strong-growing plants are healthy plants, able to withstand disease attacks better than weak specimens.

Plants which have been regularly troubled by pests or diseases in previous years should be protected against them in advance. Cultivate regularly all soils known to harbour pests.

When using liquid chemicals to protect plants or destroy pests and diseases, always spray in dull, still weather. Spray drift can contaminate nearby food crops. Don't spray or dust plants when they are in flower since you may also kill pollinating insects, such as bees. Never spray in hot sunshine – leaf-scorch will result.

▼ **Slug and snail damage** Moist shady conditions are preferred by hostas – also by slugs and snails, which can reduce leaves to skeletons. Slime trails betray their presence.

APHIDS

Plants affected Almost all cultivated plants.
Symptoms Small, mostly wingless, rather plump insects cluster in large numbers on tips of young shoots and below flower buds. Several types may occur – coloured green, grey, brown or black. They excrete a sticky honeydew which fouls foliage below the attack. Black sooty mould is a common secondary infection on the sticky leaves. Aphids multiply rapidly, sucking plant sap and thus distorting and stunting shoots.
Danger period Spring and summer.
Treatment Spray with pyrethrum, malathion or pirimicarb as soon as detected; repeat as necessary. For control over a longer period, treat with a systemic insecticide, such as dimethoate or heptenophos – before spraying ensure plants are well watered or they may be scorched.

CAPSID BUGS

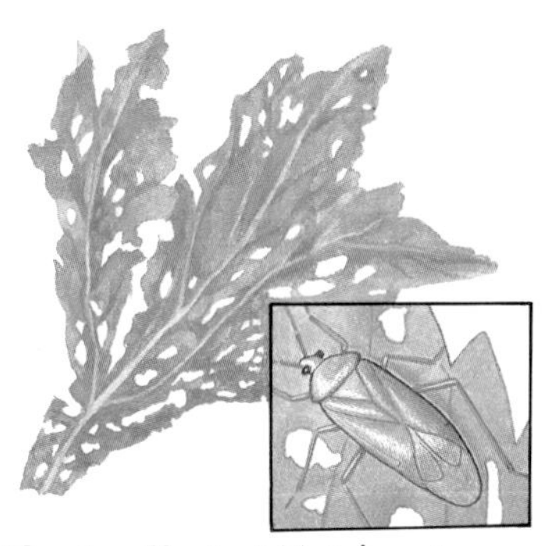

Plants affected Mainly asters, chrysanthemums, dahlias, fuchsias, pelargoniums, salvias, sunflowers and zinnias.
Symptoms Tattered holes appear in young leaves.
Danger period Late spring to late summer.
Treatment Spray with dimethoate or treat plants with fenitrothion or malathion. Kill weeds which harbour bugs.

CLUB ROOT

Plants affected Stocks, wallflowers and other members of the cabbage family.
Symptoms Roots become swollen and distorted. Plants are weakened and turn yellow.
Danger period Growing season.
Treatment Apply hydrated lime to raise soil pH to 7.5. Rake 4% calomel dust into soil before planting or dip roots in thiophanate-methyl.

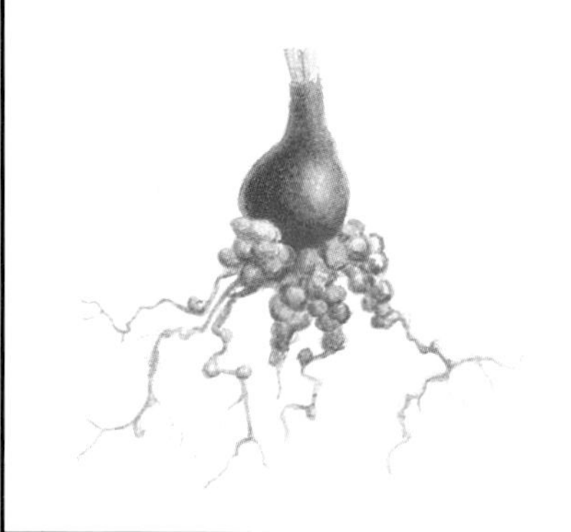

EARWIGS

Plants affected Chrysanthemums, cinerarias, dahlias, delphiniums, pansies, violas and zinnias.
Symptoms Irregular, tattered holes in leaves and petals.
Danger period Late spring to mid autumn.
Treatment Spray or dust with HCH or pirimiphos + methyl. Trap earwigs in flowerpots stuffed with straw, then destroy them.

FOOT ROT

Plants affected Bedding plants.
Symptoms Stem bases, which may be discoloured, rot and roots usually die.
Danger period Growing season.
Treatment Rotate bedding plants from year to year. Water bedding plants grown in seed boxes with Cheshunt compound or copper oxychloride when put in their planting holes.

FROGHOPPERS

Plants affected Campanulas, chrysanthemums, golden rods, perennial asters, phlox, lavender, rudbeckias and many others.
Symptoms Frothy masses of 'cuckoo spit' covering small green insects in leaf axils.
Danger period Summer.
Treatment Wash off 'cuckoo spit' with a powerful jet of water from a garden hose or spray with malathion or HCH.

GREY MOULD (BOTRYTIS)

Plants affected All plants.
Symptoms Grey, velvety mould on rotting leaves and flowers, especially under glass or in secluded sites.
Danger period Growing season.
Treatment Destroy infected plants. Don't overcrowd plants in damp, shady sites. Spray with benomyl, carbendazim or thiophanate-methyl.

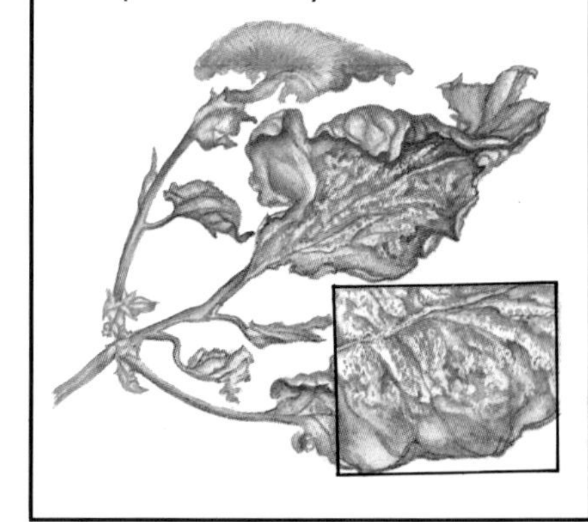

LEAFY GALL

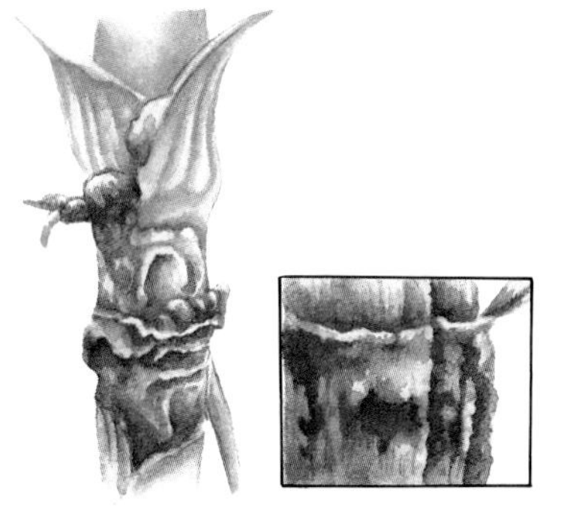

Plants affected Many types, but particularly carnations, chrysanthemums, pelargoniums and sweet peas.
Symptoms Abortive, often flattened shoots with thickened, distorted leaves develop at ground level.
Danger period During propagation and throughout growing season.
Treatment Destroy infected plants. Don't grow susceptible plants on the same site again.

PETAL BLIGHT

Plants affected Chrysanthemums; sometimes cornflowers.
Symptoms Dark, water-soaked spots or blotches spread on petals until flowers rot.
Danger period At flowering time, particularly in hot, wet summers.
Treatment Control is not easy. Destroy affected flowers immediately by cutting them off and burning them. Avoid high humidity when growing under glass; ventilate freely.

PETUNIA WILT

Plants affected Petunias; also salpiglossis and zinnias.
Symptoms Plants wilt, often as they are about to flower. Stem bases may be discoloured.
Danger period Growing season.
Treatment Rotate bedding plants from year to year so that susceptible ones are grown on a fresh site each year. Water planting holes with Cheshunt compound or copper oxychloride and drench plants with either weekly. Burn diseased plants.

POWDERY MILDEW

Plants affected Forget-me-nots, golden rods, Michaelmas daisies.
Symptoms White, floury coating mainly on leaves and shoots.
Danger period Growing season.
Treatment Spray with copper, carbendazim, propiconazole, thiophanate-methyl or spray or dust with sulphur. Repeat as necessary. Burn diseased shoots at end of season.

RUST

Plants affected Many types, but especially antirrhinums, hollyhocks and pelargoniums.
Symptoms Brown, orange or yellow powdery masses of spores develop on leaves and stems.
Danger period Growing season.
Treatment Burn all diseased leaves. Spray with bupirimate + triforine, propiconazole, mancozeb or thiram at ten to fourteen-day intervals.

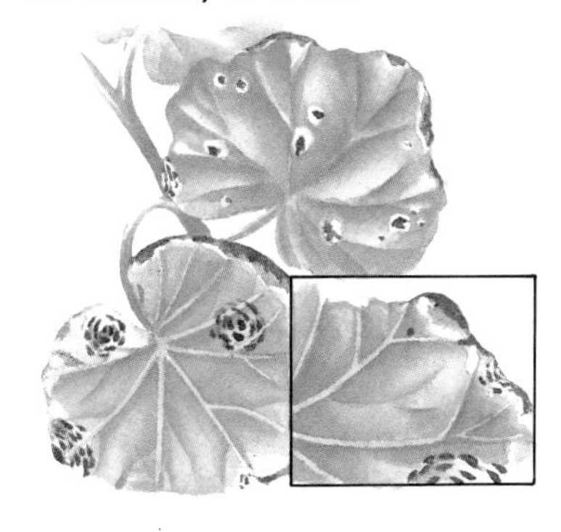

SLUGS AND SNAILS

Plants affected Anemones, delphiniums, hostas, primulas, rudbeckias, sweet peas, violets and many other plants.
Symptoms Irregular holes eaten in leaves and flowers. Slime tracks.
Danger period Growing season.
Treatment Clear up decaying plant material. Avoid heavy dressings of organic material. Sprinkle proprietary slug pellets or use aluminium sulphate sprays.

STEM ROT

Plants affected Carnations, godetias and lobelias.
Symptoms Rotting of stems, but no obvious fungal growth visible. The same fungus may cause basal rot of carnation cuttings taken from diseased plants.

Black leg disease also causes rotting of pelargonium cuttings at the stem base and collapse. Affected tissues are soft and black.
Danger period Growing season; black leg soon after cuttings are taken.
Treatment Where possible, cut out and burn affected parts; spray with Bordeaux mixture, except on pelargoniums for which no chemical treatment is available. Destroy badly affected plants. Maintain good hygiene during propagation.

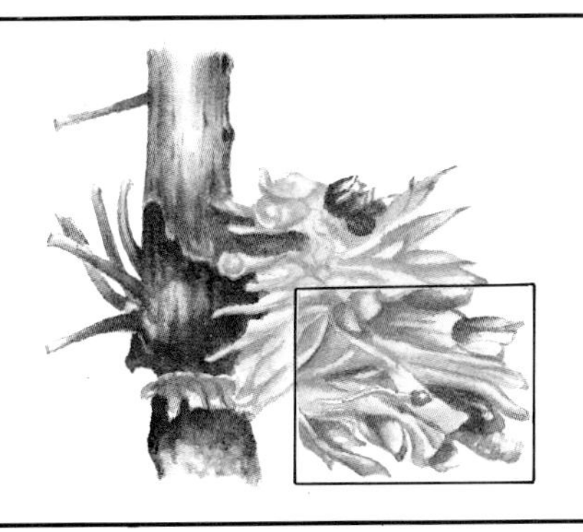

SWIFT MOTHS

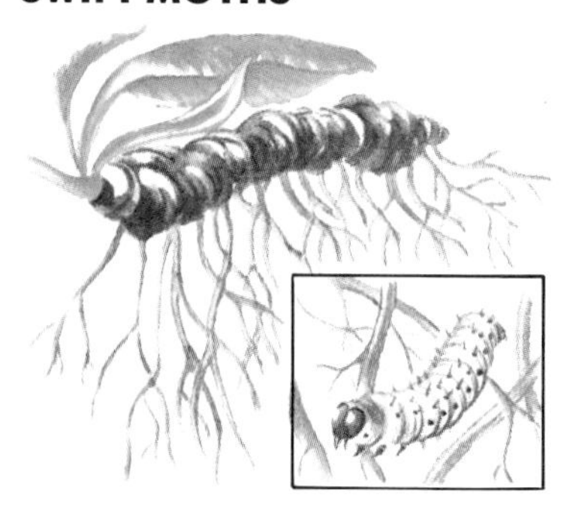

Plants affected Various herbaceous perennials.
Symptoms Off-white caterpillars of the swift moth, which live in the soil and feed on the roots. See also Cutworms, below.
Danger period Any time of year.
Treatment Weed control and cultivation reduce the risk of attack. Protect susceptible plants by working diazinon + chlorpyrifos or HCH dust into the soil.

TORTRIX MOTHS

Plants affected Many herbaceous plants, especially phlox, chrysanthemums and heleniums.
Symptoms Caterpillars eat irregular, small holes in leaves and bind them with silk webbing.
Danger period Late spring to summer.
Treatment Spray thoroughly with fenitrothion or permethrin. Destroy individual caterpillars by hand.

VIRUSES

Plants affected Many types of plant, but particularly chrysanthemums, pelargoniums, violas and wallflowers.
Symptoms Leaves crinkled, small and sometimes irregularly shaped. Flowers distorted, or colour broken – white streaks, or stripes in a lighter or darker shade. May not affect vigour.
Danger period Growing season.
Treatment Dig up and burn.

WHITEFLY

Plants affected Mainly a pest of indoor and greenhouse plants, but often appears on container bedding plants on a patio, especially regal pelargoniums.
Symptoms White -winged flies like tiny moths, on leaf undersides – often fly off when disturbed. Tiny white scale-like nymphs may also be present. No obvious damage to leaves, but plants are depleted of strength by these sap-sucking insects.
Danger period Late spring to early autumn; all year indoors or in a heated greenhouse.
Treatment Spray regularly and thoroughly with pirimiphos-methyl, permethrin or insecticidal soaps. Destroy badly infested plants by burning.

OTHER PESTS AND DISEASES

Birds , especially house sparrows, may damage flowers, buds and leaves, usually in search of seeds. Their favourite targets are low-growing, bushy, continuously flowering plants such as marigolds. Dead-head to prevent seed production. Chemical bird repellents are available, but have variable success. Keep seed beds moist and covered with black cotton to deter birds from dust-bathing.
Chafer beetle larvae are C-shaped whitish grubs with three pairs of legs and a brown head. They eat the roots of many annuals and herbaceous perennials, causing top-growth to wilt and die. Apply HCH or diazinon + chlorpyrifos to the soil before planting or work in around the roots.
Crown gall affects many herbaceous plants, mainly causing irregular, often quite large, knobbly swellings at the base of the stem. Destroy affected plants.
Cutworms are fat greyish-brown caterpillars living in the soil. They eat through young shoots at soil level and are most troublesome on light soils in dry summers. Plants keel over and die. Control weeds which encourage cutworms. Cultivate soil in winter to expose cutworms – birds then eat them. Protect susceptible young plants as for Chafer grubs.
Damping-off is a common disease of young seedlings, especially under glass. Seedlings keel over and die. Avoid overcrowding by sowing thinly. Use sterilized seed compost for sowing indoors. Don't overwater and keep well ventilated. Water with Cheshunt compound or copper oxychloride. Remove dead seedlings immediately they collapse.
Leatherjackets are the legless, greyish-brown larvae of craneflies (daddy-long-legs). They are pests of newly cultivated soil and feed on roots and stems. Young plants are damaged in spring, but attacks may occur throughout the growing season. Plants turn yellow, wilt and die. Protect plants by working HCH or diazinon + chlorpyrifos into the soil. Hoe soil regularly and improve drainage – birds eat grubs which are brought to the surface.
Red spider mites are a serious pest of house plants, but also infest outdoor bedding perennials in summer. Leaves are faintly speckled, eventually discolouring, wilting and dying. As mites swarm over the plant, very fine webbing is visible. Spray with dimethoate, pirimiphos-methyl, malathion or derris. Dig up and burn seriously infested plants. See also biological pest control, page 86.
Sclerotinia disease can affect all types of herbaceous plants, but is most common on sunflowers (*Helianthus*). A brown, wettish rot forms at the base of stems, often with a mass of white mould. Plants wilt and lower leaves turn yellow; stems may keel over. Dig up and burn infected material. Control weeds which also harbour the disease.

WATER PLANT TROUBLES

Deep water and marginal aquatic plants are susceptible to a few destructive pests and diseases, the control of which demands special care.

Most water plants are perennials and, as such, share some of the pest and disease problems associated with their terrestrial cousins. Indeed, the marginal aquatic types – those which grow in wet soil at the edge of the water with most of their foliage above the water surface – suffer from the same troubles that you would expect of border perennials.

There are two main difficulties in overcoming water plant pests and diseases – access to the plants for hand control is often impossible or at best precarious, and chemical control is usually inadvisable, especially if there are fish or other livestock in the pool. Most chemical pesticides are poisonous to fish.

To add to the problem, many water plants are scorched by chemical pesticides, so even if you don't have any fish you shouldn't spray water plants with chemicals. In many cases, pest infestations can be controlled with forceful jets from a hose to dislodge insect larvae and eggs; this is particularly effective where the pool is stocked with fish.

In general, the most effective way of dealing with serious outbreaks of pests and diseases is to cut off and destroy all the affected stems, leaves and flowers. You may have to crawl across the pool on a sturdy scaffold board, or wade in the pool to get to the plants. But never wade in any pool which is lined only with PVC, butyl rubber or glass fibre – you will puncture or crack it.

When using a scaffold board for access across a glass fibre pool, raise the ends of the board above the edges of the pool using a few bricks or paving slabs, otherwise the weight may crack the preformed liner.

Fish and other livestock can do much towards eliminating water pests, as well as adding to the tranquil charm of the pool. They eat the larvae and grubs of pests such as caddis flies and water lily beetles, together with other undesirable water-dwellers like mosquito larvae.

Fish, however, also have their predators, notably the domestic cat and herons. Small pools can be protected with a fine wire-mesh covering and herons, a protected species, which usually feed from a standing position in the water, can be deterred by stretching plastic-covered wires along the inside edges of the pool.

▼ **Water lily beetle** In early summer, water lily beetles and brown china mark moths migrate from poolside vegetation to lay clusters of eggs on water lily leaves. They hatch into larvae and caterpillars that feed voraciously on flowers and foliage.

BROWN CHINA MARK MOTH

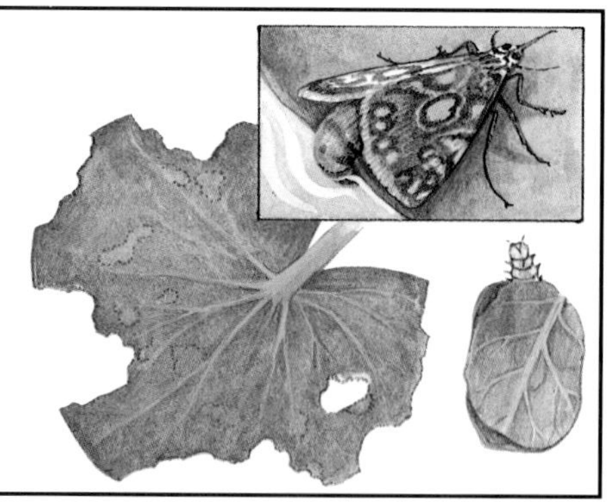

Plants affected Floating aquatic plants, especially water lilies.
Symptoms Small brown and white moths lay eggs on floating leaves. These hatch into small caterpillars, which chew oval segments out of the leaves and use them to build protective cases around themselves. At first, the cases are attached to the undersides of the leaves, but as the caterpillars grow and build larger cases they float on the water. Caterpillars feed on leaves, cutting more unsightly holes.
Danger period Eggs laid in mid to late summer; caterpillars begin eating leaves two weeks later.
Treatment Remove cases by hand. Cut off and burn the leaves of badly infested plants to promote new growth.

CADDIS FLIES

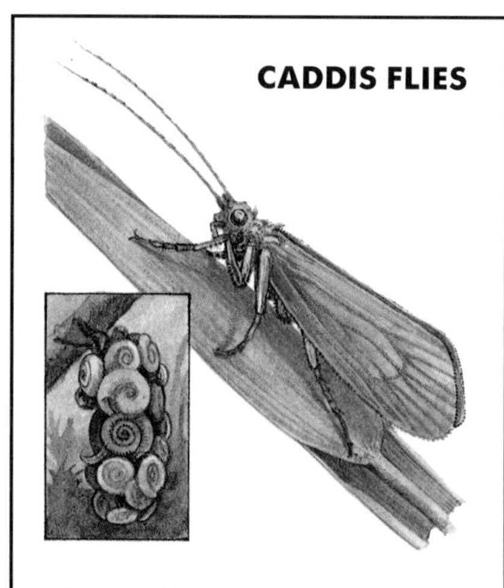

Plants affected Any aquatic or floating plants.
Symptoms Moth-like insects lay jelly-like trails of eggs in the water. Larvae build protective cases around themselves and feed on water plants. Damage is rarely severe.
Danger period Summer.
Treatment Remove by hand and destroy any larvae cases.

WATER LILY APHIDS

Plants affected Water lilies and poolside plants.
Symptoms Colonies of greyish-black aphids disfigure leaves and flowers.
Danger period Growing season.
Treatment Knock aphids into the water by squirting with a hosepipe – fish then eat them. Or drown them with sacking or weighted netting to submerge the leaves for several hours.

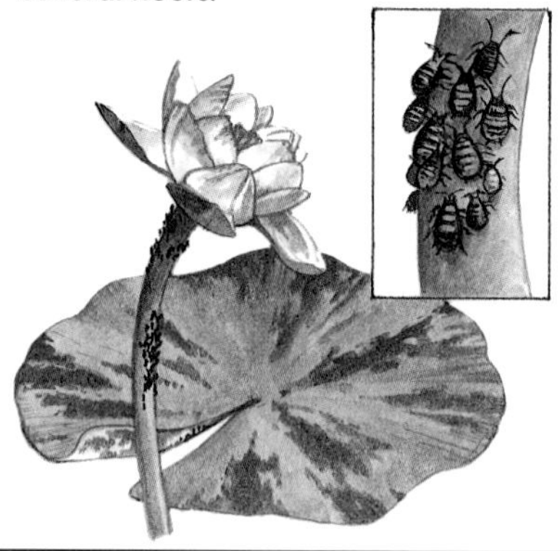

WATER LILY BEETLES

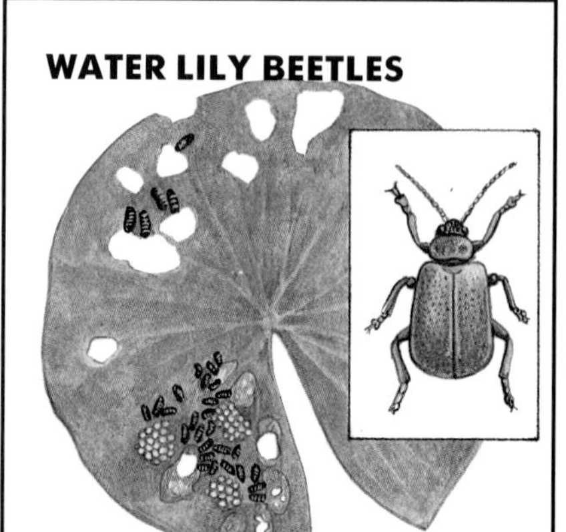

Plants affected Mainly water lilies.
Symptoms Small dark brown beetles, 6mm (¼in) long, lay eggs on the leaves. These hatch into leaf-eating, yellow-bellied, brownish black larvae.
Danger period Early to late summer.
Treatment As for water lily aphids.

OTHER POOL TROUBLES

Leaf miners – the grubs of certain midges – tunnel through the inner tissues of water plant leaves, leaving translucent trails and causing disfigurement and loss of vigour. In severe cases, the leaves can be reduced to skeletons.

Fish eat these grubs and generally keep them under control, but if you don't have any fish in the pool, pick off by hand and destroy infested leaves. False leaf-mining midges do not tunnel into the leaf tissues, but eat out serpentine lines over leaf surfaces, giving the same effect.

Leaf spot disease may affect water lilies, causing dark blotches on the leaves, which eventually rot and disintegrate. This disease occurs mainly in very humid summers.

If you don't have any fish or other livestock, spray the foliage with Bordeaux mixture. Otherwise, pick off by hand and destroy affected leaves, preferably by burning them.

Another type of leaf spot disease – which should be treated in the same way – causes brown, dried out patches on the leaves. Seriously infected leaves eventually crumble away and the disease spreads rapidly. In severe cases the whole stock will have to be replaced.

Pond snails are not pests, unless they occur in plague proportions – small numbers actually do good by eating decaying leaves, fish droppings and algae which foul the pond.

Fish eat snail eggs and generally keep them under control. Scoop out excess populations of snails using a child's fishing net.

Root rot is a fungal disease which sometimes affects water lilies. Leaves and flower stalks become black and rot spreads down to the roots which turn slimy, usually with an unpleasant smell. Destroy affected leaves or pull up the entire plant in severe cases.

Slugs and land snails devour the succulent young leaves and stems of many bog plants and marginal aquatics growing around the edges of a pool, being attracted by the constantly moist environment. They eat ragged holes and leave characteristic slime trails.

The only really effective method of control is to scatter proprietary slug pellets around susceptible plants, or to spray the ground with a slug and snail egg killer. Avoid dropping bait in the pond, especially if there are fish in it; keep pets away from treated areas.

Frogs can occasionally become a menace at breeding time in spring and may attack small and weak ornamental fish.

ROSE PESTS AND DISEASES

Roses suffer from their fair share of pests and diseases, but few pose a real threat. With routine control, serious problems can be avoided.

As with all garden plants, the surest way to keep rose pest and disease attacks to a minimum is to maintain the best possible cultural conditions. Vigorous, actively growing plants are invariably better able to cope with minor physical damage to foliage than those which are already sickly due to nutrient, light or water deficiencies.

There are a few problems, however, which nearly every rose grower will experience. Black spot, mildew, rust and aphids are, sadly, synonymous with rose growing, but they should not deter you – most healthy plants will tolerate at least minor outbreaks without undue loss of bloom or overall performance.

Certain problems, such as black spot, may be more serious in one region than another. It is less troublesome in industrial areas than in smokeless zones – country gardens may be less affected than town ones, for example.

Powdery mildew, the most common of all rose diseases, can cause particular problems where roses are grown closely together and in shady sites. Where the disease is prevalent, it may be a good idea to dig up and burn badly affected plants and replace them, in a fresh site, with varieties known to be resistant to mildew, such as 'Crimson Shower', 'Silver Jubilee' and many others.

Above all, watch out for early signs of attack and take measures to eliminate pests and diseases before they get a hold. Once a rose is neglected, it's difficult to cure it – whether by cultural or chemical means – so plan a regular programme of spraying.

Fungicides work best when sprayed evenly over both upper and lower leaf surfaces, so producing a protective barrier against infection. When actively growing, new shoots should be protected at two-week intervals, especially against mildew – fungicides are much more effective as preventative measures than as a cure. Begin spraying as soon as active growth is under way in late spring. Also spray after heavy rain, when the protection may have been washed away.

Insecticides are best sprayed less frequently. One early treatment in late spring, followed by a second dose a month later, is usually sufficient, but follow the manufacturer's instructions for rate and frequency of application. Spray once more in early autumn. Avoid continuous use of one chemical – some pests and diseases can develop resistance quite quickly – it's a good idea to keep at least two available.

There are some proprietary chemical 'cocktails' available which give combined protection against diseases such as mildew and black spot, and pests such as aphids. These make the job of regular spraying much simpler.

Many other chemicals are available which control specific pests and diseases, either by direct surface contact or by systemic action. Suitable types are recommended under each of the problems on the following pages – names of chemicals refer to the active ingredient as specified in the manufacturer's ingredients which are listed on the label of the bottle or packet, not to brand names.

◄ **Black spot** This virulent rose disease can cause the loss of most leaves, especially on heavily pruned hybrid tea roses. It overwinters on fallen leaves – rake them up and burn them.

APHIDS

Symptoms Small, mostly wingless, rather plump insects cluster in large numbers on tips of young shoots and buds. Several types may occur – coloured green, pinkish, orange or black. They excrete a sticky honeydew which fouls foliage below the attack. Black sooty mould is a common secondary infection on the sticky leaves. Aphids multiply rapidly, sucking sap and thus distorting and stunting the rose shoots.
Danger period Spring and early summer mainly, but may persist through the growing season.
Treatment Start early in the growing season, using a fine spray of malathion or pirimicarb to control initial attacks; repeat several times at three-day intervals. For control over a longer period, treat with a systemic insecticide, such as dimethoate or heptenophos. Permethrin or pyrethrum may also be effective. Before spraying systemic insecticides, ensure plants are well watered.

BLACK SPOT

Symptoms Distinct black blotches on leaves, surrounded by yellow haloes. Leaves fall prematurely. Shoots, and often the entire plant, are weakened by severe attacks.
Danger period Late spring on.
Treatment Spray regularly with mancozeb or myclobutanil, propiconazole, sulphur, triforine with bupirimate or thiram. Burn all infected leaves. Or try benomyl, carbendazim and thiophanate-methyl.

CANKER

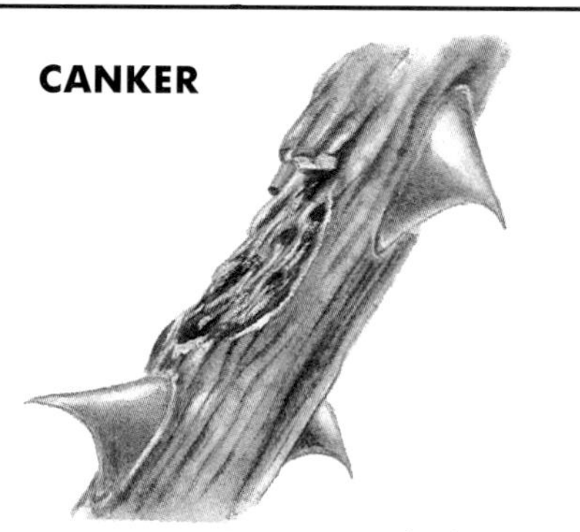

Symptoms Brown, cracked and sunken patches on stems, often with a corky edge and tiny black spots. The patches eventually encircle the stem, causing die-back and death.
Danger period All year.
Treatment Cut out and burn diseased wood. Fungus attacks through wounds to bark and stem. Paint large pruning cuts with fungicidal paint and spray with a copper fungicide.

CAPSID BUGS

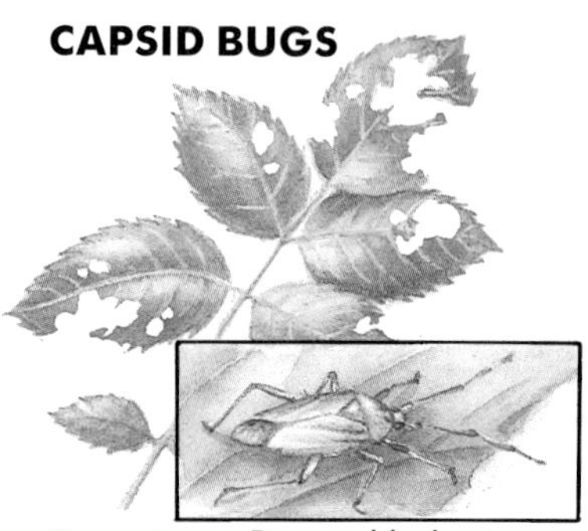

Symptoms Ragged holes in young leaves, becoming tattered. Buds and shoots distorted or dead; buds that survive form lopsided blooms.
Danger period Late spring and summer.
Treatment Spray with a systemic insecticide, such as dimethoate or treat plants with fenitrothion or malathion. Clear plant debris and weeds which may also harbour bugs.

CATERPILLARS

Symptoms Irregular, often quite large holes cut in leaves.
Danger period Mid to late spring onwards.
Treatment Remove and kill isolated caterpillars by hand. (Most active, and therefore visible, in the evening.) Spray more serious infestations with permethrin, pyrethrum or fenitrothion.

CHAFER BEETLES

Symptoms Adult beetles eat flowers, often devouring the entire side of a bloom; also eat irregular holes in leaves. Large, fat grubs of the cockchafer attack roots, sometimes killing the whole rose. Infrequent rose pest.
Danger period Adults: mid summer. Grubs all year.
Treatment Adults: remove by hand or spray with HCH or fenitrothion; avoid spraying open flowers. Grubs: treat soil with HCH or diazinon + chlorpyrifos. Eliminate weeds.

DIE-BACK

Symptoms Shoots wither and die from the top downwards. No specific cause – bad planting, black spot, canker, mildew, frost damage, mineral deficiency and waterlogging may all be responsible in part.
Danger period Spring to autumn.
Treatment Cut off dead shoots to healthy wood and spray with foliar feed. Fertilize in spring, not autumn.

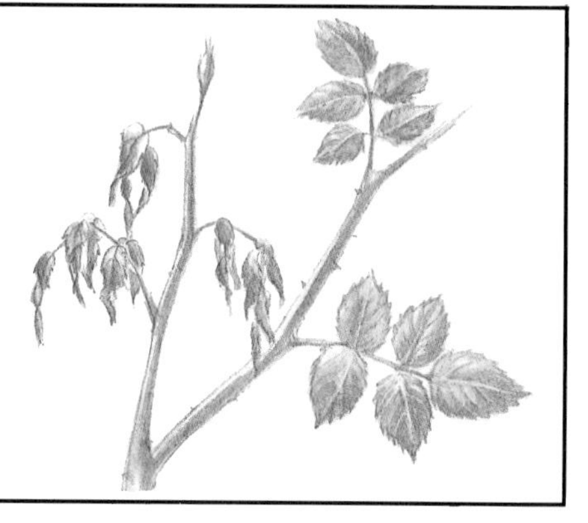

LACKEY MOTHS

Symptoms Irregular holes eaten in leaves; sometimes almost complete loss of leaves. Caterpillars spin 'tents' of silky threads.
Danger period Mid spring to mid summer.
Treatment Cut out and destroy stems bearing eggs in winter (bands of 100-200 eggs). Spray with permethrin or fenitrothion in spring and early summer. Cut out and burn 'tents' — chemicals can't penetrate them.

LEAF-CUTTER BEES

Symptoms Neat, semi-circular pieces cut from leaf edges. May weaken growth; disfigure plants.
Danger period Mid to late summer.
Treatment Destroy nests if found (in soil, rotting wood or brickwork). No effective chemical control. Never spray when in bloom – you will also kill pollinating insects.

LEAF-ROLLING SAWFLIES

Symptoms Leaves rolled downwards along length by pale green grubs. Plants disfigured and weakened.
Danger period Spring to summer.
Treatment Remove affected leaves – squeeze between fingers or burn to kill grubs. Spray with pirimiphos-methyl or fenitrothion.

LEAFHOPPERS

Symptoms Coarse white flecks on leaves. Cast insect skins often found on leaf undersides. More serious in warm spots, where leaf-fall and loss of vigour may result.
Danger period Early summer to mid autumn.
Treatment Spray with HCH, dimethoate, fenitrothion or malathion at two-week intervals.

MILDEW

Symptoms Leaves, shoots and flower buds covered with a white powdery coating; growth distorted.
Danger period Spring to autumn.
Treatment Spray with fenarimol, or bupirimate and triforine, myclobutanil or propiconazole or similar fungicide if the fungus becomes resistant to a particular chemical.

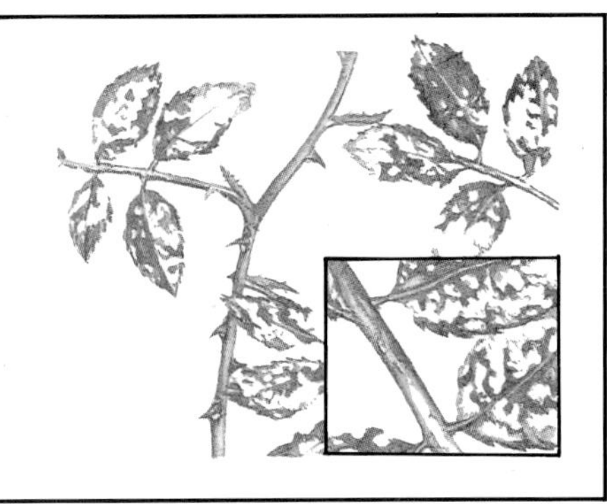

PURPLE SPOTTING

Symptoms Small, irregular, purplish spots on leaves. It is distinct from black spot in that the spots are smaller and do not have a yellow fringe.
Danger period Mid spring to autumn.
Treatment Poor cultural conditions are usually responsible, so spray with a foliar feed, improve soil drainage, and apply a mulch and compound fertilizer.

RED SPIDER MITES

Symptoms Minute yellowish green mites – like tiny spiders – suck sap by piercing leaf undersides and spin fine webs across them. In severe cases the webbing shows as a whitish halo at the edges of leaves, but the most obvious symptom is a bronzing discoloration of upper leaf surfaces. Leaves may eventually turn yellow and fall prematurely.
Danger period Late spring to autumn, especially in hot, dry weather.
Treatment Red spider mites quickly become resistant to chemicals, so use a mixture of treatments. Spray with derris, malathion, pirimiphos-methyl or dimethoate, repeating at one week intervals to kill both adults and hatching larvae. Under glass, biological control can be an effective alternative.

ROSE SLUGWORMS

Symptoms Holes eaten partly through leaf tissues, leaving transparent 'windows' of dried up tissue. Damaged areas turn brown and appear scorched. Pale yellowish green grubs may be seen.
Danger period Early summer to early autumn.
Treatment Spray with permethrin, pyrethrum or derris.

RUST

Symptoms Swellings on stems, stalks or leaf undersides burst to reveal masses of orange, powdery spores.
Danger period Mainly from mid summer onwards.
Treatment Cut out and burn affected shoots. Spray regularly with triforine and bupirimate, mancozeb, myclobutanil, propiconazole, sulphur or thiram.

THRIPS

Symptoms Flower petals blackened at the edges; also mottled/streaked with lighter colour. Flowers may darken and rot. Leaves show silvery flecking.
Danger period Early summer to early autumn, especially in hot, dry weather.
Treatment Spray with malathion, dimethoate, HCH, fenitrothion, permethrin or pirimiphos-methyl.

TORTRIX MOTHS

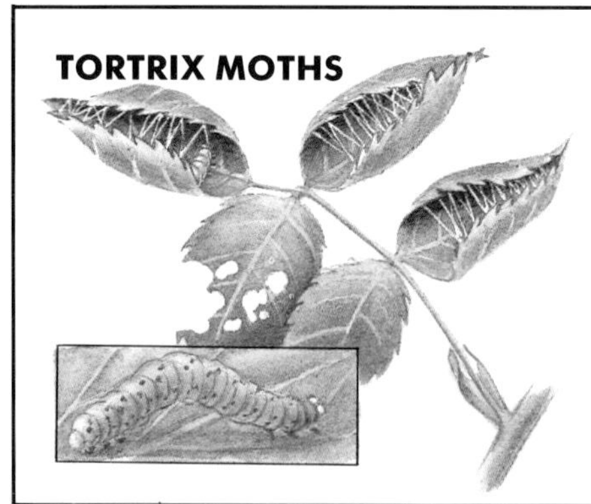

Symptoms Caterpillars of tortrix moths spin characteristic silken webs. These are used to draw together the edges of leaves, so forming a protective cover inside which they can feed in reasonable safety. Irregular small holes are eaten in the leaves and flower buds. When disturbed, tortrix caterpillars wriggle backwards, often dropping from the rose on a fine strand of silk.
Danger period Caterpillars cause most damage in late spring to early summer.
Treatment Chemical control may be rather difficult, but forceful spraying with pirimiphos-methyl may be effective. Alternatively, treat with permethrin, fenitrothion or pyrethrum. Isolated attacks are best dealt with by hand – pick off and squeeze together rolled-up leaves to crush the larvae and pupae. Burn the leaves.

OTHER PESTS AND DISEASES

Ants loosen soil around roses, especially in sandy areas. Can cause wilting or even plant death. Dust/spray with pirimiphos-methyl or HCH.
Banded rose sawfly maggots – grey-green with a yellowish-brown head – at first eat away leaf undersides in summer, leaving the top surface intact, but later eat irregular holes through leaves. They eventually bore into pithy stems or pruning cuts to pupate. Cut off and burn affected stems. Spray or dust with pyrethrum, permethrin or derris.
Crown galls are large, brown, knobbly swellings on the stem close to ground level. Can be left untreated – effects not serious. If you wish, cut out and burn unsightly galls.
Froghoppers cause little damage, but their nymphs suck sap, and may cause wilting or distortion. They engulf themselves in a white, frothy spittle around a stem or stalk – **cuckoo-spit.** Spray with malathion, using high pressure to penetrate the froth. Rub out minor infestations between finger and thumb or dislodge with tap-water from the garden hose.
Honey fungus causes the sudden death of affected plants. White fan-shaped sheets of fungal growth are found beneath the bark of roots and stems at ground level in autumn. They are up to 15cm (6in) across and usually yellowish brown. Black, bootlace-like strands may be found in the soil and on rose roots. Dig up and burn affected plants and all roots.
Robin's pincushions are red or green moss-like galls on leaves and around stems from late summer to early autumn (turn brown in winter) – inside live tiny wasp larvae. Can be left untreated or cut off and burn.
Scurfy scale may infest stems, weakening and disfiguring growth. Scales are tiny, greyish-white, flat protective discs over tiny insects. Spray with malathion or pirimiphos-methyl in early autumn to control newly hatched nymphs.

DEFICIENCIES

Correct the following deficiencies by feeding with rose fertilizer.
Iron deficiency: yellowing between veins; young leaves worst.
Magnesium deficiency: pale leaf centres brown/dead along mid-vein.
Manganese deficiency: yellowing between leaf veins – striped.
Nitrogen deficiency: poor, stunted growth and small, pale leaves, sometimes with red spots.
Phosphate deficiency: new leaves dark, small and purplish below.
Potash deficiency: poor quality, small blooms. Brown-edged leaves.

DISORDERS

Blindness is the failure of a shoot to develop flower buds. Prune shoot to half its length.
Waterlogging causes leaf yellowing – first veins, then most of leaf. Improve drainage or replant.

SHRUB TROUBLES

With good cultivation, most shrubs will be trouble-free, but learn to identify pests and diseases so that remedial measures can be taken when necessary.

All shrubs are woody-stemmed plants, generally with a well-branched, bushy habit, though the term includes many climbing or sprawling plants. They may be deciduous or evergreen, but all live for many years on the same site. As such, they often present a rather tough and undesirable food for potential pests – especially those which feed by biting into the plant tissues to suck sap – and for potential disease organisms. If a pest or disease does get a hold, however, the problem can persist for many years unless measures are taken in the early stages to eradicate it.

The young shoots of all shrubs lack protective wood and are soft and inviting to biting pests, so make regular visual checks of all shrubs in spring and early summer. Turn leaves to reveal pests which hide on the undersides. Distorted or discoloured foliage and shoots invariably indicate trouble – though some harmless viruses may be responsible for attractive distortions of plants such as the twisted branches and crimped leaves of the corkscrew hazel (*Corylus avellana* 'Contorta') and the flattened and recurved stems of the Japanese willow (*Salix sachalinensis* 'Sekka').

When buying shrubs from a nursery, remember that these plants will provide a permanent feature in the garden, so it is worth paying a little extra to ensure you get good-quality stock – vigorous, compact plants are far more immune to pest and disease attack when planted out.

Prepare the planting site, supplying adequate organic matter and fertilizers to encourage strong, healthy growth. Water shrubs regularly until well-established. Control all weed growth and remove debris in which many pests will breed. Prune all damaged or dead branches back to strong and healthy wood, to discourage the spread of fungal diseases, and also cut out weak and crossing stems.

Encourage wildlife in the garden – some birds and beneficial insects are good friends – blue tits eat caterpillars and ladybirds devour aphids and scale insects.

If some branches of a shrub are attacked by pests or diseases, the simplest and most effective cure is to cut out the infested material back to healthy wood and put it straight on the bonfire. Never put infested material on a compost heap. However, complete removal of branches may disfigure the shrub, so chemical treatment may be the only answer.

The following pages will help you to identify the major pests, diseases and disorders of garden shrubs and offer advice on the selection of a chemical treatment. Chemical names listed here refer to the active ingredient, not the proprietary name. Follow carefully the manufacturer's recommendations for application method, dilution rate and use.

◀ **Blackfly infestation** Aphids are troublesome pests of many shrubs, infesting soft young shoots, such as those of mock orange (*Philadelphus coronarius* 'Aureus'). They also excrete a sticky honeydew on the foliage near the infestation, and this in turn invites fungal diseases which further weaken the shrub.

ADELGIDS

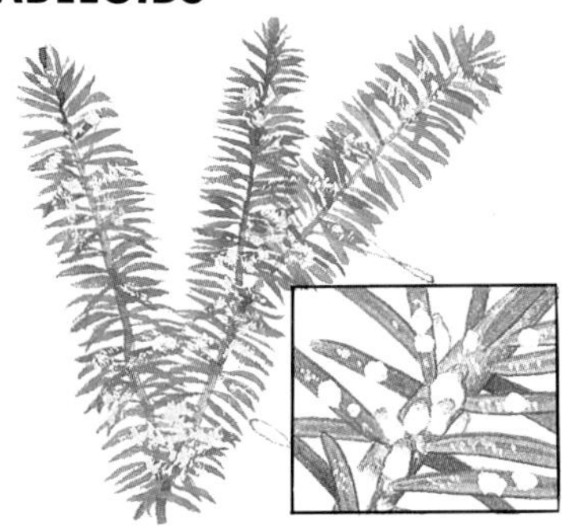

Plants affected Larch, pines, spruces, firs, etc.
Symptoms Colonies of small, dark aphid-like insects partially covered by tufts of white woolly wax infest undersides of leaves and leaf axils. Some adelgids cause galls.
Danger period Mid to late summer.
Treatment Spray thoroughly with HCH or malathion in early spring and repeat about three weeks later.

APHIDS

Plants affected Many shrubs; mainly young, soft growth.
Symptoms Colonies of small, plump, black, green or pinkish bugs; sticky honeydew excreted on to leaves, often with secondary black fungal growth.
Danger period Spring/summer.
Treatment Spray with systemic insecticides like dimethoate or heptenophos or with malathion, pirimicarb, pirimiphos-methyl or pyrethrum.

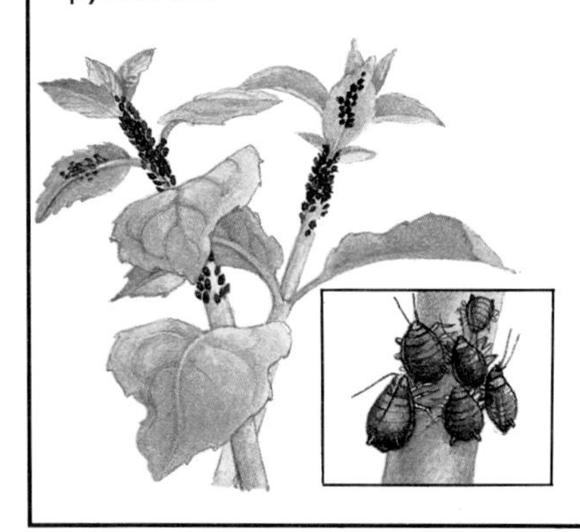

CAPSID BUGS

Plants affected Buddleias, forsythias, hydrangeas, roses, caryopteris, etc.
Symptoms Tattered holes appear in younger leaves.
Danger period Late spring to late summer.
Treatment Good general garden hygiene and weed control may reduce capsid bug infestation. Spray with dimethoate, fenitrothion, malathion or HCH as soon as the first symptoms appear.

CHLOROSIS

Plants affected Many shrubs, especially hydrangeas, ceanothus and acid-lovers on lime soils.
Symptoms Yellowing between veins on young leaves.
Danger period Growing season.
Treatment Dig in pulverized bark or crushed bracken or use acidifying chemicals. Apply a chelated compound, or tonic containing trace elements.

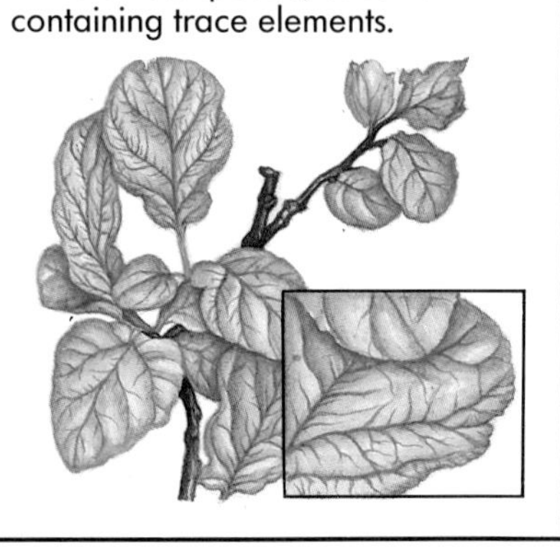

CORAL SPOT

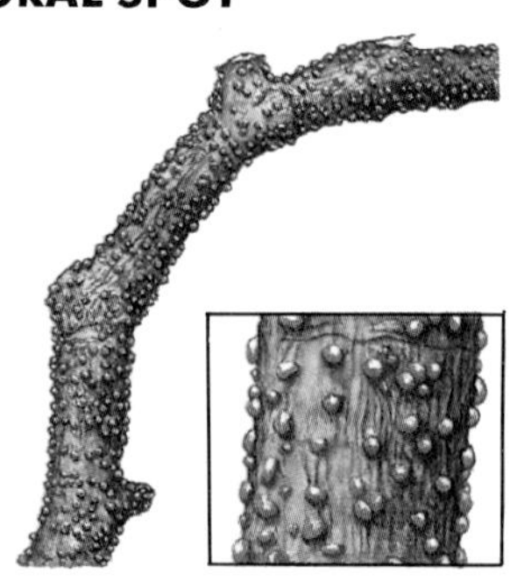

Plants affected Many shrubs, especially magnolias, currants, maples and figs.
Symptoms Die-back of branches caused by coral-red, spore-filled pustules on dead wood.
Danger period Any time.
Treatment Cut out dead shoots to well below the disease, and burn. Protect cuts with a wound sealing paint.

FIREBLIGHT

Plants affected Cotoneasters, pyracanthas, stranvaesia and chaenomeles.
Symptoms Shoots die back (particularly flowering spurs), leaves turn brown and wither, and cankers develop at base.
Danger period Flowering time.
Treatment Cut out diseased wood to 60cm (2ft) below affected tissues. Disinfect all pruning tools after use.

FROGHOPPERS

Plants affected Lavender, roses, currants, hypericums, forsythias, rubus, and many other ornamental shrubs.
Symptoms Frothy masses of 'cuckoo spit' covering small yellowish green insects about 6mm (¼in) long. Young shoots may eventually become distorted or wither, but damage is rarely severe, though infested shoots are visually rather unattractive.
Danger period Early to mid summer.
Treatment Wash off 'cuckoo spit' with a powerful jet of water from a garden hose. This may be enough to dislodge the insects, but you can also spray with malathion or HCH – use a powerful spray in order to penetrate the protective froth.

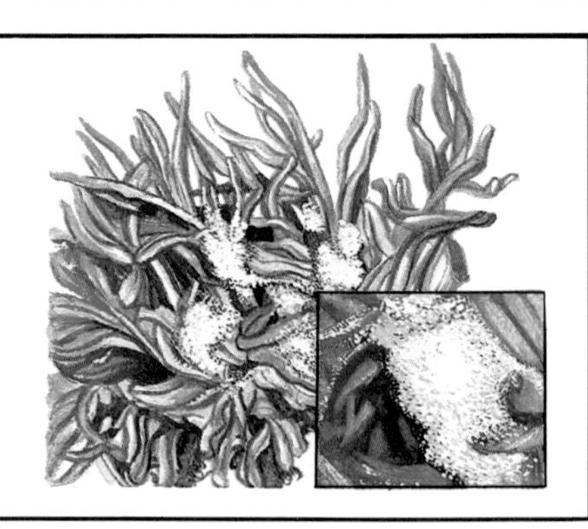

HONEY FUNGUS

Plants affected Almost all woody plants, especially those growing near old, decaying tree stumps.
Symptoms Sudden death of shrubs. White fan-shaped growths of fungus beneath the bark of roots and trunk at soil level. Brown-black, root-like structures may be found in the soil around the roots. Honey-coloured toadstools may appear at the base of a dying shrub.
Danger period All year; toadstools usually appear from mid summer to early winter.
Treatment The only effective cure is to dig up the entire plant and burn it. Even the surrounding soil should be excavated and destroyed. Do not replant shrubs or trees on the same site for at least one year. Grow only resistant shrubs.

LEAF MINERS

Plants affected Holly, honeysuckle, privet, lilac, etc.
Symptoms Small larvae tunnel within the leaves, creating blistered patches. Leaves may also be rolled.
Danger period Late spring to summer.
Treatment Cut off and burn affected leaves, or spray with HCH, malathion or pirimiphos-methyl.

LEOPARD MOTH

Plants affected Cotoneasters, cherries, lilacs, maples, rhododendrons and shrubby willows.
Symptoms Branches tunnelled by caterpillars, causing wilting of leaves.
Danger period All year.
Treatment Kill the caterpillars by pushing a piece of wire into the tunnels. Seal holes with plasticine or putty. Burn severely infected branches on the bonfire.

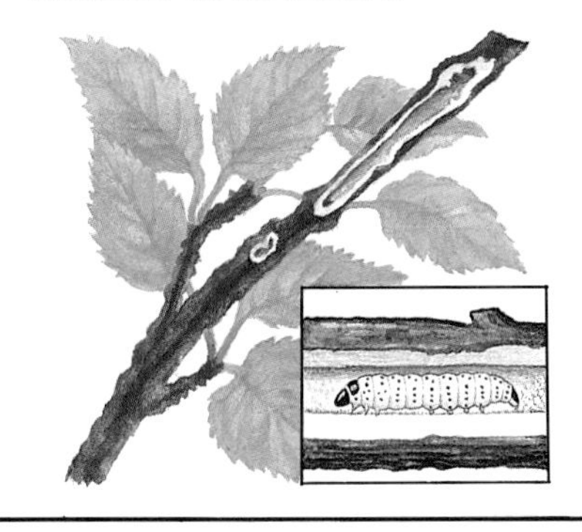

POWDERY MILDEW

Plants affected Euonymus and many other shrubs.
Symptoms A white, floury coating on leaves and shoots, and sometimes on flowers.
Danger period Throughout the growing season.
Treatment Cut out severely affected shoots in autumn. Spray as soon as seen with benomyl, carbendazim, propiconazole, sulphur or bupirimate + triforine.

RED SPIDER MITES

Plants affected Hydrangea, choisya, roses, wisteria and others.
Symptoms Older leaves turn a bronzed yellow colour, dry out and eventually die.
Danger period Late spring to early autumn.
Treatment Spray immediately after flowering with dimethoate, pirimiphos-methyl, malathion or derris.

RUST

Plants affected Mahonias, berberis, box, rhododendron, hypericum and some other shrubs.
Symptoms Brown spots appear on the foliage.
Danger period All year.
Treatment Difficult to eradicate; remove and burn diseased leaves, and spray at fortnightly intervals with bupirimate + triforine, mancozeb, propiconazole or thiram on remaining growths.

SCALE INSECTS

Plants affected Ceanothus, cotoneasters, camellias, bay laurels and many other shrubs.
Symptoms Colonies of brown, yellow or white scales on stems or leaves of older shoots.
Danger period All year.
Treatment Spray with pirimiphos-methyl, malathion or dimethoate in early summer; repeat three weeks later.

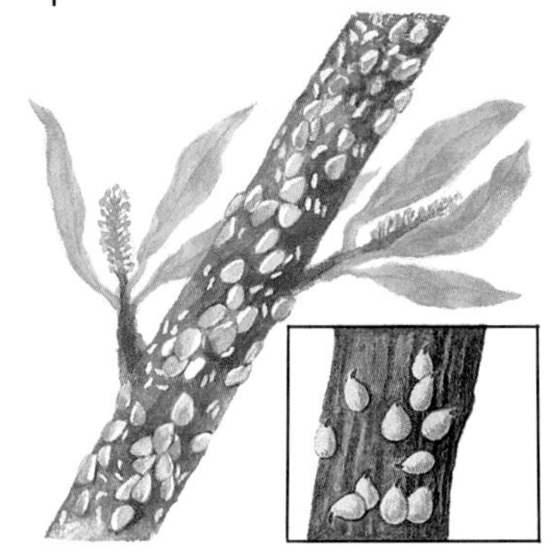

SILVER LEAF

Plants affected Prunus, lilacs and certain other shrubs.
Symptoms Some leaves become silvered. When a cut cross-section of an affected branch is moistened, a brown or purple stain appears.
Danger period Autumn to spring.
Treatment Cut out branches to 15cm (6in) below where the stain in the wood stops. Treat cuts with protective paint.

THRIPS

Plants affected Privet, lilac, honeysuckle and other shrubs.
Symptoms Leaves finely mottled with a general silvery-brown appearance.
Danger period Early summer to early autumn, especially during hot, dry weather.
Treatment Spray with HCH, malathion, dimethoate or pyrethrum when the symptoms are first seen.

TORTRIX CATERPILLARS

Plants affected Many shrubs and other garden plants.
Symptoms Irregular, small holes eaten in leaves, which are drawn together with silk webbing to form a 'tent'.
Danger period Late spring and early summer.
Treatment Spray thoroughly with fenitrothion, permethrin or pirimiphos-methyl or remove and destroy caterpillars by hand.

VINE WEEVILS

Plants affected Vines, euonymus, rhododendrons, camellias, clematis, yew and some other shrubs.
Symptoms Small, irregular notches eaten out of leaf edges at night by adult beetles. Legless, white larvae feed on roots, checking growth and sometimes causing sudden wilting and collapse of shoots and leaves, especially on small container-grown shrubs.
Danger period Spring and summer.
Treatment Remove accumulations of leaves and other plant debris, where the weevils rest by day, and spray or dust affected plants with HCH at dusk in late spring and early summer. Leaf feeding by adult weevils rarely causes severe damage, though damaged leaves are unsightly.

OTHER TROUBLES

Birds, especially bullfinches, strip dormant flower buds of certain shrubs in late winter and early spring. Forsythia, lilac, viburnum and wisteria may be badly damaged. Blackbirds and thrushes devour the berries of many shrubs in autumn and winter. Large birds such as pigeons may cause physical damage to delicate branches. Various types of bird scarer may be used, though most are unattractive in the ornamental garden and may not be effective. Chemical bird repellents give some protection.
Box suckers feed only on box (*Buxus*). Tiny yellowish or green nymphs (young insects) suck sap from shoot tips in spring, causing stunted growth with cabbage-like cupped leaves. Sticky honeydew is also excreted. Nymphs may be controlled by spraying with a systemic insecticide such as dimethoate. Kill adults before they lay eggs by spraying with HCH or malathion in mid summer.
Caterpillars of various moths eat the leaves of certain shrubs, leaving large, irregular-shaped holes. Locate, remove by hand and destroy individual caterpillars. Spray larger infestations with permethrin or derris as soon as symptoms appear.
Die-back is a disorder which causes foliage to turn brown and die, starting at the branch tip and working downwards. Prune individually damaged branches back to healthy wood. Keep remaining plants vigorous by applying a general fertilizer and mulching in spring and giving a foliar feed in summer.
Woolly aphids produce woody swellings and tufts of white wool on stems and branches of cotoneasters and pyracanthas from early summer to early autumn. Where possible, brush a spray-strength solution of malathion or dimethoate on to the affected areas or spray as soon as the pest is detected.
Phytophthora foot and root rot affects heathers, acers, rhododendrons, camellias, junipers and other shrubs. Leaves are abnormally small, yellow or sparse over all or part of the crown in broad-leaved shrubs, grey then turning brown in conifers and heathers. Partial die-back is followed by death of shrubs. A reddish-brown triangular patch shows beneath bark at ground level. Destroy affected plants and change the soil well beyond the full depth and spread of the roots. Replant with less susceptible shrubs.
Scab affects pyracanthas from spring to autumn, showing as blackish-brown spots on leaves which may fall prematurely. Fruits become covered with scabby spots, turn black and shrivel. The fungus overwinters as small scabby patches on the twigs. Rake up and burn fallen leaves and cut out infested shoots in autumn. Spray in early or mid spring and again in early and mid summer with Bordeaux mixture or other copper fungicide, mancozeb, bupirimate with triforine or benomyl, carbendazim or thiophanate-methyl.

TREE TROUBLES

Trees are sturdy and don't succumb readily to pests or diseases, but if problems do occur remedial action is essential.

Trees are woody plants with a permanent above-ground framework. The living tissues within their trunk and branches are protected to some degree from pests and diseases by a layer of coarse-textured bark. However, if this layer becomes damaged in any way parasites and diseases can enter.

For this reason it is important to trim away any damaged wood as soon as possible, leaving a clean surface which will heal quickly. The exposed sapwood is prone to disease and infection until a callous has formed over it; it can be protected by covering it with fungicidal wound paint, but this may also slow down the growth rate of the callous.

A few serious diseases – honey fungus and fireblight, for example – can infect structural wood despite the tree's built-in defences. These are long-term diseases which are carried over many years and spread from tree to tree. Early diagnosis is vital if you want to save the trees.

Since dead or rotting wood is weaker than healthy wood, infected trees not only look unsightly, but are potentially dangerous and can topple over in gales.

Leaves and soft young stems are susceptible to attack from sucking and biting insects and to fungal diseases. However, due to the sheer bulk of a mature tree, such infestations have to be widespread before major damage is done. Young trees, on the other hand, can be set back permanently.

Ecologically sound winter-wash sprays can be used on some pests. Based on tar oil and water, they are applied to deciduous trees during dormancy. Avoid spraying in windy weather.

Look out for curling or eaten leaves, sticky deposits, abnormal discolorations or growths and other unusual features, then follow the advice on the following pages.

PHYSICAL PROTECTION

In rural areas trees are frequently plagued by rabbits and squirrels. If the garden is unfenced, deer can also be a problem in some regions.

Rabbit damage to young trees – chewed bark – can be eliminated by wrapping the base of the trunk with a proprietary spiral-shaped plastic tree guard.

However, tree guards are not effective against squirrels or deer since these pests can reach the branches to chew bark, buds and leaves. The best protection against deer is to build a strong fence all round the garden.

Squirrels cannot be controlled effectively by physical barriers because they are agile climbers. Seek advice from the pest control officer for your local council if squirrels are very troublesome.

▼ **Honey fungus** (*Armillaria mellea*) This disease can infect all woody plants, causing death of branches or complete trees. It occurs chiefly in areas with many broad leaved trees. Honey-coloured toadstools around the base of a tree are the obvious signs, but the main damage is done by the brown-black, rod-like structures found in the soil around the roots.

UNUSUAL GROWTHS

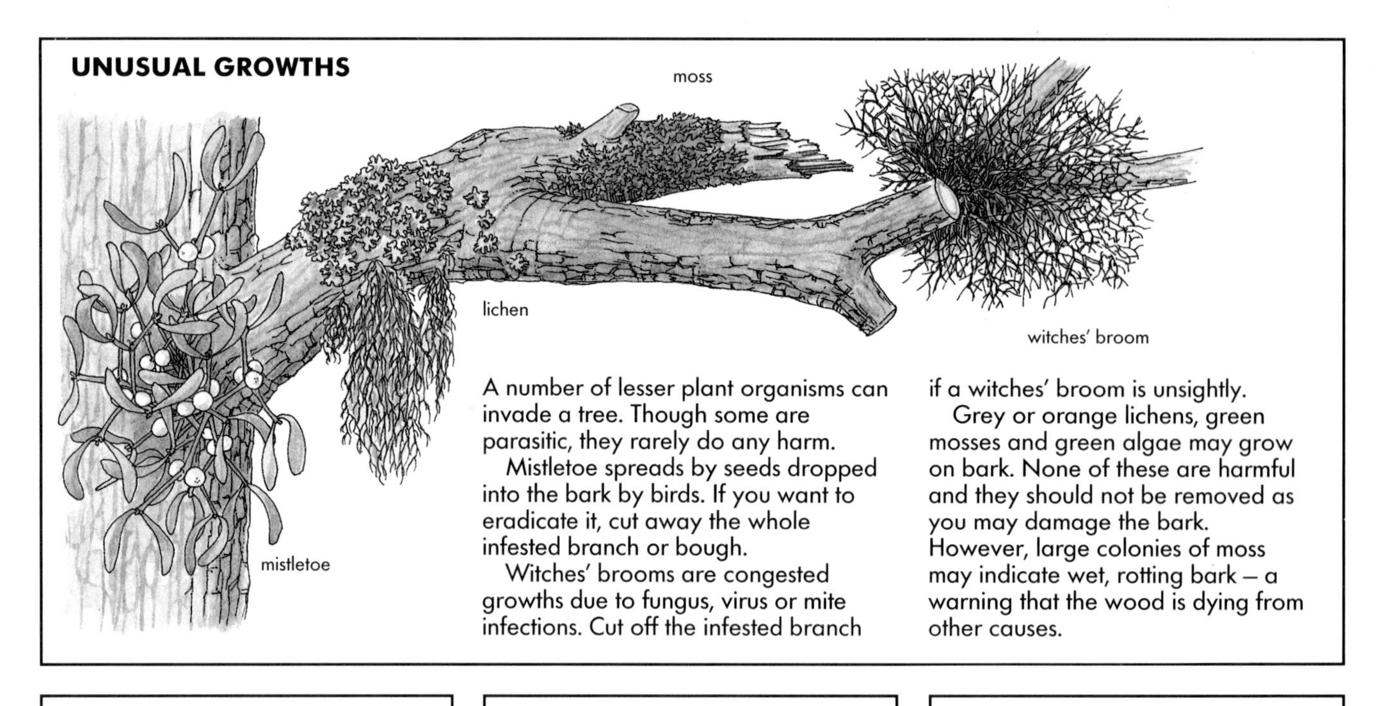

A number of lesser plant organisms can invade a tree. Though some are parasitic, they rarely do any harm.

Mistletoe spreads by seeds dropped into the bark by birds. If you want to eradicate it, cut away the whole infested branch or bough.

Witches' brooms are congested growths due to fungus, virus or mite infections. Cut off the infested branch if a witches' broom is unsightly.

Grey or orange lichens, green mosses and green algae may grow on bark. None of these are harmful and they should not be removed as you may damage the bark. However, large colonies of moss may indicate wet, rotting bark – a warning that the wood is dying from other causes.

ADELGIDS

Trees affected Firs, larches, pines, spruces and other conifers.
Symptoms Colonies of small, dark aphid-like insects covered by tufts of white woolly wax infest undersides of leaves and leaf axils.
Danger period Spring to late summer.
Treatment Spray thoroughly with HCH or malathion in early spring and repeat about three weeks later.

BARK SPLITTING

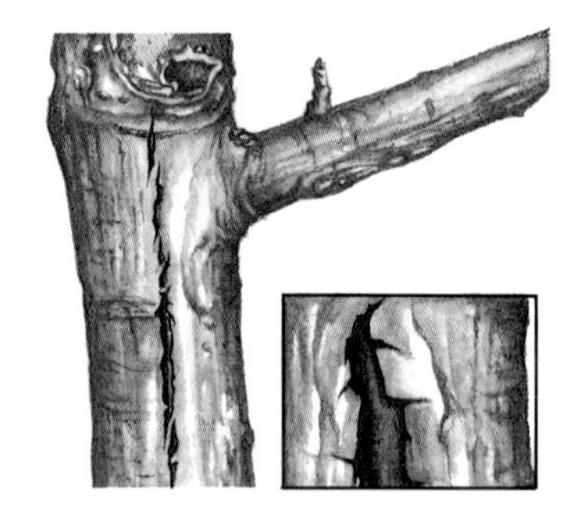

Trees affected Many types, including fruit trees.
Symptoms Bark splits and the cracks open up.
Danger period At any time of year.
Treatment Cut out any dead wood and trim away all loose bark with a disinfected pruning knife. If the tree is then fed, mulched and watered well, the wound should heal naturally; don't use wound paints.

CANKER

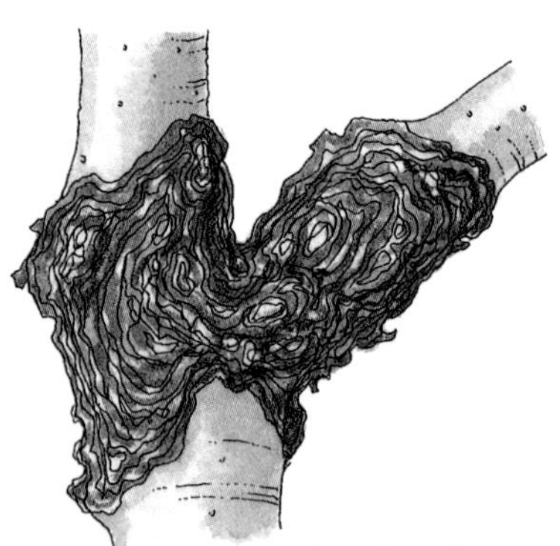

Trees affected Ashes, beeches, crab apples, poplars and sorbus.
Symptoms Oval cankers on the trunk and branches; bark shrinks in rings until inner tissues exposed.
Danger period At any time.
Treatment Cut out and burn infected spurs or small branches. On larger branches and trunks, pare away diseased material and burn it. Coat cuts with canker paint.

CATERPILLARS (winter moths)

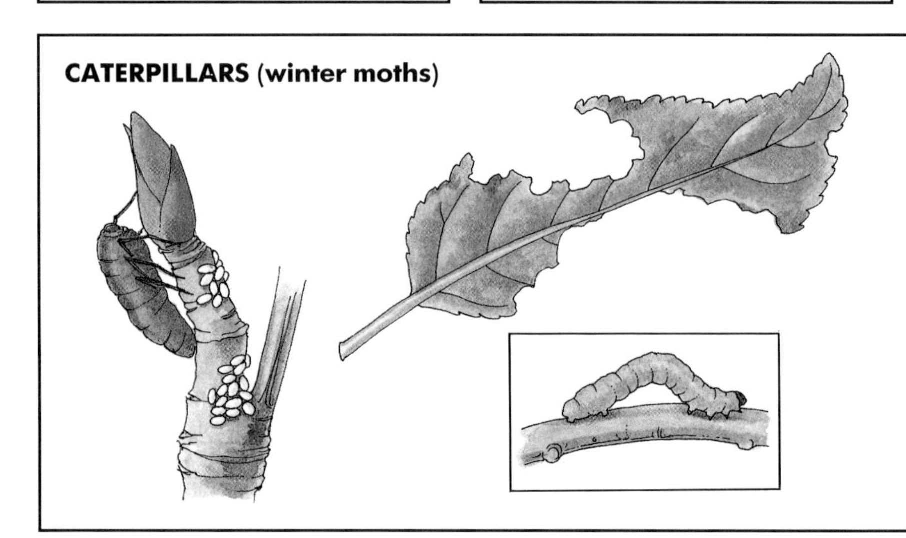

Trees affected Broadleaves.
Symptoms Young leaves and buds eaten by green, yellow-green or brown 'looper' caterpillars, leaving ragged holes and edges.
Danger period Eggs laid in winter and early spring; leaves eaten during spring and early summer.
Treatment Wrap a proprietary grease band around the trunk in mid autumn to prevent the wingless female moths from climbing up the trunk to lay their eggs. Or, spray small trees with fenitrothion, malathion, permethrin or pyrethrum as soon as buds open in spring.

CORAL SPOT

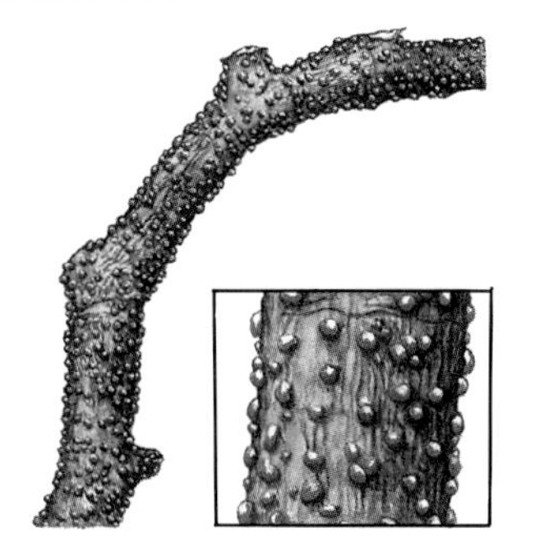

Trees affected Acers, magnolias and many other trees.
Symptoms Die-back of branches caused by coral-red, spore-filled pustules on dead wood.
Danger period Throughout the year.
Treatment Cut out dead branches or boughs to well below the diseased area, and burn. Protect cuts with a wound-sealing fungicidal paint.

FIREBLIGHT

Trees affected Cotoneasters, crab apples, hawthorns, sorbus, pears and other members of the rose family,
Symptoms Branches die back (particularly flowering spurs). Leaves turn brown and wither; cankers develop at their base.
Danger period Flowering time.
Treatment No chemical cure. Cut out and burn all diseased wood.

GALL MITES

Trees affected Mainly limes, elms, maples and sycamores.
Symptoms Minute mites feed on leaves, which react by producing small reddish or green outgrowths. These can be disfiguring, but no real damage is caused by the mites.
Danger period Spring onwards.
Treatment No effective pesticides available.

GALL WASPS

Trees affected Oaks
Symptoms Many different galls resembling peas, silk buttons and spangles growing out of leaves; other galls occur on shoots, catkins and acorns, sometimes singly, often numerous. Growth caused in response to tissue attack by tiny wasp larvae.
Danger period Growing season.
Treatment No effective treatment; damage never serious.

HONEY FUNGUS

Trees affected Most species.
Symptoms Sudden death. White fan-shaped fungus growth beneath bark of roots and trunk at soil level. Toadstools at base.
Danger period All year.
Treatment No cure. Cut down and burn the tree, including roots and surrounding soil. Do not replant trees or shrubs on the same site for at least a year. Grow resistant types.

RUST

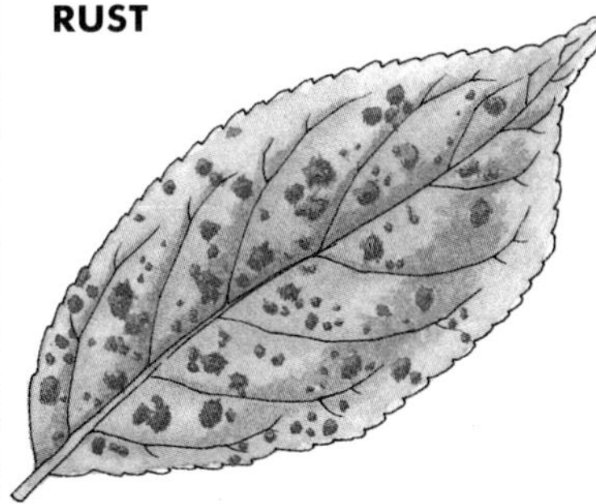

Trees affected Mainly willows, birches, poplars and plums.
Symptoms Brown, orange or yellow powdery masses develop on leaves and stems. Leaves may turn yellow in severe cases.
Danger period Summer.
Treatment Pick off and burn diseased leaves. Encourage vigour by good cultural treatment. Spray with mancozeb, bupirimate with triforine, propiconazole or thiram.

SCAB

Trees affected Crab apples, pears.
Symptoms Olive-green blotches of fungal growth on leaves, which fall prematurely. Small blister-like pimples develop on young shoots, later burst the bark and then show as ring-like cracks or scabs. Open lesions are prone to secondary infection by canker. Dark, corky scabs appear on fruits.
Danger period All year.
Treatment Cut out cracked and scabby shoots. Pick off and burn affected leaves. Start spraying when flower buds are visible and until early summer if necessary, with benomyl, carbendazim or thiophanate-methyl, though frequent use can cause resistant strains of the fungus. Or spray with thiram, Bordeaux mixture or other copper fungicide, mancozeb or bupirimate with triforine.

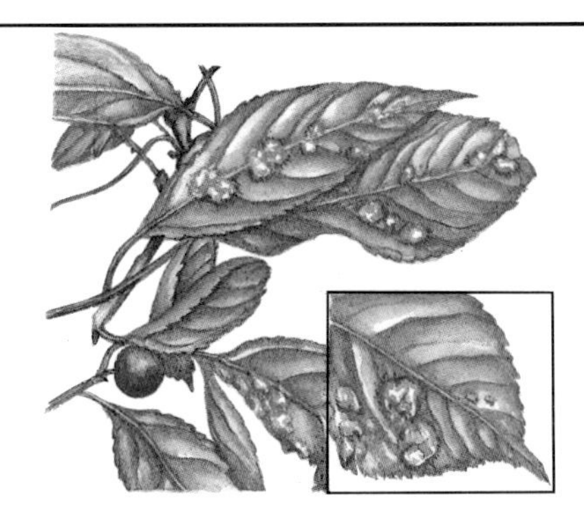

SILVER LEAF

Trees affected Crab apples, pears, plums and other prunus.
Symptoms Some leaves become silvered. When a cross-section of an affected branch is moistened, a brown or purple stain appears. A flat, purple fungus eventually develops on dead wood.
Danger period Early autumn to late spring.
Treatment Cut out branches to 15cm (6in) below the point where the stain in the wood stops. Treat cuts with wound-sealing paint.

TAR SPOT

Trees affected Acers, especially sycamores.
Symptoms Yellow patches on the upper surface of the leaves develop into large black blotches, often with a yellowish halo. Other types of leaf spot on maples show as red-brown to yellowish lesions.
Danger periods Growing season.
Treatment If possible, pick off and burn affected leaves. Sweep up and burn all fallen leaves in autumn.

WOOLLY APHIDS

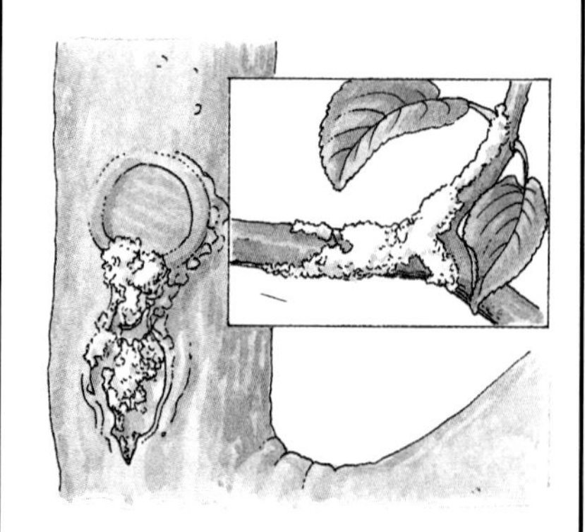

Trees affected Cotoneasters, pyracanthas and crab apples.
Symptoms Woody swellings and tufts of white wool on trunks and branches, especially in crevices around old wounds.
Danger period Mid spring to early autumn.
Treatment Where possible, brush a spray-strength solution of malathion or dimethoate on to affected areas when the wool first appears. Alternatively, spray the affected plants.

OTHER TROUBLES

Aphids – colonies of small, plump, black, green or pinkish bugs – infest leaves and young shoots, stunting, distorting and weakening growth. They also excrete sticky honeydew which frequently encourages a secondary infection of sooty mould. Lime trees are especially susceptible. Aphids may transmit virus diseases, although this is rarely a problem with trees.

Spray thoroughly with a systemic insecticide such as dimethoate or heptenophos, or with a contact type such as pirimicarb fenitrothion or malathion.

Birds – especially bullfinches – peck off flower buds in winter and early spring. There is no effective deterrent, but bird scarers of various types may give some control.

Bracket fungi produce shelf-like toadstools, each up to 30cm (1ft) across, on trunks and branches. The spores enter through dead or damaged tissues and may cause rotting of the heartwood and die-back. Fungal growth may not appear until several months after the initial spore infection.

Cut off small diseased branches. If the fungus appears on the main trunk, employ a tree surgeon to check on the safety of the tree.

Leopard moth caterpillars tunnel into the branches of acers, ashes, birches, flowering cherries, crab apples, cotoneasters, hawthorns, oaks, sorbus and willows, causing wilting of their leaves. Damage occurs at any time.

Kill the caterpillars by poking a piece of wire into the tunnels, then seal the holes with modelling clay or putty. Burn severely infested branches.

Powdery mildew forms a white powdery coating of spores on stems and leaves. Crab apples, medlars and pears are particularly susceptible and their shoots may become stunted and weakened.

Where possible, remove and burn all badly infected shoots. Spray with benomyl or thiophanate-methyl, repeating fortnightly as necessary.

Red spider mites often infest ornamental trees of the rose family – especially crab apples, hawthorns, peaches, plums and rowans. Colonies of minute red mites accumulate on leaves from spring onwards, causing speckling, bronze discoloration and drying out of tissues.

Spray trees thoroughly immediately damage is seen with dimethoate, pirimiphos-methyl or malathion.

Scale insects attack many different garden plants, including acers, beeches, cherries, cotoneasters, horse chestnuts and limes. Colonies of brown, yellow or white scales appear on older shoots at most times of year, but particularly in late spring and summer. Persistent infestations weaken the growth of the tree.

Spray or brush dormant wood with tar oil in early or mid winter. If possible, time other chemical treatments to coincide with the insect's crawling stage before their protective scales are formed, usually early to mid summer. Spray thoroughly with malathion or pirimiphos-methyl.

Scorch may affect acers, beeches and some other trees in spring. Pale brown spots appear on the young leaves which in serious cases become papery and withered.

Lay a mulch to ensure that the trees do not suffer from dry soil during the critical period. Cold drying winds may be the main cause of leaf scorch, so put up some form of windbreak to shield susceptible species from this in exposed gardens.

Verticillium wilt is a disease caused by soil-borne fungi. It enters trees through young roots or through wounds, causing brown discoloration on leaves and stems. Acers are the most commonly affected trees.

Wilt diseases are difficult to eradicate, but rarely kill trees – at worst, a few branches die back, and should be pruned away.

Troubles in the kitchen garden

Pests and diseases can have devastating effects on fruit and vegetables, seriously reducing yields and in extreme cases wiping out whole crops. Some gardeners follow a regular spraying programme to protect the kitchen garden, while others believe in avoiding all man-made chemicals, not only in the battle against weeds, pests and diseases, but also as fertilizers and soil improvers. Such an organic approach to gardening relies on soil management and good cultivation techniques to maintain a natural balance between predators and parasites.

Chemical controls are quick and usually effective, but can also kill other insects, including pollinating bees and butterflies and beneficial insects such as ladybirds. With edible crops, it is particularly important to follow manufacturers' instructions for strength of dosage and length of time lapse between spraying and harvesting.

Good cultivation methods used in conjunction with chemical control only when absolutely necessary is the most sensible approach. A regular crop rotation programme can minimize the build-up of certain soil pests and diseases, while deep digging in autumn will expose soil-dwelling grubs to the mercy of natural predators. Many fruit varieties are bred to be resistant to particular diseases and some chemical preparations are environmentally sound: for example, grease bands tied round fruit tree trunks in autumn trap insects as they crawl up to lay their eggs on fruit spurs, and a tar oil winter-wash will kill any that escaped.

Organic gardening Untouched by chemical sprays, organic-grown produce is healthy and environmentally friendly.

ORGANIC GARDENING

Organic gardening involves an attitude of mind which views plants and their place in the garden as an eco-system, and excludes man-made chemicals.

Organic gardening makes use of animal and vegetable manures, and some concentrated fertilizers of animal and vegetable origin – going back, in other words, to the fundamentals of plant culture without any short-cuts in the way of man-made chemicals.

Organic gardening also implies the total removal of chemicals from the garden scene unless they are of organic origin - that is, unless they come from plants or animals. Even then, the use of any chemical to control a pest, disease or weed or to control or improve cropping qualities is thought to be an admission of defeat, since it upsets the natural balance. Rather than using chemicals, you should ensure that the soil, light, moisture and other environmental conditions are at their best so that plants grow to the limit of their potential. Where possible, you should grow plants naturally resistant to pests and diseases.

The organic 'school' maintains that the addition of concentrated manufactured fertilizers, such as sulphate of ammonia or Growmore, is wasteful and expensive. Much of their nutrient content is leached through the soil before it is absorbed.

Some concentrated fertilizers are acceptable, but only of organic rather than mineral origin. Hoof and horn, and bone-meal are examples – they break down slowly and remain within reach of the roots for some time. The result is a better plant.

So-called ground minerals – except those of animal origin – are allowed, such as rock phosphate, which is not processed but simply supplements the minerals which may be in the soil already but in short supply. In the average garden, however, real nutrient deficiencies are rare and such fertilizers, even organic ones, seldom need to be added.

Many organic gardening notions – using natural manures, and taking measures to deter pests and diseases rather than simply destroying them with chemicals – are perfectly normal to all gardeners. But gardening organically involves looking at the garden as a whole. It takes into account, too, the condition of the soil and the weather, and evaluates all these together. Decisions

▼ **Green manure** Long before organic gardening became fashionable, farmers ploughed quick-growing crops of rape, mustard, vetches or annual lupins into the soil while still green. This type of manure helps to enrich and fix the soil's nitrogen content and to improve its texture and structure.

WEEDS AND PESTS

1 There is no truly organic method of eliminating weeds, but you can avoid using chemicals by hand-weeding and hoeing – two very effective, energetic control methods.

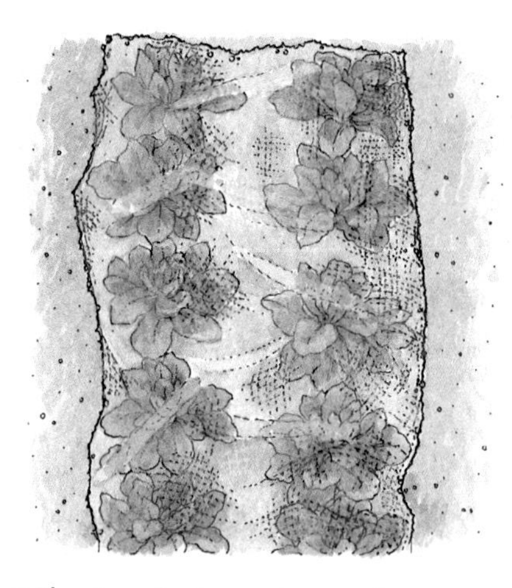

2 Floating cloches – sheets of transparent, woven plastic fibres or spun web fleece serve two functions in the organic vegetable plot – they protect seeds and young plants from adverse weather and pests. The soft material won't harm the foliage.

3 Organic control methods for slugs and snails include the use of beer traps – part-fill a watertight container with beer, sink it in the soil near to susceptible plants and prop a saucer over the top. Slugs and snails, attracted by the smell, crawl inside the trap and drown in the beer.

can then be made as to the need for improving some aspects and altering others to produce the best possible plants.

Going organic

If your approach to gardening has always been the one in which you buy weedkillers to destroy weeds, chemical insecticides to spray on greenfly and other pests, and fungicides to get rid of diseases, or if you have relied on fertilizers such as Growmore to feed plants, it takes quite a shift in outlook to attempt gardening without them.

Similarly, organic gardening may not be entirely successful at first. Indeed, in some gardens it may be essential to use chemicals to begin with in order to clean the ground and plants. If you want to try organic gardening and have never done it before, it is perhaps best to work into it a step at a time. In this way you can discover how to manage your own garden organically in the way which suits it best.

Organic gardening affects three main areas of gardening management – pest, disease and weed control; soil treatment; and cultural practices. Companion planting, in which one plant species is thought to benefit another growing alongside, is a fourth element.

Pests, diseases and weeds

If plants become severely, or even mildly, infested by a pest the normal reaction of most gardeners is to reach for the nearest spray-gun. Chemical controls are unquestionably efficient and destructive, quick and time-saving. Pests are killed rapidly by man-made chemicals and some are long-lasting.

Unfortunately, many chemicals also kill pollinating insects, such as bees, butterflies, moths and hoverflies, together with other insects which are predatory or parasitic on the very insects for which the insecticide is intended. Similarly, many garden pests and diseases – and now also some weeds – are becoming resistant to these chemicals and to successively produced new ones.

Chemicals are expensive, they need to be applied frequently in many cases, and they have effects not only on the soil, but also on discharges made into ground water and hence rivers and seas. There are a variety of ways in which pest, disease and weed problems can be overcome without the use of chemicals, and it is well worth considering them.

In a garden where no pesticides are used at all, the natural balance can operate and prevent the large and detrimental build-up of a particular insect to plague proportions. Predators and parasites can live and breed – ladybirds and their larvae, and hoverfly and lacewing larvae all feed on a variety of aphids such as greenfly, blackfly and the plum leaf-curling aphid; ground beetles and centipedes attack small insects and slugs in the soil; and the red velvet mite feeds on other mites. There are many more examples of this natural control of insects, and of larger creatures – snails by thrushes, for instance.

Fungal diseases can be prevented by applying the correct method of cultivation and taking special care with soil management. Weeds, too, can be eliminated by culural practices such as thorough hand-weeding or hoeing.

Soil treatment

Organic soil management is not quite as straightforward as organic pest control when it comes to changing over from normal modern methods. You must find out what your soil type is – remembering that it can vary appreciably in different parts of the garden – whether it is acid, alkaline or neutral, what the drainage is like, and whether it is fertile or starved of nutrients such as phosphorus.

Managing the soil organically relies heavily on the use of bulky organic manures derived from decaying animal or vegetable residues. These improve and maintain the physical structure of the soil – mixing them into the soil alters the way in which the separate soil particles stick together, ensuring that there is enough air for the roots to develop to their full extent, and for surplus water to drain into the subsoil.

Most soils benefit from the addition of bulky organics – rotting farm manures of cow, pig or horse origin, garden compost, seaweed compost, spent mushroom compost, poultry deep litter and leafmould. Peat, now considered an endangered substance, and shredded bark are also organic materials, but are less useful as soil conditioners since they contain little plant food.

Dig any of these organic composts into the soil, thoroughly mixing it in as you go, or use them on the surface as a mulch. Though some types may be difficult to obtain, garden compost can be made all the time, and has the additional advantage that it makes use of most of the garden 'rubbish' – grass clippings, leaves, soft stems, faded flowers, weeds (unless they have set seed), and even fruit and vegetable scraps.

Although the bulky organic composts are primarily used for ensuring a good soil structure, they also contain plant foods and, in a well-maintained soil, will provide sufficient nutrients to produce strong healthy plants.

▶ **Straw mulch** A surface covering of straw will keep the fruits of these courgette plants clear of the soil, while a companion edging of marigolds deters such pests as aphids.

GREEN MANURES

Green manure crops are grown for several purposes. Legume crops – clover, fenugreek, lupins and tares – fix nitrogen in their root nodules, making it available for subsequent crops. Deep rooted plants bring valuable nutrients from the subsoil to the surface and encourage bacterial activity. Their green foliage, when dug in, adds humus to the soil. Root systems break up the soil, making it easier to work. Winter crops help to prevent nutrients such as nitrogen from being washed out of the soil.

Green manure crops should be cut down and turned into the soil while they are green and soft, before they flower or set seed.

CROP	SOWING TIME	FEATURES
Buckwheat	Late spring to early summer	Deep rooted. Flowers attract hoverflies (which feed on aphids) and pollinating bees. Dig in before the leaves turn yellow in late summer
Clover, Essex red	Spring or late summer	Good nitrogen fixer. Suppresses weeds. Dig in when the land is needed; can be overwintered
Comfrey	–	Grown from root divisions taken any time except mid to late winter. Needs a plot to itself
Fenugreek	Late spring to mid summer	Fast-growing with strong roots. Fixes nitrogen. Seed from wholefood shops usually germinates satisfactorily. Dig in 10-12 weeks after sowing, before flowers appear
Lupin, annual	Mid spring to mid summer	Fixes nitrogen; fungi associated with the roots also help to make phosphates available. Dig in before flowers open
Mustard, white	Early spring to late summer	Fast-growing; useful for filling gaps in crops. Don't grow on ground infected with clubroot disease. Suppresses weeds. Dig in before the first frost
Rye-grass, grazing	Spring to mid autumn	Excellent winter green manure. Strong root system helps to break up soil. Dig in as soon as seed stalks begin to develop
Tares, winter	Late summer or spring	Fixes nitrogen. Suppresses weeds if sown in spring. Dig in during spring following a late summer sowing, or after 2-3 months if sown in spring

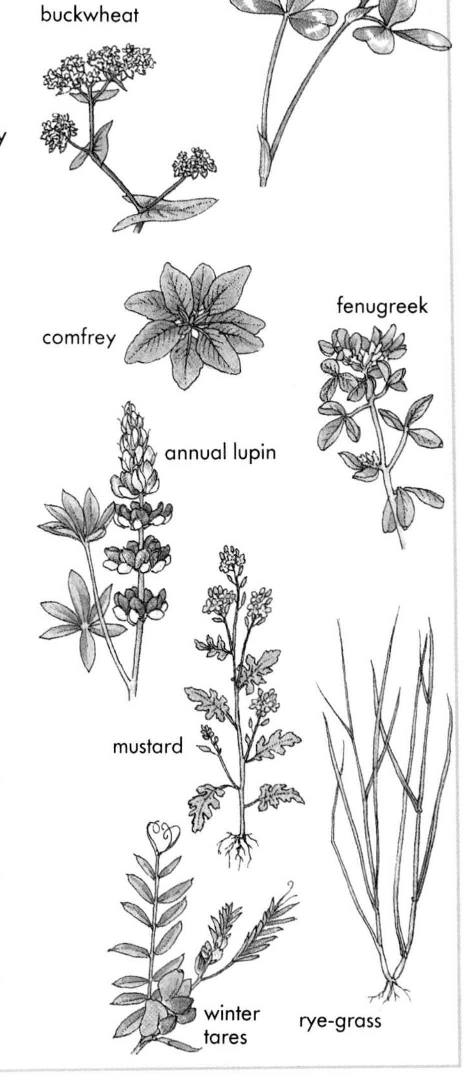

ORGANIC COMPOSTS AND FERTILIZERS

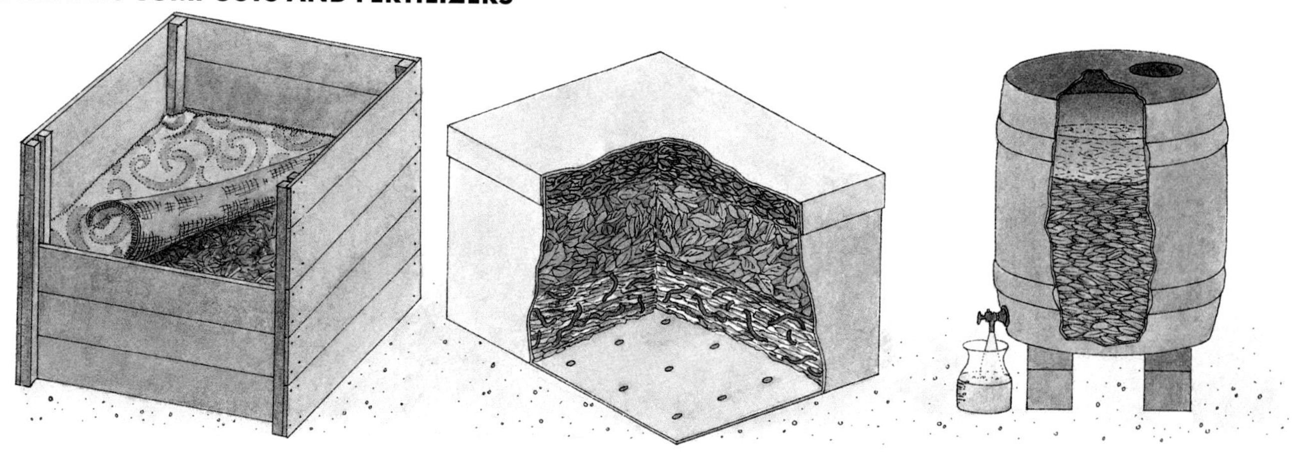

1 Organic garden compost can be made from kitchen scraps and all kinds of garden plant waste – provided it doesn't include weed seeds or diseases. Slatted timber bins keep the heap tidy, and allow air to penetrate the compost. Cover the compost with a piece of old carpet to retain heat and moisture.

2 Small amounts of garden compost can be broken down quickly in a worm box. Drill aeration and drainage holes in a wooden box, half fill with moist compost or soft leaves, then add food scraps at the sides. Cover tightly. Worms from a fisherman's shop are ideal for starting off bacterial activity.

3 Organic liquid manure can be made from shredded comfrey leaves. Cram the leaves into a barrel or bucket and cover. Depending on the temperature it will have fermented after a fortnight, when juice can be drawn off. Dilute to about half strength before applying as a foliar feed.

Think of the soil as a living organism in its own right, rather than as a lifeless substance needing digging and watering. Soil is in fact teeming with living creatures – some microscopic, all feeding, fighting, resting, breeding and dying continuously, and, in the process, having profound effects on the soil particles, gases and moisture. Anything you do to the soil – even walking on it – will alter it.

Soil improvement

Special cultural practices play an important role in organic gardening. Mulching the soil not only improves it and keeps it moist in summer, but also keeps weeds under control. But weeds are not always enemies – some provide food for the adult stages of insects whose larvae are predators on other insects, and a light cover of annual weeds will keep the soil cool and moist in summer. Provided the weeds are removed before they set seed, they will do no great harm. Exceptions are groundsel and chickweed which should be pulled up while quite young as they can harbour cucumber mosiac virus which has a wide host range and can be very destructive.

If there is space in the vegetable or fruit garden, a good way of improving the soil is to grow a 'green manure' crop such as mustard or winter tares and dig it in before it flowers. This will build up the humus content in the soil as organic manures do.

Rotation of vegetable crops does much to prevent the build-up of pests and diseases in the soil that results from growing crops in the same soil every year.

Pests and diseases can be avoided by growing plant varieties which are known to be resistant – some modern fruit and vegetable varieties are bred especially for this quality. There are rose varieties which are resistant to black spot and/or mildew, varieties of apple which defeat apple scab disease, and so on

Companion planting

One of the best ways of preventing epidemics of pests and diseases is to grow mixtures of plants, rather than blocks of one kind – a mixed herbaceous border, for instance, will be more trouble-free than a formal bedding scheme with lots of the same species blocked together. Similarly, roses mixed with shrubs or herbaceous perennials will be less likely to be plagued by greenfly. Mixing rows of vegetables is another method, such as lettuce between sweetcorn.

The theory of true companion planting goes further still – certain plants grown close together actually benefit one another, and other plants can have bad effects. Chives are claimed to control black spot disease on roses, carrots mixed with onions ward off carrot fly, and hyssop attracts cabbage butterflies away from cabbages. Gladioli, on the other hand, can inhibit the growth of nearby peas and beans, and fennel has a bad effect on tomatoes.

Falling back on inorganics

The gardener can plump for a strong decision one way or the other - to use solely organic principles, or to use inorganic methods wherever appropriate. The latter approach will probably appeal to the majority of people and there are, indeed, times when inorganic gardening is helpful and occasionally necessary. On an old, played-out site where the soil is little more than stones, sand and rubbish, quick-acting mineral fertilizers must be used at least for the first few years.

Occasionally, in spite of all one's efforts, epidemics of pests or disease do occur. The best way to deal with such problems is to apply a quick and thorough blanket spray, preferably using one of the insecticides or fungicides harmless to the 'goodies'. The aphicide pirimicarb, for instance, is specific to aphids and will not harm any other insects, including pollinating bees.

Among the choice of pesticides, many are quite harmless to humans and animals – in particular, the synthetic pyrethroid group of chemicals, for example permethrin, similar to the pyrethrum obtained from plants, but even safer and more effective.

GREEN VEGETABLE PESTS

Troubles in the kitchen garden can be disastrous as they disfigure plants and effectively reduce their cropping qualities.

Brassicas – including cabbages, Brussels sprouts, broccoli and cauliflower – and other green vegetables, such as beans, peas, celery and lettuces, produce their harvestable yield above ground and this can be damaged directly by leaf and stem pests and diseases, or indirectly by those which attack the root system.

The following pages explain how to recognize the common pests and diseases of green vegetables and how to deal with them. Though the list may appear daunting, many of these troubles can be avoided if the soil is fed and limed well so that the plants grow vigorously. It is also a good idea to dress seed drills with calomel dust or to dip the roots of young plants in a fungicide solution as a precaution against soil-dwelling pests and diseases. Thin seedlings before they become crowded to let air and light circulate freely.

General garden hygiene is particularly important when growing vegetables – rubbish and dead growth can harbour many pests and diseases. Always gather up fallen leaves and other debris and put them on the compost heap. If dead plant matter is known to contain pests or diseases, burn it rather than using it for compost.

When using chemical pesticides and fungicides follow the manufacturer's instructions carefully regarding the safety interval between spraying and harvesting – many chemicals take several days or even weeks before they disperse or become harmless to consume. Never spray vegetables which are ready for harvesting, and avoid letting spray drift pollute them when treating nearby crops.

If a particular chemical proves ineffective, try another one - the pests in one area may develop resistance to a particular substance used over a long period. Do not spray crops indiscriminately since you may destroy creatures which are beneficial – harmless insects such as ladybirds which prey on other pests, for instance. Avoid spraying crops which are in flower and alive with pollinating bees and other insects. If possible, spray on dull, still days.

▼ **Caterpillar damage** Eggs of white butterflies hatch into yellow-bodied caterpillars that feed voraciously on the leaves and hearts of cabbages and cauliflowers and in severe cases destroy entire plants.

ANTHRACNOSE

Crops affected Dwarf beans, and, occasionally, runner beans.
Symptoms Black-brown, sunken areas on the pods; brown spots on the leaves and stems. Leaves may fall prematurely.
Danger period Throughout the growing season – especially in cool, wet summers.
Treatment Destroy diseased plants. Sow seeds from a good supplier and in a fresh site.

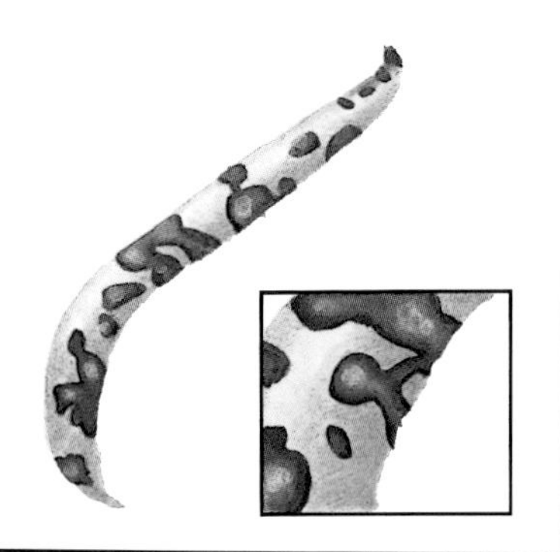

BEAN SEED FLY

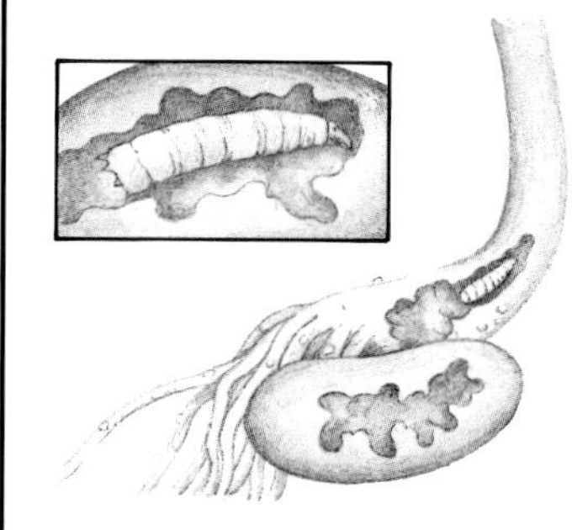

Crops affected Beans, especially runner and french, and peas; certain other crops like sweetcorn.
Symptoms Small white maggots tunnel into seeds which then often fail to germinate. Emerging seedlings wilt and become distorted.
Danger period Immediately after sowing.
Treatment Dust the seed drills with pirimiphos-methyl prior to sowing. Pull up and destroy affected seedlings.

BLACK BEAN APHID

Crops affected Broad beans.
Symptoms Small black aphids infest young shoots and suck sap.
Danger period Late spring to mid summer.
Treatment Spray with pirimicarb, pirimiphos-methyl, dimethoate or heptenophos. Pinch out growth tips once four trusses have set.

CABBAGE CATERPILLARS

Crops affected Cabbages, cauliflowers and other brassicas.
Symptoms Large, ragged holes eaten in leaves by the caterpillars of the large and small white butterflies and the cabbage moth. The last two usually burrow into cabbage hearts; the large white prefers the outer leaves. Plants may be totally destroyed, leaving just a skeleton of the tougher leaf veins.
Danger period Early summer to early autumn.
Treatment Inspect the undersides of leaves after white butterflies have been seen hovering – rub off and destroy any eggs. Remove and destroy caterpillars by hand if practicable. Spray with permethrin or pyrethrum or use biological control.

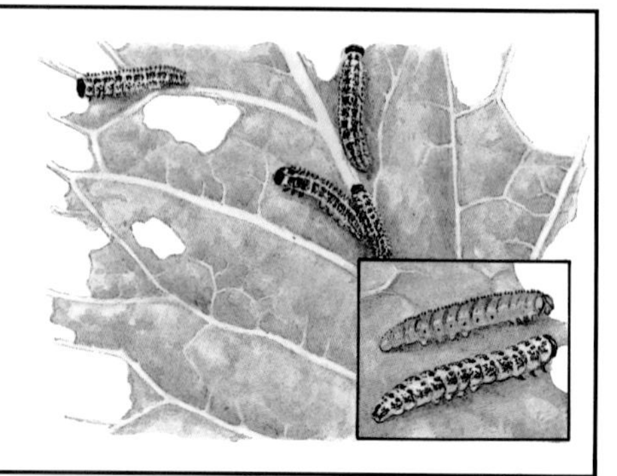

CABBAGE ROOT FLY

Crops affected Brassicas.
Symptoms Fly maggots in the soil feed on the roots, causing collapse of young plants.
Danger period Immediately after transplanting.
Treatment Mix diazinon+ chlorpyrifos in the soil when planting, or water in pirimiphos-methyl. Use proprietary brassica collars.

CABBAGE WHITEFLY

Crops affected Brassicas.
Symptoms Small white moth-like insects take off from the undersides of leaves. These may become soiled with honeydew and sooty mould.
Danger period Late spring to early autumn.
Treatment Spray with malathion, permethrin, pyrethrum or pirimiphos-methyl.

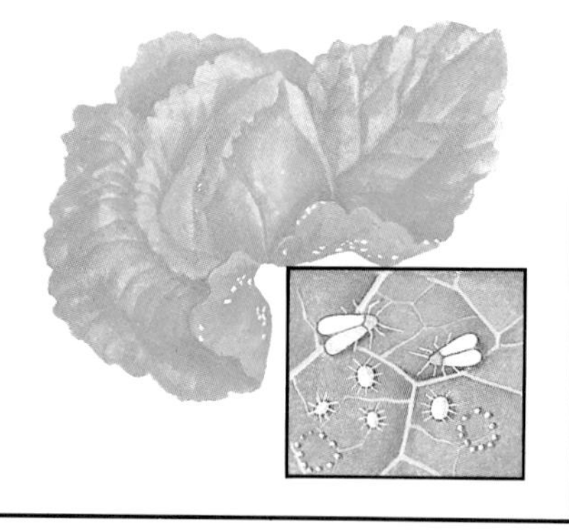

CELERY FLY

Crops affected Celery.
Symptoms Maggots burrow into the leaves causing brown blotches. Growth is checked; severe attacks cause complete plant death.
Danger period Early summer to autumn.
Treatment Spray plants with dimethoate when damage is seen, or cut off and burn affected leaflets.

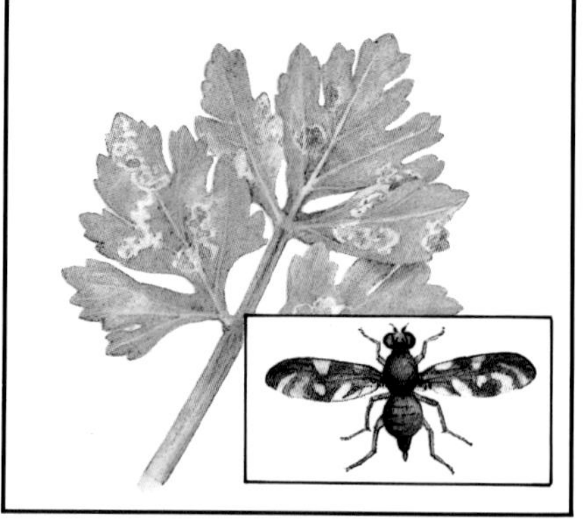

CLUB ROOT

Crops affected Brassicas.
Symptoms Swollen, distorted roots; yellowing, sickly, wilting foliage.
Danger period Throughout the growing season.
Treatment Improve drainage if necessary. Apply a generous dressing of hydrated lime to the soil; put calomel dust in the planting holes or dip roots in a solution of thiophanate-methyl. Burn infected plants.

CUTWORM

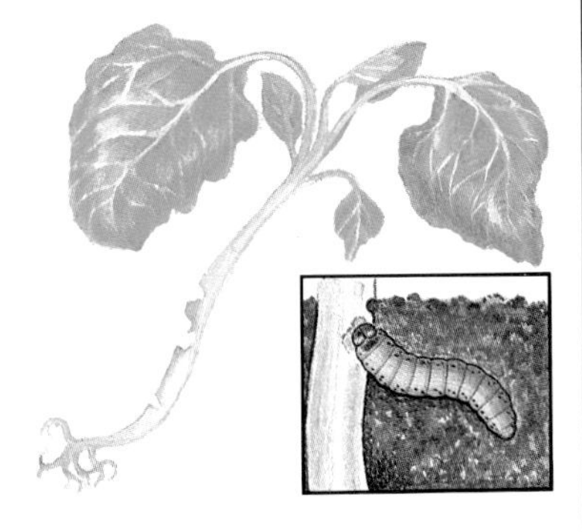

Crops affected Lettuces.
Symptoms Shoots eaten through at soil level; fat caterpillars in the soil.
Danger period Early spring and late summer.
Treatment Control weeds, which encourage cutworms, by hand or by shallow hoeing. Protect lettuces by working diazinon+ chlorpyrifos into the soil.

FLEA BEETLE

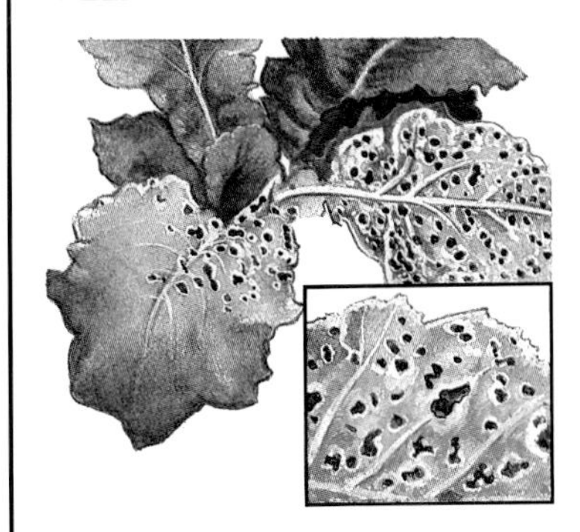

Crops affected All brassicas, swede and turnip tops; also wallflowers.
Symptoms Youngest leaves pitted with very small holes; growth of seedlings stunted.
Danger period During dry, sunny spells in late spring.
Treatment Dust seedlings with HCH, derris or pirimiphos-methyl. Good garden hygiene will often reduce the risk of attack.

GREY MOULD/BOTRYTIS

Crops affected Peas and beans; lettuces under glass.
Symptoms Grey mould on pea and bean pods or base of lettuces.
Danger period Growing season.
Treatment Prick off and destroy diseased pods by burning. Spray with benomyl, carbendazim or thiophanate-methyl.

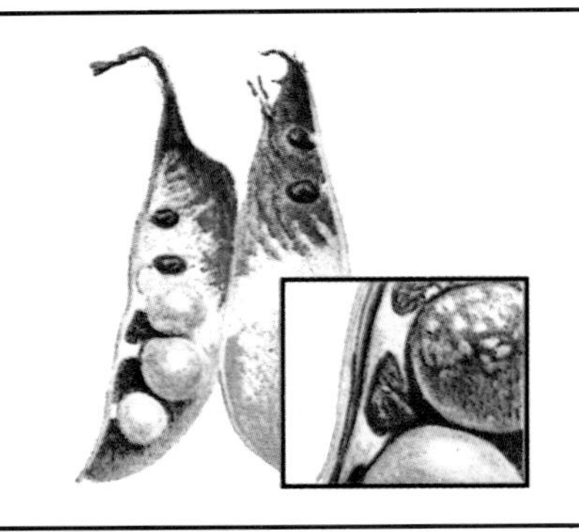

HALO BLIGHT

Crops affected French and runner beans.
Symptoms Brown spots surrounded by a halo on pods, leaves or stems. Infected seeds show raised blisters.
Danger period Growing season, especially in wet weather.
Treatment Don't plant infected seeds. Destroy diseased plants. Buy seeds from a good source.

LEATHERJACKETS

Crops affected Brassicas.
Symptoms Roots eaten by tough-skinned, fat, grey-brown, legless grubs. Plants wilt and may die.
Danger period Mid spring to early summer.
Treatment Before planting, dig deeply to expose grubs to birds. Work diazinon+chlorpyrifos or HCH into the soil.

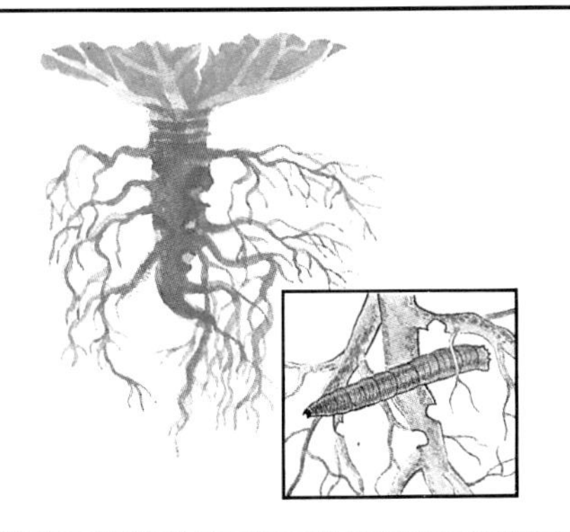

PEA AND BEAN WEEVIL

Crops affected Peas and broad beans.
Symptoms Leaf edges are eaten in a scalloped or U-shaped pattern by small beetles. Growth of young plants is retarded. Seedlings may die if the attack is severe. Pea and bean weevils can also transmit a virus disease which affects broad beans.
Danger period Throughout early spring to early summer.
Treatment Prepare the ground thoroughly before sowing to encourage rapid growth. Hoe between the young plants in mid to late spring. Apply HCH dust or fenitrothion spray to young plants as soon as the symptoms are seen. Older plants are not seriously affected and they generally recover without loss of yield. Clear away plant debris and coarse vegetation which harbour overwintering weevils.

PEA MOTH

Crops affected Peas.
Symptoms Peas inside the ripening pods are eaten and a small maggot-like caterpillar – about 6mm (¼in) long with a pale yellow body and a black head – is present, which eventually eats its way out and crawls to the ground.
Danger period Early summer to late summer.
Treatment Spray about one week after the flowers first open, and again two weeks later, with fenitrothion or permethrin. Alternatively, grow early or late-maturing pea varieties which are not in flower or pod during the critical egg-laying period. Cultivate the soil thoroughly in winter to expose the caterpillars – which overwinter in the soil in cocoons – to predatory birds and cold weather, which should destroy many of them.

PEA THRIPS

Crops affected Peas.
Symptoms Minute, elongated insects feed on the leaves and pods causing silver mottling and distortion of pods. Severe attacks result in stunted growth and few flowers.
Danger period Hot, dry summers.
Treatment Spray with dimethoate or fenitrothion as soon as symptoms appear.

ROOT APHIDS

Crops affected Lettuces, beans.
Symptoms White, waxy aphids on roots. Leaves wilt and turn yellow.
Danger period Summer and autumn.
Treatment Water infested plants with a spray-strength solution of pirimiphos-methyl. Some varieties are immune to root aphids.

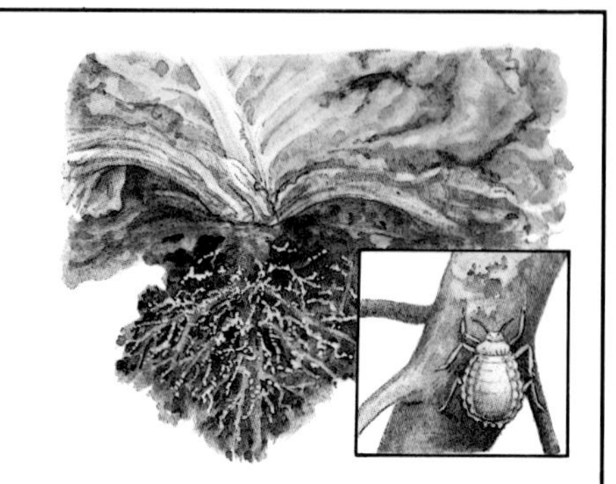

WHIPTAIL

Crops affected Broccoli and cauliflowers, mainly on acid soils.
Symptoms Leaves ruffled, thin and strap-like. This is caused by deficiency of molybdenum.
Danger period Throughout the growing period.
Treatment Lime the soil or apply a fritted trace element product containing molybdenum.

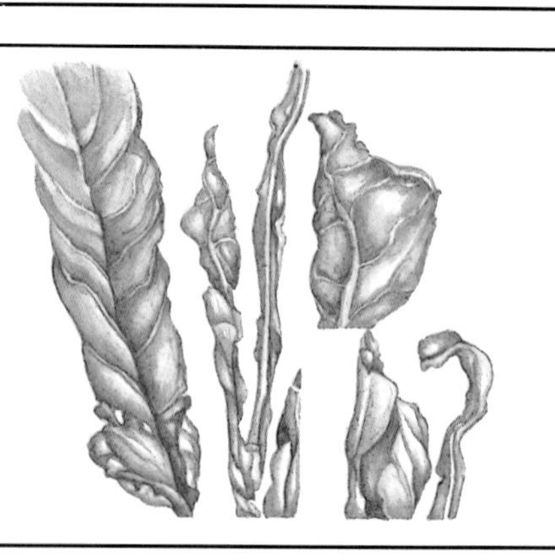

OTHER PROBLEMS

Bolting Lettuces produce tall, flower-bearing stems and fail to heart-up. This happens especially in hot weather. Avoid late transplanting and overcrowding. Keep lettuces well-watered, especially at the seedling stage.

Foot rot A fungal disease affecting peas and beans, causing discoloration and rotting of stem bases, usually leading to plant death. Water young plants with Cheshunt compound and do not grow legumes on the same site for several years.

Leaf spot Small brown or black spots, caused by various bacteria and fungi may appear on leaves of cabbages and cauliflowers, which fall prematurely. Cut off and burn diseased leaves. Where plants are growing close together, remove alternate plants to improve circulation of air.

Pigeons Brassica leaves may be torn or eaten almost completely, newly transplanted brassicas may be uprooted, and pea and bean seeds may be taken. Damage occurs throughout the year. Erect netting over crops where pigeons are very troublesome. A framework of black cotton or strings tied with glittering foil strips may also deter them.

Rabbits eat lettuces, often nibbling several plants rather than just one. Erect a 1.2-1.5m (4-5ft) high wire-mesh fence around the vegetable garden, burying 30cm (1ft) of the mesh below soil level to prevent rabbits from burrowing underneath.

Root rot Foliage discoloration, premature leaf fall, die-back of shoots or collapse of plants caused by soil that is too wet or too dry, or various fungal diseases. Any vegetable may be affected. Destroy infected plants and improve soil conditions. Employ a good crop rotation programme over a three-year cycle.

Slugs and snails Large holes eaten in foliage; young plants may be devoured completely. Slime tracks present. Most troublesome in spring and autumn during moist weather. Scatter proprietary slug bait around affected plants or sink beer traps at intervals along the rows.

Tipburn Lettuces develop brown, scorched leaf edges during sudden hot spells in spring or summer due to water loss. Try to maintain a constant soil moisture level.

White blister A fungal disease causing blisters on leaves and stems of brassicas. These blisters are filled with white powdery spores. Remove and burn diseased leaves and stems.

Wire stem A disease that affects many young plants, especially cauliflowers and other brassicas. Stem bases turn brown and shrink, causing death or stunting. Make sure that seedlings are raised in sterilized compost. Destroy diseased plants.

ROOT CROP PESTS

Unseen at first, soil-living pests and diseases seriously affect vegetable roots and tubers.

Root vegetable crops, including carrots, onions, parsnips, swedes, turnips, asparagus, Jerusalem artichokes, and especially potatoes, are susceptible to a number of pests and diseases, some quite serious. A couple of other problems – forking or 'fanging' of carrots and parsnips, for instance – are related to cultural defects such as poor soil preparation.

The edible portion of all root crops lies hidden under the ground throughout the crop's life and so it is much more difficult to catch a pest or disease problem in its early stages than with leaf or pod vegetables. Keep a constant eye on the health of the foliage and stems of root crops, since they reflect the health of the roots.

Discoloration, wilting and general stunting or lack of vigour in the top growth, with no visible signs of a pest or disease, generally indicates a soil or root-borne problem, and this is the time to take remedial action.

Ideally, however, routine preventative treatment should be carried out in advance of any such signs of attack. Soils that are known to harbour pests should be cultivated regularly with a fork or hoe to bring them to the surface and expose them to predators such as birds.

Rubbish and dead growth lying in the vegetable plot harbour pests and diseases, so put them on the compost heap or burn them - always destroy obviously diseased growth. Also, eliminate all weeds in and around the vegetable plot, since many of these form secondary hosts for vegetable pests.

Maintain a three-year crop rotation programme to minimize the build-up of persistent soil-borne pests and diseases. Promote strong, quick growth by feeding and watering regularly – weak growth tends to be more susceptible to pest and disease attack.

Never allow waterlogging problems to persist in the vegetable garden, since these conditions encourage the fungal diseases that cause various root rots. Improve the overall drainage of the bed and incorporate plenty of organic matter – if appropriate for the crops to be grown – when preparing the soil.

Follow the manufacturer's instructions when applying pesticides and fungicides, especially with regard to the safety interval between spraying and harvesting the crop. Spray crops on a calm, dull day when no rain is forecast, or in the evening, to prevent the chemical from drifting on to delicate plants or scorching foliage.

Chemical names quoted on the following pages refer to the active ingredient, rather than the proprietary name – check the instructions label on the bottle or container before buying.

▲ **Carrot fly** This pest can destroy a complete crop of parsnips and both early and maincrop varieties of carrots. The fat maggots tunnel into the roots and often cause them to rot.

▼ **Potato common scab** An unsightly rather than destructive disease affecting only the skin tissues of maincrop potatoes. Where the disease persists in the soil, grow varieties known to be resistant.

CARROT FLY

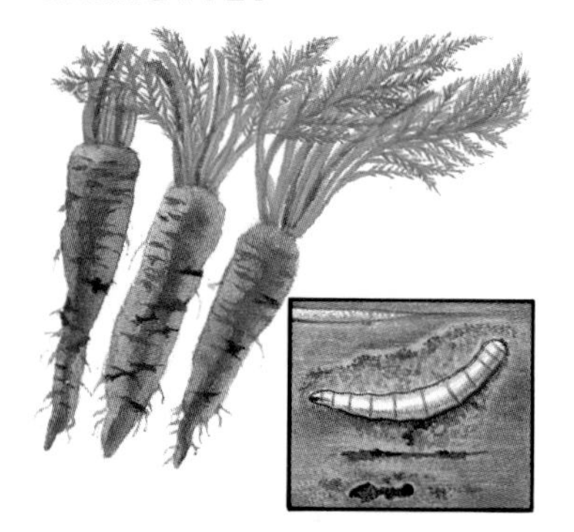

Crops affected Carrots and parsnips (also parsley and celery).
Symptoms Fly maggots tunnel into the roots.
Danger period Throughout the growing season.
Treatment Where prevalent, sow thinly in late spring. Treat the rows with diazinon+chlorpyrifos. Water late-season carrots with spray-strength pirimiphos-methyl in mid to late summer.

CRACKING

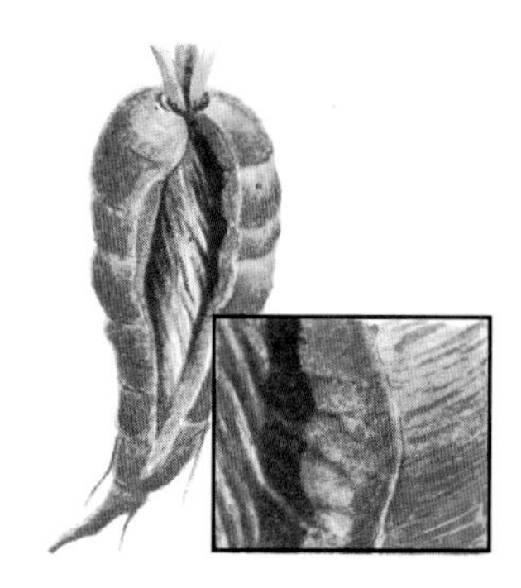

Crops affected All types of root vegetables, especially carrots and parsnips.
Symptoms A physiological problem causing lengthwise splitting of the edible root. No symptoms above ground.
Danger period Throughout the growing season.
Treatment Avoid erratic growth of the plants by watering before the soil dries out completely.

MILLIPEDES

Crops affected All types of root vegetables.
Symptoms Feed inside roots and extend damage caused by other pests. Millipedes differ from beneficial centipedes by having more legs, grey-black colouring and slower movement.
Danger period Late summer to autumn.
Treatment Maintain good garden hygiene. Cultivate deeply.

ONION FLY

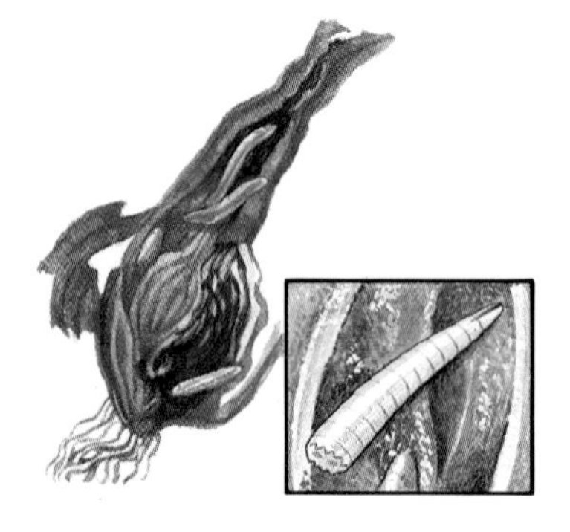

Crops affected Onions, shallots and leeks.
Symptoms Mushy bulbs. Small white maggots in rotting tissues.
Danger period Late spring to late summer.
Treatment Before sowing apply diazinon+chlorpyrifos granules or water with spray-strength pirimiphos-methyl two or three times during growth. Destroy affected plants.

ONION NECK ROT

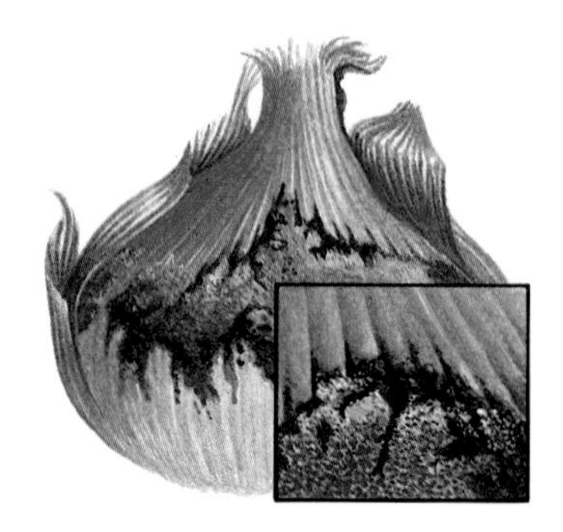

Crops affected Onions.
Symptoms A grey, velvety mould develops near the neck of stored onions, which rot rapidly.
Danger period Growing season; symptoms only appear in storage.
Treatment Buy treated seed or dust with carbendazim. Store only well-ripened, hard onions and put them in a dry, airy place. Destroy diseased onions.

ONION WHITE ROT

Crops affected Onions; occasionally leeks, shallots and garlic.
Symptoms The bulb base and roots are covered with a white fungus, and rot.
Danger period Throughout the growing season.
Treatment Grow on a new site each year – the disease contaminates soil for eight years or more.

PARSNIP CANKER

Crops affected Parsnips.
Symptoms Brown, orange-brown or black cankers on the roots (parsnip canker refers to several fungal diseases affecting parsnips), causing rot to different degrees.
Danger period Throughout the growing season.
Treatment Sow seeds early in deep, lime-enriched loamy soil, adding a balanced fertilizer. Parsnips with small roots may be less susceptible, so close spacing in the rows may be beneficial. Rotate crops regularly; grow resistant varieties, such as 'Avonresister', 'Gladiator' and 'Tender and True'. Destroy diseased plants. There is no satisfactory chemical control method. Do not store any parsnips which show signs of canker.

POTATO BLACK LEG

Crops affected Potatoes.
Symptoms A black rot develops at the base of a main stem. Leaves turn yellow, and stems soften and die. A common problem.
Danger period Early to mid summer.
Treatment Destroy all affected plants. Lift the remainder of the crop carefully and take care to store only completely healthy tubers.

POTATO BLIGHT

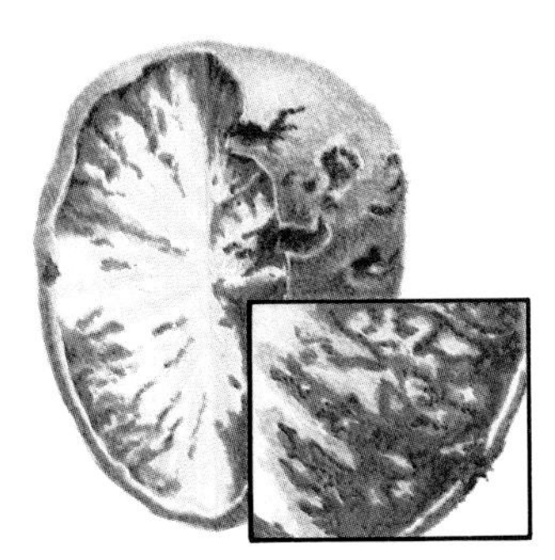

Crops affected Potatoes.
Symptoms Yellow-brown patches on leaves; eventually die. Red-brown discoloration under skin of tubers spreads inwards but shows through skin as a grey patch. Often secondary infection of evil-smelling soft rot.
Danger period Mid summer on.
Treatment Earth up potatoes well. Spray maincrops in mid summer with mancozeb or Bordeaux mixture.

POTATO COMMON SCAB

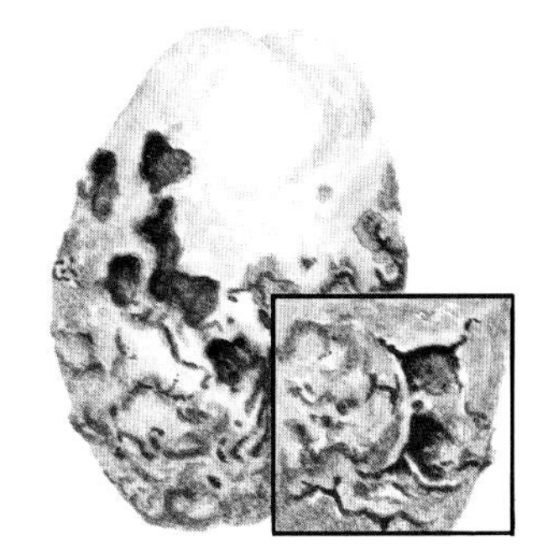

Crops affected Potatoes.
Symptoms Ragged-edged scabs on tubers.
Danger period Growing season.
Treatment Don't apply lime before planting. Dig in plenty of humus; keep growth even by watering before the soil dries out. If trouble persists, grow resistant potato varieties such as 'Arran Pilot', 'King Edward' and 'Maris Peer'.

POTATO INTERNAL RUST SPOT AND HOLLOW HEART

Crops affected Potatoes.
Symptoms Scattered brown marks appear within the flesh of the edible tuber (internal rust spot); or tubers develop brown, hollowed-out hearts (hollow heart). Affected potato tubers may rot in storage.
Danger period Throughout the growing period. Hollow heart may occur after a prolonged wet spell following a dry spell at any time in summer.
Treatment Dig in plenty of humus, and try to keep the growth even by watering before the soil dries out completely. There is no satisfactory chemical treatment for either of these disorders.

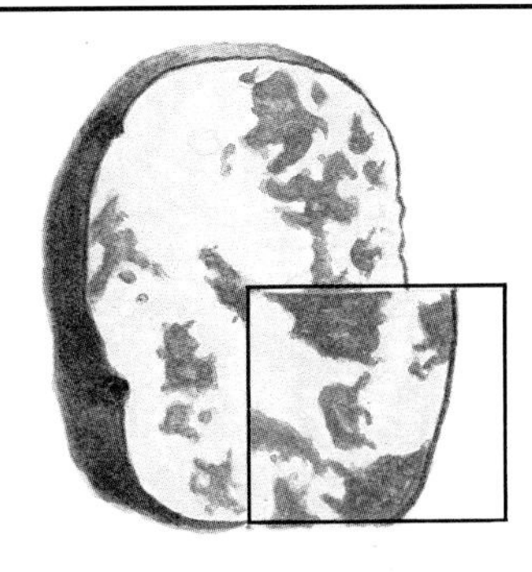

POTATO POWDERY SCAB

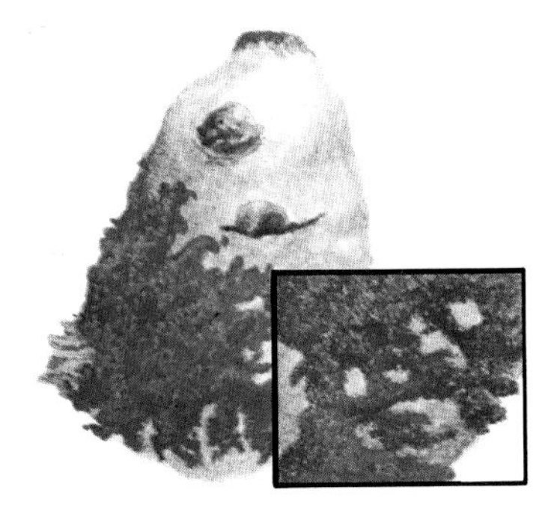

Crops affected Potatoes.
Symptoms Uniform round scabs, at first raised but later bursting open to release powdery spores. Affected tubers may be deformed in shape and have an earthy taste.
Danger period Throughout the growing season.
Treatment Destroy diseased tubers. Don't plant potatoes in the same site for several years.

POTATO SPRAING

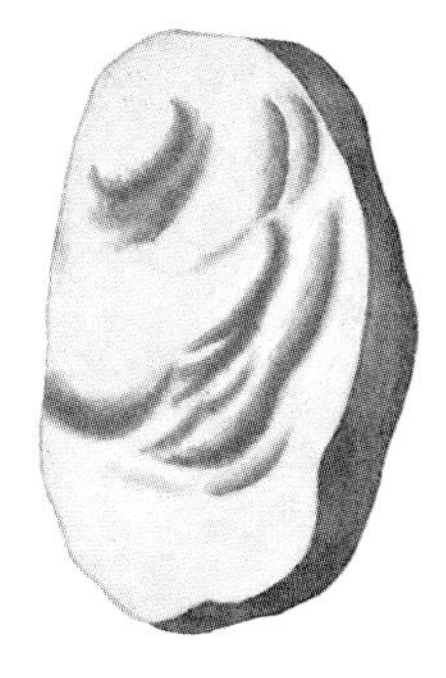

Crops affected Potatoes.
Symptoms Brown, curving stains in the potato tuber's flesh. The outer skin remains unblemished.
Danger period Throughout the growing season, but symptoms only evident when potatoes are prepared for cooking.
Treatment Burn infected tubers. Don't plant potatoes in the same site for several years. 'Pentland Dell' is susceptible.

SLUGS

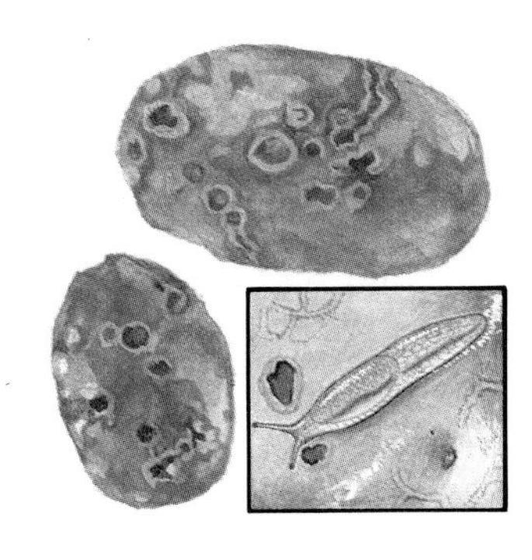

Crops affected Potatoes (as well as many other garden plants and crops).
Symptoms Irregular holes and tunnels eaten into tubers.
Danger period Throughout the growing season.
Treatment Apply proprietary slug baits or water with aluminium sulphate-based products in spring. Lift maincrop potatoes early.

SWIFT MOTH CATERPILLARS

Crops affected Carrots and parsnips.
Symptoms Off-white, soil-living caterpillars with distinctive brown heads feed on the edible roots, hollowing out the inner tissues. Caterpillars may be seen in the soil during cultivation.
Danger period Throughout the growing season; rarely serious.

Treatment Destroy by hand any caterpillars found during soil cultivation. Maintain good garden hygiene and eliminate weeds, especially docks and stinging nettles, which frequently harbour these pests. Protect ornamental and crop plants by incorporating diazinon+chlorpyrifos granules into the surrounding soil as a routine operation at the time of sowing.

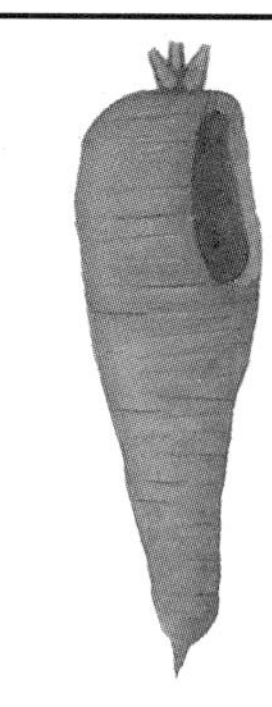

VIOLET ROOT ROT

Crops affected Carrots, parsnips and asparagus.
Symptoms Roots covered with violet fungal threads that eventually kill the plants
Danger period Throughout the growing season.
Treatment Burn affected plants; do not store diseased tubers. Don't plant susceptible crops in the same position for several years.

WILLOW-CARROT APHIDS

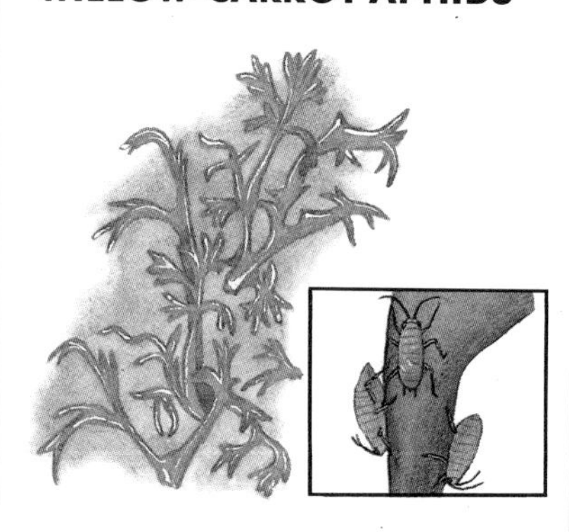

Crops affected Carrots, parsley, parsnips.
Symptoms Foliage stunted and sticky. Aphids also transmit motley dwarf virus, causing yellow leaf mottling and a reduced yield. Eggs overwinter on willows.
Danger period Late spring and early summer.
Treatment Spray with dimethoate, fenitrothion, heptenophos.

WIREWORMS

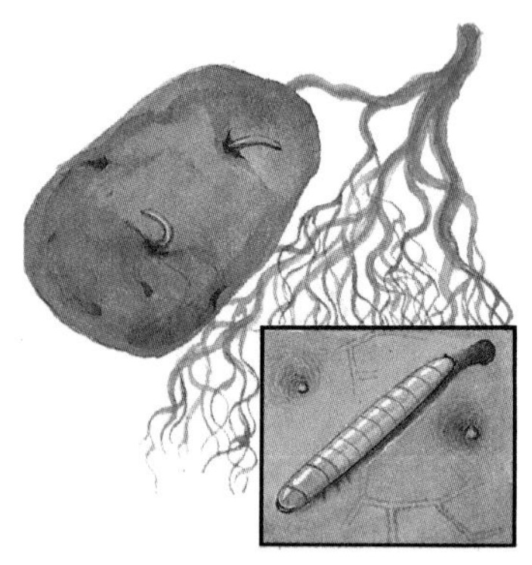

Crops affected Potatoes, carrots and certain other vegetables.
Symptoms Roots tunnelled by yellow-brown worm-like larvae.
Danger period Early spring to early autumn.
Treatment Cultivate soil thoroughly before planting. Control weeds. Apply diazinon+ chlorpyrifos to the soil around plants.

OTHER PROBLEMS

Bacterial soft rot can occur in the garden or in store, and may be serious, especially after a wet season. It affects swedes, turnips, parsnips, onions and potatoes, and often follows damage to tissues by another pest or disease. Small, water-soaked lesions break out around a wound. These spread and the tubers, stems or leaves rot into an evil-smelling, slimy mass. Improve soil drainage, control other wound-forming pests and diseases, maintain a good crop rotation and don't use too much manure. Keep lifted tubers and bulbs in a dry place. Don't store affected crops.

Club root is a serious infection of turnips and swedes, striking during the growing season. Roots swell and distort, and the leaves turn yellow and sickly. Improve drainage, especially on acid soils; rotate the crops. Apply a liberal dressing of hydrated lime and rake in 4% calomel dust before sowing.

Cutworms may attack the stems of young carrots, turnips, swedes and potatoes, especially on light soils during dry spells. Shoots are eaten through at ground level by fat caterpillars. Control weeds, which encourage cutworms, and protect susceptible plants by working a little diazinon+chlorpyrifos into the soil at the time of sowing.

Eelworms can be serious pests of onions and potatoes, as well as many other plants. The leaves, stems and bulbs of onions become bloated and distorted as a result of attacks by these minute worm-like creatures. The potato cyst eelworm causes pinhead-size yellow or brown cysts to grow on roots, resulting in wilting and death of plants. Where infestations are severe, do not plant the same crop on that site for several years. Dig up and burn badly affected plants. Chemical control of all types of eelworm is very difficult, and no safe and effective compounds are available for use by amateur gardeners. Some potato varieties are resistant to or tolerant of cyst eelworm attacks.

Fanging is a disorder of carrots and parsnips in which the edible root divides into two or more forks. It is caused by too much compost in the soil, or by stony or poorly prepared soil, not by a pest or disease. Use soil which has been manured for a previous season's crop. Take care not to compress the seed bed too much.

Sclerotinia disease is a fungal disease that over winters in the soil. It attacks many root crops in store, especially carrots and parsnips, and is frequently restricted to the topmost part of the root. It consists of a white, fluffy mass containing hard, black structures of resting fungal growth. The roots soften and decay. Store sound roots only. Check stored roots regularly, and burn all affected material.

SOFT FRUIT PESTS

Succulent berry fruits can be ruined by birds, pests and diseases unless they are properly protected.

The softest of all fruit crops, strawberries are particularly susceptible to attack from birds and other pests. Once injured, their tissues soon succumb to further infection by fungal diseases. Other soft and bush fruits – including blackberries, raspberries, loganberries, blueberries, cranberries, blackcurrants, red currants, white currants, gooseberries and grapes – are also troubled by a range of pests and diseases.

Rhubarb, though not a true fruit (it is a leaf-stalk), is usually included in this group of crops and is prone to a number of pest and disease problems characteristic of soft edible tissues.

Larger animals, especially birds and squirrels, can devastate a soft fruit crop. By far the most effective way of avoiding trouble is to construct some sort of cage over the entire plant or group of plants. Plastic netting is readily available with a small mesh to prevent access by birds. You can drape it over rows of strawberries, anchoring it in the soil with galvanised wire pegs, or throw it over fruit bushes. You will have to undrape the netting whenever you need to attend to the plants, but this inconvenience is rewarded by increased fruit yields.

You can also stretch the netting tautly on a support framework of canes so that it covers the whole area. Alternatively, you can buy rigid, ready-made walk-in fruit cages, or you can construct your own from timber posts, with plastic-coated wire netting attached to battens. Such fruit cages allow easy access to the bushes, for soil cultivation, pruning, spraying and harvesting. It is advisable to take the netting down every winter to prevent damage from gales and heavy snowfalls.

Smaller pests, including many insects, are not deterred by a fruit cage and you will need to prevent undue damage – unless you are a dedicated organic gardener – by operating a routine chemical spray programme. With all pesticides and fungicides, however, it is best to avoid using the same chemicals year after year, since certain pests and diseases can develop resistance to them. Never use chemicals indiscriminately: remember that not all insects are pests – some pollinate the flowers and others are predators of the real pests.

Good garden hygiene is important in the fruit garden, especially around low-growing crops such as strawberries. Decaying debris must be cleared from the ground – it harbours fungal spores as well as insects and other pests.

Follow the manufacturer's instructions when using chemicals in the fruit garden, paying special attention to the recommended safety period before harvesting and eating the crops.

▲ **Blister aphids** These tiny pests cause characteristic red blistering on the leaves of red and white currants or yellowish blistering on blackcurrants. Young leaves are worst affected and the pests can easily deplete the fruit bush's energy, with reduced yield.

▼ **Grey mould** Also known as botrytis, this troublesome disease affects strawberries and raspberries in wet summers. The fungus spreads rapidly and persists on plant debris all year. Good hygiene is essential.

BLISTER APHIDS

Crops affected Red and white currants; also blackcurrants.
Symptoms Irregular, raised red/green blisters on leaves.
Danger period Late spring and early summer.
Treatment Spray with tar-oil wash in mid winter to kill eggs. Apply insecticides such as dimethoate or heptenophos in spring, just before flowering. Repeat after flowering if necessary.

CANE SPOT

Crops affected Raspberries and loganberries.
Symptoms Purple spots on canes become white and split down the cane. Leaves and fruit are distorted.
Danger period Spring to autumn.
Treatment Destroy badly affected canes. Spray with a copper fungicide, benomyl, carbendazim or thiophanate-methyl, following the manufacturer's instructions.

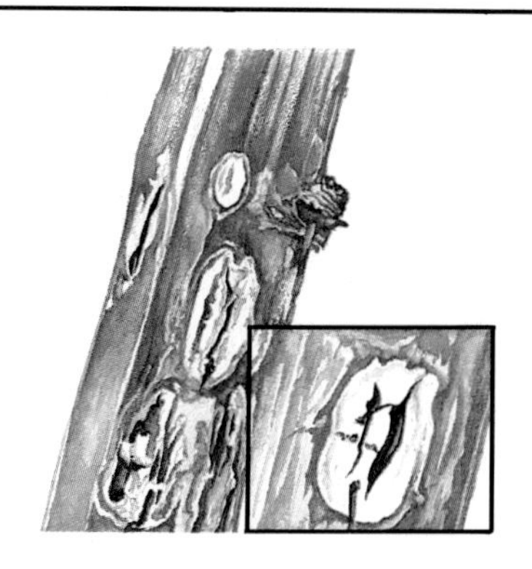

CHLOROSIS (lime-induced)

Crops affected Raspberries.
Symptoms Yellowing of the leaves.
Danger period Growing season.
Treatment Make the soil more acid by digging in pulverized bark or acidifying chemicals. Apply a chelated compound or fritted trace elements, following the manufacturer's recommendations for application rate.

CORAL SPOT

Crops affected Red currants (also many ornamental shrubs and trees).
Symptoms Red, cushion-like masses of fungal spores (pustules) on dead branches and stems. Die-back of shoots or large branches may result. Severe coral spot attacks may kill entire plants.
Danger period Any time.
Treatment Cut out and burn all dead wood. Cut diseased but living shoots back to at least 15cm (6in) below the infected area, using a sterilized pruning knife; treat all cuts with a fungicidal wound-sealing paint. Feed, mulch, water and/or improve drainage of the soil as necessary to encourage vigour – healthy fruit bushes are less likely to be attacked by this parasitic fungus.

CROWN ROT

Crops affected Rhubarb.
Symptoms Rotting of the main bud, then of the whole crown, in which a cavity may develop. Spindly and discoloured leaves die down early, or don't develop at all.
Danger period Growing season.
Treatment Dig up and burn the entire plant. Don't plant rhubarb again in the same spot.

EELWORMS

Crops affected Strawberries.
Symptoms Young growth and buds stunted, distorted and scarred by microscopic, leaf-boring eel-like worms.
Danger period Growing season.
Treatment No effective chemicals are available. Destroy infested plants. Purchase healthy stock from reputable nurseries.

GALL MITES

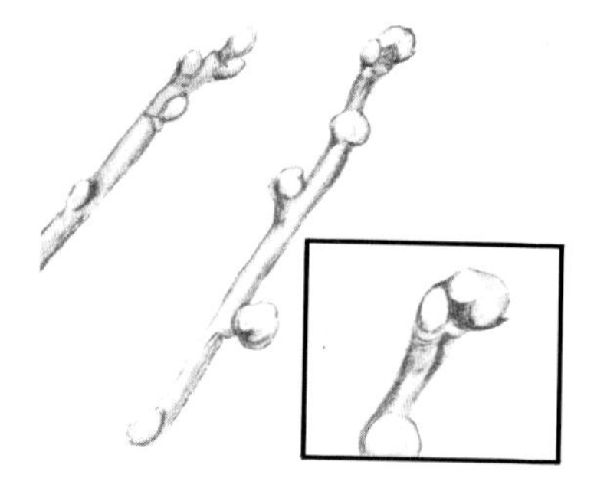

Crops affected Blackcurrants.
Symptoms Infested buds swell up and fail to develop, forming characteristic 'big buds'.
Danger period Late winter and early spring.
Treatment Remove and burn affected buds in very early spring and spray with the fungicide carbendazim when the first flowers open, repeating after about three weeks.

GOOSEBERRY SAWFLIES

Crops affected Gooseberries, currants.
Symptoms Leaf tissues eaten away, with many or all of the leaves reduced to a skeleton of veins.
Danger period Mid spring to late summer.
Treatment Spray thoroughly with derris, pyrethrum, fenitrothion or malathion when caterpillar damage first occurs.

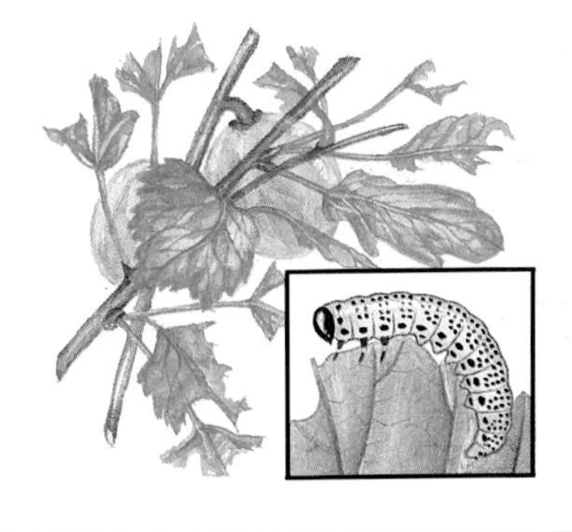

GREY MOULD

Crops affected Mainly strawberries and raspberries.
Symptoms Fruit rots and becomes covered with a grey, velvety mould (also called botrytis).
Danger period Flowering time; symptoms appear on fruits.
Treatment Spray with benomyl, thiophanate-methyl or carbendazim as the first flowers open, repeating two or three times at 14-day intervals. Remove all diseased fruits.

LEAF MIDGE

Crops affected Blackcurrants.
Symptoms Small maggots feed on young leaves causing them to twist tightly and fail to expand. Severe attacks may check growth.
Danger period Mid spring to early autumn.
Treatment Spray with dimethoate just before flowering; repeat three weeks later.

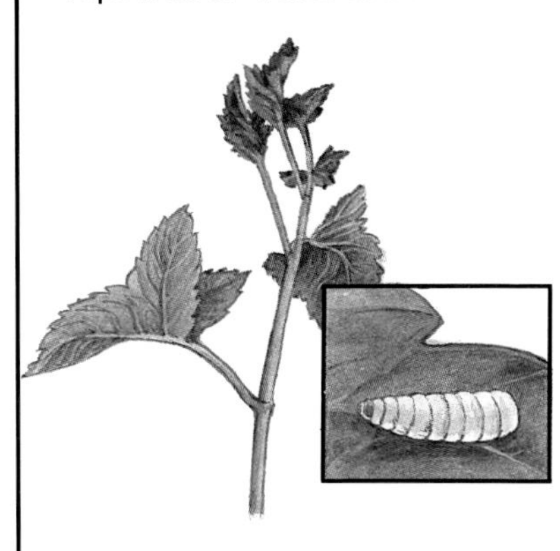

MEALYBUGS

Crops affected Greenhouse grapes.
Symptoms Foliage and stems covered with patches of mealy wax threads covering colonies of bugs or eggs.
Danger period Any time.
Treatment Spray with pirimiphos-methyl or malathion before fruit swells, and/or apply tar oil to dormant vines. Or use biological control.

RASPBERRY BEETLES

Crops affected All cane fruit.
Symptoms Beetle grubs feed on ripening fruit.
Danger period Summer.
Treatment Spray at dusk with fenitrothion, derris or malathion as soon as fruits turn pink (raspberries); 80% petal fall (loganberries); first open flowers (blackberries).

POWDERY MILDEW

Crops affected Grapes, strawberries and gooseberries.
Symptoms A white powder that turns brown on gooseberries but may show as loss of colour on strawberries. Grapes may split.
Danger period Growing season.
Treatment Spray with benomyl, carbendazim, thiophanate-methyl, bupirimate with triforine or sulphur (except on gooseberries).

REVERSION

Crops affected Blackcurrants.
Symptoms Leaves are smaller than normal and with fewer lobes. Flower buds lack their normal hairs and are magenta in colour. Affected bushes fail to produce a good crop. Be careful not to confuse the symptoms with those of frost damage or potassium deficiency (poor leaves and crop yield, but flower buds not affected in the same way).
Danger period Only obvious on long basal shoots in early or mid summer.
Treatment Dig up and burn the entire plant in winter – there is no cure for this serious disease. In the following spring, replant only bushes certified to be free of virus.

Control the blackcurrant gall mite that is primarily responsible for spreading this disease, as a routine precaution (see page 166).

SPUR BLIGHT

Crops affected Raspberries and loganberries.
Symptoms Canes bear purple to silver blotches, spotted with black. Spurs on these die back.
Danger period Spring and summer.
Treatment Cut out infected canes after fruiting. Spray new canes with benomyl, carbendazim, thiophanate-methyl or a copper fungicide.

STRAWBERRY BEETLE

Crops affected Strawberries.
Symptoms Shiny black ground beetles eat chunks out of ripening fruits (birds cause similar damage). They may be found scuttling beneath the fruit and under the straw.
Danger period Early summer.
Treatment Maintain good garden hygiene, removing all debris and leaf litter. Keep down all weeds. Methiocarb slug pellets give some control.

STRAWBERRY MITES

Crops affected Strawberries.
Symptoms Tiny, hardly visible mites (tarsonemid mites) attack plants causing brittle leaves with curled-down margins. Terminal buds killed.
Danger period Spring and summer.
Treatment There is no effective chemical control. Maintain good garden hygiene. Burn infested plants and obtain new stock from a reputable supplier.

VIRUS

Crops affected Many soft fruits.
Symptoms Variable. Yellow-blotched, often distorted, leaves on raspberry, blackberry and strawberry bushes (mosaic virus illustrated); gooseberry leaves discoloured along veins (vein banding mosaic virus); strawberry leaves develop yellow mottling (mottle virus), puckered with red/purple-spotting (crinkle virus), or have yellow margins and dwarfed leaves (yellow edge virus). Harmless yellow blotches on raspberry leaves are often caused by leaf and bud mites.
Danger period Growing season.
Treatment Dig up and burn affected plants. Re-plant virus-free stocks. Maintain hygiene. Eliminate pests which transmit viruses.

OTHER TROUBLES

American gooseberry mildew is a fungal disease that attacks leaves, shoots and fruits of gooseberries during the growing season, giving them a white, powdery coating; it also attacks blackcurrants late in the season. Tips of diseased shoots are distorted. Prune bushes to give free circulation of air. Cut off and burn diseased shoots in late summer. Spray with sulphur (except yellow-fruited varieties), or with benomyl, carbendazim or thiophanate-methyl or triforine with bupirimate.

Aphids of many kinds attack soft fruits, mainly causing distortion and stunting of young growth, weakening the plant. They may also spread virus diseases. There are aphids specific to gooseberries, raspberries and strawberries; others are more general in their attack. Spray affected garden plants with pirimicarb, dimethoate, heptenophos, fenitrothion or malathion.

Cane blight disease afflicts raspberries. Leaves wilt and wither in summer; canes discolour and snap off at ground level. Cut diseased canes below ground level and burn them. Spray new canes with Bordeaux mixture or other copper fungicide.

Capsid bugs feed on the sap of currants from mid spring to late summer, and inject toxic saliva. Ragged holes appear in younger leaves and fruits are misshapen and discoloured. Maintain good garden hygiene and eliminate weeds. Protect susceptible bushes by spraying with dimethoate, fenitrothion or malathion when symptoms appear.

Leaf spot affects blackcurrants and gooseberries, causing brown spots on the leaves from late spring onwards, which then fall prematurely; worse in wet seasons. Remove diseased leaves and burn them. Spray with mancozeb, benomyl, carbendazim, thiophanate-methyl or triforine with bupirimate after flowering, or a copper fungicide after harvesting. Repeat two weeks later.

Red spider mites attack currants, cane fruits and strawberries during the growing season, especially when grown under glass. Leaves show a very fine, light mottling on their upper surfaces, followed by general yellow discoloration. Maintain a humid atmosphere in greenhouses, spraying plants with water if necessary. Spray with dimethoate, pirimiphos-methyl or malathion. Biological control is effective.

Slugs and snails eat holes in ripening strawberry fruits, leaving characteristic slime trails. Sprinkle proprietary slug baits, following the manufacturer's recommendations regarding timing.

Strawberry tortrix moth Caterpillars spin silken webs over strawberry leaves, pulling the leaf margins together like a tent. Remove and destroy affected leaves by hand. Or spray with fenitrothion or permethrin before flowering; repeat again after harvesting the fruit.

TOP FRUIT TROUBLES

Apples, pears and all stone fruit grown on bush trees, cordons, espaliers or fans are subject to injury.

Apples, pears, cherries, plums, damsons, gages, apricots, peaches and other top fruits are prone to a number of pests, diseases and disorders which can ruin the edible fruits or damage the foliage. Severe leaf damage reduces the yield of fruit.

Birds often damage buds and fruits. The main protection is to cover trees with 2.5cm (1in) mesh nylon or polythene netting. Fans, cordons, and espaliers are the easiest to protect by means of temporary cages. Other means are muslin or polythene bags, stockings, newspaper cones or plastic sleeves, put over each fruit. Less effective are bird scarers, bird-repellent sprays or cotton threads tied among the branches.

Fungal diseases and insect pests, which can seriously damage or kill trees, are the other main problems in fruit growing.

There are many fungicides and insecticides that can be sprayed on fruit but they should not be used indiscriminately. Regular spraying is not advisable – it kills beneficial insects, such as pollinating ones, as well as enemies. Also, the pest or fungus concerned can develop a resistance to the chemical used. Some red spider mites, for instance, are resistant to all, or most, of the common sprays traditionally used to combat them.

Researchers now advocate the use of predators and parasitic wasps to control pests where possible. However, these are not always suitable for outdoor use, so some chemical control is necessary.

Keep a keen watch for pests and diseases, and use chemical treatment only when they can be seen or, in some cases, if the plant was attacked the previous year. Confine treatment to the affected plant, and those nearby.

When using chemicals, always follow the manufacturer's instructions regarding dilution and application rate and for the safety period before fruit can be harvested and eaten. When spraying high up into a tree, wear a face mask to protect yourself against falling spray drift. Never spray on a windy day. Spray in the morning or late afternoon/early evening when pollinating insects are less likely to be on the wing.

Good garden hygiene also helps to keep pests and diseases under control. Never leave old prunings lying about, and in autumn and winter pick off any old, rotting and mummified fruit. Prune out all dead spurs and cankered branches. Burn these together with any rotten fruit which can spread the fungus disease brown rot. Sweep up fallen leaves and apply a tar-oil winter wash as a regular routine.

▲ **Peach leaf curl** This common disease affects peaches and nectarines. It reduces the vigour of trees and impairs fruit yield after repeated, unchecked attacks.

▼ **Bird damage** Blackbirds, thrushes, jays and magpies devour chunks or take pecks out of ripening fruit. Wasps extend the damage and spores of brown rot enter the wounds and render the fruit inedible.

APPLE BLOSSOM WEEVILS

Crops affected Apples.
Symptoms Flower buds almost reach maturity but fail to open; petals then die. A small weevil larva, pupa or brown/black beetle can be found inside each bud on close inspection. (Similar symptoms, but with no such insects inside the buds, suggest frost damage.)
Danger period Mid to late spring.
Treatment Spray with HCH, fenitrothion or pirimiphos-methyl just before the flower buds start to open in order to kill the female weevils before they lay their eggs. Minor attacks can be ignored since they merely assist the natural thinning process, reducing the amount of fruit which sets, but increasing the size of those remaining.

APPLE CANKER

Crops affected Apples.
Symptoms Oval cankers on the trunk or branches; bark shrinks in rings until inner tissues exposed.
Danger period Any time.
Treatment Cut out and burn infected spurs. On larger branches and trunks, pare away diseased material. Seal with canker paint. Spray with Bordeaux mixture or carbendazim just before and at 50% leaf fall.

APPLE CAPSID

Crops affected Apples; sometimes pears.
Symptoms Irregularly shaped raised bumps and corky patches on the ripening fruits.
Danger period Mid spring to late summer.
Treatment Spray with a proprietary tar oil or wash during the dormant period to kill overwintering eggs, and/or spray with dimethoate just before the trees start to flower.

APPLE SAWFLY

Crops affected Apples.
Symptoms Caterpillars eat into the cores of young fruitlets, which then drop prematurely. This pest also causes superficial scarring of mature fruit.
Danger period Late spring to early summer.
Treatment Spray thoroughly with fenitrothion, pirimiphos-methyl or permethrin one week after petal fall.

BACTERIAL CANKER

Crops affected Cherries, plums.
Symptoms Elongated, flattened canker-bearing exudations of gum on dying shoots.
Danger period Autumn and winter; symptoms don't appear until next spring or summer.
Treatment Cut out infected branches. Seal wounds. Spray with Bordeaux mixture or copper fungicide in late summer, early and mid autumn.

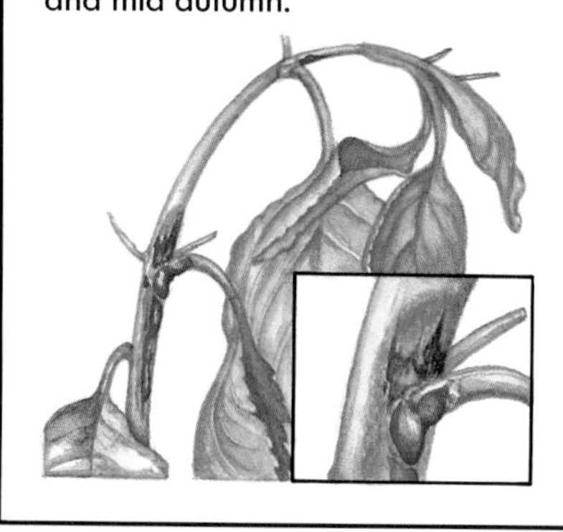

BROWN ROT

Crops affected All top fruit.
Symptoms Fruit turns browny white, often covered with concentrically ringed fungus spores, then withers and shrinks.
Danger period Summer; also during storage.
Treatment Destroy all rotten and withered fruits. Cut out any dead and cankered shoots during maintenance pruning. Inspect stored fruit regularly.

BULLFINCHES

Crops affected Plums, pears, apples and cherries.
Symptoms Small pink-chested birds, often in flocks, eat flower buds before they open.
Danger period Late autumn to mid spring.
Treatment Cover susceptible plants with 2.5cm (1in) mesh netting. Spraying with a proprietary bird repellent may give some control.

CHERRY BLACKFLY

Crops affected Cherries.
Symptoms Leaves at the tips of young shoots curled and twisted by black aphids. Foliage below sticky with honeydew which encourages sooty mould.
Danger period Late spring to mid summer.
Treatment Spray thoroughly with a systemic insecticide, such as dimethoate or heptenophos immediately after flowering. Also apply a tar-oil winterwash after leaf-fall.

CODLING MOTH

Crops affected Apples.
Symptoms Caterpillars eat into the cores of ripening fruit.
Danger period Summer.
Treatment Spray thoroughly with fenitrothion, permethrin or pirimiphos-methyl in the second or third week of early summer and again three weeks later to kill the young caterpillars before they penetrate the fruit. Pheromone traps capture male moths and reduce the mating success of females.

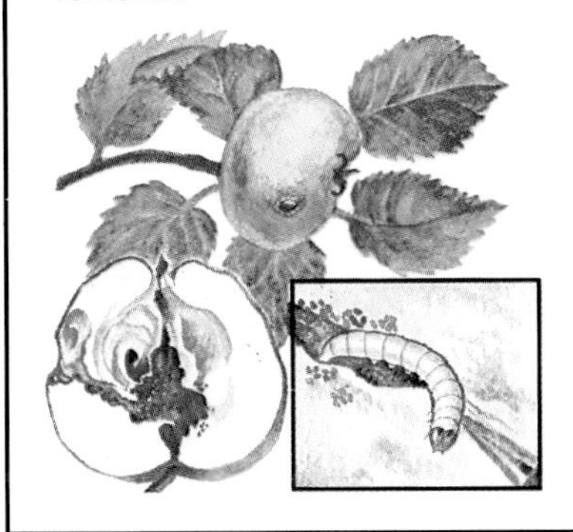

CRACKING

Crops affected Apples, pears, plums and gages.
Symptoms A physiological disorder causing the fruit's skin to split open, exposing the inner flesh. Fruit looks unpleasant and secondary infection by moulds and rot diseases may result.
Danger period Throughout the growing season.
Treatment Try to avoid irregular growth by mulching to conserve moisture, and by never allowing the soil to dry out.

GUMMING

Crops affected Cherries.
Symptoms Gum exudes on branches and trunks and gradually hardens.
Danger period All the year, but the trouble is worst in summer.
Treatment With good feeding, mulching and watering, the gumming should stop, but gum may have to be removed so that the dead wood beneath can be cut out.

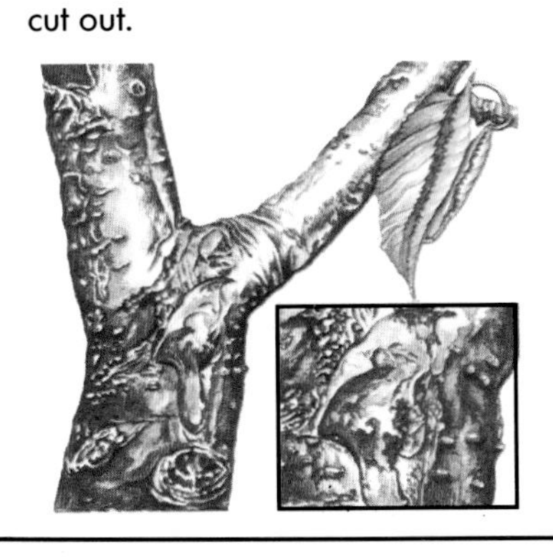

LEAF-CURLING APHIDS

Crops affected Plums, apples, pears, peaches and damsons.
Symptoms Young leaves puckered and curled.
Danger period Mid spring to mid summer.
Treatment Spray with a systemic insecticide, such as dimethoate or heptenophos in early spring, before the tree blossoms, and after flowering if necessary. Also apply a winter wash.

PEACH LEAF CURL

Crops affected Peaches and nectarines (also almonds).
Symptoms Leaves with large red blisters become white, then brown, and fall prematurely.
Danger period Before bud-burst.
Treatment Spray with Bordeaux mixture or other copper fungicide in mid to late winter. Repeat two weeks later and again just before leaf-fall. Destroy diseased leaves before they whiten.

PEAR LEAF BLISTER MITE

Crops affected Pears; occasionally apples. (Ornamental mountain ash, whitebeams and cotoneasters may also be hosts.)
Symptoms Tiny mites feed in leaves causing numerous pink or yellow blisters (pustules) to appear on both sides of the young leaves in spring. As the leaves age, these blisters turn brown. Badly infested leaves may fall. Vigour and fruiting ability generally not affected.
Danger period Mid spring to late summer.
Treatment Pick off affected leaves and burn them if heavily infested. No chemical treatment available for garden use.

SCAB

Crops affected Apples and pears (also ornamental pyracanthas).
Symptoms Brown or black scabs on the fruit, which may, in severe cases, crack when the scabs have merged and become corky. Olive-green blotches of fungal growth also appear on leaves, which fall prematurely. Small blister-like pimples may develop on young shoots, later burst the bark and then show as ring-like cracks or scabs.
Danger period Growing season.
Treatment Cut out all cracked or scabby shoots when pruning. Spray regularly with benomyl, carbendazim, thiophanate-methyl, mancozeb or triforine with bupirimate, starting when the young flower buds are visible, and until mid summer if necessary.

SHOTHOLE

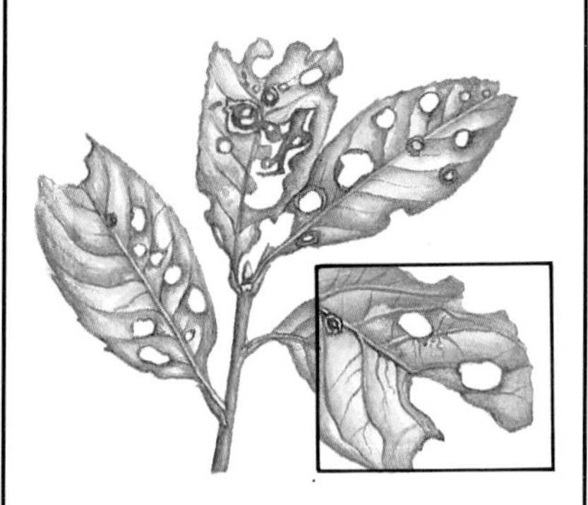

Crops affected Plums, peaches and cherries.
Symptoms Brown patches on leaves, then irregular holes caused by a fungus.
Danger period Throughout the growing season.
Treatment Feed trees yearly; mulch to prevent soil drying out. Foliar-feed small trees. If trouble recurs, spray with Bordeaux mixture in summer.

STONY PIT VIRUS

Crops affected Old pear trees.
Symptoms Fruit pitted and deformed in shape, with patches of dead, stony cells in the flesh, making it inedible. Symptoms first appear on one branch and over the years gradually spread until all the fruit on the tree is affected.
Danger period Any time throughout the year.
Treatment Cut down and burn diseased trees.

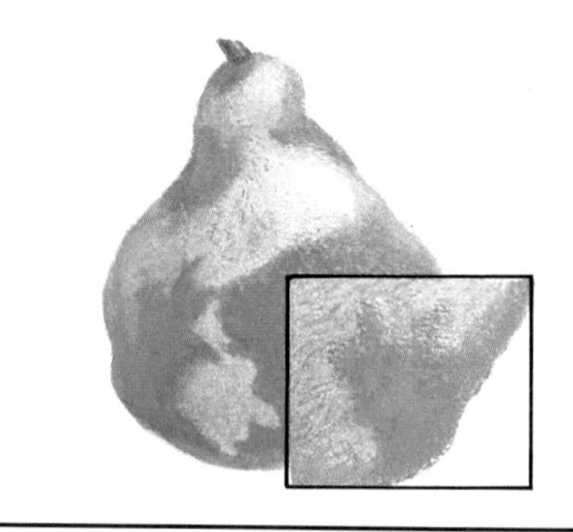

WOOLLY APHIDS

Crops affected Apples.
Symptoms Woody swellings and tufts of white wool on trunks and branches. Swellings may crack and cankers appear.
Danger period Mid spring to early autumn.
Treatment Brush spray-strength malathion, pirimiphos-methyl, dimethoate or heptenophos on to affected areas when wool first appears.

OTHER TROUBLES

Bitter pit affects apple fruits, causing slightly sunken brown spots beneath the skin and throughout the flesh. It occurs throughout the growing season, but is not apparent until harvesting or in store. Feed and mulch trees, and never allow the soil to dry out. In early summer, spray with calcium nitrate, taking care to follow the manufacturer's instructions.
Capsid bugs are small yellowish, green or brownish beetle-like insects, which eat tattered holes in the young leaves of apples. They may also injure the fruits of apples and pears, causing small bumps and irregularities on the skin. Good garden hygiene and weed control may reduce capsid damage. Protect susceptible trees by spraying with a systemic insecticide such as dimethoate. Or use fenitrothion or malathion as soon as the symptoms are seen.
Die-back is a disorder of fruit trees, causing foliage to turn yellow or brown, wilt then die, starting at branch tips and working back. Prune branches to healthy wood. Feed and mulch to keep other branches healthy. Spray with a foliar feed.
Fruit tree red spider mites infest apples, plums and pears. Older leaves turn bronze-yellow, dry out and die. If red spiders were troublesome the previous year spray immediately after flowering with dimethoate, pirimiphos-methyl or malathion.
Pear suckers, related to aphids, feed on the sap of pear shoots, leaving sticky excretions on young growth in spring, which becomes distorted. Spray with dimethoate, permethrin or malathion shortly after petal-fall.
Plum sawfly caterpillars tunnel into plum fruits, causing serious reduction in yields. Holes eaten in the fruits exude a sticky, black ooze. Infested fruits drop prematurely. Control as for apple sawfly.
Scale insects – tiny creatures each covered with a flat or rounded, yellow or brown scale – occur in colonies on older shoots of peaches and apples, particularly in late spring or summer. Spray with pirimiphos-methyl, malathion or dimethoate just before mid summer, repeating about three weeks later.
Split stone is a disorder of peaches and nectarines, causing the stone to split in two and the fruit skin to crack open at the stalk end during the growing season. Feed and mulch the tree. Water regularly and add lime if the soil is acid. Pollinate the flowers by hand.
Tortrix moth caterpillars eat holes in young leaves of apples and pears, and draw together the edges of the leaves by silk threads. Fruits may be nibbled. These small caterpillars have the characteristic habit of wriggling backwards when disturbed. Destroy caterpillars by hand, or spray forcibly with permethrin, pirimiphos-methyl or fenitrothion.

INDEX

ACKNOWLEDGEMENTS

Photographer's Credits
A-Z Botanical Collection 116(tl,bl); Bernard Alfieri 139; Biofotos/Heather Angel 53, 69; Brian Carter 133; Bruce Coleman Ltd 120(bl); Collections/Patrick Johns 125(t); Eric Crichton 14, 18, 25, 40, 51, 57, 72, 85, 95, 169(b), 114(tr), 116(tr,br), 117(bl), 118(tr), 119(tl,tr,bl); Samuel Dobie and Son Ltd 107; Philippe Ferret 41; Garden Picture Library (Brian Carter) 28, (Bob Challinor) 6, 56, (David Russell) 19, 36, (Ron Sutherland) 4-5, 67, (Brigitte Thomas) 112, (Didier Willery) 45, (C Woodyard) 70; John Glover 54, 128, back cover; Hall's Homes and Gardens Ltd 105; Holt Studios 117(tr); Jacqui Hurst 114(tl), 115(tl,tr); Photos Lamontagne 129; Andrew Lawson 49; S and O Mathews 152; Tania Midgley 33; Natural Image/R Fletcher 24; Natural Selection/ Paul Morrison 114(bl); Nature Photographers (D Hawes) 115(br), (Paul Sterry) 113, (D Washington) 120(tl); Clive Nichols front cover, 2-3; Simon Page-Ritchie/ Eaglemoss 125(b); Perdereau/Thomas 21; Photos Horticultural 11, 13, 15, 44, 52, 59, 73, 77, 89, 103, 114(br), 115(br), 117(br), 118(tl), 119(br), 121, 143, 147, 161, 165(t); Reader's Digest Magazine/ Julian Nieman 8; Reed Consumer Books/ Michael Crockett 63; Annette Schreiner 121; Harry Smith Collection 9, 21, 27, 29, 32, 37, 47, 48, 50, 117(tl), 118(bl,br), 120(tr,br), 137, 157, 169(t); Sue Stickland 153, 155; Elizabeth Whiting and Associates 81, 165(b), (Michael Dunne) 99; Steve Wooster 102.

Illustrators
David Ashby 58, 71, 104-6; Elisabeth Dowle 11-13, 20-23, 30-31, 34-35, 38-39, 42-43, 46, 90-94 124(b); Christine Hart-Davies 26-27, 60-62, 74-76, 78-80, 82-84, 96-98, 100-101, 122-123, 124(t), 148-150, 154-156; John Hutchinson 64-66; Stan North 86-88, 108-109; Reader's Digest 130-132, 134-136, 170-172; Ann Winterbotham 1, 16-17, 138, 144-146, 158-160, 166-168; Clare Wright 140-142.

Index compiled by Christine Bernstein

Typesetting SX COMPOSING, ESSEX; Printing & Binding PRINTER INDUSTRIA, GRÁFICA S.A. BARCELONA
Separations COLOURSCAN OVERSEAS CO PTE LTD, SINGAPORE; Paper PERIGORD-CONDAT, FRANCE

53-006-2